THE POWER OF
WOMEN

CELEBRATING WOMEN FROM WESTERN AND CENTRAL MASSACHUSETTS
FROM THE 1600s TO THE PRESENT DAY

Wayne E. Phaneuf & Joseph Carvalho III, Eds.

The Republican.   HERITAGE BOOK & TRAVEL SERIES

Acknowledgements

PEOPLE AND ORGANIZATIONS PARTICIPATING IN THIS PUBLICATION:

Contributing Institutions and Organizations

Adams Historical Society

African Hall Steering Committee, Springfield Science Museum, Springfield Museums

Bay Path University

Belchertown Historical Association, Stone House Museum

Edward Bellamy Memorial Association, Chicopee, MA

Berkshire Athenaeum, Pittsfield, MA

The Berkshire Eagle, Pittsfield, MA

Blandford Historical Society

Boston Public Library

Chicopee History Room, Chicopee Public Library

Community Foundation of Western Massachusetts

Elms College, Archives

Michele & Donald D'Amour Museum of Fine Arts, Springfield Museums

Forbes Library, Northampton

French Canadian Heritage Center, Chicopee, MA

George Walter Vincent Smith Art Museum, Springfield Museums

Greenfield Public Library

Historical Journal of Massachusetts, Westfield State University

Holyoke History Room, Holyoke Public Library

Jones Library, Amherst, MA

Library of Congress

Longmeadow Historical Society

Massachusetts League of Women Voters

Massachusetts State Archives, Boston

MassHumanities, Northampton, MA

Mount Holyoke College

Old Sturbridge Village, Sturbridge, MA

PAHMUSA (Pan African Historical Museum USA), Springfield, MA

Pioneer Valley History Network

Plainfield Historical Society

Polish Center of Discovery & Learning, Chicopee, MA

El Pueblo Latino, Springfield, MA

The Republican newspaper Archives and Library

Paul Robbins Associates, Inc.

Sophia Smith Archives, Smith College

Southwick Historical Society

Special Collections, University of Massachusetts (Amherst) Library

Springfield Armory Museum, National Park Service, Springfield, MA

Springfield City Library

Springfield College

The Springfield Museums Association

Springfield Regional Chamber of Commerce

State Library of Massachusetts, Boston

Storrowton Village, Eastern States Exposition

University of Massachusetts at Amherst, Library and Special Collections

Western New England University, Law Library

Westfield Athenaeum

Westfield State University, Institute for Massachusetts Studies

Wilbraham Monson Academy

Williamsburg Historical Society

Wisteriahurst Museum

Lyman & Merrie Wood Museum of Springfield History, Springfield Museums

Worcester Historical Museum

Worcester Polytechnic Institute

Worcester Public Library

Worcester Women's History Project

Contributing Individuals:

Janice Beetle

Andrea Canavan

Gayle Elizabeth Carvalho

Tricia Canavan

Gary Cook

Mara Dodge, Ph.D.

Donald D'Amour, Ph.D.

Alison M. Duffy

Mark A. French

David Gordon

Russ Held

Michelle Johnson

Stephen Kaplan

Ed Klekowski, Ph. D.

Leah Lamson

Marianna McKee

Eugene Michalenko
Robyn Ann Newhouse
Curtis Panlilio
Chrystina (Xtina) Geagan Parks
Stas Radosz
Paul Robbins
John Simpson
David Starr
David Tebaldi
Don Treeger
Mary E. Walachy
R. Lyman & Leslie Wood

Authors:

Jason J. Alves
Holly Angelo
Paul Anthony
Barbara Bernard
Ralmon Jon Black
Marcia Blomberg
Monica M. Borgatti
Garry Brown
Rosemary Brown
Ted Brown
Marge Bruchac
Heather Cahill
Patricia Cahill
Cynthia A. Campbell
Kathleen Carreiro
Joseph Carvalho III
Natasha Clark
Fred Contrada
Nancy F. Creed
Eileen Crosby
Scott J. Croteau
Melissa Cybulski

Tina D'Agostino
Daria D'Arienzo
Jeanette DeForge
Phil Demers
Peter L. DeRose
Kate Deviny
Chris Dondoros
Jeanne Douillard
Laurel Davis Ferretti
Anne-Gerard Flynn
Janine Fondon
William Freebairn
David M. Fuller
Richard C. Garvey
James S. Gleason
Peter Goonan
Ronni Gordon
Coralie Gray
Joanne M. Gruszkos
M. Susan Guyer
Heather Haskell
Thomas L. Higgins, M.D.
Lujuana Hood
Margaret Humberston
Talene Jermakian
Judith E. Kappenman, SSJ
Jane Kaufman
Judith Kelliher
Jim Kinney
Ted LaBorde
Sonya Lawson, Ph.D.
Diane Lederman
Darlyn Diaz Lindsay
Elise Linscott
Mary Ellen Lowney
Jacqueline T. Lynch

Robert Magovern
Marsha Marotta, Ph.D.
Penni Martorell
Cliff McCarthy
Betsey McKee
Suzanne McLaughlin
Marie Meder
Manon L. Mirabelli
Kathleen Mitchell
Janet Moran
Nancy L. Nelson
Meredith Perri
Alex Peshkov
Wayne E. Phaneuf
Dennis Picard
Damaris Perez-Pizarro
Teresa E. Regina
Romola "Mimi" Rigali
Elizabeth Román
John Sampson
Susan Sawyer
Thomas Sawyer
Ellen Savulis
Marilyn J. Schmidt
Shira Schoenberg
Mary Serreze
Catherine Shannon, Ph. D.
Tom Shea
Cynthia G. Simison
Jonathan Stankiewicz
David Stier
Greg Swanson
Cori Urban
Michelle Williams
Shannon Young
Katie Allen Zobell

Book Designed by: Michelle Johnson and Curtis Panlilio
Fonts used: Filosofia and Montserrat
Printed by: Bang Printing · Published by *The Republican*, 1860 Main Street, Springfield, MA 01102-1329

Introduction

The Power of Women

BY CYNTHIA G. SIMISON

When regional historians Wayne E. Phaneuf and Joseph Carvalho III undertook an effort to document "The Power of Women" and share a history of women in Western and Central Massachusetts, it was no easy task, made more difficult perhaps by the course of American history itself and how women have been regarded in society over the past four centuries. The resources to which they turned for research weren't always rich in documentation of either women's roles at any particular time or the achievements of individual women.

Among the Puritans who settled the Massachusetts Bay Colony in the 1600s, for example, it was the male settlers who led the government and distributed the lands among themselves. Thus, the male version of history in Massachusetts can be more easily tracked than the path of those who, simply because of their sex, were relegated to "supporting roles." Still, despite the regard with which they were held at any one time in history, women across the generations nonetheless worked right in plain sight to make a difference in their communities.

From the Native Americans who populated our region long before the Mayflower made landfall forward to 21st century role models of all faiths, races, gender identity and ethnicity, women have toiled to improve the lives of every person.

From teachers to nurses.

From soldiers to poets.

From abolitionists to suffragists.

From scientists to politicians.

In 1776, the year our nation was formed, Massachusetts' own Abigail Adams wrote to her husband, the then future president, John Adams, "I desire you would Remember the Ladies, and be more generous and favorable to them than your ancestors. Do not put such unlimited power into the hands of the Husbands. Remember all Men would be tyrants if they could. If particular care and attention is not paid to the Ladies we are determined to foment a Rebellion, and will not hold ourselves bound by any Laws in which we have no voice, or Representation."

At most every step along the way to this day in history, women faced limits on what they could do, what was expected of them, how they should conduct themselves and, sadly, how they would be credited for their accomplishments.

This book is an effort to establish a record with more than 800 biographical sketches of women of significant achievement in all fields of endeavor and from all periods of history, from the colonial era to modern day.

This region of Massachusetts, thanks in large part to the existence of women's colleges and its progressive history, can claim a rich legacy of women of achievement, women, who as Carvalho says, "could see the big picture" and who led the way on social issues of their day, from abolition to temperance to suffrage. Each generation has coped with the evolution of how women should behave and how they could take on new roles in the workforce. In the 19th and early 20th centuries, for instance, the wives of wealthy men, educated in their own right, could easily tread the leadership paths open to them thanks to their husbands' wealth and position. They were often women who wanted to do more with their lives than housekeeping tasks to which many were often relegated.

As the sexual revolution arrived in the 1960s and 1970s and family life took on an entirely new dynamic, women experienced perhaps the most remarkable changes in achieving equality of opportunity and achievement. Still, for as progressive and forward-thinking as our state may be regarded, Massachusetts is in many ways still very puritanical in terms of accepting women as leaders without regard for their gender.

Consider these facts. It wasn't until the early 20th century, in the 1920s, when the first woman was elected to serve in the Massachusetts House of Representatives and the first woman from the Bay State took a seat in the U.S. Congress. It wasn't until 1987 that a woman was first elected to statewide office in Massachusetts when Evelyn Murphy took office as lieutenant governor, and it wasn't until the 21st century, 2001, when Massachusetts had its first woman serving as governor, and only then when Lt. Gov. Jane Swift became acting governor.

It's further evidence that along with the social burdens like race, ethnicity, religion and social status which are confronted by their male brethren, women continue to face the added challenge of their sex.

This book is intended to "set the table" for future research. As it is being published, the story of women's achievements in Western and Central Massachusetts is still being written by a new generation of women (and men) who are inspired by those who came before them.

SPONSORS

GOLD SPONSORSHIP

Baystate Health

Pride

BRONZE SPONSORSHIP

Bay Path University

Elms College

Springfield Museums

COMMUNITY PROFILE

104th Fighter Wing, Barnes Air National Guard Base

Behavioral Health Network, Inc.

Big Y World Class Markets

SPONSORS

Bulkley, Richardson & Gelinas

Holyoke Medical Center

Health New England

Senator Eric P. Lesser

Massachusetts General Hospital

Mercy Medical Center

Congressman Richard E. Neal

New England Farm Workers' Council

PeoplesBank

The Republican

Springfield College

Springfield Regional Chamber of Commerce

Springfield Symphony Orchestra

VA Central Western Massachusetts Healthcare System

The Zonta Club of Springfield

Table of Contents

Editors' Note: In this book we have attempted to include as many historical and contemporary women of note in the Berkshire, Hampden, Franklin, Hampshire and Worcester counties of Massachusetts. Close to 1,000 women are among those listed, but we are sure that are others who deserve recognition but did not come to our attention. It is hoped future historians can use this data base to further research and expand the narrative of women's contributions to our region and nation.

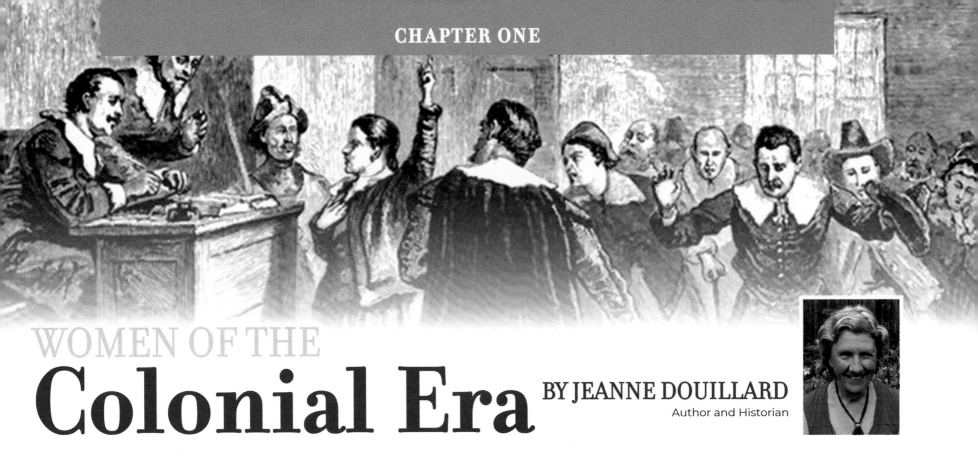

CHAPTER ONE

WOMEN OF THE
Colonial Era

BY JEANNE DOUILLARD
Author and Historian

People shape history and history shapes people. Through my reading and research, I have come to realize that an understanding of history is essential. Not the history of names and dates to be memorized, not the history of conqueror over conquered, but History as Story.

For thousands of years, women's stories have been pushed into the background of history. Women were at once playthings and family caretakers, as well as legal property, first of their fathers and then of their husbands. It was thought that women couldn't think clearly enough to be scientists, mathematicians, or leaders. Their role as mothers did not allow them to develop seriously as writers and artists; which begs the question: has this always been part of the historical narrative?

In *High Tide in Tucson*, Barbara Kingsolver notes, "If we can divine religion from relics, it seems pretty clear that... (ancient) human societies stood most in awe of female power..." If in our ancient past, women were honored and revered in society, what caused the changes that we struggle with today?

Was it that women's roles became diminished when men realized they also had an essential part to play in the conception of a child? Did a change occur in the transition from hunter/gatherer societies to agricultural communities? Animals roamed free in the wild, hunted by men. In villages, men became "owners" of animals, which gradually became a commodity that could be handed down from father to son. Women were thus left out. From partner, woman became property and this narrative has been carried down through history, touching the lives of most women. This book attempts to set the record straight by bringing to light unknown stories from America's past.

If we dig deep, as the writers of this chapter have done, we find surprising tales of women who helped shape the early years of Western and Central Massachusetts. This first chapter illuminates the lives of some of these women, from all races and backgrounds: slaves, free women of color, Native American women and English women who inhabited these areas in the early years. We find stories of women who were captured in Native/French raids and were brought to Canada and chose to remain there; stories of women who were eventually bought back and returned to New England. There are tales of captured English women who were brought to Native villages, became enculturated and chose to live with the Native peoples for the rest of their lives; stories of valiant women accused of witchcraft and tales of the spurious reasons why they were accused... important stories that make history come alive.

This chapter also highlights several Native women who were involved in land "sales" to Englishmen in early Western and Central Massachusetts. Granted, there were many misunderstandings in these transactions, for the concept of land ownership was foreign to Native peoples. In most cases, the Natives believed they were offering to "share" this land with the Europeans and these "misunderstandings," as history reveals, led to tremendous suffering for the indigenous peoples of New England and elsewhere.

Wayne Phaneuf, Executive Editor of *The Republican*, wrote: "In today's world we are at an historical moment that is being led by women whether it be the fight for equal pay and opportunity or an end to sexual harassment. They follow in the footsteps of centuries of struggle to end slavery, to secure the vote and assure rights that were reserved only for men. This book will help to tell the story of their accomplishments and struggles."

Women of the Colonial Era
Mary Bliss Parsons

"Jury Finds Mary Parsons Not Guilty of Witchcraft, May 13, 1675"

Colonial Massachusetts has a well-deserved reputation as a litigious culture; fortunately it was also a record-keeping one. County courthouses are full of 300 year-old documents — depositions, trial transcripts, judges' orders — that allow historians to reconstruct the stories of the people accused of witchcraft. One of the best documented, and most unusual, is the case of Mary Bliss Parsons of Northampton.

Mary Bliss and Joseph Parsons married in Hartford in 1646. After several years in Springfield, the Parsons family, which now included three children, moved to Northampton, a brand new settlement some 20 miles up the Connecticut River. Joseph Parsons soon became one of Northampton's leading citizens. A successful merchant, he served as a selectman and on the committee to build the first meetinghouse. Since the Parsons also owned the first tavern in town, they were right in the thick of things.

Another couple, Sarah and James Bridgman, followed a similar route but had a very different experience than the Parsons. They also wed in Hartford, moved to Springfield, and then on to Northampton, where a feud developed between the two families.

Soon after arriving in Northampton, Mary Parsons gave birth to a son, the first English child born in the town. That same month, Sarah Bridgman had a baby boy. When he died two weeks later, she claimed it was the result of Mary's witchcraft. Rumors began to swirl about the town. Joseph Parsons decided to go on the offensive. He charged James Bridgman with slander for spreading rumors about Mary Parsons' alleged witchcraft.

Even though juries usually sided with the plaintiff in such cases, Joseph Parsons was taking a risk by bringing rumors to the attention of officials. Authorities might decide there was merit to the accusations, and the plaintiff could suddenly find herself the defendant.

The case was heard at the Magistrates' Court in Cambridge in October 1656; 33 depositions were given. Almost half of Northampton's 32 households sent a witness; a few others came from Springfield.

Sarah Bridgman related her tale of how in May 1654 she heard a "great blow on the door" and immediately sensed a change in her newborn. Then she saw "two women pass by the door with white cloths on their heads." The women disappeared, and Bridgman concluded her son would die because "there

[was] wickedness in the place."

Such testimony was the norm in witch trials. An argument took place, and when something went awry later, people attributed the problem to witchcraft. One Northampton woman testified that the yarn she had spun for Mary Parsons ended up full of knots. Since the yarn the woman spun for others had no knots, she concluded that Mary's witchcraft was the cause. Another woman blamed Mary Parsons when her daughter fell ill shortly after she had refused to let the girl work for Parsons. One man stated that the day after "some discontent[ed] words passed" between himself and Mary Parsons, he found his cow in the yard "ready to die," which it did two weeks later.

A number of people testified in Mary Parsons' defense. Three women described Sarah Bridgman's baby as "sick as soon as it was born." A neighbor stated that the cow in question had died of "water in the belly." The court ruled in favor of the Parsons. The Bridgmans were given the choice of paying a fine or making a public apology. They paid the fine.

The feud and Mary Parsons' ordeal resumed 18 years later, in 1674, when the Bridgmans' son-in-law filed a new complaint. He "strongly suspect[ed] that [his wife] died by some unusual means, viz, by means of some evell Instrument." The instrument he had in mind was Mary Bliss Parsons.

On January 5, 1675, the county magistrates summoned Mary to appear before them. Women searched her body for "witch's teats," unexplained (to seventeenth-century eyes) protrusions where "imps" were said to suck. The record is silent as to what they did or did not find, but in March the Court of Assistants in Boston sent Mary Parsons to prison to await trial. The records from this trial do not survive, but we know that on May 13, 1675, a jury found her not guilty.

The Parsons returned to Northampton, but in 1679 or 1680, they moved back to Springfield, perhaps to escape the rumors that continued to dog them. Mary Bliss Parsons was in her mid-80s when she died in 1712.

Although Mary Parsons occupied a far more secure social position than almost all of the other women charged with witchcraft in early New England — after all, she was the wife of one of the richest, most respected men in Western Massachusetts — her experience fit the norm in other ways. Middle-aged women were the most likely to be accused of witchcraft. The issues of jealousy, personal animosity, and family feuds that were so evident in her case would fuel the Salem witch hysteria of 1692 as well.

The horror that began in Salem Village (present day Danvers) and spread to almost every town in Essex county saw women, children, and men, including the former minister of Salem Village, hauled before magistrates. At one point some 170 accused witches were being held in jails in Ipswich, Salem, Boston, and Cambridge. Between June and September of 1692, authorities hanged 19 people and pressed one to death; four more died in prison, awaiting trial. In 1693 the madness ended. There would be no more convictions and executions for witchcraft in New England, although it would be another century before the belief in witches lost its hold on the people of the region. – *Mass Moments*, Mass Humanities

Lucy Terry Prince

(B. CA. 1730 IN AFRICA; D. 1821 IN SUNDERLAND, VT) Lucy Terry Prince's obituary is noteworthy first because of its length — obituaries at that time were generally brief, especially for women — and second because newspapers rarely took note of a black person's passing. Lucy was living in Vermont when she died, and her obituary was originally published in the *Vermont Gazette*. The fact that it was reprinted in a Greenfield, Massachusetts paper suggests that, while she had left the state years before, she had not been forgotten.

Born in Africa, Lucy was kidnapped as a small child and brought to Bristol, Rhode Island, where merchants grew rich from Rhode Island's flourishing slave trade. She was about four when Ebenezer Wells, a tavern owner from Deerfield, purchased her and took her to live with him and his wife in Western Massachusetts.

The Wellses were childless, and Lucy may have been more integrated into their household than most "servants for life," as New Englanders called their enslaved men and women. Records show that Lucy was baptized in 1735 and became a church member nine years later.

On the morning of August 25, 1746, Deerfield came under assault from the Abenakis. The settlement had endured violent raids before, but things had been quiet from the mid-1720s to the 1740s. The attack on Deerfield by the French-allied Abenaki in 1746 found "the English colonists woefully unprepared to war." Five whites were killed, along with two Abenaki. At 21, Lucy already had a reputation as a gifted storyteller. It surprised no one when she composed a poem, "The Bars Fight," about the traumatic events of that day.

The poem opened: "August 'twas the twenty-fifth, / Seventeen hundred forty-six; / The Indians did in ambush lay, / Some very valiant men to slay." She names the casualties of the attack along with some information about how they met their fate.

The poem drew on the African tradition of oral narrative. Although Lucy Terry was literate, scholars have speculated that she may not in fact have written "The Bars Fight" down at all but told and re-told the story and others repeated it. The earliest print version found is from a lecture given in 1819. The poem first appeared in a book when it was included in a history of Western Massachusetts published in 1855.

Sometime around 1750, Abijah Prince, an enterprising formerly enslaved man who had served in the Massachusetts Bay militia,

Deerfield captives, 1704.

moved to Deerfield. He and Lucy married on May 17, 1756 and moved onto land owned by the Wells family. At some point, Lucy gained her freedom. It is possible that Ebenezer Wells gave Lucy her freedom or the hard-working Abijah may have purchased it. In any case, she, and therefore her children, were free by the time the first of their six children was born in 1757. Two of their sons would serve in the American Revolution.

By 1785 the family had left Deerfield and were living on their own land in Guilford, Vermont. Twenty years older than Lucy, Abijah died in 1794, and the family struggled to retain the property it had worked so hard to acquire. Lucy died on July 11, 1821, at the age of 97. She was an important enough figure that the principal speaker at her funeral was the Rev.

Lemuel Haynes, the first African American to be ordained in the Congregational Church.

Over time, a number of legends developed about Lucy Terry Prince. One has it that she confronted the trustees of Williams College when they refused to admit her son. No documentation exists and the encounter is highly unlikely. Another is that she appeared before the U.S. Supreme Court, an event that new research has shown did not occur. However, in 1803 she did successfully argue an appeal of a land case before the Vermont Supreme Court — remarkable evidence of the eloquence and assertiveness of Lucy Terry Prince. – *Mass Moments*, Mass Humanities

Eunice Williams

On January 23, 1800, a man named Thomas Thorakwaneken Williams arrived in Longmeadow, Massachusetts, after a long journey from his home near Montreal. His hosts were his third cousin and her husband Nathaniel Ely. Thomas had brought his two sons, 11-year-old Eleazer and seven-year-old John, to live with the Ely family while attending the local school.

This was not an unusual arrangement for the time; it was common practice for parents to send their children to live in the homes of friends and relatives for a few years. There was, however, something very unusual about this particular situation. Thomas Williams and his sons were members of the Kanienkehaka Mohawk tribe.

The story begins in the winter of 1704 in Deerfield, Massachusetts, an outpost on the Massachusetts frontier. For nearly 30 years, this small Connecticut River Valley village had endured intermittent attacks by the French and their Native American allies who had joined forces to resist the spread of English settlement. Deerfield was attacked seven times during King Philip's War. When a new war broke out between France and Britain in the fall of 1700, the village was an obvious target. Disaster struck on February 29, 1704. In the predawn hours, as the watchman slept, a party of 50 French soldiers and about 200 Iroquois, Abenaki, Huron, and Mohawk warriors, staged a raid on Deerfield. The French goal was to devastate the village, and they succeeded. Seventeen houses were burned to the ground. Barns were also torched, with a heavy loss of livestock, tools, and provisions.

There were heavy casualties on all sides. Two Frenchmen were killed, another 22 wounded. Eight Indians died and about 20 were wounded. Some of the wounded did not survive the rigors of the return march. Forty-eight Deerfield residents were slain in the raid; 112 were taken captive and force-marched to Canada. Over 20 of the captives — mostly young children and women weakened by pregnancy and childbirth — perished on the journey north.

The Indian fighters were primarily interested in taking prisoners and getting them safely back to Canada where they could be ransomed. Ransoming captives was one way to bolster an economy weakened by the collapse of the beaver trade. Other captives would be adopted into Native American families, thus helping to replace members of the tribe who had been lost to war and disease.

The French generally measured victory in terms of property destroyed and enemy killed, but at Deerfield, they, too, were seeking prisoners of war — one in particular, the town's respected minister, John Williams. The French believed that if they could take Williams captive, they could exchange him for an important French prisoner the English were holding.

The Williams home was one of the first attacked. It was ransacked and the family seized; two of the children and an enslaved woman were killed at once. Mrs. Williams, only recently delivered of her eighth child, died on the second day of the march. But the minister and five of his children reached French Canada in safety. After prolonged diplomatic negotiations, Reverend Williams and four of

Brookfield raid, 1675.

the children returned to Massachusetts. One of the Williams children, seven-year-old Eunice, could not be "redeemed." In spite of pressure from French officials, the Mohawks of Kahnawake refused to give her up, claiming they "would as soon part with their hearts." The Kahnawake were known to treat adopted members of the tribe with love and devotion. Eunice no doubt enjoyed the same nurturing and gentle discipline as children born into Mohawk culture. Within two years she had forgotten how to speak English; she lived the life of any Kahnawake girl.

In 1707 the Williams family received word that "she is in good health but seems unwilling to return." By 1713 she had married a Native American. When an agent hired by her father arranged to meet with Eunice, she refused to speak to him. He reported that her Indian relatives "leave her to act her liberty respecting her return."

It was nearly a decade after the Deerfield raid before John Williams himself traveled to Canada to see his daughter. He was heartbroken that "she is yet obstinately resolved to live and dye here, and will not so much as give me one pleasant look... After John Williams' death, his sons continued to make overtures to their "captive" sister but got no response. Finally, in 1740, 36 years after her capture, they met with Eunice and her husband in Albany. Several visits to Massachusetts followed.

The Williamses tried in vain to persuade Eunice to settle among them in Massachusetts — to finally be "redeemed." Although she felt affection for her English siblings, she had no desire to return to her childhood home. She died in the Mohawk village of Kahnawake, surrounded by her Indian family, at the age of 89. Her descendants live there still.

Thomas Williams, the man who traveled to Longmeadow in January 1800, did not share his grandmother's feelings. He arranged for his sons to be educated in Massachusetts. When they arrived, the boys could not speak a word of English; they were wearing Native dress, and their manner and behaviors were described as "wild" and "curious." The boys gradually adopted the dress, language, and manners of their new community. John returned to Canada, while Eleazer remained in the United States. – *Mass Moments*, Mass Humanities

Mashalisk (aka Mishalisk)
(B. CA. 1610; D. AFT APRIL 1674)
Algonquian Native American elder of the Pocumtucks of the upper Pioneer Valley. The following is the text as transcribed by historian Harry Andrew Wright of a deed to John Pynchon of Springfield of lands which became part of present day Deerfield, MA:

"These presents testifie, That Mashalisk (the old woman, Mother of Wuttawwalunincksin [aka Wallauckinksin]) doth hereby Bargaine sell & allienate a Tract of Land in ye Southerly side of Pacomtuck River & so lying all along by Quinetticot River side downe to ye Lower Point of ye Hill called Wequomps & by ye English Sugarloafe hill: all ye Tract of Land between ye greate River Quinetticot on ye east & ye ledge of Mountaines on ye west, & on ye Northward fro Pacomtuck River Mouth, Mantehelant downe southward to Wequomps & to ye very Point of land where ye hills come to ye greate River called Tawwat or Tawwattuck Togither wth all ye Islands in ye greate River, called Mattampash, AUinnack, or AUinnackcooke, Taukkanackcoss, or by whatever other names they may be called, all ye whole sd Tract of Land Mantehelant Mattampash downe to Tawwat or Tawwattuck & so by ye ledge of Mountaines lie fro greate River westward. The sd Mashalisk Doth sell all to John Pynchon of Springfield to him his heires & assignes forever, flor & in Consideration of a debt of ten large Severs & other debts of Wuttawolunicksin her sons wch shee acknowledges her self engaged for ye Payment off to John Pynchon aforesd: for the said Just and due Debts & moreover for & in consideration of sixty fada of wampum. 2. cotes some cotton & Severall other small things all wch ye sd Mashalisk acknowledge to have Reed & to be therwth fully satisfied & contented. Doe fully clearly & absolutely give Grant Bargaine & sell unto John Pynchon of Springfield aforesd, hereby giving granting & resigning up to him all my right Title & interest in ye aforesd land: To Have & to Hold all the sd land to ye only proper use & Behoofe of him ye sd John Pynchon his heires & assigns for ever, wth all ye profits advantages & comoditys thereoff & theretmto belonging whatsoever, & that for ever: And ye sd Meshalisk doth hereby covenant & promise too & wth ye sd John Pynchon, that shee will ye sd Pynchon save harmless of & from all manner of claimes right title & interest of any other person whatsoever unto ye sd Land hereby sold & will defend ye same from all or any Molestation or Incumbrance of Indians right to all or anypart thereof : and as having full right & lawful Power thus to doe, Doth in witness thereof! here unto affix her hand & scale this 26th day of August 1672."

Elisabeth "Betty" (Parsons) Allen
(B. MAR. 25, 1716 IN NORTHAMPTON, MA; D. JAN. 10, 1800 IN NORTHAMPTON, MA)
was a celebrated mid-wife in Northampton for over 50 years and "assisted in bringing 3000 children into the world," according to D. A. R. registrar Lottie S. Corbin. Seven of her sons fought in the American Revolution, many becoming officers. The Daughters of the American Revolution chapter for Northampton is named the "Betty Allen Chapter." – Joseph Carvalho III & Cynthia G. Simison

Margaret Bliss

(B. JULY 15, 1595 IN GLOUCESTERSHIRE, ENGLAND; D. AUG. 28, 1684 IN THE LONGMEADOW SECTION OF SPRINGFIELD, MASSACHUSETTS BAY COLONY) Widowed in Hartford, Margaret Bliss moved her family in 1645 to Springfield/ Longmeadow and managed her affairs "with great prudence and Judgement". She acquired land and a house that stood for 200 years after her death in 1684. She defended her property rights in court on several occasions including bravely suing William Pynchon, the local magistrate and leader of the "plantation" for raising the level of a dam which flooded her property.
– Joseph Carvalho III & Robert Magovern

Mary (Pynchon) Holyoke

(B. 1623 IN ESSEX, ENGLAND; D. OCT. 20, 1657 IN SPRINGFIELD, MASSACHUSETTS BAY COLONY) was the daughter of William Pynchon [founder of Springfield], wife of Elizur Holyoke, and one of the most prominent and wealthy women of the early Springfield settlement.
– Joseph Carvalho III

Kesquando Pomatikenio

daughter of Squakeage Sachem Mashepetott, Algonquian Native-American members of the Squakheages in the area now known as Northfield, MA. She was mentioned in a deed of land (parts of today's towns of Bernardston, Gill, and Northfield) to Joseph Parsons and William Clarke of Northampton on June 15, 1695. – Joseph Carvalho III

Kewenusk

(B. CA. 1595 LIVED IN AGAWAM [LATER PART OF MASSACHUSETTS BAY COLONY]; Algonquian Native American of the Agawam clan, mother of Cuttonus "the right owner of Agawam & Quana," and wife of Wenawis (d. bef. 1636). She is mentioned in the July 15, 1636 deed of land to William Pynchon, Henry Smith and Jehu Burr, English settlers from the

Bliss House at Main and Loring Streets in Springfield, MA (built in 1645).

Massachusetts Colony. Cuttonus signed the deed "in the name of his mother."
– Joseph Carvalho III

Majessett

Algonquian Native American, daughter of Sachem Quanquan (d. before 1672) and "Sarah," was mentioned in the Deed of land to the town of Hatfield on Oct. 19, 1672.
– Joseph Carvalho III

Masconomo

an Algonquian Native American of the Nipmuc people of what is now Worcester and Middlesex Counties, was referred to as "the squaw Sachem of Nashobah" in colonial documents ca. 1632. The term Nashoba is the Nipmuc name for the area that would later be settled by the English as Littleton, MA. However, in that Masconomo was regarded by the colonial authorities as the only representative of the Nipmucks at the colonial "General Court," she may have had wider influence beyond the immediate Nashoba village amongst the much larger Nipmuck community of that time period.
– Joseph Carvalho III

Mary (Pynchon) Holyoke headstone, Springfield Cemetary, Maple St. in Springfield, MA.

Mattabauge

an Algonquian Native American mentioned in a deed of land to the town of Hatfield dated Oct. 19, 1672. – Joseph Carvalho III

Mary (Dickinson) Mattoon

(B. MAR. 10, 1758 IN AMHERST, MA; D. JULY 30, 1835 IN AMHERST, MA) was the influential wife of Revolutionary War General Ebenezer Mattoon. They owned large tracts of land in North and East Amherst, Leverett, and Pelham, MA. She was in charge of the family's affairs whenever Her husband was away in service to the Patriot cause, and in support of General William Shepard defending the U.S. Arsenal at Springfield during Shay's Rebellion. While her husband was away in Springfield with his Amherst militiamen, Mary had the occasion to defend her home from an interloping Shaysite

by forcing him back out of the window with her broom. The D.A.R. chapter of Amherst is named in her honor, Mary Mattoon Chapter. – Joseph Carvalho III

Mauhammetpeet

was a noted Mahican Native American member of the Schaghticokes, wife of Fiahpuhcaumin and granddaughter of Ohweemin respected female leader of the clan. She and her sister Mequnnisqua "who were the true Sole and rightful owners of the land [as described in the deed]" deeded land (now parts of the towns of Charlemont, Ashfield, Buckland, Colrain, Florida, Hawley, Heath, Monroe, Rowe, and Savoy) to the Massachusetts Bay Colony on Aug. 9, 1735. – Joseph Carvalho III

Niarum

(B. CA. 1600; LIVED IN AGAWAM IN 1636 [LATER PART OF MASSACHUSETTS BAY COLONY]; D. CA. 1652) Algonquian Native American of the respected elders of the Agawam clan, was

the wife of Coa, a sachem of the Agawams and one of the signatories to the deed of land to William Pynchon, Henry Smith and Jehu Burr leaders of the first English settlers to the Pioneer Valley, dated July 15, 1636. Her husband Coa also deeded land [now part of Longmeadow, MA] to John Pynchon of Springfield on April 14, 1652. – Joseph Carvalho III

Paupsunnuck

Algonquian Native American member of the Woronoco, wife of Pauneasum, deeded Woronoco land on the northeast side of the Woronoco River to John Pynchon of Springfield, May 4, 1663. – Joseph Carvalho III

Potucksisq

(b. ca. 1600 in Agawam region; d. after 1666), Algonquian Native American of the Agawam clan and referred to as "owner" (most probably on behalf of her clan) of land called "the higher meadow" along the Agawam river (now called the Westfield River) in what is now Agawam, MA, referred to in a deed to the town of Springfield dated June 20, 1666. – Joseph Carvalho III

Quan

a Stockbridge Native American woman, was a signatory to a deed of land (parts of today's Egremont and Alford) to the Colony of Massachusetts Bay on Oct. 29, 1756. – Joseph Carvalho III

Mary (White) Rowlandson

LATER MARY TALCOTT (B. 1637 IN SOMERSET, ENGLAND; D. JANUARY 5, 1711 IN MASSACHUSETTS BAY COLONY) was a colonial English woman who was captured by Native Americans during King Philip's War and held for 11 weeks before being ransomed. Mary White was born c. 1637 in Somerset, England. Her family left England sometime before 1650, settled at Salem in the Massachusetts Bay Colony and moved in 1653 to Lancaster, on the Massachusetts frontier. There she married Reverend Joseph Rowlandson of Ipswich, Massachusetts, in 1656.

At sunrise on February 10, 1675, during King Philip's War, Lancaster came under attack by a war band of Narragansetts, Wampanoags and Nashaway/Nipmucs. During the attack, the Native American raiding party killed 13 people and took at least 24 people captive. Rowlandson and her three children, Joseph, Mary, and Sarah, were among those taken in the raid. Rowlandson's 6-year-old daughter, Sarah died from her wounds after a week of captivity.

For more than 11 weeks, Rowlandson and her children were forced to accompany the war band as they travelled through the wilderness to carry out other raids and to elude the English colonial militia. On May 2, 1676, Rowlandson was ransomed for £20 raised by the women of Boston in a public subscription and paid by John Hoar of Concord at Redemption Rock in Princeton, Massachusetts. In 1682, six years after her ordeal, *The Sovereignty and Goodness of God: Being a Narrative of the Captivity and Restoration of Mrs. Mary Rowlandson* was published. This text is considered a seminal American work in the literary genre of captivity narratives. It went through four printings in 1682 and garnered readership both in the New England colonies and in England, leading it to be considered by some as the first American "bestseller."
– Joseph Carvalho III

"Sarah," Christian

English name of Algonquian Native American "ye wife of Quanquan Sachem late deceased," mentioned in a deed of land to the town of Hatfield dated Oct. 19, 1672.
– Joseph Carvalho III

Seconsk

Algonquian Native-American member of the Woronoco (native-American clan living in the area now the city of Westfield, MA) was the wife of Kenip, a Sachem of the Woronoco, and mentioned in the April 20, 1641 land deal between William Pynchon and the Woronoco.
– Joseph Carvalho III

Marguerite Stebbins

(NEE ABIGAIL STEBBINS, B. DEERFIELD, MASSACHUSETTS BAY COLONY; D. 1740 IN QUEBEC PROV. CANADA)
was married to a French-Canadian "Coureurs de bois" named Jacques de Noyon. They lived in Deerfield when it was attacked by a raiding party made up of French and Native Americans on Feb. 29, 1704. Abigail was captured and brought to Canada. She was baptized as a Catholic in 1708 and her name was changed to Marguerite. Her husband left his family to pursue his frontier adventures, leaving Marguerite to fend for herself. She proved to have excellent "business skills" and she petitioned the French colonial court to allow her to transact business in her own name, French law dictated that men and women owned marital property equally. Either spouse could apply to the courts for a "separation of goods," if the other spouse was not a responsible fiscal partner. English common law did not give women this right. In this Marguerite was better off in Canada than in New England. She conducted several real estate transactions and the family did well financially until she died in 1740 at which time Jacques returned and left the estate in arrears at the time of his death in 1745.
– Jeanne Douillard

Mariah "Mary" Swinck

(B. CA. 1639 IN NEW AMSTERDAM ?; D. NOV. 24, 1708 IN SPRINGFIELD, MA)
was the first known African-American woman to live in Western Massachusetts. She was the wife of Peter Swinck, the first free black settler in Western Massachusetts.
– Joseph Carvalho III

Lydia (Chapin) Taft

(FEBRUARY 2, 1712 MENDON, MA; NOVEMBER 9, 1778 UXBRIDGE, MA)
was the first woman known to legally vote in colonial America. This occurred at a Town Meeting in the town of Uxbridge in Massachusetts Bay Colony. Given the important nature of the vote, the landowner and taxpayer status of Josiah's estate, and the fact that young Bazaleel, Caleb's younger brother, was a minor, the townspeople voted to allow Lydia, "the widow Josiah Taft," to vote in this important meeting. Taft voted at the Uxbridge town meeting on October 30, 1756, becoming the first recorded legal woman voter in the American colonies.
– Joseph Carvalho III

Deborah (Thayer) Wheelock

(B. DEC. 12, 1741 IN MENDON, MA; D. NOV. 15, 1815 IN UXBRIDGE, MA)
was the wife of Simeon Wheelock, 1st Lieutenant of the Uxbridge militia company of minutemen who answered the call for the defense of Lexington and Concord. After the war, Simeon answered the call to arms in Shay's Rebellion but never returned home. Deborah was left to provide for her family by herself with her youngest child being only 2 years old. The D.A.R. chapter for Uxbridge is named after her. – Joseph Carvalho III

Woolauootatimesqua

Native American member of the Schaghticokes, sister of Schaghticoke sachem Nepuscauteusqua, and mother to sons Ompontinnuwas, Penewanse, Cockiyouwah, and Wallenas. Her sons were signatories on her behalf to a deed of land (lands which are now parts of today's towns of Athol, Barre, Dana, Gardner, Hubbardston, Petersham, Phillipston, Princeton, Rutland, Templeton, and Westminster) to the Colony of Massachusetts Bay dated Aug. 29, 1735.
– Joseph Carvalho III

The Bars Fight

BY LUCY TERRY PRINCE

August, twas the twenty-fifth,
Seventeen hundred forty-six,
The Indians did in ambush lay,
Some very valiant men to slay
Twas nigh unto Sam Dickinson's mill,
The Indians there five men did kill.
The names of whom I'll not leave out,
Samuel Allen like a hero foute,
And though he was so brave and bold,
His face no more shall we behold.
Eleazer Hawks was killed outright,
Before he had time to fight,
Before he did the Indians see,
Was shot and killed immediately.
Oliver Amsden he was slain,
Which caused his friends much grief and pain.

Simeon Amsden they found dead
Not many rods from Oliver's head.
Adonijah Gillett, we do hear,
Did lose his life which was so dear.
John Sadler fled across the water,
And thus escaped the dreadful slaughter.
Eunice Allen see the Indians comeing
And hoped to save herself by running:
And had not her petticoats stopt her,
The awful creatures had not cotched her,
Not tommyhawked her on the head,
And left her on the ground for dead.
Young Samuel Allen, Oh! lack-a-day!
Was taken and carried to Canada.

– *transcribed by the Pioneer Valley History Network*

Wompely

wife of Nenpownam, Algonquian Native American members of the Squakheages mentioned in a deed of land (parts of today's towns of Bernardston, Northfield, and Warwick) to the town of Northfield on May 24, 1686. – Joseph Carvalho III

At left: Woodcut image of Mary Rowlandson
Above: Algonquian woman in diorama at the Springfield Science Museum, Springfield Museums, Springfield, MA

CHAPTER TWO

WOMEN IN
Education

BY TERESA E. REGINA
Retired Administrator, Springfield School Dept.

Education - essential for society's development - ensures individual growth and enlightenment. Through 1960, 40 years after women received the right to vote in the United States, women had few basic choices at the end of their formal education. In spite of these views, women in Western Massachusetts excelled in schools in areas that were traditionally professions for men.

Northampton School for Girls, the library ca. 1945.

From the early settlement years, education aimed to prepare one for life, which included spiritual, economic, and creative needs. In the 17th century, the Puritan community in Springfield sought to have children learn to read and write to discover God's word. In the 18th and 19th centuries, students' preparation for life meant learning to read not only for religion and salvation, but to prepare for careers, such as doctors, lawyers, teachers, machinists, clerks, and scholars.

Education for all children was important from the beginning in Western Massachusetts. Settlers came from the eastern colony where Harvard College was established for men in 1636, the same year that Springfield was settled. Five years later in 1641, Springfield selectmen ordered teaching of reading to enable children to learn their catechism.

Although the selectmen also ordered a

school building that would be maintained by the community, resources were not available from the new, small settlement. Dame schools emerged where females taught in private homes and were paid with produce in the summer and with firewood in the winter.

When the town was destroyed in 1675 during the King Philip's War, a school was operated in the meeting-house tower. By 1679, a one room schoolhouse was built, mostly attended by boys ages 5-18.

During the 1700s, progress in education was slow. Many young men, instead of going to school, patrolled the woods north of Springfield for Indian raiding parties and helped families on the farms. The Indian Wars and the American Revolution took the boys from schools. By 1785, the Williamstown Free School, which would become Williams College in 1793, was established. Although for men,

Mary Lyon, the formidable founder of Mount Holyoke College in South Hadley, MA.

this initiative would establish the need for future schools for both men and women. In an unsuccessful attempt to relocate Williams College to Amherst, Amherst College was founded in 1821.

With urbanization, formal and coordinated education was needed. Although considered experimental in the 1820s, the first high school opened in Springfield in 1828. The second floor held a girls' private school. The public high school emphasized grammar, spelling, arithmetic, U.S. history, and algebra. In 1856, the first high school class received diplomas with eight girls and one boy.

A new and changing country affected by wars, a depressed economy, and a changing ideology of women's roles in society developed educational opportunities, especially with a liberal education and in areas of study which previously were considered reserved for men. Mount Holyoke Female Seminary, founded in South Hadley in 1837, had rigorous academic requirements for entrance and a demanding course of study, which excluded the domestic areas.

Mary Lyon, the founder, worked diligently to raise funds for the school and to prove that women could excel in what may be considered male studies, like chemistry.

Other schools for women opened later in the 19th century and many developed in the early 20th century. Smith College opened in Northampton in 1875 with 14 students. Sophia Smith left her large inheritance to establish the college for women to rival any school for males. In 1897, the Bay Path Institute opened in Springfield at State and Dwight Streets to focus on business skills. By 1920, the school moved to 100 Chestnut Street. In 1945, the Institute became the Bay Path Secretarial School for Women in Longmeadow with expanded business opportunities. The Elms College, co-founded in 1897 in Pittsfield by the Sisters of St. Joseph and the Diocese of Springfield, was a girls' preparatory academy and moved to Chicopee in 1899 as St. Joseph's Normal College. The school's charter, approved in 1928 as a women's liberal arts college specializing in education, was named the College of Our Lady of the Elms.

It is in this historical context that women who lived, learned, and worked in Western and Central Massachusetts developed and contributed to society. Not accepting gender limits, these women did not limit their own aspirations. Women made a mark in public and private education. All believed in education, in liberal arts, in expanding critical thinking skills that would lead their students to develop in diverse fields and to make their own contributions to a "new" nation.

Women's Colleges and Girls Schools

Mary Lyon and Mount Holyoke College

BY PATRICIA CAHILL

Mary Lyon, the formidable founder of Mount Holyoke College in South Hadley, grew up on a farm in Buckland. She was born in 1797, one of eight children. Her father died when she was six years old. She learned the skills needed on a farm.

But Mary Lyon wanted more.

She would become famous for the college she founded in 1837, which in her lifetime was called Mount Holyoke Women's Seminary. It is the oldest in a circle of Northeast colleges known as the Seven Sisters, revered for their high standards and their success in turning out women leaders.

It seems incredible that, in her day, a lone woman could achieve all that. But Mary Lyon had an insatiable thirst for knowledge, the heart of a lion, and a deep belief that women's intellect was equal to that of men

And she was born, after all, in the "Age of Enlightenment," which brimmed with revolutionary ideas about science and politics. She also lived at a time when education was a subject of great concern to thinking Americans. She met proponents of women's education and of teacher training.

As a child, Mary Lyon went to schools in Buckland and Ashfield. She began teaching in Shelburne Falls at age 17. She taught in different schools in different seasons, in eastern and western Massachusetts. In between, she used her earnings to further her own education.

It was a grueling schedule. Teachers often had to board with local families to be near a school. One family Lyon lived with was that of Edward Hitchcock, celebrated science professor and eventually president of Amherst College, who encouraged her love of science.

While teaching in Ipswich, Mary Lyon met Zilpah Grant, who, like her, wanted to further the cause of women's education. They teamed up to establish two schools for girls, in Derry, NH, and Ipswich, MA.

Neither of those schools lasted long, and in 1834, Mary Lyon decided to forge ahead on her own. By then she had developed a large network and a fine reputation as a teacher. She hit the road to gather support and raise funds for her new project. She traveled hundreds of miles, often by stagecoach.

The result was Mount Holyoke, which opened in 1837 with 80 students. Its four-story building housed dormitories, an assembly hall, dining room, library, and living space for teachers. There was a large office area for Mary Lyon, founder and principal, as the president was then called. She also taught chemistry. She insisted students have good study habits, prayer, and exercise. She had a system for assigning them chores, from setting tables to washing windows, not only to teach self-discipline, but to bring down the price of tuition.

Most important, Mary Lyon implemented an academic curriculum that was every bit as rigorous and varied as that of men.

Twelve years later, the founder of Mount Holyoke was dead at age 52. Even her robust farm-bred strength could not withstand the diseases of the time.

But her school survived – and lived up to her legacy. Outstanding scholars continued to join the faculty, including scientists of renown, such as zoologist Cornelia Clapp and botanist Henrietta Hooker, who have buildings on campus named after them.

Alumnae brought glory to their alma mater. Mary E. Woolley, 11th president of Mount Holyoke (1901-1937), gave the college international stature with her support of such causes as suffrage and arms control.

Many women's colleges have gone co-ed

Mary Brigham Hall, Mount Holyoke College, South Hadley, MA

in the past century. But in 1971, Mount Holyoke College made a decision. It declined.

Smith College

BY JANE KAUFMAN

Founded by the daughter of a farmer from Hatfield, Smith College began with an ambitious and elite mission.

Sophia Smith inherited a fortune from her penurious brother Austin Smith at the age of 65. In her will, she designated funds to start the college in Northampton "to furnish for my own sex means and facilities for education equal to those which are afforded now in our Colleges to young men."

Christian higher education would help young women, she wrote: "...[T]heir 'wrongs' will be redressed, their wages adjusted, their weight of influence in reforming the evils of society will be greatly increased, as teachers, as writers, as mothers, as members of society, their power for good will be incalculably enlarged."

Founded in 1871, Smith College was the first women's college to receive a charter in Massachusetts, although Mount Holyoke

Sophia Smith, founder of Smith College in Northampton, MA

had already opened as a seminary. Smith opened in 1875 with 14 students. Admissions requirements included knowledge of classics in Greek and Latin as well as algebra, geometry and rhetoric. From its beginning the college prepared women to teach, and in 1926 the nearby Campus School was established as a laboratory elementary school.

"Knowledge is forgotten, but the faculties it has strengthened abide, and serve for higher acquisitions," wrote its first president, Laurenus Clark Seelye. Students studied classics, Romance languages, mathematics and sciences. They could take electives in art and music. Daily chapel attendance was mandatory. Tuition was $100; room and board were $250. To house students, Smith set up home-like cottages rather than dormitories, and there was a 10 o'clock lights out rule.

By 1885, half of the professors were women.

In 1893, Smith held the first women's college basketball game, and basketball was an early favorite sport at the college. In winter, students coasted downhill on rugs and hassocks and engaged in snowball fights.

The purchase of an organ in 1891 allowed students to study church music. With the completion of the Lyman Plant House in 1896, Smith could offer classes in botany. In 1897 the psychology department was added.

Smith's second president, Marion LeRoy Burton, began the college's honors program.

Under Smith's third president, William Alan Neilson, the major field of study was introduced, along with interdepartmental majors in science, landscape architecture and theater.

During World War I, Smith students and alumni went to Chateau Roblecourt at Grecourt in what had been recently occupied France. The Smith College Relief Unit offered aid and made daily deliveries of bread, milk and tools to 16 towns.

As soldiers returned from World War I, Smith offered courses that led to nursing and opened a coeducational graduate program in psychiatric social work. The model for that program remains largely unchanged.

Between the two world wars, Neilson brought distinguished faculty from Europe, and he instituted the Junior Year Abroad program in 1924.

Soon after the 1941 bombing of Pearl Harbor, the college provided facilities for the first Officers' Training Unit of the Women's Reserve, or WAVES. Smith added a summer term from 1942 to 1945, so students could graduate early and go on to government, hospital or military service.

The pall of McCarthyism hung over the campus during the 1950s, and Smith's president, Benjamin Fletcher Wright, was a defender of intellectual freedom during that era.

During the 1960s, Smith President Thomas Corwin Mendenhall overhauled the curriculum, abandoning college-wide requirements and encouraging independent study.

Jill Ker Conway became Smith's first woman president in 1975. Under her administration, the Ada Comstock Scholars Program expanded. That program allows women beyond traditional college age to earn a four-year degree.

Under Smith President Mary Maples Dun, five new majors were introduced, along with courses in non-Western and neglected American cultures.

Ruth Simmons, who became Smith's president in 1994, was the first African-American woman to head an American top-ranked college or university. Simmons oversaw many changes to the curriculum: a program that allows every Smith student to elect an internship funded by the college; an engineering program; the establishment of a poetry center and a peer-reviewed journal for scholarly works by and about women of color; and intensive seminars for first-year students and programs to encourage speaking and writing skills.

In 2004, 19 women graduated as part of the first class of engineers.

During Carol T. Christ's administration, a blueprint for the future included focus on the following subjects: international studies, environmental sustainability, and community engagement.

Today, Smith College offers a full range of undergraduate programs and a host of graduate programs. Graduate programs include studies in biological sciences, master's and Ph.D. programs in social work, dance, exercise and sport studies, playwrighting, interdisciplinary studies, teaching, and a mathematics post-baccalaureate degree program.

As of 2013, Kathleen McCartney is Smith's 11th president.

"Smith is a national leader in its number of Fulbright fellowships," she stated. "Among liberal arts institutions, Smith is one of the top recipients of National Science Foundation funding. Our alumnae have broken barriers and changed the landscape for women everywhere."

From Horace Mann's Normal School to Today's Westfield State University

BY PATRICIA CAHILL

Westfield State University has an important place in the history of women and education. It was the first public co-educational Normal School in the country.

First, an explanation of the curious name. A Normal School was a teachers' college. Nothing strange about that – except that at the start of the 1800s, the concept of teaching teachers must have seemed outlandish to Americans. After all, wasn't the only thing teachers had to do was stand up and tell children what they knew about a subject?

But in the decades after the Revolutionary War, it became clear something was lacking. One-room schoolhouses, home schooling, unruly classrooms and ill-prepared instructors would not help the young country move forward with an educated population.

A Normal School would establish what elementary and high school students were expected to master, and how to achieve that end. It would involve hands-on experience. Teachers in public schools were abysmally paid. A Normal School would give them the stature of professionals.

Supporters of the Normal School movement included Horace Mann, an Ivy-League lawyer and legislator who devoted his life to public education.

In 1838, the Massachusetts Board of Education decided to give it a try. It chose Lexington and Barre as sites for Normal Schools. Lexington Normal School for Females evolved into Framington State College.

In Barre, the Normal School was co-ed. It moved to Westfield in 1844, after its young principal died. Principal Samuel P. Newman had sacrificed a post at Bowdoin College in Maine for the many-layered, exhausting job at the Normal School.

"His health broke down," writes Westfield history professor Robert T. Brown, author of *The Rise and Fall of the People's College: The Westfield State Normal School 1839-1914.*

The school at Barre had opened in 1839 with 12 women and eight men. In 1859, in Westfield, it had 260 students. Applicants to the Normal School had to pass tests, provide character references, and pledge to teach for at least two years after graduation. In addition to their education courses, they had to study such areas as writing, logic, history, arithmetic, algebra, geometry, astronomy, geography, grammar, and "principles of piety and morality."

Alumnae of the Normal School spread seeds of knowledge throughout the nation and abroad. An alumna named Harriet E. Davis reported in 1855 that she had taught for a year in Sterling, two years in Holyoke, and two in Westfield, before marrying and raising three sons. Others made teaching a lifetime career.

Two of the alumnae of 1877, sisters Mary and Frances Allen of Deerfield, gained fame for their photography in the period between 1890 and 1920.

The school opened its first residence hall in 1874, with 68 bedrooms for 175 students. In 1956, Westfield State left its downtown location and moved to its current expansive, leafy Western Avenue campus.

The Normal School was re-named Westfield State Teachers College in 1932. In 1956 it became Westfield State College, and could grant four-year degrees that were not expressly for teaching. In 2010 it became Westfield State University.

Vicky Carwein became the first woman president of Westfield State in 2004. Today the number of male and female students is about equal, but in the past women outnumbered men, especially in wartime. From 1898 to 1902, no males enrolled.

"Because the overwhelming majority of our students were women, and I was working in an era of growing interest in women's history," wrote Professor Robert Brown in the introduction to his 1988 book *The Rise and Fall of the People's College: The Westfield State Normal School 1839-1914.* "I came to see the Normal Schools as playing a significant roles in the history of American women."

The College of Our Lady of the Elms

BY PATRICIA CAHILL

The College of Our Lady of the Elms in Chicopee was founded by and for women.

The Catholic Diocese in Springfield bought the land in Chicopee for the purpose of starting a female academy in 1899, but the Sisters of St. Joseph staffed it from the start and are considered the founders.

Today the Elms (as it is often called) is a co-educational liberal arts college on a 27-acre campus in Chicopee, offering 37 majors to students of varied faiths. It started out on a small scale, serving about 20 girls of mostly Irish descent. In the early years they wore black uniforms, according to Elms professor Thomas Moriarty, in a history he wrote for the college's centennial in 1999. Throughout its history, some students have been residential, some commuters.

A parish priest, Father John J. McCoy, originally proposed acquiring the Chicopee property for the academy. The Diocese had tried before. In 1897 it had established a St. Joseph Academy in Pittsfield. Instead of becoming the Elms, the Pittsfield institution evolved into St. Joseph Central High School and survived until 2017.

In the early years the Academy of Our Lady of the Elms, as the Chicopee school was then called, were Mother Mary Albina (born Annie Murphy) and Bishop Thomas Beavan. The names of the original teachers, all nuns, are also on record: Sisters Mary Valerian, Mary Justinian, Mary Emmanuel, Mary Alacoque, Mary Chrysostom, Mary Genevieve, and Mary Simeone.

At the turn of the century, "academy" referred to a school for children of elementary or high school age. By 1902, the Elms was offering courses beyond the high school level, according to Moriarty. By 1910, it included a two-year Normal School program (teacher's college) designed for those students who planned to become teachers after graduating. The Elms building it was housed in was called St. Joseph's Normal School.

In the years that followed, more buildings on campus were bought, inherited, or constructed. More faculty came, with advanced degrees, and more courses were added. As it grew, the academy sought confirmation of its evolution. In 1927, it petitioned the commonwealth for the right to award four-year degrees like other colleges of its kind.

In 1928, that right was granted and the school officially became the College of Our Lady of the Elms. Bishop Thomas S. O'Leary became its first president.

Like his predecessor, Bishop O'Leary had a partner in the Sisters of St. Joseph. His co-founder was Sister John Berchmans, born Margaret Frances Somers. With the assistance of the Elms vice president, it was Berchmans who guided the college in its long quest to gain accreditation by the New England Association of Schools and Colleges in 1942.

The building that dominates the campus and holds the president's office was re-named Berchmans Hall in 1983.

The college would wait until 1958 to appoint its first woman president, Sister Rose William. There have been five male presidents since then, and three female: Sister Mary A. Dooley (1979-94), Sister Kathleen C. Keating (1994-2001), and Sister Mary Reap, Ph.D (2009-17).

Dr. Reap was succeeded by Dr. Harry E. Dumay, who has a Ph.D in higher education administration from Boston College. Quite a different preparation than that of the little band of nuns, daughters of Irish immigrants, who, armed with courage and their Catholic faith, took on a new century and a created a new world of learning.

COLLEGE OF OUR LADY OF THE ELMS (CHICOPEE) WOMEN PRESIDENTS: Sister Rose William Murphy SSJ (1958-65); 3rd President, Sister Mary A. Dooley SSJ (1979-94; 6th President, Sister Kathleen Keating SSJ (1994-2001); 7th President, Sister Mary Reap, IHM, PhD. (2009-2017); 10th President

Bay Path University

BY JANE KAUFMAN

Founded in 1897, Bay Path's first home was at the corner of State and Dwight streets in downtown Springfield. First known as the Bay Path Institute, the co-educational business school was known for its accelerated 48-week format and strong education programs, particularly business management, accounting, teaching, and finance. Bay Path moved in 1920 to 100 Chestnut St, growing to 1,200 students by 1941.

During World War II, as young men enlisted, young women were working on the factory floor to company offices. Thomas Carr, a Springfield businessman, bought Bay Path in 1945. He shifted the school to all-women, changing the name to Bay Path Secretarial School for Women, and relocated Bay Path to Longmeadow. In 1949, Bay Path Junior College was chartered by the Commonwealth of Massachusetts to award the Associate in Science degree. President Carr increased the number of academic majors.

In 1968, President Thomas Carr stepped down from the presidency. He was succeeded by President Douglas Perkins. In 1971, Dr. A. Randle Elliott became Bay Path's third president. Elliott was dedicated to enhancing the college's academic reputation as well as broadening offerings to the community and non-traditional women.

The fourth president of Bay Path came from the faculty. In 1979, Dr. Jeannette Wright took the helm and petitioned the Commonwealth to allow Bay Path to award bachelor's degrees. The name was officially changed to Bay Path College. Wright served until 1994.

Dr. Carol A. Leary was selected as the fifth president of Bay Path University. Under her leadership, Bay Path has undergone momentous changes including the launching of the annual Women's Leadership Conference in 1995.

The Women's Leadership Conference, which takes place at the MassMutual Center in downtown Springfield, has hosted as keynote speakers the likes of Jane Fonda, Barbara Walters, Queen Latifah, Gloria Estefan, Marlee Matlin and a host of other prominent and respected celebrities. The conference includes a full program of breakout sessions and opportunities for women to network.

The college has expanded in many ways since the turn of the 21st century. In 1999, the college established the One Day A Week College for adult women. In 2000, the college founded a co-educational graduate school, which now has more than 25 degrees and certificates. In 2014, it opened The American Women's College, the first all-woman, all online Baccalaureate program in the United States.

In 2016, the college established the Strategic Alliances division, providing innovative learning experiences for people, businesses and organizations. In 2017, Bay Path launched an Occupational Therapy Doctorate program.

As of July 1, 2014, the name was changed to Bay Path University. This began a new evolution, one that included multiple campus sites, over 3,220 students, and an online international presence.

Other Educational Institutions of Note:

MARY A. BURNHAM SCHOOL FOR GIRLS

was founded in Northampton in 1877 by the former head of the English Department at Wellesley College, Mary A. Burnham. Its original name was The Northampton Classical School for Girls and it was "one of the oldest schools in the United States to prepare girls for college." With Burnham's death in 1885, her friend and former head of the Chemistry Department at Wellesley College, Bessie Talbot Capen, became principal of the school and changed the name of the school to the Mary A. Burnham School for Girls at that time.
– Joseph Carvalho III

Burnham School, Northampton, MA

THE ELMS SCHOOL FOR GIRLS, HADLEY AND SPRINGFIELD, MA

Charlotte Williams Porter established a school for girls called The Elms in Hadley, Massachusetts in 1866. The school was moved to Springfield in 1881. Porter served as the "Headmistress" for fifty years.
– Joseph Carvalho III

FOXHOLLOW SCHOOL FOR GIRLS, LENOX, MA

By the 1940s, Foxhollow was generally considered to be "one of the most serious Girl's School's in the region." Preparatory courses geared to prepare students for the "leading Women's colleges," with it's "emphasis upon independent thinking and the creative arts."
– Joseph Carvalho III

MISS HALL'S SCHOOL IN PITTSFIELD, MA

is one of the foremost college-preparatory schools for girls in the country. Established in 1898, the School combines a traditional college-preparatory curriculum with two innovative, nationally acclaimed programs. Miss Hall's School is accredited by the New England Association of Independent Schools and Colleges and is a member of the Association of Schools in New England, the National Association of Independent Schools, the Association of Boarding Schools, the National Coalition of Girls' Schools, and the Secondary School Admission Test Board.

JULIA HAWKES (b. ca. 1800) opened a school for young women in Springfield in 1829 and ran it until 1831. – Joseph Carvalho III

HOWARD SCHOOL FOR GIRLS, SPRINGFIELD, MA

Catherine Lathrop Howard (b. 1833 in Springfield; d. 1897 in Springfield) studied in Cambridge under noted scientist Professor Alexander Agassiz. Returning to Springfield, Howard, with help from her sisters Lucinda and Sophia, founded the Howard School for Girls in 1863. She was a pioneer in the teaching of girls and women in Western Massachusetts. Upon her death in 1897, the *Springfield Republican* called her "a singularly interesting and valuable personality in the life of Springfield, and said of her that "the ultimate view of her career as teacher, the essential and extraordinary merit was character...." The newspaper said of her school that it was "a school for girls of a character so individual and rare that no other can be said to exactly parallel it or take its place." – Joseph Carvalho III

THE MACDUFFIE SCHOOL FOR GIRLS

Dr. John and Abby (Parsons) MacDuffie founded the MacDuffie School for Girls in Springfield. Abby MacDuffie was one of the most prominent local activists for women's voting rights and often campaigned widely through Springfield and neighboring towns speaking from her automobile, a novel approach at that time. She was also one of the founders of the local branch of the League of Women Voters. – Joseph Carvalho III

DOLLY (BLAIR) NICHOLS

(b. 1795; d. 1864) and her husband Rev. George Nichols (b.1796; d. 1841 in Springfield, MA) opened a school for young women ca. 1834 on Main Street in Springfield. – Joseph Carvalho III

Foxhollow Riders in front of the "Mount" (Edith Wharton Estate).

THE NORTHAMPTON SCHOOL FOR GIRLS

was founded in 1924 by Dorothy M. Bement and Sarah Whitaker. In its first 25 years, over 600 of its students entered college with more than half that number attending Northampton's Smith College. The course of study began with eighth grade and consisted of six years of college preparatory studies. For many years it was "the only New England school for girls devoted exclusively to college preparation." – Joseph Carvalho III

NORTHFIELD SCHOOL FOR GIRLS

was founded in 1879 by famed evangelist Dwight L. Moody who lived there. Its stated mission was "to help young women with limited financial resources to gain education." The School began in the home of Rev. Moody with a first year's enrollment of 25 girls. By 1950, the school had an enrollment of approximately 500 students with classes held in eight buildings and students housed in 12 dormitories spread over 200 acres. In 1912 the school was merged administratively with the Mount Herman School for Boys, however, separate campuses were maintained. The merged entity was re-named The Northfield Schools. – Joseph Carvalho III

OREAD INSTITUTE was a women's college founded in Worcester, MA in 1849 by Eli Thayer. It had three levels of instruction: primary, academic, and collegiate. According to the Worcester Women's History Project, the four year collegiate program, "offered a classical, college-level curriculum and is thought to be the first institution of its kind exclusively for women in the country." The college closed in 1881. – Joseph Carvalho III

PITTSFIELD FEMALE ACADEMY/PITTSFIELD YOUNG LADIES SEMINARY

In 1800, Nancy Hinsdale established a "select female school" in Pittsfield. With the financial support of Joshua Danforth, Joseph Merrick, and Ezekiel Bacon, Hinsdale incorporated the school in 1806 as the Pittsfield Female Academy. She served as the Academy's principal until 1813. Eliza Doane of Boston led the school from 1814 to 1818, followed by a series of women who served for shorter terms. In 1826, the trustees erected a three story building for the Academy. In April of 1827, the seminary was opened as a boarding school, and the standard of education was raised. Circa 1838, the seminary "appears to have been abandoned as a corporate institution." Nancy Hinsdale's niece, Fanny Hinsdale revived "a select school" until 1844. In 1845 Clara Wells took over the leadership of the school and operated the school with success until 1870. After Wells' death, Mary E. Salisbury assumed the leadership of the Seminary and according to contemporaries restored the Pittsfield Young Ladies Seminary "to the prosperity of its best days." – Joseph Carvalho III

PITTSFIELD YOUNG LADIES INSTITUTE

was established by Rev. Wellington Hart Tyler in 1841, and was at one time regarded as "the most noted and successful institution of learning which ever existed in Pittsfield." Rev. Tyler operated the school until his retirement from education in 1852. Rev. C. V. Spear conducted the school from 1857-1860. The school later was operated briefly under the name Maplewood Young Ladies Institute. – Joseph Carvalho III

Stoneleigh-Prospect Hill School for Girls, 1963

MRS. SEDGEWICK'S SCHOOL FOR YOUNG LADIES

was established in Lenox, MA prior to the Civil War.

MISS STEARNS' SCHOOL FOR GIRLS

was opened in the early 1840s in Worcester, MA. – Joseph Carvalho III

STONELEIGH-PROSPECT HILL SCHOOL FOR GIRLS OF GREENFIELD, MA

traces its origins to two predecessor schools: the Prospect Hill School founded in Greenfield in 1869 and the Stoneleigh School for Girls founded by Caroline Sumner and Isabel Cressler in Greenfield. The schools were united in 1930. – Joseph Carvalho III

WORCESTER DOMESTIC SCIENCE SCHOOL

[for women] was established in 1898 by Henry D. Perky and operated until 1904 in the building which formerly housed the Oread Institute. After Perky's death in 1904, the school closed but in later years the school was revived with the same name, by Frank M. Weathered who had previously been a teacher under Perky's administration. – Joseph Carvalho III

WORCESTER STATE NORMAL SCHOOL

was "turned over entirely to female students" in 1915. – Joseph Carvalho III

SPRINGFIELD PUBLIC SCHOOLS NAMED IN HONOR OF WOMEN

Alice B. Beal School, 285 Tiffany Street

Mary A. Dryden Veterans Memorial School 190 Surrey Road

Margaret C. Ells School, 319 Cortland Street

Rebecca Johnson School, 55 Catherine St.

Mary M. Lynch Elementary School 315 North Branch Pkwy.

Mary O. Pottenger School, 1435 Carew St.

Mary M. Walsh School, 50 Empress Ct.

WESTERN AND CENTRAL MASSACHUSETTS PUBLIC SCHOOLS NAMED IN HONOR OF WOMEN

Roberta G. Doering School, Agawam

Anna E. Barry School, Chicopee

Mary E. Finn School, Southborough

Sarah W. Gibbons Middle School Westborough

Elsie A. Hastings Elementary School Westborough

Dr. Marcella R. Kelly School, Holyoke

Rita E. Miller Elementary School, Westford

Margaret Neary Elementary School Southborough

Marguerite E. Peaslee Elementary School Northborough

Fannie E. Proctor Elementary School Northborough

Pearl E. Rhodes Elementary School, Leyden

Florence Roche School, Groton

Mary Rowlandson Elementary School Lancaster

Saint Bernadette School, Northborough

Saint Mary Elementary School, Shrewsbury

Helen Mae Sauter Elementary School, Gardner

Florence Sawyer School, Bolton

Mary D. Stone Elementary School, Auburn

Lt. Clayre T. Sullivan Elementary School, Holyoke

Marion E. Zeh Elementary School Northborough

Education and Educators

Sophia Smith

(B. AUG. 27, 1796; D. JUNE 12, 1870)

Unlike Mary Lyon, the founder of Mt. Holyoke Seminary in nearby South Hadley, Sophia Smith was not a social reformer or educator. Her father was a prosperous farmer prominent in town affairs. Educated mostly in the local schools, she was always an avid reader. She never married and rarely ventured far from home, especially after she lost her hearing at the age of 40. She lived in the house where she was born with her unmarried sisters and brother. When the last of them died in 1861, she found herself a very wealthy woman.

She turned to her young pastor, John Morton Greene, a graduate of Amherst College, for guidance. Greene and his wife, who had attended Mt. Holyoke, both believed education was the key to salvation. Vassar College had just been chartered, but there was still no true college for women in New England. Sophia Smith had sorely missed attending such a college, and she decided to endow one.

When Sophia Smith, the last surviving member of a wealthy Connecticut Valley family, died in 1870, she left her fortune to endow a new college for women. Smith believed that by giving women access to higher education, "what are called their 'wrongs' will be redressed, their wages will be adjusted, their weight of influence in reforming the evils of society will be greatly increased." Although she stated clearly that she did not wish "to render my sex any the less feminine," her idea of giving women an education equal to men was a daring one.

Once the location was secure, serious financial challenges lay ahead. The trustees soon discovered that Smith's $390,000 bequest was not enough to implement the plan. They engaged a fundraiser to visit "friends of women's education" in eastern Massachusetts, where they expected to find supporters — and donors — for their project.

They also appealed to the people of Northampton to contribute $70,000 towards the cost of constructing the first building. The college would be the pride of the town, "A college of high character is such a benefit to every interest of a town and community," they argued, "that it is just and right that people even make a sacrifice to secure it. How many families of taste and refinement, and wealth, it will cause to enter here? What an element of culture it will introduce into our social life?" The next serious challenge was to assemble a student body qualified to study a liberal arts curriculum as demanding as those at male colleges, with courses in classics, modern languages and literature, mathematics, and natural sciences. To gain admission, students had to pass examinations in geography, English, Latin, and Greek grammar and literature, arithmetic, algebra, and geometry. Very few young women were prepared for such a rigorous admission process; 14 entered with the first class in 1875.

The greatest controversy surrounded the very idea of higher education for women. As colleges began to accept women, commentators worried that it would "unfit women for domestic life." Others feared that advanced study would ruin a woman's health. There were also concerns about women living outside the sphere of family influence. One contributor to *Scribner's Magazine* insisted that "no consideration would induce us to place a young woman — daughter or ward — in a college which would shut her away from all family life for a period of four years. The system is unnatural, and not one young woman in ten can be subject to it without injury... There is no reason for exposing hundreds of girls to the perils of college life as they at present exist." The Smith trustees responded by deciding to "erect a number of smaller dwelling-houses around a central academic building. Each forms a separate establishment with its own

domestic life." A "lady-in-charge" and a female faculty member resided in each house. At the end of the first year, the college proudly reported that "the standard of study has been well maintained." Equally important, "there has been no sickness among the students living in the college boarding house."

Smith College has been a nationwide leader in women's liberal arts education for over 125 years. Among its many distinguished alumnae are Barbara Bush, Julia Child, Betty Friedan, Madeleine L'Engle, Margaret Mitchell, Nancy Reagan, and Gloria Steinem. In 1942, the Sophia Smith Collection at Smith College was established as a repository of manuscripts, archives, photographs, periodicals, and other primary sources in women's history. In 2000, Sophia Smith was inducted posthumously into the National Women's Hall of Fame.
– *MassMoments*, Mass Humanities

ALPHABETICAL LISTING OF NOTABLE WOMEN IN EDUCATION

Auretta Roys Aldrich
(B. 1829 IN FLETCHER, VT; D. 1920) Springfield's Aurelia Aldrich was the first advocate for kindergarten education programs in Western Massachusetts. She became interested in the educational movement while travelling in Germany. Milton Bradley published her first book on the subject, *Kindergarten Handbook*, in 1877. A few years after the publication, Aldrich founded the Springfield Kindergarten Club. During the 1840s and 1850s, Aldrich lived in the utopian community of Hopedale, MA.
– Joseph Carvalho III

Shirley Alvira
became the first Latina principal in Chicopee and went on to become the assistant superintendent of schools in Chicopee before becoming the first Latina superintendent of schools in Westfield. Alvira remains the only

Latina to have served in that role in Westfield.
– Elizabeth Román

Mary Ames
(B. 1835 IN MA; D. AFTER 1880)
was a teacher from Springfield, MA who volunteered to travel to Edisto Island off the coast of South Carolina soon after the Civil War in May of 1865 to teach African-American children of former slaves. Part of the Freedman's Bureau effort in post-war South Carolina led by General Rufus Saxton of Greenfield, Ames spent more than a year in that position joined by her fellow educator from Springfield, Emily Bliss.
– Joseph Carvalho III & Wayne E. Phaneuf

Emily Bliss
was a teacher from Springfield, MA who volunteered to travel to Edisto Island off the coast of South Carolina soon after the Civil War in May of 1865 to teach African-American children of former slaves. Part of the Freedman's Bureau effort in post-war South Carolina led by General Rufus Saxton of Greenfield, Bliss spent more than a year in that position joined by her fellow educator from Springfield, Mary Ames.
– Joseph Carvalho III & Wayne E. Phaneuf

Mary Ann Brigham
(B. DEC. 6, 1829 IN WESTBOROUGH, MA; D. JUNE 29, 1889 IN NEW HAVEN, CT)
was an American educator who was the 8th President (President Elect) of Mount Holyoke College in 1889. After teaching for a few years, "she was elected President of Mount Holyoke Seminary and College in 1889, but died in a railway accident before she could take up her appointment." She was educated at Mount Holyoke Female Seminary, as part of the 1849 class. Brigham began her academic career in 1855, teaching at Mount Holyoke. In 1858 she was named assistant principal at Ingham University, remaining in that post until 1863. From 1863 to 1889 she served as a teacher

Above left: Mary Brigham **Above right:** Shirley Alvira

and associate principal at Brooklyn Heights Seminary. She served for several years as president of the Mt. Holyoke Alumnae Club in New York City, and shortly after the 1888 charter of Mount Holyoke College, she was elected as 8th President of her alma mater. On June 29, 1889, as she was traveling from New York to South Hadley, Massachusetts to assume her post, the train crashed at New Haven, Connecticut. She died in the wreck. In 1897 a dormitory was erected by the New York Alumnae Club on the Mt. Holyoke campus. It was named The Mary Brigham Hall.
– Joseph Carvalho III

Angeline Brooks

(B. APR. 2, 1836 IN WEST SPRINGFIELD, MA; D. 1927 IN SPRINGFIELD, MA) established the Willow Street School in the 1880s, a free kindergarten for African-American children, paying all the bills herself. When the school did not succeed financially, she offered to provide the same service as a public school for the City of Springfield without salary for a year.

Despite the backing of the Milton Bradley Company which offered to provide all of the necessary kindergarten supplies, her offer was declined by the School Department and she then moved to New Haven, Connecticut to found the Connecticut Valley Kindergarten Association. She returned to Springfield after authoring *The Kindergarten and the School*.
– Joseph Carvalho III

Jennie Cora (Clough) Busby

(B. JAN. 17, 1857 IN WORCESTER, MA; D. 1928 IN WORCESTER, MA) was the first African American woman to attend the Worcester Normal School (now Worcester State University) and later became the first African-American woman to teach in the Worcester public school system. She began her teaching career teaching first grade at the Thomas Street School, known as Worcester's "School for Colored Children" although the majority of the school's students were Irish immigrants. She later taught at the Providence Street School in Worcester for eight years until 1894

when she married George Alfred Busby. As married women were not allowed to teach in public schools at that time, this ended her teaching career. – Joseph Carvalho III

Carol Tecla Christ

(B. MAY 21, 1944 IN NEW YORK CITY) is a widely respected scholar of Victorian literature and served as the 10th president of Smith College from 2002 to 2013. She was awarded Yale University's Wilbur Cross Medal in 2007. In 2017, Christ was appointed the 11th chancellor of the University of California/Berkeley and the first woman to hold that post.
– Joseph Carvalho III

Anne Laura Clarke

(B. JULY 4, 1787 IN NORTHAMPTON, MA; D. AUG. 15, 1861 IN NORTHAMPTON, MA) Northampton teacher who "re-invented herself" as a public lecturer from 1822-1834. From Baltimore to Boston, Clarke spoke on western history and the history of clothing, advertised as "Miss Clarke's Historical Lectures." Using a "slide projector" and hand painted maps and charts, she was on the cutting edge of the public lecture circuit of that era. – Joseph Carvalho III

Ada Louise Comstock

(B. DEC. 11, 1876 IN MOORHEAD, MN; D. DEC. 12, 1973 IN NEW HAVEN, CT) completed her high school education at the age of 15 and went on to college. In 1895 she transferred from the University of Minnesota to Smith College, where she completed her last two years of undergraduate study. After graduating from Smith in 1897, Ada went on to a graduate program at Moorhead State Normal School, where she became certified to teach, and then entered Columbia University for graduate work in English, history and education. In 1907, after teaching rhetoric at the University of Minnesota, she was appointed the university's first dean of women. In 1912, Ada came to Smith to serve as the first dean of the college and to teach English. In 1917, when the presidency of Smith College became vacant, Ada was given the responsibility of Smith's operation for approximately six months. The chance to become the president of a women's college presented itself in 1923, when Radcliffe offered Ada the position of its first full-time president. Under President Comstock, Radcliffe launched a nationwide admission program, improved student housing, constructed new classroom buildings and expanded the graduate program. She served in that capacity until 1943. In retirement Comstock was involved with the Smith College Board of Trustees.

Smith College named The Ada Comstock Scholars Program in her honor. Ada Comstock Scholars range in age from their 20s to their mid-60s, with varying backgrounds and life paths, whether they chose to begin work, start families or travel after high school. They have come to Smith from all parts of the United States and as far as Asia and Africa. A common denominator for all Ada Comstock Scholars is that they reached a point where they wished to complete their education and fulfill their potential in new and creative ways. – excerpted from the Smith College website

Jill Ker Conway

(B. OCT. 9, 1934 IN HILLSTON, NEW SOUTH WALES, AUSTRALIA; D. JUNE 1, 2018 IN BOSTON, MA) is an author and educator who served as Smith College's first woman president from 1975 to 1985. In 1975, Conway was named by Time as a Woman of the Year. Since 2011, Conway has served as the Board Chair of Community Solutions. In 2013, she received a 2012 National Humanities Medal from President Barack Obama. – Cynthia G. Simison

Mary-Beth A. Cooper, PhD, DM

(B. 1961) became the 13th president of Springfield College in August 2013. Cooper earned her Doctor of Philosophy in education administration from Michigan State University,

and a Doctor of Management from Case Western Reserve University. She previously served as senior vice president for student affairs at Rochester Institute of Technology and as chair of the YMCA of Greater Rochester Board of Directors. Cooper co-led the RIT President's Commission on Women to improve the campus climate for women. Known for her volunteer leadership, President Cooper has been named to the National Association of Independent Colleges and Universities (NAICU) Committee on Policy Analysis and Public Relations, as well as to the board of trustees of the Council for Adult and Experiential Learning. She was appointed by Massachusetts Governor Charlie Baker to serve on the Special Commission to Study the Incorporation of Safe and Effective Pain Treatment and Prescribing Practices Into the Professional Training of Students That May Prescribe Controlled Substances. She also serves on the boards of the Association of Independent Colleges and Universities in Massachusetts (AICUM), the Community

Top left: Ada Louise Comstock.
Top: Roberta G. Doering (Courtesy *The Republican*)
Bottom: Mary-Beth A. Cooper

Sister Mary A. Dooley, Ph.D.

(B. MAR. 5, 1923 IN CAMBRIDGE, MA;
D. NOV. 2013 IN HOLYOKE, MA)
was a Sister of St. Joseph, and served as
the sixth president of Our Lady of the Elms
College in Chicopee, MA from 1979 to 1994.
Sister Mary Dooley taught at St. Joseph
High School in North Adams from 1947 to
1965 and at Elms College from 1968 to 1971.
From 1971 to 1980, she served as president of
the Sisters of St. Joseph. Sister Mary Dooley
also served as president in the Leadership
Conference of Women Religious, and in 1978
was their official delegate to the installations
of Popes John Paul I and John Paul II in Rome.
Among her many honors, she was awarded
the Pynchon Medal. – Joseph Carvalho III &
Suzanne McLaughlin

Mary Maples Dunn

(B. APR. 6, 1931 STURGEON BAY, WI; D. MAR. 19,
2017 IN WINSTON-SALEM, NC)
was an American historian and noted college
administrator. Serving as its 8th president
from 1985 to 1995, Dr. Dunn "led Smith
College through exciting and challenging
times. During her tenure, the college raised
more than $300 million, constructed two
major buildings and renovated many more,
enhanced communication on and off campus,
attracted record numbers of applicants and
doubled the value of its endowment."
– Joseph Carvalho III

Anna Cheney Edwards

(B. JULY 31, 1835 IN NORTHAMPTON, MA; D.
1930) served as Associate Principal of Mount
Holyoke Seminary, 1872-1888; and as Professor
of Theism and Christian Evidences, 1888-1890.
From 1876, served as vice-president of the
Hampshire County Branch of the Woman's
Board of Missions.
– Joseph Carvalho III

Foundation of Western Massachusetts, the
Springfield Museums, DevelopSpringfield, the
Naismith Memorial Basketball Hall of Fame,
and the Willie Ross School for the Deaf. She
is a member of the Economic Development
Council of Western Massachusetts; and serves
on the steering committee for the FutureCity
Economic Development Strategy initiative
for the City of Springfield, as well as on the
leadership advisory committee of Read!
Reading Success by 4th grade.
– Wayne E. Phaneuf & Jack Flynn

Roberta G. Doering (B. JAN. 12, 1925 IN

SYRACUSE, NY; D. MAR. 27, 2016 IN SPRINGFIELD,
MA) Long-time Agawam School Committee
Woman, 1970-2016. In 2010, Doering was
awarded the Thomas P. "Tip" O'Neill Lifetime
Achievement Award by the Massachusetts
Association of School Committees. She was
also a long-time member of the Springfield
Science Museum's Advisory Committee and
served for many years as its chairperson. The
Roberta G. Doering Middle School in Agawam
was named in her honor in 2010.
– Jim Kinney & Joseph Carvalho III

Top: Sister Mary Dooley. **Bottom left:** Mary Maples Dunn.
Center: Anna Cheney Edwards.

Margaret C. Ells

(B. AUG. 4, 1882 IN VT; D. NOV. 13, 1971 IN MONTGOMERY, MA) distinguished Springfield educator, is credited with being "primarily responsible for establishing women's vocational education in the United States. She was in charge of Women's vocational training courses at the highly regarded Springfield Trade School from 1934-1952. Ells was the only educator from New England selected by President John F. Kennedy to help revise the vocational education act which provided more vocational training for American youth. She was referred to as "the first lady of vocational education." Her honors included: 1943 William Pynchon Award, 1947 honorary degree from American International College, 1960 scholarship in her honor at A.I.C., Springfield named an elementary school after her in 1960, and the Margaret Ells professorship of education in the School of Education was established at A.I.C. in 1969.
– Joseph Carvalho III

Susan Mabel (Hood) Everson

(B. MAY 10, 1876 IN RED WING, MINNESOTA; D. IN MA)
A graduate of Smith College, Emerson served as principal of the Mary A. Burnham School in Northampton beginning in 1939. She also served for a time as headmistress of the Stoneleigh-Prospect Hill School (for girls) of Greenfield, MA. – Joseph Carvalho III

Mary Salome Cutler Fairchild

(B. JUNE 21, 1855 IN DALTON, MA; D. DEC. 30, 1921 IN TAKOMA PARK, MD)
was a pioneering American librarian and library educator. – Joseph Carvalho III

Mary V. Flynn

(B. 1920 IN STOCKBRIDGE, MA)
began teaching in 1943 spent 36 years teaching in Central Berkshire Regional School District. She was elected head of

Above left: Margaret C. Ells. **Above right:** Susan Mabel (Hood) Everson.

the Berkshire County Teachers Association in 1965. She was named the first director of Chesterwood in 1960. Retiring in 1979, Flynn was also elected to head the Berkshire County Retired Teachers Association in 1981. Active in local politics, Flynn was elected to the executive committee of the Berkshire County Democratic Association in 1972 and elected chairman in 1980. She first ran for the Select Board in Stockbridge in 1978 and was the first woman to serve on the board. In 1980, Flynn was elected to the executive board of the Berkshire County Selectmen's Association.
– James Gleason & Joseph Carvalho III

Gretchen Holbrook Gerzina

(B. 1950 IN SPRINGFIELD, MA)
an author, historian, and educator, is the Dean of the Commonwealth Honors College at the University of Massachusetts. Prior to assuming this position in 2015, she was the Kathe Tappe Vernon Professor of Biography, and Chair of the Department of African and African-American studies at Dartmouth; Professor of English and Director of Africana Studies at Barnard College, Columbia University; and Professor of English and Associate Dean of Faculty at Vassar College. Gerzina's book *Mr. and Mrs. Prince: How an Extraordinary 18th-century Family Moved out of Slavery and into Legend* was nominated for the Pulitzer Prize, the National Book Award, the Frederick Douglass Book Prize and the NAACP National Image Award. In 2016, she was named the Paul Murray Kendall Chair in Biography at the University of Massachusetts. Among her historically-grounded biographical studies are *Carrington: A Life* (1989); *Black England: Life Before Emancipation* (1995) a *New York Times* "notable book of the year" that was

also published in the United States as *Black London*; and *Frances Hodgson Burnett: The unexpected life of the author of The Secret Garden* (2004). She also is the editor of three books: *Black Victorians/Black Victoriana* (2003); the *Norton Critical Edition of The Secret Garden* (2005) and *The Annotated Secret Garden* (2007). From 1997 to 2012, Gerzina hosted the nationally-syndicated public radio program "The Book Show," and has done commentaries on National Public Radio and Vermont Public Radio. In 2016, She completed a ten-part BBC Radio 4 series on Britain's Black Past. – Diane Lederman & Wayne E. Phaneuf

Lucille D. (Campbell) Gibbs

(B. AUG. 8, 1926 IN BOSTON, MA;
D. OCT. 16, 2011 IN AGAWAM, MA)
was a graduate of the Westfield State Teachers College (today's Westfield State University), the only African-American in the Class of 1948. She began her teaching career in the Boston public school system but soon moved to Springfield in 1951 to begin teaching in the Springfield elementary schools including the William N. DeBerry and Alice B. Beal schools. In 1969 she temporarily left the classroom to serve as interim administrator of a federal program that encouraged local elementary children to discuss racial, ethnic, and social differences and introduced them to ways of resolving conflicts. Lucille returned to teaching elementary school until 1983 when she was appointed, with tenure, to Springfield Technical Community College as an Academic Guidance Counselor retiring in 1991. Gibbs held many leadership positions within a wide variety of public and private organizations including Baystate Medical Center, Dunbar Community Center, Urban League Guild, League of Women Voters, Springfield Planning Board, Springfield Education Association, Westfield State College Board of Trustees, Westfield State College Alumni Association, Westfield State Foundation, Friends of the University of Massachusetts Fine Arts Center and Stage West. Lucille served as a mentor to many local young people through her work with the STCC Afro-American Cultural Club, YMCA, YWCA, Springfield Girls' Club Family Center and the Girls Scouts of Central and Western Massachusetts. In recognition of her life of service to the community, Gibbs received the James F. Hennessey Award from the Springfield branch of NAACP (2001), the Pioneer Valley Women of Distinction from the Pioneer Valley Girl Scout Council (2001), the Door Openers Award from the Black Leadership Alliance (2008), and the Living

Left: Gretchen Holbrook Gerzina
Above: Lucille D. Gibbs

Legends Community Service Award from Bethel African Methodist Episcopal Church (2009). – Joseph Carvalho III & Cynthia G. Simison

Cecelia A. Gross, Ph. D.

(B. APR. 20, 1934; D. OCT. 30, 2013 IN SPRINGFIELD, MA) was a history professor at Springfield Technical Community College, a historian of African-American history, and creator of the African American Heritage Trail in Springfield, MA. – Joseph Carvalho III

Alice L. Halligan

(B. 1893; D. 1967 IN SPRINGFIELD, MA) originator of the famous "Springfield plan for Education and Democracy." She later founded the Springfield Adult Education Council, and was awarded the William Pynchon Medal in 1948. Following her death in January of 1967, the *Springfield Union* wrote of her: "She was nationally known for her leadership in establishing courses in democracy and in the adult training field which achieved country-wide fame for Springfield."
– Joseph Carvalho III

Priscilla (Kane) Hellweg

(B. MAR. 27, 1958) is the Executive Artistic Director of Enchanted Circle Theater (ECT), a non-profit, multi-service arts organization based in Holyoke, MA. She has performed, taught, written, directed, and designed arts integrated programs at Enchanted Circle for almost 40 years. A regional leader in arts integration, ECT works in public schools throughout Western Massachusetts, and collaborates with over 60 community partner organizations to make arts inspired learning accessible to all. Under Hellweg's direction, ECT was awarded the Commonwealth Award, Massachusetts' highest honors in the arts, sciences and humanities. Hellweg was named a Champion of Arts Education by the Massachusetts Alliance for Arts Education and received the Milestone Award from the

Above left: Priscilla (Kane) Hellweg. **Above right:** Rebecca Mary Johnson.

National Guild for Community Arts Education for her contributions to the field. She serves on the Massachusetts Arts Education Advisory Council, and the Holyoke Early Literacy Initiative. She has been training teachers, teaching artists, community-based educators and college students to integrate theater arts across the curriculum for decades, and is currently developing The Institute for Arts Integration, a soon-to-be hub of innovation in education in Western Massachusetts
– Kathleen Carreiro

Barbara Howell Jefferson

(B. APR. 19, 1938 IN PITTSBURGH, PA; D. SEPT. 14, 2016 IN NORTH CAROLINA) was an educator and school administrator in the Springfield, MA public school system from 1961 to 2002. She served as principal of the William N. DeBerry School and under her leadership that school was the first to implement the TABS (Team Approach to Better Schools) program which

was used as an example for educators at National Education Association conferences nation-wide. – Joseph Carvalho III

Rebecca Mary Johnson

(B. JULY 10, 1905 IN SPRINGFIELD, MA; D. OCT. 4, 1991 IN SPRINGFIELD, MA) was the first African American principal in the Springfield Public School System and in the Commonwealth of Massachusetts. She was a graduate of Fisk University in Nashville, Tenn., and received a master's degree from Columbia University Teachers College. She also completed graduate work at Springfield College and Northwestern University. Prior to coming to Springfield, Johnson taught in South Carolina schools for 16 years. She began as a teacher in Springfield, MA in 1943 and retired as a principal of the Lynch Elementary School in 1975. Johnson was first named acting principal of Washington Elementary School in 1945. At the time of her appointment, Springfield Superintendant

Dr. John Granrud called her "one of the most brilliant teachers in the system." In 1948, she was appointed principal of the East Union Street School. Later, she was to serve as principal of DeBerry Elementary School, the East Union Street Elementary School, and Tapley Elementary School. The Rebecca M. Johnson School in Springfield is named in her honor. – Joseph Carvalho III & Wayne E. Phaneuf

Sister Kathleen Keating, Ph. D.

(B. FEB. 22, 1931 IN SPRINGFIELD, MA), a Sister of St. Joseph, served as the 7th president of Elms College in Chicopee, MA from 1994 to 2001. She was assistant professor of history at Elms College from 1966 to 1975. She also served as chair of the college's Division of Social Sciences. From 1975 to 1978, she was president of the National Assembly of Women Religious in Chicago and was president of the Congregation of Sisters of St. Joseph

Above: Sister Kathleen Keating
Left: Dr. Carol A. Leary

of Springfield from 1979 to 1987. From 1989 to 1993, she ministered in Nicaragua as an associate member of the Maryknoll Sisters working as a pastoral minister and a professor of English at the Jesuit University of Central America in the city of Managua.
– Joseph Carvalho III

Marcella R. Kelly, Ph. D.

(B. SEPT. 23, 1906 IN MA; D. JAN. 23, 1994 IN HOLYOKE, MA) was an educator who began her career in the Holyoke Public Schools in 1931, becoming a principal in 1938. Kelly was promoted to Assistant Superintendent of Schools in 1946, and ultimately appointed as Holyoke's first female Superintendent of Schools in 1963. Under her leadership, Holyoke built three new elementary schools, a junior high school, the innovative West Street School, and Holyoke High School. A pioneer in bilingual education, Kelly also instituted a wide range of curriculum reforms and new programs including the School of Licensed Practical Nursing at Holyoke Trade High School. In 1973, Kelly wrote one of the first collective biographical women's history books for a Western Massachusetts community, *Behind Eternity: Holyoke Women Who Made a Difference* in 1973. – Joseph Carvalho III

Carol A. Leary, Ph.D.

(B. MAR. 29, 1947)
became president of Bay Path University, in Longmeadow, MA in 1994. A Phi Beta Kappa graduate of Boston University, she earned her doctorate of philosophy degree at The American University - Washington, D.C. She previously served as a vice president at Simmons College. Leary has served on the boards of numerous state and national organizations, among them, the Community Foundation of Western Massachusetts, The Beveridge Family Foundation, Inc., the Women's College Coalition, the Association of Independent Colleges and Universities of Massachusetts, and the WGBY Public

Television Board of Tribunes. At Bay Path, she has added new baccalaureate programs and professional certificates; established over 25 graduate and post-graduate degrees; introduced the One Day A Week Saturday Program for adult women and created two additional campus locations in Sturbridge and Concord; launched The American Women's College, the first all-women, all-online baccalaureate program in the nation; and expanded and renovated major campus buildings, including the Philip H. Ryan Health Science Center for allied health programs. She has received numerous awards and honors related to her work in the community.
– Jane Kaufman

Maud S. Mandel, Ph. D.

(B. JUNE 14, 1967) became the 18th president of Williams College on July 1, 2018. Prior to her appointment she served as Dean of Brown University, the university's senior undergraduate academic officer. She began as a faculty member at Brown in 2001. Mandel was chair of the Judaic studies program at Brown University from 2012 to 2014. Her publications include *In the Aftermath of Genocide: Armenians and Jews in Twentieth-Century France* (Duke University Press, 2003); *Muslims and Jews in France: History of a Conflict* (Princeton University Press, 2014); and as co-editor of *Colonialism and the Jews* (Indiana University Press, 2017).

As Brown's dean, Mandel was deeply involved in efforts to advance diversity and inclusion, leading a collaborative process with students and staff to open the First-Generation College and Low-Income Student Center, the first center at any Ivy League school to be dedicated to first-generation students.

The Center provides communal, academic and social support to first-generation and low-income students and serves as a home base for student-centered organizations such as First-Gens@ Brown and the Undocumented and DACA student initiative. Mandel also has promoted programs to foster retention for historically underrepresented students in the STEM fields, including the New Scientist Collective, an academic support and mentorship program for students in these fields. – Joseph Carvalho III

Kathleen McCartney

(B. 1956 IN MEDFORD, MA) is the 11th president of Smith College, installed on Oct. 19, 2013. She is the former dean of the Harvard Graduate School of Education, is an internationally recognized authority on child development and early education. McCartney was the recipient in 2009 of the Distinguished Contribution Award from the Society for Research in Child Development. In March 2015, she was elected to the Board of Directors of the American Council on Education.
– Joseph Carvalho III

Dr. Mary Elizabeth (Cannon) McLean

(B. SEPT. 25, 1912 IN NEW JERSEY; D. AUG. 19, 1995 IN SPRINGFIELD, MA) Moving to Springfield in 1939, she was one of Springfield's earliest African-American educators and the city's first Director of Special Education. McLean also taught at Westfield State College (now University) and at American International College in Springfield. An active member of the local branch of the NAACP, she also served as the Chairperson of the John Brown Archives Committee at St. John's Congregational Church in Springfield, MA.
– Patricia Cahill & Joseph Carvalho III

Top left: Maud S. Mandel, Ph. D. **Top right:** Dr. Mary Elizabeth McLean. **Bottom left:** Miriam E. Nelson. **Bottom right:** Sister Mary Reap.

Above left: Dorothy (Jordan) Pryor. **Above right:** Dr. Christina Royal.

Sister Rose William Murphy

(NÉE THERESA, B. DEC. 18, 1894 IN HOLYOKE, MA; D. MAR. 11, 1966 IN SPRINGFIELD, MA) was a Sister of St. Joseph and served as the third president of Our Lady of the Elms College in Chicopee, MA from 1958 to 1965. She was the first woman president of that college. She taught at Springfield's Cathedral High School from 1923 to 1943 when she joined the faculty at the Elms. Appointed Dean in 1948, she served in that capacity for ten years prior to being selected as president of the college.
– Joseph Carvalho III

Miriam "Mim" E. Nelson

A health and nutrition scholar, scientist, university professor, higher education administrator and government policy adviser who was named the seventh president of Hampshire College and assumed that position on July 1, 2018. She had previously served as the director of the Sustainability Institute at the University of New Hampshire. Nelson has been health and nutrition adviser to the U.S. Department of Health and Human Services and the U.S. Department of Agriculture. She was a senior adviser to Michael Pollan's Emmy-nominated documentary "In Defense of Food" and chief scientific adviser to PBS NOVA's "Marathon Challenge" film.
– Diane Lederman

Dorothy (Jordan) Pryor

(B. DEC. 4, 1923) of Springfield, MA. Now retired professor emeritus at STCC, Pryor was a long-time educator in Springfield, MA and for many years taught English at Springfield Technical Community College. She began working at the U.S. Armory in Springfield, and was an affirmative action officer. Pryor was one of the early African-American teachers in the Springfield School system. STCC has honored her by creating their annual Dorothy Jordan Pryor Award given to those considered "living Treasures" in the college community.
– Elise Linscott

Olive Augusta Rainey

(B. DEC. 21, 1875 IN GEORGETOWN, SC; D. 1964 IN SPRINGFIELD, MA) was the daughter of Joseph Hayne Rainey, the first African-American Congressman (1870-1879) from South Carolina. She was one of the first African-American teachers in the Springfield School System and taught there for over 35 years. Rainey also served on the Board of Directors of the Dunbar Community Center of Springfield, and was the Youth Advisor of the Springfield NAACP. – Joseph Carvalho III

Sister Mary Reap, Ph.D.

(B. SEPT. 8, 1941 IN ARCHIBALD, PA) was president of Our Lady of the Elms in Chicopee, MA from 2009 to 2017, their 10th president. She is credited with overseeing the funding and construction of the college's $13.5 million Center for Natural and Health Sciences building. She joined the Congregation of Sisters, Servants of the Immaculate Heart of Mary, in 1961 and was the longest serving president of her alma mater, Marywood University in Scranton, PA leading that college from 1988 to July of 2007 before coming to Elms College. She served two terms as a member of the Presidents and Bishops Education Committee for the United States Conference of Bishops. – Jeanette DeForge & Joseph Carvalho III

Teresa E. Regina

(B. APRIL 25, 1941 IN BUENOS AIRES, ARGENTINA) became the first woman to serve as superintendent of Schools for the City of Springfield, MA when she was appointed interim superintendent from 2000-2001. She began teaching in the Springfield School system in 1965, and was successively promoted to Supervisor of English, Assistant Principal, Supervisor of Public Relations including operating the schools' television station WTER (her initials), and Executive Assistant to the Superintendent.
– Joseph Carvalho III

Christina Royal, Ph.D.

(B. IN NEW YORK) became the fourth president of Holyoke Community College in Holyoke, MA in January 2017 and is the first woman to hold that position. Earlier in her career in higher education, she served as the Associate Vice President of eLearning & Innovation at Cuyahoga Community College in Cleveland, and had district-wide oversight over one of the largest distance learning programs in the State of Ohio. In recognition of her work in that field, she was the recipient of the 2012 United States Distance Learning Association International Award for Outstanding Leadership by an Individual. In June of 2017, Royal was appointed to the board of directors of the non-profit Massachusetts Technology Collaborative. – Michelle Williams

Janis M. Santos

(B. FEB. 16, 1937 IN LUDLOW, MA) is the executive director of the Holyoke-Chicopee-Springfield Headstart program. She began working for Headstart in 1973 when she opened the Ludlow Headstart program. Santos became the executive director of the area program in 1979 which grew to become the 2nd largest Headstart program in Massachusetts by 2012. The National Head Start Association presented Santos with the Head Start Pioneer Award in 2013.
– Elizabeth Román

Mary Fletcher (Benton) Scranton

(B. DEC. 9, 1832 IN BELCHERTOWN, MA; D. OCT. 8, 1909 IN SEOUL, KOREA) was a Methodist Episcopal Church missionary to Korea who founded the Ewha Womans University, one of the most prestigious women's schools in Asia. – Joseph Carvalho III

Sisters of St. Joseph

Seven Sisters of St. Joseph came to Chicopee Falls, MA from New York in 1880 to open a school. In just three years, a new community

was established in Springfield. Over the years, the Sisters opened elementary and high schools in Central and Western Massachusetts, Rhode Island, and Uganda, Africa, as well as establishing Our Lady of the Elms College in Chicopee. Following the Second Vatican Council, the Sisters of St. Joseph restructured their community life. Their ministries expanded to pursue work in prisons, parishes, homeless shelters and other social services. In the mid-1970s, the Fall River community merged with Springfield; and in 2001, the Rutland, VT group joined the Springfield group.
– Sister of St. Joseph Judith E. Kappenman

Ruth Jean (Stubblefield) Simmons

(B. JULY 3, 1945 IN GRAPELAND, TX) was chosen as Smith's ninth president in December of 1994 serving until 2001. With a long and distinguished career in higher education behind her, Simmons was the first African-American woman to head any top-ranked American college or university. Simmons "galvanized the campus through an ambitious campus-wide self-study process that resulted in a number of landmark initiatives," including Praxis, a program that

allows every Smith student the opportunity to elect an internship funded by the college; the first engineering program at a women's college; and programs in the humanities that included the establishment of a poetry center and a peer-reviewed journal devoted to publishing scholarly works by and about

Above left: Janis M. Santos. **Above:** Mary Fletcher Scranton.

Cheryl Stanley, Ed. D.

is the Dean of education at Westfield State University. She joined the faculty at WSU in 1993 and was appointed dean in 2011. Stanley was instrumental in the University's Reach to Teach initiative with the Springfield Public Schools which was developed to help fill educator staffing needs in critical shortage areas and hard-to-staff schools. She is president of the Massachusetts Association of Colleges for Teacher Education (MACTE). Stanley served on the Massachusetts Board of Early Education from 2011 to 2014, and now serves on the state's Black Advisory Commission which addresses issues of importance to the black community with a focus on economic inclusion, equality, and equity in education. She received a "Black Women of Excellence" Award from the Urban League of Springfield in 2018.
– Joseph Carvalho III

Sophia Dana (Hazen) Stoddard

(B. JULY 23, 1820 IN HARTFORD, VT; D. MAR. 4, 1891 IN NORTHAMPTON, MA)
graduated from Mount Holyoke in 1841. She taught at the Seminary for nine years and was Associate Principal from 1849-1850. She joined her first husband as a missionary to Persia in the 1850s. – Joseph Carvalho III

Ann M. Southworth

(B. AUG. 23, 1947)
of Springfield, a longtime Springfield educator and school administrator, was appointed as the new principal at Saint Martha School in Enfield, Connecticut in 2016. After the devastating tornado of 2011, Southworth came out of retirement to serve as president of Cathedral High School from 2011 to 2016. Southworth is a former teacher, principal, and assistant superintendent in the Springfield public school system. – Peter Goonan

women of color. From October 2001 to June 2012, Simmons served as the president of Brown University, their first female president. In December of 2017, she was appointed president of Prairieview A&M University in Texas, also the first woman to serve as president. In 2009, President Barack Obama appointed Dr. Simmons to the President's Commission on White House Fellowships.
– Joseph Carvalho III

Anna Louise Smith

(B. 1855 IN CT; D. 1921 IN SPRINGFIELD, MA)
was one of the founders of the Springfield Day Nursery and was "instrumental" in establishing a tuberculosis hospital in Springfield. – Joseph Carvalho III

Top left: Ann M. Southworth. **Top right:** Sophia Dana Stoddard. **Left:** Ruth J. Simmons.

Anne Sullivan

(B. APRIL 14, 1866 IN FEEDING HILLS, AGAWAM, MA; D. OCT. 20, 1936 IN QUEENS, NY)
was orphaned and institutionalized as a youngster who suffered limited vision. Overcoming that disability, Sullivan eventually graduated as valedictorian from the Perkins Institute for the Blind in 1886. The following year, she began her lifelong association as teacher and companion to the deaf and blind Helen Keller, who became college educated thanks, in part, to Sullivan who attended every class with her. Sullivan became an advocate for those with disabilities. The child-centered approach Sullivan used in teaching Keller ultimately became and remains standard practice in teaching children with these handicaps. The Agawam St. Patrick's Committee gives an award in her memory each year. – Dr. Catherine Shannon

Hattie Twitchell

(B. 1855 IN MA; D. AFTER 1923 IN MA)
founded the Springfield Normal Kindergarten Training School in 1896, also serving as its principal. She was known nationally as one of the "earliest and most capable trainers of kindergarten teachers" in the country. Twitchell led the effort to establish the Springfield Free Kindergarten Association.
– Joseph Carvalho III

A.M. Wells

was the first principal of Worcester's "Female High School" established in 1831, then referred to as a "finishing school." – Joseph Carvalho III

Mary Emma Woolley

(B. JULY 13, 1863 IN SOUTH NORWALK, CT; D. SEPT. 5, 1947 IN WESTPORT, NY)
was appointed president of Mount Holyoke College in 1901. She was the first woman

Right: Helen Keller and Anne Sullivan.

senator of Phi Beta Kappa (1907), and was the first woman to represent the United States at a major diplomatic Conference, the Geneva Conference on Reduction and Limitation of Armaments (1932). – Joseph Carvalho III

Jeanette (Tornow) Wright, Ph.D.

(B. SEPT. 8, 1927 IN MILWAUKEE, WI; D. MAR. 8, 1994 IN LONGMEADOW, MA)

was the 4th president of Bay Path College (now University), serving from 1979 to 1994. During her tenure, Wright "ushered in an era of profound changes" from re-engineering the curriculum to petitioning the Commonwealth of Massachusetts to allow Bay Path to award bachelor's degrees. It was under her leadership that the institution transformed into Bay Path College. She also served as a commissioner for the Governor's Commission on the Status of Women, and served on the New England Association of Schools and Colleges, the state Board of Regents, and the Connecticut Department of Education. Additionally, Wright was a former president of the National Council of Independent Junior Colleges; a member of the Western Massachusetts American Personnel and Guidance Association and the American Psychological Association, and a fellow of the Massachusetts Psychological Association. Prior to her work at Bay Path, Wright was a Fulbright Scholar to China, and a licensed psychologist in Massachusetts, where she maintained a private practice for many years.

– Bay Path University & Joseph Carvalho III

Mary Emma Woolley

CHAPTER THREE

WOMEN
Social and Political Activists

BY LEAH LAMSON

Long-time journalist and editor of
the *Worcester Telegram & Gazette*

The woman's rights movement begin at Seneca Falls in 1848. That meeting spurred interest in forming a national movement.

In May of 1850, women from the Seneca Falls meeting who were attending an anti-slavery convention in Boston got together to plan a National Woman's Rights Convention. Nine met, with seven of them chosen to do the work. They selected Worcester as the location. Paulina Wright Davis wrote the call to the convention, presided over it, created the first permanent woman's rights organizations, and founded the first woman's rights newspaper.

The convention, held on October 23 & 24, 1850, attracted approximately 1,000 people. Of this number 268 "declared themselves" which meant they could vote. Of that number, 84 were from Worcester. The Worcester convention resolved to support "equality for all, without distinction of sex or color," setting it apart from others of its day. Contemporaries saw it as the beginning of the organized women's rights movement.

In 1851, the second National Woman's Rights Convention was also held in Worcester. Historians believe it probably had more to do with geography than the political climate of the city. But at the same time, Worcester was, as Reverend Higginson had said, a seething centre of all the reforms, a sympathetic place to hold a convention on such a radical topic as equal rights for women.

THE BLIND GODDESS !   CAN THIS BE JUSTICE ?

Massachusetts Woman's Suffrage Association
585 Boylston Street.

Social & Political Activists

The First National Woman's Rights Convention

(Oct. 23-24, 1850) The first national convention for woman's rights was held in Worcester. The first day of the convention, the streets surrounding Brinley Hall in Worcester were overflowing with delegates. The *New York Tribune* reported that "above 1,000 people were present, and if a larger place could have been had, many more thousands would have attended." For two days, more than 1,000 delegates from 11 different states had filled Brinley Hall to overflowing. Speakers, most of them women, demanded the right to vote, to own property, to be admitted to higher education, medicine, the ministry, and other professions. Many newspaper reporters heaped scorn on the convention. Although derisive, the press coverage actually helped bring the convention to the attention of a broad national audience and build support for the movement. Other national conventions followed, but change was slow. It took another 70 years — long after most of the delegates to the Worcester Convention had died — before American women won the right to vote.
– *MassMoments*, Mass Humanities

The Places Where Worcester's Reformers Met

- Brinley Hall
- Mechanics Hall
- Central Exchange Building
- Worcester County Kansas League
- A.M.E. Zion Church
- Worcester Female Employment Society
- American Temperance House
- Horticultural Hall
- The Reform Book Store

- Worcester Children's Friend Society
- Oread Institute
- Ladies Collegiate Institute
- Saint Elizabeth's Hospital
- Worcester Water Cure Institution
- Botanic and Clairoyant Institution

[excerpted from the Worcester Women's History Project booklet, Worcester Women's History Heritage Trail: Worcester in the Struggle for Equality in the Mid-Nineteenth Century]

Susan Brownell Anthony

(B. FEB. 15, 1820 IN ADAMS, MA; D. MAR. 13, 1906 IN ROCHESTER, NY) was one of the most important American social reformers and women's rights activists in American history. Anthony played a pivotal role in the movement for women's suffrage in America. She met Elizabeth Cady Stanton in 1851 and their life-long friendship led to a number of significant collaborations beginning with their founding of the New York Women's State Temperance Society.

In 1856, Anthony became the New York state agent for the American Anti-slavery Society. In the midst of the Civil War, Anthony and Stanton founded the Women's Loyal National League in 1863 conducting the largest petition drive in U.S. history up to that time, collecting close to 400,000 signatures in support of the abolition of slavery. Campaigning for equal rights for women and African-Americans, they created the American Equal Rights Association in 1866. Two years later, Anthony and Stanton began to co-publish a women's rights newspaper, *The Revolution*. Splitting from other efforts, they formed the National Woman Suffrage Association in 1869, and would not merge with their rival American Woman Suffrage Association until 1890 when the two organizations became the unified National American Woman Suffrage Association with Anthony as its leader.

In 1878, Anthony and Stanton presented the U.S. Congress with an amendment giving women the right to vote introduced by Sen. Aaron A. Sargent (R-CA). The amendment became known as the "Susan B. Anthony Amendment." Forty-two years later, It was finally ratified as the Nineteenth Amendment to the U.S. Constitution in 1920.
– Joseph Carvalho III

Lucy Stone

(B. AUG. 13, 1818 IN WEST BROOKFIELD, MA; D. OCT. 18, 1893 IN DORCHESTER, MA) The Stone family farm, on Coy's Hill, was smack in the middle of

Massachusetts, but there was nothing middle-of-the-road about Lucy Stone. As William Lloyd Garrison wrote after first meeting her, she had "a soul as free as the air" and she chose a "very firm and independent" course.

She was almost 30 years old when she graduated from Oberlin College with honors in the summer of 1847. Invited to write a commencement address, she refused because she would not be allowed to read it herself. Oberlin was the first American college to educate women alongside men, but even there, women did not participate in public exercises with men.

A few months later, Lucy Stone gave her first public address from the pulpit of her brother's church in Gardner. Soon, she began traveling the state as an agent for the American Anti-slavery Society. On weekends she lectured on abolitionism; during the week, she spoke out for woman's rights. In 1850, she helped organize the first national woman's rights convention. Held in Worcester because the city was easily accessible by train and known to be hospitable to reform, the convention drew more than a thousand people to a downtown hall. Both hostile and sympathetic reporters from all over the country covered the two-day event.

Over the next few years, Stone proved to be a powerful and popular orator. She earned a good living and a national reputation giving public lectures on the injustices faced by blacks and women. She toured the country,

The staff of the Women's Fund of Western Massachusetts includes, left to right: Donna Haghighat, chief executive officer; Julie Holt, office manager; Jorene Lomenzo, development associate; Ellen Moorhouse and Christine Monska, program officers; and Monica Borgatti, director of philanthropy. Not pictured is Nikai Fondon, youth development coordinator. (Photo by Janice Beetle)

Women's Fund of Western Massachusetts

(WFWM) is a public foundation supporting women's leadership and nonprofit organizations that work on behalf of women and girls. Inspiration for WFWM came from a group of local women who attended the 1995 United Nations Conference for Women in Beijing, China. The organization was incorporated in 1997 and its first grants to organizations in the state's four western counties were made in 1998. WFWM develops strong relationships with grantees and encourages their success through impact evaluations that track accomplishments and help minimize challenges. To date, WFWM has awarded over $2.5 million in grants to about 150 different organizations, impacting over 400,000 women and their families.

Under the leadership of CEO, Donna Haghighat, WFWM advances gender equity by supporting women and girls through:

- Grantmaking: multi-year grants to nonprofit organizations in the four counties of western Massachusetts (since 1998)
- Leadership Institute for Political and Public Impact: a non-partisan program providing adult women across the Commonwealth with tools, mentors, and the confidence to become effective civic leaders and elected officials (since 2011)
- Young Women's Initiative Springfield Partnership: activating young women, ages 14-24, to identify systemic barriers and recommend policy solutions to address structural issues that impact the lives of area youth (launched 2017)

The mission of the Women's Fund of Western Massachusetts is to fuel progress toward gender equity by funding the most promising solutions, collaborating with results-oriented partners, and by elevating the collective power of local women to take charge and to lead with purpose.
– Monica M. Borgatti

organizing anti-slavery and woman's rights conventions, collecting petitions, lobbying legislators, and, whenever she had the opportunity, speaking to state legislatures.

In May 1851, she addressed the Massachusetts legislature on behalf of an amendment to the state constitution giving full civil rights to women. In the gallery that day was Henry Brown Blackwell, the son of a reform-minded family from Cincinnati (two of his sisters were pioneer physicians). Blackwell set out to persuade Lucy Stone to overcome the objections she had long held to marriage. After a two-year courtship, he succeeded. At their wedding in April 1855, they read a protest "against the present laws of marriage [which] refuse to recognize the wife as an independent, rational being." Stone promised to love and honor her husband but omitted the word "obey" from her vows, and she further defied custom by keeping her own name.

After her marriage, Lucy Stone continued to lecture, drawing large and enthusiastic audiences. In 1857 she gave birth to her only child, Alice Stone Blackwell. When the baby was a few months old, Stone refused to pay the bill for the taxes on her house on the grounds that it was "taxation without representation." The town responded by auctioning off her household goods. Stone curtailed her lecturing during the first years of Alice's life and was just returning to the lecture circuit when the Civil War began.

Like her fellow reformers, when war came Stone devoted all her energies to the Union cause. As the end of the war neared, she called for political rights, including the vote, for newly emancipated slaves and women. When the 14th Amendment passed Congress, it gave equal protection under law to men who had been slaves but, to the dismay of woman suffragists, in doing so it introduced the word "male" into the Constitution for the first time. Although Stone was deeply disappointed, she supported ratification of both the 14th and the 15th Amendments; the latter gave black men the right to vote.

Stone's old friends and allies Susan B. Anthony and Elizabeth Cady Stanton opposed ratification. The result was a bitter division in the woman suffrage movement, which lasted for more than 20 years. Stanton and Anthony led one wing; Stone and Blackwell the other. From her base in Boston, Lucy Stone founded the American Woman Suffrage Association, and, with the help of her husband and later her daughter Alice, published *The Woman's Journal*, the influential paper which was known as "the voice of the woman's movement." The two factions were not reconciled until 1890, three decades before American women cast their first votes in a national election.

Lucy Stone died at her home in Dorchester on October 18, 1893. Her last words sum up her life's work: "Make the world better," she whispered to her daughter. She was mourned around the world. "The death of no woman in America had ever called out so general a tribute of public respect and esteem," her old adversary Elizabeth Cady Stanton wrote. Stone had planned her own funeral. Six men and six women were pallbearers. Her casket was taken to Forest Hills Cemetery where, two months later, Lucy Stone would be the first person in Massachusetts to be cremated.
– *Mass Moments*, Mass Humanities

Sojourner Truth

(NÉE ISABELLA BAUMFREE, B. CA. 1797 IN SWARTEKILL, NY; D. NOV. 26, 1883 IN BATTLE CREEK, MI) spent much of her life as a roaming preacher who spoke the truth about slavery and other evils as she received it from God. When she went looking for a place to call home, however, Truth brought her ideals and preaching skills to the Florence section of Northampton.

Truth, who gained world fame in the 19th century through her memoirs, *The Narrative of Sojourner Truth*, spent a dozen years in Florence during the height of the abolitionist movement, fighting for an end to slavery.

Born into slavery herself in 1797, Truth dropped her given name, Isabella, and left her home in upstate New York in 1827 when slavery in that state came to an end.

For years, Truth walked the roads between Connecticut and Long Island preaching about her relationship with God to anyone who would listen. The practice made her a powerful speaker who could mesmerize a crowd with her passionate rhetoric. As the abolitionist movement grew, Truth learned that there were others who were speaking out against slavery, sexism and other injustices. One such group had formed a utopian community called the Northampton Association of Education and Industry, based in the village of Florence.

In 1843, Truth came to Florence, attracted by like-minded thinkers such as William Lloyd Garrison, Frederick Douglass and David Ruggles. For more than a decade, she carried on her causes from a home on Park Street. Several houses in the area also served as stops on the Underground Railroad.

While she found a home with her fellow utopian thinkers, Truth created a stir in the greater community, which was taken aback by the sight of a corncob pipe-smoking black woman. When one local church-goer informed her that she would never get into heaven with tobacco on her breath, Truth reportedly replied, "Well, I don't expect to have my breath with me when I go."

The Northampton Association disbanded in 1846, but Truth remained in Florence until 1857, when she moved to Michigan. She spent her later years working with former slaves in a newly created community called Freeman's Village in Washington, D.C. By the time she died in 1883, Truth's memoirs had made her a legend in her own time. – Wayne E. Phaneuf

Sojourner Truth with Abraham Lincoln.

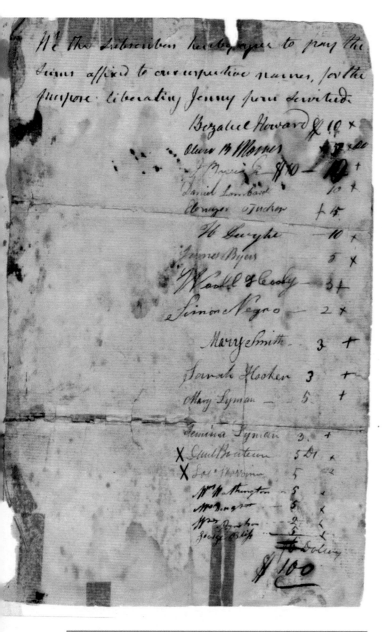

"Bill of Sale" Feb 16, 1808. List of Springfield residents who donated money to purchase Jenny Williams' freedom from New York slavery. (Courtesy Lyman and Merrie Wood Museum of Springfield History, Springfield Museums)

Jenny Williams Rescued from New York Slavery

BY WAYNE E. PHANEUF

By 1800 slavery in the north was a dying institution. All the New England states had either banned it outright or launched what was known as "gradual abolition" with the newborn sons or daughters of slaves declared free.

From the very pulpits of churches where ministers a generation before were slave owners the abolition movement gained some of it biggest boosters who were instrumental in the struggle for freedom. One isolated drama in that struggle took place in Springfield in 1808.

Around the beginning of the 1800s, a young black woman named Jenny arrived in Springfield, which was then a town of about 2,200 people who mostly lived in an area where the present downtown section is located. Jenny had a secret. She had escaped from slavery, not from the Deep South, but from New York state, where slavery was still legal.

Jenny settled in this town by the Connecticut River, fell in love with a man named Jack Williams, and was married in First Church on Court Square in 1802. She settled down with her husband in a small cabin on what was then the outskirts of town on the banks of Goose Pond, almost the present day center of Mason Square.

Connecticut Valley Historical Society President Henry Morris, in a paper presented in 1879, described Jenny as "an honest, industrious and useful person. Everybody knew Jenny, and everybody liked her." Much to the horror of local residents, a man named Peter Van Geyseling from Schenectady, N.Y., appeared in Springfield in 1808 with legal papers proving that Jenny was his escaped slave. Morris wrote that the slaveholder was about to separate Jenny from her husband and family and drag her back to bondage to the state from which she had escaped.

Although Massachusetts outlawed slavery in 1780, the state of New York was in a state of "gradual abolition" which did not end until 1827. The news of Jenny Williams' plight spread quickly through the town. People wanted to help, but the law was on the side of the New York man. It looked as though Jenny's fate was sealed. But then, someone had an idea that they shared with Peter Van Geyseling. Wouldn't he rather have a reasonable sum of money than a discontented slave who had tasted freedom in Massachusetts and would most likely run away again? A bargain was struck, and the townspeople went into action.

The Rev. Bezaleel Howard, the minister who presided over Jenny's marriage six years before, drew up a bill of sale and the people of Springfield quickly raised Van Geyseling's asking price of $100. He signed over his right to Jenny to the Springfield selectmen, who set her free to live out her life with her husband and family on the shores of Goose Pond.

The bill of sale was dated Feb. 16, 1808, and was signed by 18 residents of Springfield, black and white, who pledged the money for Jenny Williams' freedom. That document still exists in the collection of the Wood Museum of Springfield History proof of a town that cared and would not sit by and see slavery take one of its own. [Editors' note: Jenny (Cumfrey) Williams, b. ca. 1770 in New York; d. ca. 1840 in Springfield, MA]

Fighting Against Domestic Violence in the U.S. and Japan: The Yoko Kato Story

BY JANE KAUFMAN

Possessed with an indomitable spirit, Yoko Kato became an international advocate for victims of domestic violence after her daughter, Sherry A. Morton, 23, and grandson Cedric, 18 months old, were murdered.

Kato remembers the day of the brutal

stabbings by Sean D. Seabrooks, Sherry's estranged boyfriend and Cedric's father.

Kato and Sherry spoke on the telephone twice each day after Cedric was born. On January 11, 1993, they spoke during Sherry's lunch hour. Sherry told Kato that Seabrooks had failed to provide child support, and Kato encouraged Sherry to allow Kato to pursue the matter with a lawyer rather than engaging Seabrooks directly.

Rather than calling as she was about to retire, Sherry called at 7 p.m. to say she was going out with friends and would be home too late to call.

The doorbell rang at 4 a.m. the next morning at Kato's Westhampton home. Then-Detective Russell P. Sienkiewicz and Officer Robert Dunn were there. They asked to see her then-husband, Rad Nutting. When he entered the room, Sienkiewicz told Kato to sit down.

"Is it Sherry?" she asked.

Sienkiewicz nodded.

"Is it Cedric?" she asked.

Sienkiewicz nodded and told her that the two had been killed and that the suspect, Seabrooks, was in custody.

She left the room and vomited.

At 6 a.m., she turned on the local news on Channel 40. Eileen Curran was the anchor. Curran reported the double homicide without naming the victims. Kato, who knew Curran, called the newswoman after the broadcast to inform her of who the victims were.

"She lost it," Kato remembers, and Curran came to see Kato later that morning.

Six days later, Kato stood on Main Street in Northampton as part of a vigil against domestic violence. That was her first stand in what became her raison d'etre.

Kato doesn't recall when she first told her story – perhaps because she has done it so frequently over the last 25 years. Her message to domestic violence victims is to reach out for help. She defines abuse as physical, emotional, financial and isolation (total control).

"Women get brainwashed," she said.

Masuo Nishibayashi, left, consul general of Japan, hands Yoko Kato of Westhampton a special award for her work on domestic violence in Massachusetts and Japan during a ceremony at the First Churches in Northampton. The award was part of a celebration of the 150th anniversary of U.S.-Japan relations (May 25, 2004). Photo by Mieke Zuiderweg, courtesy *The Republican*.

Her impact has reached Japan, where a documentary was made by public television station NHK highlighting Kato's story in 1997. Prior to that time, domestic violence was not recognized as a problem in Japan. In 2001, the first domestic violence law passed in Japan. Of the many honors and awards Kato has received, she is most proud of the recognition she won from the Japanese government in 2004.

Kato was invited to Japan several times to speak – to women members of Japan's Diet (equivalent to U.S. Congress), to Japan's Parliament and to the public. On one visit, Northwestern District Attorney Elizabeth Scheibel and Assistant District Attorney Susan Loehn, accompanied her. In addition, she invited Japanese social workers, professors, lawyers and attorneys to Massachusetts to see how victims of domestic violence are supported here.

Kato was born on January 15, 1944, in Yokohama, Japan. At home, she chafed at the male-dominated culture. Each morning her father sat at the king's place at the table facing north, while her mother served him. Kato had

no interest in living a similar life.

She dated an American serviceman, James Morton, and as soon as she was of age to leave Japan, she did so. In order to prove that she would return, she had to show savings of the cost of round-trip airfare. She borrowed money from friends for a single day. After showing U.S. Embassy officials that she could afford the round trip, she returned the money and flew to California on a one-way ticket. She was 21. She married Morton, gave birth to two daughters, and moved to South Hadley with him. When his drinking gave way to what she calls financial and physical abuse, Kato separated, taking a job as a dressmaker in Troy, N.Y. The two divorced in 1975 when Sherry was 6 and Jeannie was 9.

With her daughters, Kato moved to Northampton opening Fashions by Yoko at Thornes Market in 1980. Without a budget for publicity, Kato copied Princess Diana's wedding dress. She then placed a single phone call to Channel 40. The story got picked up nationally and internationally, and Kato's business was launched. She closed her business in 2007.

At 74, Kato is active in domestic violence issues, retaining her membership on the board of the Northwestern Children's Advocacy Center. She has served on the boards of the Massachusetts Office for Victim Assistance, Safe Passage in Northampton, the Men's Resource Center in Amherst, and the Garden of Peace, a memorial to victims of homicide in Boston.

Jeannie and husband Paul Banas live across the street from Kato with their daughter, Aryn. Their son, Trevor, lives in Kato's house.

Kato visits Sherry and Cedric's graves at least once a week at Spring Grove Cemetery in Florence, adding seasonal ornaments and flowers in the summer.

"I go to talk to her," she said. "That's healing for me, too."

(Opposite page) Yoko Kato at 20th anniversary graveside ceremony, Northampton, MA, Jan. 11, 2013. (*The Republican*)
Above left: Emma (Curtiss) Bascom. **Above right:** Zara Cisco Brough (Princess White Flower)

ALPHABETICAL LISTING OF NOTABLE WOMEN SOCIAL & POLITICAL ACTIVISTS:

Frances Matilda (Dresser) Baker
(B. AUG. 20, 1822 IN STOCKBRIDGE, MA; D. DEC. 29, 1904 IN CHICAGO, IL) was the first president of the Worcester Women's Club founded on Dec. 9, 1880. – Joseph Carvalho III

Emma (Curtiss) Bascom
(B. APRIL 20, 1828 IN SHEFFIELD, MA; D. FEB. 27, 1916 IN WILLIAMSTOWN, MA) was a 19th-century American educator, suffragist and reformer. She was a charter member of the Association for the Advancement of Women and for many years was an officer of its board.
– Joseph Carvalho III

Zara Cisco Brough
(B. 1919 IN GRAFTON, MA; D. JAN. 7, 1988 IN WESTBOROUGH, MA), often spelled as Zara Ciscoe Brough, commonly referred to as "Princess White Flower", was the daughter of Sarah Cisco Sullivan and the granddaughter of James Lemuel Cisco. She served as the Chief of the Nipmuc Native Indian Tribe for 25 years from 1962 until 1987. She is best known for her work to preserve Nipmuc heritage, especially her letter of intention to petition for federal recognition of the Nipmuc as a legally distinct Native American people, which resulted in the Nipmuc being placed on "active consideration" for the status of Federally recognized tribe by July 11, 1995. During her lifetime she worked as an electronics engineer, fashion designer, drafter, technical writer, and supervisor of

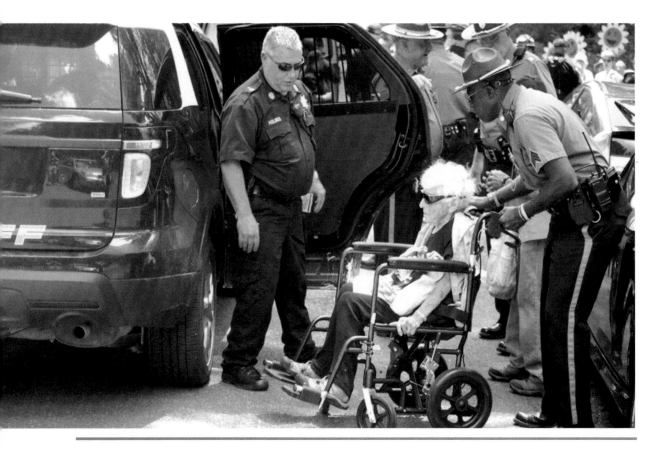

Frances H. Crowe

government projects. She held the post of "State commissioner for Indian Affairs" from 1974 to 1984. In January 2009 a Department of Youth Services facility located at 288 Lyman Street in the town of Westborough was formally named as the Zara Cisco Brough "Princess White Flower" Facility through the House Bill 3231. It had previously been named in 2007 but the official act was passed in 2009. – Joseph Carvalho III

Marie-Louise (DeRoy) Chevalier

(B. MAR. 12, 1888 IN HOLYOKE, MA; D. MAY 26, 1973 IN CHICOPEE, MA) founded the Circle des Grand 'Mamons in 1952, serving as its first president. In 1953, she founded the Franco-American Women Voters Association which became a powerful political force in Chicopee, MA where she lived later in life. From 1947 to 1949, Chevalier served as president of the Circle des Dames Francaise, an influential cultural association in the Greater Springfield Area. – Joseph Carvalho III

Hilda Colón

(B. AUG. 9, 1957) a concerned mother of three children in the Westfield School system in the 1990s, became a member of the Long Range Planning & Building Committee, and was part of the committee that pressed for the establishment of a school volunteers office. Colon attended every school committee meeting for two years, before becoming the first Latina to earn a seat on the Westfield School Committee in 1993. She is a founding member of the Westfield Spanish American Association. – Elizabeth Román

Frances H. Crowe

(B. MAR. 15, 1919 IN CARTHAGE, MO) is a long-time and much respected peace and environmental activist from Northampton, MA. During WWII, Crowe worked for Bell Labs, and became an anti-war activist after hearing about the bombing of civilian populations in Japan. In the 1960s and early 1970s, Crowe counseled conscientious objectors avoiding Vietnam and later served a month in federal prison for spray-painting "Thou Shalt Not Kill" on the casings of missile tubes at a nuclear submarine base in Connecticut. Crowe was first arrested for civil disobedience in the early 1970s at Westover Air Force Base in Chicopee. In 2011 and 2014, police in Vermont arrested Crowe a total of nine times for trespassing near the Vermont Yankee Nuclear Power Station during protests of that facility. In 2015, Smith College awarded Crowe an honorary degree for her work. As a Quaker and mother of three, Crowe, one of the region's so-called "raging grannies", has long been an active force in the American Friends Service Committee, and co-founded the Traprock Peace Center in Deerfield and the Northampton chapter of the Women's International League for Peace and Freedom. A collection of Crowe's papers is kept at the Sophia Smith Collection at Smith College. Crowe is the recipient of the Courage of Conscience Award from the Peace Abbey in Sherborn and the Joe E. Callaway Award for Civic Courage from The Shafeek Nader Trust for the Community Interest. Her most recent protest has been opposition to the natural gas pipeline that is planned to traverse the Otis State Forest at Sandisfield, MA, where she was arrested for trespassing in her wheelchair on June 29, 2017. She is the author of *Finding My Radical Soul*. – Phil Demers & Mary Serreze

Hannah Maria Tracy (Conant) Cutler

(B. DEC. 25, 1815 IN BECKET, MA; D. FEB. 11, 1896 IN OCEAN SPRINGS, MS) was an active abolitionist and women's rights advocate as well as a leader in the temperance movement. Cutler served as president of the Ohio Woman Suffrage Association and the American Woman Suffrage Association (AWSA). Cutler helped to shape the merger of two feminist factions into the combined National American Woman Suffrage Association (NAWSA).
– James S. Gleason

Paulina (Kellogg) Wright Davis

(B. AUG. 7, 1813 IN BLOOMFIELD, NY; D. AUG. 24, 1876 IN PROVIDENCE, RI) was an abolitionist, suffragist, and educator. Davis wrote the call to the Worcester Convention held on Oct. 23 and 24, 1850, presided over it and delivered the opening address. In 1853, she founded the first women's rights newspaper, *The Una,* serving as its editor from 1853 to 1855. All but one year from 1850 to 1858, she served as president of the National Woman's Rights Central Committee. She was one of the founders of the New England Woman Suffrage Association in 1868. In 1870, she organized the 20th anniversary Women's Suffrage Meeting and published *The History of the National Woman's Rights Movement*. She was posthumously inducted into the National Women's Hall of Fame in 2002.
– Joseph Carvalho III

Waleska Lugo DeJesus

(B. 1977 IN PUERTO RICO; RAISED IN SPRINGFIELD, MA) A longtime community activist representing the interest of Latinos and women in the region, Lugo DeJesus has over 20 of experience working in the private, nonprofit sector, and in higher education.

Above left: Elizabeth G. Dineen. **Above right:** Paulina Wright Davis.

She also works as an independent consultant promoting inclusion, civic engagement, leadership and educating communities about 21st century race relations and is the Director of the Healing Racism Institute of Pioneer Valley. In 2011, she served as interim Dean of Multicultural Affairs at Westfield State University. Massachusetts Governor Deval Patrick appointed her as a commissioner for the Commonwealth Service Corps.
– Elizabeth Román

Elizabeth G. Dineen

(B. NOV. 24, 1955) of East Longmeadow, MA is the executive director of the YWCA headquartered in Springfield, MA, appointed in 2016. A strong advocate for women and children, for twenty-seven years she served as an Assistant District Attorney in the Hampden County District Attorney's Office. As a prosecutor, her caseload focused primarily on sexual assaults, domestic violence, physical and sexual child abuse, and child homicide cases. After leaving the District Attorney's Office, Attorney Dineen served as Chair of the Department of Criminal Justice at Bay Path University. In February of 2018, Dineen was appointed to the Massachusetts Governor's Council to address sexual assault and domestic violence by Governor Charles Baker.

During her career, Dineen has received a number of awards, including Elms College Alumna of the Year (2017); Top Women of Law (2013); Massachusetts Governor's Award for Service to the Commonwealth (2008); and first female recipient of the Massachusetts Bar Association: Access to Justice Award — Prosecutor of the Year (2003).
– Talene Jermakian

Katharine (Forbes) Erskine

(B. SEPT. 23, 1890 IN WESTBOROUGH, MA; D. JAN. 26, 1990 IN WORCESTER, MA) moved with her family to Worcester at the age of nine. She studied economics at Vassar College and while there developed a keen interest in the Women's suffrage movement. Graduating from Wellesley with a masters degree, she taught at the University of Wisconsin for three years before returning to Worcester to marry attorney Linwood M. Erskine who worked as a lawyer assisting local women's suffrage advocates. Katherine became a charter member of the League of Women Voters, and after the passage of the 19th Amendment held the first organizational meeting of the local chapter of the League at her home. She continued to advocate for women's rights throughout her life, also serving as the president of the Worcester YWCA twice.
– Joseph Carvalho III

Abby Kelley Foster

(B. JAN. 15, 1811 IN PELHAM, MA; D. JAN. 14, 1887 IN WORCESTER, MA) was an American abolitionist and radical social reformer active from the 1830s to 1870s. She was an active fundraiser, lecturer and committee organizer for the influential American Anti-Slavery Society, where she worked closely with William Lloyd Garrison and other radicals. Foster was the founder of the *Anti-Slavery Bugle* and organizer for the Webster Anti-Slavery Society. She was one of the first women admitted to the American Anti-Slavery Society. For fifteen years, Foster spoke across the country at fairs and anti-slavery societies and was never intimidated by hostile mobs that gathered at many of her public appearances. In 1850, Foster worked with Lucy Stone to organize the first National Woman's Rights Convention in Worcester. In 1845, she married fellow abolitionist and lecturer Stephen Symonds Foster. Together they worked for equal rights for women and for slaves/African

Abby Kelley Foster

Americans. Her former home of Liberty Farm in Worcester, Massachusetts was a "stop" on the Underground Railroad and has been designated a National Historic Landmark.
– Joseph Carvalho III

Frances A. Frederick

(B. MAY 27, 1858 IN SPRING BAY, IL; D. SEPT. 25, 1948 IN HOLYOKE, MA), social activist, founded the Walnut Street Settlement in Holyoke's Ward IV modelled after Hull House in Chicago. Working there for over twenty years, Frederick was the first woman to be honored with the William Dwight Award for Outstanding Service to the Holyoke Community.
– Joseph Carvalho III

Worcester Woman's Suffrage League

was formed on Oct. 4, 1886 with Mrs. Mary C. Harris elected as president. Sarah Henshaw was elected president in 1887 and served in that capacity until 1902. The League disbanded in 1917 and turned over its accumulated funds to the Massachusetts Women's Suffrage Association with its members becoming members of the state organization.
– Joseph Carvalho III

Young Women's Christian Association

The Worcester YWCA was created on June 13, 1885. Under the presidency of Mrs. Charles G. Reed, YWCA rooms were opened on Feb. 1, 1886. Their headquarters building was built in 1890. Springfield's YWCA was established in 1893 and was one of the charter members of the national YWCA. The Brookside Young Women's Camp (Springfield YWCA) was established before 1919 and located in Chester, MA.
– Joseph Carvalho III

Elizabeth Freeman

OF STOCKBRIDGE, MA (B. CA. 1744; D. DECEMBER 28, 1829), also known as "Bet" or "MumBet", was the first black slave to file and win a freedom suit in Massachusetts. The Massachusetts Supreme Judicial Court ruling, in Freeman's favor, found slavery to be inconsistent with the 1780 Massachusetts State Constitution. Her suit, *Brom and Bett v. Ashley* (1781), was cited in the Massachusetts Supreme Judicial Court appellate review of Quock Walker's freedom suit. When the court upheld Walker's freedom under the state's constitution, the ruling was considered to have implicitly ended slavery in Massachusetts. – Joseph Carvalho III

Betsy Gaberman

of Longmeadow, has been a teacher, a businesswoman, and activist, and a philanthropist. She has held national and local leadership roles in the Council of Churches, the Jewish Federation of Greater Springfield, the United Way, Israel Bonds, the Jewish Council for Public Affairs, and the Jewish Endowment Foundation of Western Massachusetts. She has chaired the United Way of the Pioneer Valley's Leadership Division, and chaired the former Heritage Academy's Capital Campaign. She has served on the Board of the Jewish Council of Public Affairs (JCPA), an umbrella organization for Jewish Federations. Gaberman was one of the JCPA's representatives at the Women's Conference in China. She has been on the National Advisory Board on Admissions and Chair of the Secondary School Committee for the University of Pennsylvania. In addition, she chaired Operation Moses (a fundraising campaign for the covert evacuation of Ethiopian Jews from Sudan in 1984), Bosnian relief, and hosted a variety of political fundraisers and programs on Headstart, interfaith issues, AIDS, domestic violence, and community relations. In 2013, Gaberman was honored by the Women's Philanthropy of the

Above left: Marie Weis Hazen. **Above right:** Betsy Gaberman.

Jewish Federation of Western Massachusetts. – Jane Kaufman

Constancya Gulewski

(B. 1902 IN NORTHAMPTON, MA) was one of the founders of the influential Mater Dolorosa Society of the Polish Women's Alliance of America in Holyoke, MA in 1912. – Joseph Carvalho III

Marie (Weis) Hazen

(B. NOV. 11, 1895 IN OHIO; D. FEB. 27, 1986 IN HOLYOKE, MA) was a Holyoke activist for child welfare. She was appointed to the White House Conference on Children and Youth by President Harry S. Truman in 1950. IN the late 1940s, she was appointed to the Massachusetts State Committee on Juvenile Delinquency whose work resulted in the establishment of the Massachusetts Youth Service Board, Hazen served on that board for six years. She also was the "prime mover" in the founding of the Child Guidance Clinic (later re-named the Area Mental Health Clinic), and served as the president and director of that organization. IN 1958, Hazen was honored with the William G. Dwight Award for Distinguished Service to the Holyoke Community. – Joseph Carvalho III

Margaret Goddard Holt

(B. OCT. 4, 1911 IN SWARTHMORE, PA; D. JAN. 1, 2004 IN AMHERST, MA) was a painter, writer, educator, prolific letter-writer, and long-time peace and justice activist. She and her husband Lee Holt moved to Springfield in 1947, her parents were originally from Worcester, MA. At that time, she worked part time teaching art therapy with handicapped people at United Cerebral Palsy and Monson State Hospital. Margaret and Lee Holt coordinated a 1967-1972 Vigil in Springfield against the U.S. war on Vietnam; Margaret co-founded the Springfield chapter of the Women's International League for Peace and Freedom and was a delegate of women from all over the world who visited Pope John XXIII in Rome, Italy calling for a world without war; she marched in the Poor People's Campaign of 1963 in Washington, D.C., she was a "back-bone" member of the Gray Panthers of the Pioneer Valley; and her concern for prisoners and prison-related issues led to many years of weekly correspondence with three Texas Death Row "grandsons." Margaret and Lee Holt also helped establish the Amherst Vigil for a Nuclear Free World in 1979 and for 24 years, come rain, shine or snow, they and others gathered at the Amherst Common every Sunday noon for a Vigil addressing a wide array of local to global peace and justice issues. – Tom Shea

Helen Fiske Hunt Jackson

(B. OCT. 15, 1830 IN AMHERST, MA; D. 1885) A lifelong friend of Emily Dickinson and a talented poet in her own right, Helen Fiske Hunt Jackson would become one of the most admired and prolific authors of her time. Her poems, essays, travel sketches, and children's stories were widely published in the 1860s. Jackson made regular trips east to maintain contact with other authors and

Margaret Goddard Holt

The Quota Club's beginnings in Massachusetts:

In 1927, Quota received the attention of U.S. President Calvin Coolidge, who sent his greetings to that year's convention attendees. Headquarters was on the move to the nation's capital — Washington, D.C. — and a permanent home. Each year, headquarters had moved with the current president and now with a pledge of support from each club ($1,700 total), Quota would have a permanent home from which to do business. By 1929's annual convention in Worcester, Massachusetts, Quota International could boast a membership of 2,500 — a real achievement in only ten years. Quota International, Inc. is a non-profit organization empowering women, children, the deaf, hard of hearing, and speech impaired in local communities around the world. In 1919, five business women inspired to serve, founded Quota International as the first international women's service organization, one year before women in the United States won the right to vote. Today, more than 5,000 Quota members, women, men, and youth, come together to help women and children overcome poverty, educational, and workforce challenges in 14 countries.

publishers. It was during a visit to Boston in 1879 that she heard Chief Standing Bear and other representatives of the Ponca and Omaha Indian tribes describe how the federal government had confiscated their peoples' land and forced them to relocate to Indian Territory. She immediately became a convert to the cause of Native American rights.

She learned everything she could about the issue. She began writing letters to newspaper on the question at the heart of her work: "Has the Indian any rights which the white man is bound to respect?" After months of research, in 1881 she published her path-breaking exposé of Indian mistreatment, *A Century of Dishonor: A Sketch of the United States Government's Dealings with Some of the Indian Tribes.* "President after president has appointed commission after commission to inquire into and report upon Indian affairs, and to make suggestions as to the best methods of managing them," she wrote. "The reports are filled with eloquent statements of wrongs done... They counsel a trial of telling the truth, keeping promises, making fair bargains, dealing justly in all ways and all things. These reports are bound up with the Government's Annual Reports, and that is the end to them."

Jackson continued as a crusader for Native American rights and devoted the rest of her life to that cause.

– Mass Moments, Mass Humanities

Ellen Holbrook (Cheney) Johnson

(B. DEC. 20, 1829 IN ATHOL, MA; D. JUNE 28, 1899 IN ST. SAVIOUR SOUTHWARK, LONDON, ENGLAND) earned her place in history as the woman who reformed the prison system of the late 19th Century. She was a founder of the New England Women's Auxiliary Association and was tasked by the U.S. Sanitary Commission during the Civil War to distribute funds to the dependents of soldiers. She often visited correctional institutions as part of her duties and was appalled at the conditions

Helen Fiske Hunt Jackson

of the prisoners and was scandalize by the contemporary practice of incarcerating both men and women in the same facility.

As an advocate for prison reform, she put her full energies into gathering an astounding 7,000 signatures in a petition presented to the legislature. As a direct result, a bill creating the first prison for women in Massachusetts was signed into law in June of 1874. Located in Dedham, MA, the facility was named the "Temporary Asylum for Discharged Female Prisoners." In 1877, a second prison for women was opened in Framingham with Johnson

Above left: Clara Temple Leonard. **Above right:** Mary Reardon Johnson.

serving as superintendent. It was here that she implemented her concept of combining reform with traditional discipline, work, and education with a goal of preparing inmates for their eventual re-introduction into free society. Johnson famously wrote that "the prisoner must learn to do right without compulsion or she will cease to do right when the compelling force is gone." The women's prison in Framingham and its program under Johnson made it "a national model which changed the way women were treated under the nation's penal system."
– Joseph Carvalho III

Mary Reardon Johnson

(B. 1950), Executive Director of the YWCA of Western Massachusetts retired in 2016. Johnson joined the YWCA of Springfield in 1983. Under Johnson's management and leadership, the YWCA expanded beyond Springfield and evolved into a solvent nonprofit with $18 million in assets, a $13 million positive fund or net asset balance,

and an endowment of $5 million. It became the state's largest provider of both domestic violence services and services to pregnant and parenting teens with an operating budget by 2016 of more than $6 million annually.
– Anne-Gerard Flynn

Carmenceita Osceola (Pascoe) Jones

(B. NOV. 6, 1925 IN ORLANDO, FLA; D. JULY 11, 2008 IN SPRINGFIELD, MA) was an activist for racial equality and for education reform in Springfield, MA. Jones grew up in Georgia and was the first African-American woman to work in an all-white office in downtown Atlanta. Moving to Springfield in 1963, she immersed herself in community activities becoming the President of DeBerry School's Parent Teacher Association. She organized the Quality Integrated Education Committee and served as Chairwoman. This committee assisted the Peaceful Integration of Springfield's elementary schools in 1974 after winning a vital desegregation suit.

Jones also was a vocal member of the panel formed by the Massachusetts Commissioner of Education to arbitrate between the School Committee and Title I parents. As a three term member of the Greater Springfield Community Council, she participated in several studies of United Way member agencies. She was elected by her peers in Western Massachusetts as a delegate to the International Women's Year Conference held in Houston, TX. The state delegation elected her as Vice-chair of the Delegation. As a Vice chair, she was invited along with the Chairs and Vice-Chairs, to the White House to present the Women's Platform to President Carter. Chairman of the Old Hill Neighborhood Council for ten years. During this time the neighborhood saw many improvements. Chief among those was Quincy Street Project where a million dollars in housing rehabilitation was expended.

In 2002, she retired as a Program Coordinator from City's Office of Housing. Prior to working for the City, she worked at St. John Congregational Church first as a Secretary and later as the Director of the Church's Inner-city Counseling & Development Center.
– Joseph Carvalho III

Clara Temple Leonard

(B. DEC. 19, 1828 IN GREENFIELD, MA; D. DEC. 22, 1904 IN SPRINGFIELD, MA) was an advocate for the humane treatment of women prisoners in the 1860s and 70s. She lobbied the Massachusetts legislature to establish a separate reformatory prison for women and as a result a bill was passed to that effect. Leonard was one of three women appointed to the advisory board to the Commissioners of Prisons on the condition and treatment of women in the state penitentiary system. In 1878, Leonard was appointed the first President of the Hampden County Children's Aid Association serving in that capacity until 1885. In 1880, Massachusetts Governor Long appointed her to the Board (first woman to hold that post) of Health, Lunacy, and Charity. Ironically, she was a known anti-suffragist and her writing on the subject was often used by the Anti-Woman Suffrage League in their lobbying efforts on both state and federal levels. – Joseph Carvalho III

Betty Medina Lichtenstein

(B. OCT. 12, 1952 IN NEW YORK CITY) A social activist and community organizer, Medina Lichtenstein was first elected to a seat on the Holyoke School Committee in November of 1985. According to the Center for Puerto Rican Studies at Hunter College in New York City, she was the first Puerto Rican woman elected to public office in the state of Massachusetts. For more than 20 years she has been the executive director of Enlace de Familias, a social service agency in Holyoke, MA dedicated to promoting healthy relationships in families. In 2013, she received the Sister Agnes Broderick Justice & Peace Award from the Providence Ministries for the Needy. – Elizabeth Román

Dr. Ruth Bertha (Stewart) Loving

(B. MAY 27, 1914 IN PHOENIXVILLE, PA; D. NOV. 25, 2014 IN SPRINGFIELD, MA) grew up in New Haven, CT, and after marrying Minor Loving in 1943, moved to Springfield, MA. She was the founder and editor of the *Springfield Negro Post*, and was a featured columnist in other local newspapers including *Springfield's Point of View*. During her long career, she held various positions at the Springfield Council on Aging, the Martin Luther King, Jr. Community Center in Springfield, and in the Springfield Assessor's Office. Since her first campaign as a Democratic candidate for Springfield School Committee in 1960, Loving was politically active, encouraging people to vote, especially in the minority communities. She was a poll worker for over 50 years. An active and vocal member of the Springfield branch of the NAACP beginning in the 1950s, she served as its president and "during the turbulent

Civil Rights decades of the 1960s and 1970s ... could be found on the front line with the NAACP." For many years, she was the host of the "Spotlight on Springfield" WMAS 1450 radio program. Along with her husband, she was a founder of the Gardner Memorial A.M.E. Church. Governor Paul Celluci appointed her to the Massachusetts African-American Advisory Committee. In 1994, WGBY Channel 57 public television honored her with an "Eyes on the Prize" award for her work in Civil and Human Rights. – Joseph Carvalho III

Lucy Walker Mallory

(B. 1861 IN MA; D. 1932 IN SPRINGFIELD, MA) was a life-long advocate for immigrant rights especially education, housing, and health. In 1912, she became a "consecrated" Congregational missionary to the foreign-born of the diverse ethnic population of the city of Springfield. It was reported that she made almost 2,000 family visits annually to help guide and counsel these families. She received the William Pynchon Medal for her life's work in 1928 and has been honored by having Springfield's first public housing development named after her in 1942. – Joseph Carvalho III

Rose "Arky" (Aisenberg) Markham

(B. JULY 19, 1915 IN WORCESTER, MA) of Northampton is a famed social justice and peace activist. She enlisted in the Women's Army Corps in WWII. As an air traffic controller, she directed pilots as they ran practice bombings in the desert of the American West, 50 miles from Los Angeles. After the war, Markham came north to work as a social worker at the U.S. Department of Veterans Affairs Medical Center in Leeds. She met George Markham when she was in her 50s, and their first date was a Vietnam War protest. Over the next several decades, the

Dr. Ruth Bertha Loving

59

Above: Lucy Mallory. At left: Sister Jane F. Morrissey.

the Sisters of St. Joseph. After graduating from the Elms College in Chicopee, MA she worked among the poor in Columbia, Peru, Bolivia, and Guatemala. Morrissey also worked for a time in refugee camps in Nepal and in Africa. In 1984, she help found Gray House, a social service agency and community center in Springfield's North End. She and Sister Maureen Broughan, SSJ started Homework House in Holyoke, MA. – Anne-Gerard Flynn

Juliette Hanh Nguyen

(B. DEC. 29, 1949 IN SAIGON, SOUTH VIETNAM) was one of the first Vietnamese immigrants to relocate to Springfield, MA area during the Vietnam War. She holds a Master's degree in Education from Cambridge College, Boston. Massachusetts Governor Paul Cellucci appointed Nguyen to head the Health & Human Services for the Commonwealth of Massachusetts in August of 1999. As Commissioner, Nguyen was in charge of the Massachusetts Office of Refugees & Immigrants. In this position she helped to craft and implement the state Wilson & Fish Alternative Project which included several state-administered programs and involved the coordination with HHS and other governmental agencies, on legal, policy and budgetary issues. Among various programs there was a Minority Small Business with Individual Cash Saving Account. This special program received a matching grant from the Federal, and State/Federal Micro-enterprise Development to assist in the managing and training of minority farmers in collaboration with United States Department of Agriculture. Under Nguyen's leadership, the Massachusetts Office of Refugees & Immigrants was named one of the top ten Refugee Resettlement Programs in the country, with over 70% of refugees securing employment within eight months of arrival to the U.S. She was re-appointed by Governor Jane Swift, and Governor Mitt Romney.

two of them fought for social justice causes until George Markham's death in 2009 at the age of 100. She co-founded the Markham-Nathan Fund for Social Justice, which provides grants to organizations helping vulnerable citizens, advocating for peace and working to protect the environment.
– Fred Contrada

Mary Lucina (Sears) McHenry

(B. DECEMBER 30, 1834 IN NEW BOSTON VILLAGE, IN THE TOWN OF SANDISFIELD, MA; D. JULY 26, 1912 IN OKOBOJI, IOWA) was an American community organizer. She became the eighth president of the Women's Relief Corps in 1890, which at the time, was the largest fraternal association in the country.
– Joseph Carvalho III

Sister Jane F. Morrissey

(B. JUNE 30, 1941 IN WESTFIELD, MA), SSJ, a social justice activist, served as president of

Nguyen was the Founder and Executive Director for the Vietnamese American Civic Association (SVACA) in Springfield – one of the first non-profit community based organizations to serve the Vietnamese population in Western Massachusetts, and the first Vietnamese Organization non-profit to be recognized and to receive funding by the United Way in the United States. SVACA was recognized by the then-U.S. Secretary of State, Colin L. Powell, for working with the State Department to help citizens understand the importance of U.S. foreign policies.

Nguyen retired in 2005 and is now a resident of Charlotte, North Carolina. She is serving as Vice-Chair of the Vietnamese Senior Services in Charlotte, a non-profit organization Nguyen and her husband Hoi Tran, founded. – Joseph Carvalho III

Linda Matys O'Connell

(B. 1947) is the co-president of the Springfield unit of the Northampton Area League of Women Voters. As a journalist, O'Connell helped start a revolution in print in 1973 when she founded the *Valley Advocate,* one of the first alternative newsweeklies in the country mounting a challenge to traditional journalism. The *Advocate* grew to a six-newspaper chain. Linda was also a pioneer in broadcast journalism as the host Connecticut Public Television's Womankind, one of the country's first talk shows devoted to women's issues. In her career as a journalist, O'Connell held ranking editorial management positions for the *Times-Mirror*, *Tribune* and *Gannett* newspaper chains. She was also a senior TV producer for Connecticut-based SimonPure Productions. She currently serves as the Social Action Chair of the United Methodist Women of Western Massachusetts and Connecticut. – Joseph Carvalho III

Maria L. Owen was the first president of

the Springfield Women's Club.
– Elizabeth Román

Above: Maria L. Owen
Above right: Juliette Hanh Nguyen
Below right: Linda Matys O'Connell

Lucy Waters Phelps

(B. NOV. 17, 1876 IN SUTTON, MA; D. MAY 21, 1965) of Sutton, MA was the first woman in Sutton to register to vote and became an ardent suffragist. She was an active member of the Worcester Equal Franchise Club which later became the local League of Women Voters. "A pillar in her community," Phelps was one of the organizers of the West Sutton Community League for the "betterment of West Sutton." in 1928. She taught at the West Sutton School for 21 years. – Joseph Carvalho III

Emma A. (Greene) Porter

(B. OCT. 25, 1851 IN CAMBRIDGE, MA; D. MAR. 6, 1915 IN WORCESTER, MA) was the first President and one of the founders of the Levana Club of Worcester in 1905. The Levana Club was an association of teachers and a forerunner of the modern parent-teachers associations common today. Porter was the principal of Worcester's Ward Street School. – Joseph Carvalho III

Abigail Persis Blanchard Gleason Rawson

(B. 1811 IN PRINCETON, MA; D. 1895 IN WORCESTER, MA) of Worcester was a social activist who was one of the founding members of the Ladies Washingtonian Temperance Society, serving as its first president. in 1843. She was a member of the First National Women's Rights Convention held in Worcester in 1850. She served as one of the managers of the Worcester Children's Friend Society for 37 years.
– Joseph Carvalho III

Maria (Fletcher) Reynolds

(B. 1804 IN WEST SPRINGFIELD, MA; D. AFTER 1845) was the first African-American woman colonist from Western Massachusetts to settle in Liberia at the Cape Palmas settlement established by the American Colonization Society. The Reynolds were early advocates of returning to Africa to re-establish their ancestral roots in a free African nation. Mary, her husband William and their four children arrived in Monrovia aboard the brig *Roanoke* on Feb. 17, 1833. Two of her children died of fevers in that first year. Maria was widowed in 1841, however, she remained in the settlement to raise her two surviving children. She was the daughter of Archelaus Fletcher, Jr. of West Springfield who was a veteran of the American Revolution. – Joseph Carvalho III

Barbara Eleanor (Coakley) Rivera

(B. SEPT. 26, 1935 IN CHICOPEE, MA; D. FEB. 10, 2005 IN SPRINGFIELD, MA) She may have been an Irish-American, but Rivera was adopted by the Puerto Rican community in Springfield, as one of their own. A lifelong community activist,
Rivera fought for the rights of women and children, Puerto Ricans and other underrepresented people in the city's North End neighborhood. She served as the director of the New North Citizens Council for 31 years. Her daughter Cheryl Rivera-Coakley went on to become the first Latina woman to be elected to the Massachusetts Legislature in 1998. – Natalia Muñoz

Sara Tappan Doolittle (Lawrence) Robinson

(B. JULY 12, 1827 IN BELCHERTOWN, MA; D. NOV. 15, 1911 IN LAWRENCE, KANSAS) She married Charles Robinson on Oct 30, 1851 and established their home in Fitchburg, MA where her husband edited a newspaper and practiced medicine. Sara and her husband were both active abolitionists and became

very involved in the New England Emigrant Aid Society after the passage of the Kansas-Nebraska Act in 1854. Charles travelled to Kansas Territory in July of 1854 to select a site for free-state emigrants from New England. Sara joined her husband in the spring of 1855. Charles had already been chosen "president" of the Lawrence Town Company and soon became the "pre-eminent leader of the free-state movement in Kansas Territory." Sara used her considerable literary skills for the cause, publishing in October 1856 a book entitled Kansas: Its Interior and Exterior Life that described in vivid detail the social and political situation of "Bleeding Kansas." Contemporary observers considered her book "second only to Uncle Tom's Cabin in importance to the anti-slavery cause." – Joseph Carvalho III

Ruth Sienkiewicz-Mercer

(B. 1950; D. 1998 IN NORTHAMPTON, MA), disability rights activist, resident of infamous Belchertown State School in the 1960s and 1970s. – Joseph Carvalho III

Tekla Starzyk

(B. CA. 1892 IN IN RUSSIA/ POLAND; D. 1955 IN CHICOPEE, MA) was one of the founders of the influential Mater Dolorosa Society of the Polish Women's Alliance of America in Holyoke, MA in 1912. – Joseph Carvalho III

Agma M. Sweeney

is a former staff assistant for U.S. Rep. Richard E. Neal and a Westfield City Councilor. Sweeney has spent many years advocating for the Latino community, particularly the immigrant population. She is passionate about immigration reform and access to quality early education for all children. She is a member of the Westfield Spanish American Association and is now a math teacher at Pope Francis High School in Chicopee. – Elizabeth Román

Elizabeth Lois (Jones) Towne

(B. MAY 11, 1865 IN PORTLAND, OREGON; D. IN HOLYOKE, MA) [See also her other listing in Authors and Publishers Chapter]. Served as president of the Holyoke League of Women Voters for six years, and as a director of the Massachusetts League of Women Voters from 1927-1930. – Joseph Carvalho III

Eleanor Pickering Townsley

(B. JULY 17, 1876 IN SPRINGFIELD, MA; D. JAN. 19, 1954 IN FLUSHING, NY) founded the precursor

organization to the Springfield Girl's Club, called the Ferry Street Settlement in 1897. In 1905, the Ferry Street Settlement Association was formed and the Girl's Club section was attended to by Townsley every day of the week for many years. The Association was re-organized as the Springfield Girl's Club in 1916. – Joseph Carvalho III

Sirdeaner L. Walker

(B. APR. 23, 1965 IN SPRINGFIELD, MA; D. OCT. 5, 2016 IN SPRINGFIELD, MA) of Springfield, MA was motivated by her son's (Carl Joseph Walker-Hoover) tragic suicide in 2009 to become one of the nation's most effective crusaders against bullying. She brought the issue to the highest levels of American government as well as to the homes of families in her hometown of Springfield. Before succumbing from breast cancer, her campaign against bullying went all the way to President Barack Obama and the White

House and gained his support for national efforts to combat bullying. She worked as Program Director of Homeless Services for the M.C.D.I. in Springfield, MA. – Joseph Carvalho III

Eliza Rose Whiting

(B. APR. 10, 1846 IN DALTON, MA; D. OCT. 5, 1938 IN SPRINGFIELD, MA) was a social welfare, journalist, and women's voting rights activist who initiated one of the first "Women's sections" in an American newspaper at *The Republican* in 1888. – Joseph Carvalho III

(Opposite page) **Left:** Lucy Waters Phelps. **Right:** Sara Tappan Doolittle (Lawrence) Robinson.

(This page) **Above left:** Elizabeth Lois Towne and her magazine *Nautilus*. **Above right:** Sirdeaner L. Walker.

(Next two pages) Women's March, Northampton, MA on Jan. 20, 2018 (*The Republican*). Women's March, Boston Common, Boston, MA, Jan. 20, 2018 (*The Republican*)

TWO PEDESTALS

DODO

FIDO

TANGO

ANTI SUFFRAGE

IGNORANCE
IDLENESS
IRRESPONSIBILITY
INFERIORITY

SHAM CHIVALRY

JUSTICE — EQUAL SUFFRAGE

SCHOOL VOTE
RED CROSS
TEACHING
GUARDIANSHIP
PROFFESSIONS
PROPERTY

MOTHERHOOD
SISTERHOOD
CO-OPERATION
SERVICE
COMPANIONSHIP
LOVE

EDUCATION
RELIGION

B. Ames
1915.

Which will the Voters choose For ▬ Women on Nov. 2ⁿᵈ

1920 -- 75th Anniversary of Woman Suffrage -- 1995
Drawn by Blanche Ames (1878-1969). Published in *Boston Transcript*, Sept., 1915,
and *Blanche Ames and Woman Suffrage* by James Kenneally, 1993.
Original at Sophia Smith Collection, Smith College, Northampton, Mass.

Zonta International

founded in 1919, actively promotes and improves the status of women across the globe. The Springfield chapter was one of the first to be organized. Their mission is "to promote peace, justice, and respect for human rights and freedoms." Their longstanding relationship with The United Nations has led to international service projects in over twenty countries providing training in education, sanitation, agriculture, and health as well as "micro-credit assistance." On April 19, 1934, two enthusiastic, Springfield Zontians, Beatrice Latourneau and Elizabeth Klages, organized the Zonta Club of the Northampton. Their first big project was the Chesterfield Lodge, a large summer home where sick mothers could recuperate either alone, or with their small children. Until this project was lost in the activities of World War II, an annual hope chest lottery provided the funding for it. During the organization's first decades, the clubs of Western and Central Massachusetts focused on helping flood victims, war relief efforts, and hospital projects. According to club president and historian Marilyn J. Schmidt, the Northampton Chapter's earliest international commitments included contributions and books for a Chinese medical student, Christmas boxes to war victims, adopting a Belgian girl, and sending CARE packages "to any country not under Russian domination." – Joseph Carvalho III

Timeline of Woman Suffrage in Massachusetts

1848
Women's Rights Convention held in Seneca Falls, NY.

1850
The National Women's Rights Convention is held at Brinley Hall in Worcester, Massachusetts on October 23 & 24. Men and women from across the country are in attendance. Of the 268 names of those who signed-in, 186 were from Massachusetts.

1851
Second National Women's Rights Convention held in Worcester, MA.

1866
The first meeting of the American Equal Rights Association is held at the Meionaon in Boston. The first petition to the Massachusetts Legislature, asking that women might be allowed to serve on school boards, is presented by Samuel E. Sewall of Boston. The same petition is presented again in 1867.

1868
New England Women's Club is founded at a convention at Horticultural Hall in Boston. By 1872 the New England Women's Club Standing Committee of Education states that "the most pressing business was securing the appointment of women on the school committee." Around this time women are elected to school committees in the small Franklin county towns of Ashfield and Monroe. The cities of Lynn, Worcester and Boston are soon to follow.

1869
A joint special committee on Woman Suffrage is formed by the Massachusetts State Legislature. The State House of Representatives votes on the question of municipal suffrage for women: 68 "yeas" (33.8%) vs. 133 "nays". The American Equal Rights Association changes the name of their organization to the National Women Suffrage Association. The American Woman Suffrage Association is also formed.

1870
The Massachusetts Woman Suffrage Association is formed at a meeting at Horticultural Hall in Boston. *The Woman's Journal: a Woman's Suffrage Newspaper* is set-up by the New England Association in 1869 and in 1870.

1871
In his address before the Massachusetts State Legislature, William Clafin becomes the first governor of the state to speak directly on the subject of women's rights. Clafin recommends a change in the laws regarding suffrage and property rights of women.

1874
Boston elects three women to serve on the school committee.

1875
U.S. Senator from Massachusetts George Frisbie Hoar argues that, for church, state and community to work well, the active participation and influence of women is necessary.

1876
Susan B. Anthony, Matilda Joslyn Gage, Sara Andrews Spencer, Lillie Devereux Blake and Phoebe W. Couzins present the "Declaration of Rights of the Women of the United States" on July 4, 1876. As published in the Declaration of Rights of the Women of the United States by the National Woman Suffrage Association, July 4, 1876.

1879
The Massachusetts Legislature votes to allow women to vote for school committee members. At the first annual elections for School Committee about 5,000 women in Massachusetts became registered voters.

1881
Massachusetts State House of Representatives again votes on the question of municipal suffrage for women: 76 "yeas" (38.3%) vs. 122 "nays". Harriet H. Robinson's *Massachusetts in the Women's Suffrage Movement: A General Political, Legal and Legislative History from 1774 to 1881* published in Boston, Massachusetts.

1892
In June 1892, the poll tax for women in Massachusetts is abolished. This enables all women citizens of Massachusetts who can read and write the right to vote for local school committee members. The percentage of registered women voters continues to remain quite low. Women are only allowed to vote for school committee members until 1920. Many women feel that a broader franchise would encourage more women to vote.

Top right: Political cartoon of Susan B. Anthony chasing President Grover Cleveland (Courtesy Library of Congress).
Top left and bottom left: Courtesy of Library of Congress.

The Massachusetts School Suffrage Association surveys the number of women elected to school boards in Massachusetts. In addition to 4 in Boston, 157 women serve in 112 cities and towns.

1893-1894

Josephine St. Pierre Ruffin founded the Woman's Era Club for black women in Boston. Its motto is "Make the World Better". In 1895 the Woman's Era club publishes *The New Era*, the first newspaper/magazine published for and by black women. Its readers are urged to become involved in public issues such as suffrage and civil rights.

1895

Massachusetts holds a non-binding referendum concerning municipal suffrage for women. Although women are allowed to vote on this non-binding topic, the vote statewide is overwhelmingly rejected. Ninety-six percent of women vote in the affirmative (23,000 out of 24,000; there were 600,000 eligible women voters), versus only 32% of male voters (87,000 of 274,000).

1915

Massachusetts males are asked to vote by referendum on women's suffrage as an amendment to the United States Constitution. As in 1895, the referendum is once again defeated by Massachusetts voters. The only community in the state of Massachusetts to vote in favor of suffrage is Tewksbury with a vote of 149 to 148. Statewide, only 35.5% were in favor. Four states in the east vote on full suffrage for women: Massachusetts, New Jersey, Pennsylvania and New York. All four states vote in the negative.

1920

It is not until 1920 with the passing of the Nineteenth Amendment to the United States Constitution that women in Massachusetts were availed full voting privileges.

Brief History of the League of Women Voters

In her address to the National American Woman Suffrage Association's (NAWSA) 50th convention in St. Louis, Missouri, President Carrie Chapman Catt proposed the creation of a "league of women voters to finish the fight and aid in the reconstruction of the nation." The League of Women Voters was formed within the NAWSA, composed of the organizations in the states where suffrage had already been attained.

The next year, on February 14, 1920 – six months before the 19th amendment to the Constitution was ratified – the League was formally organized in Chicago as the national League of Women Voters. Catt described the

purpose of the new organization:

The League of Women Voters is not to dissolve any present organization but to unite all existing organizations of women who believe in its principles. It is not to lure women from partisanship but to combine them in an effort for legislation which will protect coming movements, which we cannot even foretell, from suffering the untoward conditions which have hindered for so long the coming of equal suffrage. Are the women of the United States big enough to see their opportunity?

Maud Wood Park became the first national president of the League and thus the first League leader to rise to the challenge. She had

steered the women's suffrage amendment through Congress in the last two years before ratification and liked nothing better than legislative work. From the very beginning, however, it was apparent that the legislative goals of the League were not exclusively focused on women's issues and that citizen education aimed at all of the electorate was in order.

Since its inception, the League has helped millions of women and men become informed participants in government. In fact, the first League convention voted 69 separate items as statements of principle and recommendations for legislation. Among them were protection for women and children, right of working women, food supply and demand, social hygiene, the legal status of women, and American citizenship. The League's first major national legislative success was the passage of the Sheppard-Towner Act providing federal aid for maternal and child care programs. In the 1930s, League members worked successfully for enactment of the Social Security and Food and Drug Acts. Due at least in part to League efforts, legislation passed in 1938 and 1940 removed hundreds of federal jobs from the spoils system and placed them under Civil Service.

During the postwar period, the League helped lead the effort to establish the United Nations and to ensure U.S. Participation. The League was one of the first organizations in the country officially recognized by the United Nations as a non-governmental organization; it still maintains official observer status today. Three months after the national League was founded, the League of Women Voters of Massachusetts (LWVMA) was organized, on May 27, 1920. Many Massachusetts League members had also been part of the National Suffrage movement. Right from the beginning, LWVMA studied issues and took action, trying to influence legislation and improve our community.

LWVMA has focused on many issues, including: election laws, natural resources, women's health, children's issues, civil rights, equal rights amendment, campaign finance reform, the open meeting law, state budget and finances, public education, gender equity, administration of justice, public safety, community preservation, casino gambling, redistricting, and many, many more.
Today, the League of Women Voters of Massachusetts continues to be a respected and trusted voice for citizen participation in our democracy. – *from the Massachusetts League of Women Voters*

Today's Massachusetts League of Women Voters:

CENTRAL MASSACHUSETTS:

League of Women Voters Grafton

League of Women Voters of Harvard, MA

League of Women Voters of Shrewsbury

League of Women Voters of the Worcester Area *(serving towns without their own chapter)*

WESTERN MASSACHUSETTS:

Amherst League of Women Voters

League of Women Voters – Central Berkshire Unit

League of Women Voters of Franklin County, Greenfield, MA

LEAGUE OF WOMEN VOTERS OF THE NORTHAMPTON AREA

(serving Northampton, Springfield, Holyoke, Easthampton, Westhampton, Southampton, and Williamsburg)

LEAGUE OF WOMEN VOTERS OF WILLIAMSTOWN

[from League of Women Voters Website]

Springfield Women's Club
132 Years of Service

BY ELIZABETH ROMÁN
[excerpted from article that appeared in
The Republican July 6, 2016]

They were wives, mothers and fine ladies who were also fierce suffragettes, social activists, artists and community leaders. The women who have been members of the Springfield Women's Club in its 132-year history were not afraid to stand up for what was right and help those in need.

"Many of the women in the club have done outstanding things that have impacted the quality of life for the residents of Springfield over the years," said Frances Gagnon, a past president of the club who also served as its archivist.

About 30 women gathered for their final meeting. It was an opportunity to celebrate the rich history of the club. For over 100 years, the club donated hundreds of thousands of dollars to community organizations, helped clothe and feed the homeless, beautified parks and public spaces and fought for the rights of those in need.

At the group's final meeting in Springfield, Gagnon shared some of the history of the group. Founded in 1884 by women like its first president, Maria L. Owen, the Springfield Women's Club was a place where women could make a difference. While they had high tea and garden parties, fundraising galas and luncheons, the club was about so much more. Since its inception, the club strongly supported the suffrage movement and openly fought for women's right to vote. It was the city's only

Mayor (now U.S. Congressman) Richard E. Neal of Springfield with leaders of the Springfield Women's Club at Merrick Park in front of the Deacon Samuel Chapin Monument. (Courtesy *The Republican*)

FOUNDED IN 1884 BY WOMEN LIKE ITS FIRST PRESIDENT, MARIA L. OWEN, THE SPRINGFIELD WOMEN'S CLUB WAS A PLACE WHERE WOMEN COULD MAKE A DIFFERENCE.

Springfield Women's Club meeting at the home of Mrs. John Hooker, June 1885. (Courtesy of the Lyman and Merrie Wood Museum of Springfield History, Springfield Museums, Springfield, MA)

organization specifically for women. The 19th amendment, ratified in 1920, granted women the right to vote.

"All of this activism sharply contrasts with the club's image as a venerable old social group for affluent ladies," Gagnon said. Among its many accomplishments, the club's 1894 sponsorship of an Emergency Society led to the formation of a Red Cross chapter in Springfield. The club also funded and ran the city's Vacation School for Boys in the North End during 1900, an effort that was incorporated into the regular school program by 1918. Early in the 20th century, they opened Camp Mishnoah on the Congamond Lakes in Southwick to serve disadvantaged girls during the summer months. The camp, now owned and operated by the Springfield Boys and Girls Club Family Center, remains in operation at Lake Siog in Holland. One particular project the club is proud of was the restoration of Merrick Park, the small stretch of land on the corner of State and Chestnut streets. For its 100th anniversary, the club donated $9,500 to beautify the park, which features the "The Puritan" sculpture created by Irish-American sculptor Augustus Saint-Gaudens.

The club also started the historic preservation movement in the city.

"We said no, we can't just be tearing everything down because it's old, we can fix it, we can learn to appreciate it," Gagnon said. Kathleen Moorehead, a club member, sat on a study commission that went on to form the city's Historical Commission in 1973.

The club also petitioned city government to include assembly halls in all new school buildings and petitioned the state Legislature to authorize the appointment of the first woman probation officer in Springfield, a position first held by Emma Fall in 1912. The club paid her salary until the county agreed to do so 15 years later, Gagnon said. "They rose to the occasion during wars, floods and the Great Depression. They stitched garments and surgical dressings and also set aside money

for the hungry and sick," Gagnon wrote in a speech for the group's 112th anniversary in 1996.

The club held clothing and food drives as well as fundraisers for college scholarships. However, over the years, the work became too much for the small group.

Once boasting more than 600 members, the club membership dwindled over the years to a few hundred and later a few dozen. In May 2016, the club voted to donate more than $43,000, all of the money left over from its fundraising efforts the past few years, to the Community Foundation of Western Massachusetts.

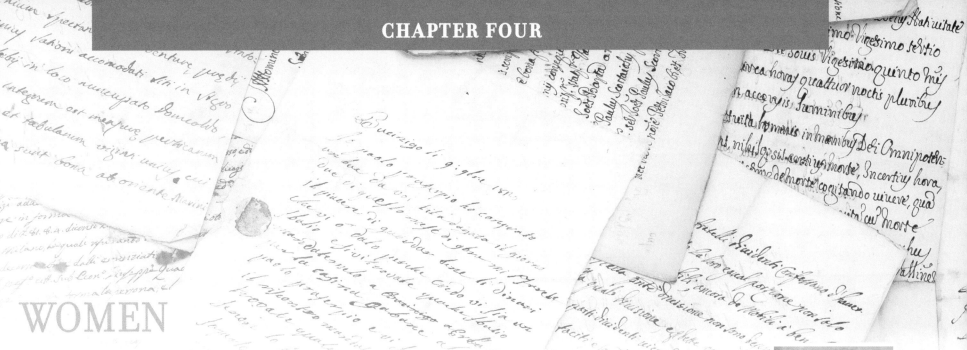

CHAPTER FOUR

WOMEN

Authors, Poets, Editors & Publishers

BY MARY ELLEN LOWNEY

Assistant Professor of Communications,
American International College

As a lifelong reader, I've appreciated my Western New England home for the wealth of bookstores here, the libraries that are the centerpieces of so many communities, and the seasons that encourage me to hole up during a snowstorm or on a rainy day with the latest bestseller, or stretch out on the beach with my book club's next title.

But there's another element that makes living here even more of a bonus for booklovers: It's hard to toss a paperback without hitting the home city or town of authors known regionally, nationally or internationally. And it's a place that's especially rich in females who've put pens to paper or fingertips to keyboards for centuries.

Here, Emily Dickinson gazed out upon Amherst in the 1800s and was inspired to write poetry that continues to affect and inspire readers the world over.

Emma Helen Blair, who grew up in Westfield, made her mark as an historian, journalist and editor, known perhaps best for her comprehensive documentary history of the Philippine Islands, spanning four centuries. She also edited journals from the Lewis and Clark expedition.

Springfield-based novelist Maria Susanna Cummins gave the world the wildly popular *The Lamplighter*, published in 1854 to immediate acclaim.

Fast forward to present day, when not co-running a publishing company in an old Easthampton mill, Kelly Link writes and edits (and was a 2016 Pulitzer Prize finalist for) fabulous fantasy. Her nomination came in 2017 for *Get in Trouble: Stories*.

Nearby Hatfield is the home of Jane Yolen, author and editor of more than 365 books, including world-famous *Owl Moon*.

Holyoke is the home of Lesléa Newman, author of 70 books for readers of all ages, among them the landmark children's book *Heather Has Two Mommies*.

Anita Shreve wrote so much of her backlist while living in Longmeadow. Fans of women's fiction treasure any new delight she publishes, from an early *work* published in 1998 *The Pilot's Wife* to her newest, *The Stars are Fire*.

Yet another prolific Western Massachusetts modern-day author is Suzanne Strempek Shea of Bondsville, who has mastered many forms of the craft, from journalism, essays, and short stories, to novels and non-fiction work. Frequently, her hometown as well as other familiar places like the Quabbin Reservoir, Chicopee and Springfield find their way into her pages. Among my favorites are her first, *Selling the Lite of Heaven*, the 1994 work inspired by a classified advertisement for a used engagement ring, *Songs from a Lead-Lined Room*, published in 2003 and describing her journey through breast cancer, and *This is Paradise*, the amazing story of an Irish mother's grief over a lost son and subsequent life mission providing health care in a small village in Malawi, Africa.

The list continues, to the delight of readers everywhere. Truly, there is a treasure trove of locally written copy by women of note, spanning the centuries.

Are Western and Central Massachusetts magnets for women authors?

For some, it's a matter of simple geography. They were born or grew up here, or came to college here, and never left. But many of those same authors have been known to sing high praises for the part of the planet that features the Connecticut River and its gorgeous valley, the Berkshire Mountains, and so many wonderful communities, large and small.

For all of these prolific and hard-working women, I am grateful.

I say, thank you for the words you put together for the pleasure of all readers, including and especially this one.

Authors, Journalists, Poets, Editors & Publishers

"Emily Dickinson"

Emily Dickinson was born on December 10, 1830, in the Connecticut Valley village of Amherst, where her grandfather had helped to found Amherst College. The daughter of a prominent lawyer and his wife, she attended a local academy and then Mount Holyoke Female Seminary in nearby South Hadley. Early on, she showed intellectual curiosity and a flair for writing. "Her compositions were unlike anything ever heard — and always produced a sensation — both with the scholars and Teachers," her brother Austin wrote after her death. "Her imagination sparkled — and she gave it free rein."

After a year at Mt. Holyoke, she rejoined her parents, brother, and sister Lavinia at the Homestead, their comfortable home in the center of Amherst. The 18-year-old enjoyed an active social life; sugaring and sleighing parties, lectures, readings, social gatherings, and new friendships filled her days. When she began writing poems in the 1850s, she circulated them among friends, often including one with a letter or gift. None were submitted for publication, but several appeared in print anonymously.

Many people perceived what her brother described as her "peculiar personal sensitiveness." He explained that "as she saw more and more of society... she could not resist the feeling that it was painfully hollow." When she was in her early twenties, she suffered from some kind of emotional disorder. Around the time she turned 30, she seemed to experience

Pictured left: Emily Dickinson

an unidentified trauma. Her handwriting changed, and she wrote an astonishing number of poems, most expressing a profound sense of loss.

Gradually, Emily Dickinson withdrew from public life. Until the mid 1860s, she was still taking long walks around Amherst with her beloved Newfoundland by her side; her observations of nature found their way into her work. After her dog died in 1866, she rarely ventured beyond the Homestead. She read voraciously, however, and carried on an active correspondence. And she wrote what are still some of the most spellbinding poems in the English language.

There were hints, never substantiated, that unrequited love had driven the young woman into the seclusion of her childhood home, where she lived out her life with her immediate family close at hand and protected from the outside world. Emily Dickinson did not answer the doorbell or meet people face to face — even Mabel Todd, although she enjoyed corresponding with her and loved to listen to her piano playing, albeit from another room.

Mabel Loomis Todd had moved to Amherst in 1881 with her husband David, the new director of the Amherst College Observatory. Attractive, vivacious, well-read, and an accomplished pianist and painter, Mabel was soon socializing with the leading families of Amherst, including that of Austin and Susan Dickinson, who lived in the Evergreens, the house they built next door to the Homestead. The Dickinsons' marriage had been troubled for a long time; within a year, Mabel and Austin, who was 27 years her senior, had begun a passionate love affair that lasted until Austin Dickinson's death.

The relationship was hardly a secret. Both spouses knew. David Todd tolerated the situation with grace; Susan Dickinson did not. Austin's sisters were supportive of the lovers, who often met at their home. Many years later, Mabel's daughter wrote that Emily "was glad that Austin had found some comfort . . . In my mother's words, 'Emily always respected real emotion.'"

Mabel Todd was one of the first people to recognize the brilliance of Emily Dickinson's poetry. Critics have since admired its compactness, tension, and wit. Full of emotional and intellectual energy, the poems were unorthodox in style and punctuation.

When the poet died in 1886 at age 56, Lavinia Dickinson found a box of hand-stitched booklets full of her sister's poems. Devoted to Emily and her writing, Lavinia turned to Mabel Todd for help. She "knew I always had faith in the poems," Mabel wrote in her journal, "and she begged me to copy and edit them — put them all into shape."

The task was enormous. There were almost 800 poems — eventually 1,800 would turn up. Mabel reported, they had "wonderful effect on me, mentally and spiritually. They seemed to open the door into a wider universe than the little sphere surrounding me." With the best of intentions, she changed "words here and there... to make them smoother" and tidied up the punctuation. She convinced the Boston editor Thomas Wentworth Higginson to help her get them published.

Higginson was a logical person to enlist in the project. Emily had asked his opinion of her writing more than a decade earlier. He called her his "eccentric poetess," corresponded with her regularly, and visited her in Amherst on at least two occasions.

Because the poems were so unconventional, Higginson was not optimistic but he submitted the manuscript to Houghton Mifflin. The publisher promptly rejected the collection as "queer — the rhymes are all wrong." Another agreed to publish the book, but only on the condition that Lavinia Dickinson pay most of the costs. The first volume came out in November of 1890; within six months, it was already in its sixth edition. Mabel Todd prepared a second series for publication a year later, and in 1894 brought out two volumes of the poet's letters.

Although scholars have worked to un-do Mabel Todd's changes, it seems clear that, without her, Emily Dickinson's poems might never have reached print and her letters would probably have disappeared. American literature would have lost one of its most singular voices.
– *MassMoments*, Mass Humanities

Louisa May Alcott
(B. NOV. 29, 1832 IN GERMANTOWN, PA; D. MAR. 6, 1888 IN BOSTON, MA)

Louisa May Alcott, author of the American classic *Little Women*, is best known for stories about happy, wholesome, conventional families. However, her own family hardly fit this description. Louisa's father Bronson, the Concord philosopher, teacher, and friend of Emerson and Thoreau, was determined that he and his family would live by his ideals, no matter how impractical they might be.

In 1843 when Louisa was ten years old, Bronson Alcott founded a utopian community he called "Fruitlands." For his wife and daughters, the move to a communal farm in the central Massachusetts village of Harvard marked the beginning of an unusual and ultimately disastrous experiment.

Bronson Alcott was a leading member of the Transcendentalist movement that emerged in the 1830s. Transcendentalists rejected institutionalized religion; they believed that knowledge of the divine came from intuition, and that individuals could find this knowledge through observing and experiencing nature. Alcott began as a teacher, setting up experimental schools based on the idea that children are born good and simply need to be allowed to let their innate knowledge unfold, like a rose blooming, as they grow.

In time, Alcott and other Transcendentalists came to view social institutions as corrupting man's true goodness. They considered money and commerce to be demeaning, industrial

work to be soul-deadening, and the desire for material possessions to be degrading. Like other Transcendentalists, Alcott rejected many institutions and customs he considered oppressive. Slavery was the great crime, but any exploitation of one creature's labor by another was unacceptable. Everywhere he looked, Bronson Alcott saw people appropriating the work of their fellow human beings and of animals in a way he believed was immoral. He introduced a vegetarian diet to the family; eventually, he also eliminated caffeine and other foods he considered artificial stimulants.

By the 1840s Bronson Alcott was convinced it was impossible to live a moral, spiritual life while a member of mainstream society. He visited several utopian communities, such as Brook Farm in Roxbury and the Shakers in Harvard, but none met his standards. In 1843 with Ralph Waldo Emerson as a trustee, backing from an English disciple named Charles Lane and financial help from his brother-in-law, Alcott founded "Fruitlands," his own utopian experiment.

The site Alcott and Lane chose was indeed idyllic. Louisa's 12-year-old sister Anna described it "a beautiful place surrounded by hills, green fields, and wood... Wachusett and Monadnoc Mountains are in sight." With his faith in the power of nature, Alcott was delighted with the spot.

The goals for the community were straightforward, if extreme. The members would practice subsistence farming, live off the fruit of the land, and so avoid any contact with the market or money. They would eschew "pollutants" such as manure-fed crops; they would purify their bodies by denying themselves stimulants such as alcohol, caffeine, warm water, and sex. They would purify their spirits by living morally and avoiding any form of exploitation, which meant no bought goods, no products of slavery, no animal products or animal labor, no private property. A regimen of days spent laboring on the land and evenings in philosophical discussion would lead them to greater knowledge of their own souls and of the divine "oversoul."

The group that gathered at Fruitlands in June of 1843 was indeed a motley lot. There were 12 adults, all of whom shared at least one trait: they had rejected conventional society. Over the next seven months, ten men and two women — Bronson's devoted wife Abigail and Ann Page, a teacher from Providence — would call Fruitlands home. The group included a baker looking for spiritualism who would eventually become a Catholic priest, a nudist, a farmer who bucked social values by refusing to cut his beard, a man who inverted his name to proclaim his freedom from social control, a cooper who had previously been in an insane asylum, and a man who rebelled against the status quo by swearing at everyone he met. Alcott and Lane were the acknowledged leaders.

Living strictly by their principles meant dressing only in linen clothes — tunics and bloomers for men and women alike — and wearing canvas shoes, as cotton was the product of slave labor, wool belonged to the sheep, silk to the worm, and leather to the cow. They ate no meat, fish, milk, eggs, butter, or cheese; in fact, their diet was limited to whole-grain bread (made by Bronson himself), fruit, vegetables, and water. They used no sweeteners, as sugar was a slave crop and honey belonged to the bees. They worked the fields without the help of draft animals, since hitching an animal to a plow was an appropriation of its labor.

After Ann Page was expelled for eating a piece of fish, Abby Alcott was burdened with all the woman's work. When a visitor asked if there were beasts of burden at Fruitlands, she replied "Only one woman."

It is hardly surprising that problems soon arose. Some members objected to Alcott's strict, some said despotic, rule and felt that the regimen was too severe. Others complained that Lane and Alcott spent too much time traveling and philosophizing and not enough time farming.

For his part, Charles Lane complained that Bronson Alcott was too devoted to his wife and that Abby Alcott favored her children. But the greatest problem was one of practicality: only one of the participants had ever farmed, and without draft animals or manure, the community simply could not produce enough to survive.

By the end of the summer, the community had dwindled to the Alcotts, Lane and his son,

Pictured above: Louisa May Alcott

and the bearded farmer Joseph Palmer. Lane and Alcott went off to recruit new members, leaving Palmer and Abby Alcott to bring in the meager harvest. As cold weather approached, it became clear that they could not survive the winter at Fruitlands with little food, less firewood, and thin linen clothing.

Finally, in the depths of winter, Abby took her four young daughters and, with help from her brother, rented a small farmhouse in a nearby village. Shortly afterward, the Lanes joined the Harvard Shaker community. Deeply depressed, Bronson Alcott took to his bed alone in the house at Fruitlands. Only after weeks of anguish could Abby persuade him to join her and the children. The family eventually returned to Concord.

In 1914 author and preservationist Clara Endicott Sears restored the Fruitlands farmhouse to her vision of its condition in 1843 and opened it as a museum devoted to Bronson Alcott's utopian experiment and the Transcendentalist movement. Today Fruitlands Museums also houses Clara Sears's collections of Shaker, Native American, and New England art and culture. – *MassMoments*, Mass Humanities

"Holyoke's Minnie Ryan Dwight : Journalist and Community Leader"

BY EILEEN M. CROSBY

Minnie Ryan Dwight

was born on June 22, 1873 to Irish immigrants Patrick and Catherine (Reilley) Ryan in the rural town of Hadley, Massachusetts and was educated at Hopkins Academy. A contemporary reported that although Miss Ryan graduated first in her class, the men in charge of naming the valedictorian were loath to bestow the honor on an Irish girl and chose not to give the honor to anyone that year. Upon graduation, she took up teaching at the Russellville one-room schoolhouse in North Hadley. The Ryan's family doctor had a son, William G. Dwight, who in 1888 had become the sole owner and publisher of the *Holyoke Daily Transcript*. Dr. Dwight, noticing Minnie Ryan's intelligence and love of writing, encouraged her to go to work for his son's newspaper. On March 3, 1891 she began work as an office assistant and reporter at the *Transcript*, the paper of record for the burgeoning industrial city. Initially, Minnie Ryan was assigned to write the social column and report on South Hadley news. After her marriage in 1896 to William G. Dwight, still the paper's publisher and editor, she began to write for the editorial page and it was in this capacity that she developed her influence as a community leader.

Minnie Ryan Dwight, or M.R.D, as she signed her editorials, was a champion of the women's suffrage movement and her efforts in advancing opportunities for women reached far beyond Holyoke. She began with energizing the Holyoke Equal Suffrage League when she was elected vice president 1913. By 1915, the League was canvassing, organizing parades, and hosting speakers on suffrage from all over the country. The *Holyoke Transcript* ran a 24-page special section on women's suffrage in September, 1915, timed to show support for an equal suffrage amendment in Massachusetts that was on the November ballot. Although the amendment was soundly defeated, she continued to advocate for passage of political rights for women. Immediately after U.S. women won the right to vote in 1919, she became a member of the Republican State Party and worked her way up into leadership positions. Never afraid to speak out, she used her power as an editorialist to criticize the party when she felt necessary. In addition to serving on the Republican State Committee for 14 years, she was a delegate to national conventions and, in the 1930s, declined the post of National Republican Committeewoman from Massachusetts.

Her leadership role in numerous organizations and progressive initiatives became legendary in her lifetime. Her vote on a Massachusetts commission to study old age pensions helped establish pensions in the state before the advent of Social Security. Her progressive views and leadership made their mark on local organizations, including the Holyoke Playground Commission (the first such commission in the state), the Mount Tom State Reservation Commission, the Hampden County Home Improvement League, the Holyoke Child Welfare Commission, the Holyoke Association for the Prevention and Cure of Tuberculosis, and the Holyoke Community Chest, among many others. As with these examples, her work for such organizations in their infancy, often as a founding member, enabled them to make lasting contributions to civic life.

Women's clubs abounded in urban communities in the first half of the twentieth century, but Minnie Ryan Dwight's role in them was unique. A founder of the Holyoke Women's Club and the Hampden County Women's Club, she also helped organize the Holyoke Business and Professional Women's Club and was a member of many smaller social and neighborhood clubs. While herself an avid gardener and the hostess of an annual tulip party, she wrote an editorial urging the 1000-member Holyoke Women's Club to exercise their powers for the benefit of women and the community, rather than channeling all their energies toward organizing garden parties and other entertainments. As a working woman herself, as well as a mother of four children, she became a strong advocate for equal pay for equal work for women.

After her husband's sudden death in 1930, she became publisher, as well as editor and owner, of the *Holyoke Daily Transcript*. In her new role, her "phenomenal capacity" for work and her voracious reading habits served

her well. Even when residing at the second family home in Key West, she was known for her disciplined work schedule and a writing desk layered with reading material from the *Congressional Record* to a range of daily newspapers and magazines. She was still working on the day before her death on July 31, 1957. Of her work as an editorialist, one noted that "she was a shrewd realist, [but] she acted on the belief that you could encourage your opponents to come around to your side.... There was no drop of malice, meanness, or smallness. She had a hearty sense of humor of the kind that gives no pain."

After her death, letters and telegrams poured in from business, religious, and political leaders from all over the country, as well as from most of the nation's major newspapers and wire services, sharing their remembrances of a remarkable woman and leader.

ALPHABETICAL LISTING OF WOMEN AUTHORS, JOURNALISTS, POETS, EDITORS & PUBLISHERS:

Maria Luisa Arroyo

(B. IN MANATI, PUERTO RICO; RAISED IN SPRINGFIELD, MA)
is a poet and educator. Arroyo was named Springfield's first poet laureate in 2015. She has received a Massachusetts Cultural Council Fellowship and New England Public Radio's Arts & Humanities Award. Along with Magdalena Gomez, Arroyo edited the 2012 anthology *Bullying: Replies, Rebuttals, Confessions and Catharsis* in response to the 2009 suicide death of 11-year-old Springfield boy Carl Joseph Walker-Hoover. She is the author of *Gathering Words/Recogiendo Palabras* published in 2008.
– Elizabeth Román

Jane Goodwin Austin

(NEE MARY JANE GOODWIN,B. FEBRUARY 25, 1831 WORCESTER, MA; D. MARCH 30, 1894) was a popular American writer in the late 19th Century. She authored 24 books and numerous short stories. Her friends throughout her life were some of the most well-known American authors, including Ralph Waldo Emerson, Nathaniel Hawthorne, and Louisa May Alcott. Austin's most popular works were her Pilgrim stories, for which she relied on family lore, archival research, and a creative imagination. Four of her books: *Standish of Standish, Betty Alden, The Nameless Nobleman,* and *Dr. Le Baron and his Daughters* are her interpretation of the New England experience from the landing of the Pilgrims in 1620 to the American Revolution. – Joseph Carvalho III

Victoria Aveyard

(B. JULY 27, 1990 IN EAST LONGMEADOW, MA) is the author of the popular Young Adult book series, *Red Queen*.

Michele Plourde Barker

(B. MAY 16, 1960) of East Longmeadow, MA is a historian, preservationist, city planner, and author. Former city planner for the City of Chicopee, Barker helped to organize the Chicopee Historical Society. She writes both historical works and is a novelist. A graduate of Elms College, earlier in her career she worked as a historian/archivist at the Connecticut Valley Historical Museum (now the Lyman & Merrie Wood Museum of Springfield History), and for many years was a costumed interpreter at Old Sturbridge Village.
– Joseph Carvalho III & Ray Kelly

Andrea Barrett

(B. NOV. 16, 1954 IN NORTH ADAMS, MA) is an American novelist and short story writer. Her collection *Ship Fever* won the 1996 U.S.

Above left: Jane Goodwin Austin. **Above right:** Victoria Aveyard. **Opposite page:** Minnie Ryan Dwight.

National Book Award for Fiction, and she received a MacArthur Fellowship in 2001. Her book *Servants of the Map* was a finalist for the 2003 Pulitzer Prize for Fiction, and *Archangel* was a finalist for the 2013 Story Prize.
– Joseph Carvalho III

Ruth Mary (Haskins) Bass

(B. JULY 18, 1934 IN SPRINGFIELD, MA) of Amherst, MA is a respected journalist, newspaper editor, and author. In her long distinguished career, she was employed as a police and court reporter for *The Berkshire Eagle*, 1956-1961; editor of *Berkshire Week* magazine, 1963-68; as editor of the *Berkshire Sampler*, 1977-1987; as associate Sunday editor and Sunday editor for the *The Berkshire Eagle*, 1987-1996; and editor of *The Paper*, Hillsdale, N.Y., c. 1999-2004. She has also been a weekly columnist for the *Berkshire Sampler* and *Berkshire Eagle*, 1983-.; and a freelance travel writer. Bass has published ten cookbooks in the *Fresh from the Garden* series, Storey Publishing Co., 1996-1998; and three novels, *Sarah's Daughter* (2007), *Rose* (2010), and *A Silver Moon for Rose* (2016). Her first experience in journalism was the creation of a school newspaper when she was in the sixth grade, followed by being part of the staff of the *Westfield High School Herald*. Among her numerous awards, she was honored as the United Press International's "Best Columnist

Top left: Barbara Bernard
Top center: Jeanette Davis-Harris
Top right: Emma Helen Blair
Bottom left: Andrea Barrett
Bottom center: Madeleine Blais
Bottom right: Thyra Bjorn

in New England" in 1987; and as "Woman of the Year" by the Professional and Business Women's Association of Pittsfield. Among her many community service efforts, Bass served on the Richmond, MA Board of Selectmen for six years, also serving as chairman; and was past-president of the Community Health Association of Richmond and West Stockbridge, MA. – Joseph Carvalho III

Suzanne "Suzy" Becker

(BORN 1962, BOLTON, MA)
is an American author, illustrator, entrepreneur, educator, and social activist and is best known for her 1990 internationally bestselling book *All I Need to Know I Learned from My Cat*, which sold two million copies and spent 28 weeks on the *New York Times* bestseller list, with several weeks at #1.
– Joseph Carvalho III

Barbara C. Bernard

(B. JULY 1927 IN NORTH ADAMS, MA)
most recently a columnist with *The Republican*, has a more than 60-year career in journalism and is also recognized for her work in the community in her adopted city of Holyoke and as a philanthropist who supports the arts and community theater. In 2017, she was the recipient of its William G. Dwight Distinguished Service to Holyoke Award, given by the Holyoke Rotary Club.

The Dwight Award was not the first time Bernard, a native of North Adams, who moved to Holyoke in 1950 with her late husband, George J. Bernard, was recognized for community service. She was honored by the Holyoke St. Patrick's Parade in 2009 with its citizenship award, and she became the first person from Holyoke in 2010 to be a recipient of the William Pynchon Medal by the Advertising Club of Western Massachusetts for distinguished public service. The Italian Progressive Society and United Veterans of Holyoke also honored her with citizenship awards, and the YMCA of Greater Holyoke

presented her the Lou Oldershaw Award in recognition of her community work.

Bernard is credited with having organized the first independent Golden Age Club in the United States, considered a forerunner to senior centers and Councils on Aging now found in most American cities and towns. In 2009, she was the recipient of a lifetime achievement award from the Valley Press Club which honored her then more than six decades of work in the media, including radio, television and newspaper journalism.

A 1948 graduate of Mount Holyoke College, she began her career as a reporter for the former *Holyoke Transcript-Telegram* newspaper. She worked for WHYN radio and eventually hosted her own show, "The Barbara Bernard Show" on WHYN-TV, the predecessor of today's Western Mass News, where she interviewed guests the likes of entertainers Nat King Cole and Robert Goulet.

Her community service includes having served on the boards of the Holyoke Public Library, Holyoke Medical Center and the University of Massachusetts Fine Arts Center. She is a member of the YMCA of Greater Holyoke, the Italian Progressive Society and the Holyoke St. Patrick's Parade Committee. She is a past, longtime trustee of PeoplesBank, where she now is an honorary trustee.

Together with her late husband, who died in 1998, Bernard was among the founding group for the Mount Holyoke Summer Theater and the New Century Theater. She is a longtime supporter of the Majestic Theater in West Springfield, Panache Productions in Springfield and the Chester Theater. – Cynthia G. Simison

Martha Gilbert (Dickinson) Bianchi

(B. NOV. 30, 1866 IN AMHERST, MA; D. DEC. 21, 1943 IN NEW YORK CITY) was an author, editor and poet. She edited several important collections of Emily Dickinson's works. Bianchi was the niece of that famous American poet.

Thyra (Ferre) Bjorn

(NÉE THYRA MARIA CHARLOTTA FERRE, B. SET. 12, 1905 IN MALMBERGET, GALIVARE, NORRBOTTENSLAN, SWEDEN; D. FEB. 14, 1975 IN LONGMEADOW, MA) was a novelist, author of nine books including *Dear Papa* (TV version appeared on "Matinee Theatre"), *Mama's Way,* and *The Golden Acre*. She lived in Springfield and Longmeadow for most of her life.
– Joseph Carvalho III

Emma Helen Blair

(B. SEPT. 12, 1851 IN MENASHA, WI; D. SEPT. 25, 1911 IN WISCONSON) historian, journalist and editor who attended high school in Westfield, Massachusetts.

Madeleine H. Blais

(B. AUG. 25, 1947) is an author, and journalist. She is a journalism professor at the University of Massachusetts in Amherst received a Pulitzer prize for Feature Writing in 1980 while working for the *Miami Herald*.
– Mary Ellen Lowney

Catherine Sanderson Blakeslee

(B. SEPT. 3, 1895 IN CT; D. APR. 27, 1981 IN LONGMEADOW, MA) co-authored *Women of Springfield's Past* (1976), one of the first women's history studies for Greater Springfield. – Joseph Carvalho III

Caroline (Clapp) Briggs

(B. MAY 14, 1822 IN NORTHAMPTON, MA; D. OCT. 15, 1895 IN SPRINGFIELD, MA) author of *Reminiscences and Letters* (1897), was a keen observer of society in Western Massachusetts in the 19th Century. – Joseph Carvalho III

Fidelia H. Cook

(B. 1818 IN MA) assistant to Josiah Gilbert Holland at *The Republican* newspaper in 1860, continued after his retirement as the newspaper's literary editor for 10 years.
– Joseph Carvalho III

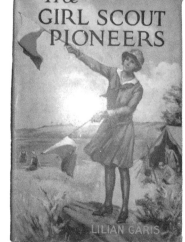

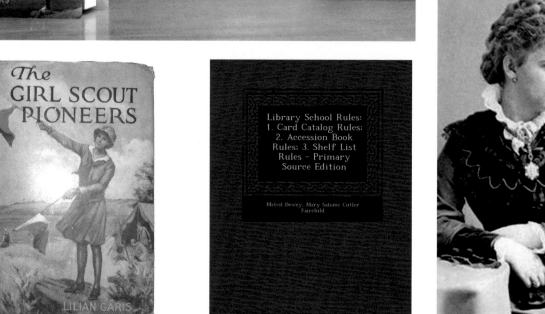

Top left: Corinne Demas
Top right: Dr. L. Mara Dodge
Center right: Ella Menkel DiCarlo
Bottom left: *The Girl Scout Pioneers* by Lillian Garis
Bottom center: Alice Morse Earle
Bottom right: Jane Dyer

Jeannette G. Davis-Harris

(B. JUNE 23, 1945 IN GLASTONBURY, CT; D. AUG. 29, 2017 IN EASTHAMPTON, MA) was an author and historian of Western Massachusetts African-American history. She wrote the first published treatise on African-Americans in Springfield and Western Massachusetts in 1976. Harris worked as a missionary and bacteriologist in Liberia. In 2017, she was honored with the Who's Who Lifetime Achievement award for her work in the field of education. A long-time resident of Easthampton, she served as a town selectman. – Joseph Carvalho III

Corinne Demas

(B. NEW YORK CITY) of Amherst, MA is an author of children's, teens, and adult books. An English professor at Mount Holyoke College since 1978, she began publishing her work in 1981. Demas is also a fiction editor of the *Massachusetts Review*. Her awards include: Aesthetica Creative Writing Award, Fiction Winner 2015; SPCA Henry Bergh Children's Book Award for Saying Goodbye to Lulu; PEN Syndicated Fiction Competition winner; Lawrence Foundation Prize for the best story to appear in *Michigan Quarterly Review*; and the Breakthrough Contest winner, University of Missouri Press.
– Mary Ellen Lowney

Ella Merkel DiCarlo

(B. JULY 11, 1919 IN PLAUEN, GERMANY; D. JULY 21, 1996 IN HOLYOKE, MA) respected journalist, author of local history of Holyoke and Western Massachusetts. DiCarlo's journalism career began in earnest when she was hired as a reporter for the *Holyoke Transcript-Telegram* in 1968. In the early 1970s, she was promoted to wire editor (the first woman wire editor in New England), columnist, and then to Assistant to the Editor and Editorial page Editor. In 1970, she won the Associated Press Award for the best news story in a New England newspaper and was a finalist for numerous other journalism awards. While her work as an editorialist and columnist was wide-ranging, local history was a passion and her depth of knowledge in this area remains unsurpassed. Her columns on local history topics did much to raise public awareness of Holyoke's rich past and her donated materials became core collections of the Holyoke History Room of the Holyoke Public Library, where she volunteered and served on the Library Board. In 1982, she compiled her research into a book: *Holyoke-Chicopee: a perspective*. She consulted on the development of Holyoke Heritage State Park and was instrumental in establishing the Holyoke Historical Commission. DiCarlo was also a vociferous proponent of civil rights. In 1962, she was at the forefront of a local initiative to host students from Prince Edward County, VA, whose public schools closed down in order to avoid compliance with desegregation orders following the Supreme Court's decisions in Brown vs. The Board of Education (1954, 1955). A charter member of the Holyoke Council for Human Relations, her service in this area earned her the NCCJ's Human Relations Award in 1972. DiCarlo also worked on many levels for equal rights for women. In 1973, she led the charge against a Massachusetts state law (passed in 1969) that a woman's husband's name and occupation be listed when she was chosen for jury duty, in case his work "affected her thinking." After much effort and lobbying, the law was changed.

In addition to her work in journalism and civil rights, DiCarlo was active in the Holyoke Women's Club and served on the board of the YMCA. She was a lay preacher for the First Unitarian-Universalist Church of Springfield.
– Eileen M. Crosby

L. Mara Dodge, Ph.D.

(B. MAR. 13, 1960) is a historian, educator, author, and editor who currently serves as the chairman of the History Department, and editor of the *Historical Journal of Massachusetts* at Westfield State University in Westfield, MA. She is the noted author of numerous articles and books on women's history, union history, gay/lesbian and GLBT history, Massachusetts history, and prison reform. Among her many honors, Dodge was awarded the King Hostick Research Award (1996) and the 2003 Book Award for Superior Achievement from the Illinois State Historical Society; the 1997 Dissertation Award from the American Association of University Women; and the first Massachusetts History Commendation Award from the Massachusetts Historical Society and the UMass Public Policy History Program in 2010.
– Joseph Carvalho III

Jane R. Dyer

(B. MAR. 7, 1949) of Cummington, MA is a highly esteemed children's book illustrator who has illustrated over 50 books. – Fred Contrada

Alice (Morse) Earle

(NEE, MARY ALICE MORSE, B. APR. 27, 1851 IN WORCESTER, MA; D. FEB. 16, 1911 IN HEMPSTEAD, NY) was an author and historian who wrote extensively on colonial New England history and culture. Among her sixteen published books are: *Curious Punishments of Bygone Days* (1896), *Home Life in Colonial New England* (1893); *Two Centuries of Costume in America, 1620-1820* (2 vols., 1903); and *Diary of Anna Green Winslow, A Boston School Girl of 1771* (1894).
– Joseph Carvalho III

Sherri Browning Erwin

(B. OCT. 8, 1968 IN HOLYOKE, MA) is a novelist, author of historical and paranormal romance novels, and "literary mashups," eg. *Janye Slayre* (2010), a parody of Charlotte Bronte's *Jane Eyre*, and *Grave Expectations* (2011). Her first published novel was *The Scoundrel's Vow,* published by Dell in 1999. – Joseph Carvalho III

Top left: Cynthia M. Gorton
Top center: Sherri Browning Erwin
Top right: Magdalena Gomez
Bottom left: Gretchen Holbrook Gerzina
Bottom center: Lilian Garis
Bottom right: Constance Green

Elizabeth Ware (Rotch) Farrar

noted author, lived in Springfield when she wrote her memoirs in 1865, *Recollections of Seventy Years*. – Joseph Carvalho III

Rachel Lyman Field

(B. SEPT. 18, 1894 IN NY; D. MAR. 15, 1942 IN LOS ANGELES, CA)
author of *Hitty: Her First Hundred Years* which was awarded a Newberry Medal for children's literature; *Fear is the Thorn*, and *Taxis and Toadstools; All This and Heaven, Too*; numerous poems published in the *New Yorker*. [married Arthur S. Pederson June 20, 1935 in Manhattan, NY] She attended Central High School in Springfield, MA, and Mount Holyoke College in South Hadley, MA.
– Joseph Carvalho III

Esther Louise Forbes

(B. JUNE 28, 1891 WESTBOROUGH, MA; D. AUGUST 12, 1967 IN WORCESTER, MA)
was an American novelist, historian and children's writer who received the Pulitzer Prize and the Newberry Medal. She moved with her family to Worcester, Massachusetts, in 1898. She attended Bancroft School in Worcester, and, from 1909 to 1912, she attended Bradford Academy, a junior college in Bradford, Massachusetts. In 1916, she joined her older sisters Cornelia and Katherine in Madison, Wisconsin where she attended classes at the University of Wisconsin. While in Wisconsin, she joined the editorial board of the *Wisconsin Literary Magazine*, along with another future Pulitzer Prizewinner, Marjorie Kinnan Rawlings. Her first novel, *O Genteel Lady!* was published in 1926 and was selected as the second book for the Book of the Month Club. In 1947, she received the Metro-Goldwyn-Mayer novel award of $150,000 for her then forthcoming book, *The Running of the Tide*, published in 1948. In 1949 she was elected a Fellow of the American Academy of Arts and Sciences. *Rainbow on the Road* was published in 1954. In 1960 Forbes became the first woman elected to membership in the American Antiquarian Society.
– Joseph Carvalho III

Linda K. Fuller, Ph.D.

(B. MAY 14, 1942) of Wilbraham, MA, Professor of Communications at Worcester State University and a Senior Fellow at Northeastern University is the author/co-editor of more than twenty books and over 250 professional publications and conference reports. She has also been the recipient of Fulbright awards to teach in Singapore and to do AIDS work in Dakar, Senegal. – Joseph Carvalho III

Frances Gagnon

(B. IN INDIAN ORCHARD, SPRINGFIELD)
noted historic preservationist, and prolific local historian who authored over one hundred local history articles in local newspapers, most frequently in the *Springfield Journal*. A life-long Historic preservationist, Gagnon served as Chairman of the Springfield Historical Commission for many years. She served for over a decade as a trustee of the Springfield Library & Museums Association (now the Springfield Museums Association) and was Chairman of the Board for one term. [See entry in Appendix listing for Pynchon Award Recipients]
– Wayne E. Phaneuf

Lilian Garis

(B. OCT. 20, 1873 IN AMHERST, MA; D. APR. 19, 1954 IN NEW JERSEY), author of juvenile fiction who under the pseudonym Laura Lee Hope wrote early volumes in the Bobbsey Twins series..
– Joseph Carvalho III

Gretchen Holbrook Gerzina

an author, historian, and educator is the Dean of the Commonwealth Honors College at the University of Massachusetts. [See full biographical entry in Chapter on Education and Educators]

Magdalena Gómez

(B. IN NEW YORK CITY) is a poet, playwright, arts educator and co-founder of Teatro V!da, launched in 2007 as Springfield's first "intergenerational Latino theater project." Gomez edited the 2012 anthology *Bullying: Replies, Rebuttals, Confessions and Catharsis* in response to the 2009 suicide death of 11-year-old Springfield boy Carl Joseph Walker-Hoover. She continues to write, act and direct plays in the region. Gómez is also known for her work as a jazz poet. She traveled and performed with her performance partner, jazz saxophonist Fred Ho for ten years. Gómez is the founder of the Ferocious Women's Group, a group dedicated to promoting the voices of girls and women through writing and performing arts. The multi-generational Ferocious Women's Group meets regularly to support and empower each other, produce theatre, and mentor young women and girls.
– Anne-Gerard Flynn & Joseph Carvalho III

Cynthia M. (Roberts) Gorton

(PEN NAME, IDA GLENWOOD, B. FEB. 27, 1826 IN GREAT BARRINGTON, MA; D. 1894 IN FENTON, MI) was a blind American poet and author. She has been referred to as "The Blind Bard of Michigan." – Joseph Carvalho III

Hannah Flagg Gould

(B. SEPT.3, 1789 LANCASTER, MA; D. SEPT. 5, 1865 IN NEWBURYPORT, MA) was an American poet. Her father, Benjamin Gould had been a soldier in the American Revolutionary War, and after her mother's death, she became his constant companion, which accounts for the patriotism of her earlier verses. – Joseph Carvalho III

Roberta M. Grahame

(B. OCT. 11, 1908 IN MINNESOTA; D. MAR. 22, 1998 IN NORTHAMPTON, MA) co-authored *Women of Springfield's Past* (1976), one of the first women's history studies for Greater Springfield. – Joseph Carvalho III

Constance (McLaughlin) Winsor Green

(B. AUGUST 21, 1897 IN ANN ARBOR, MICHIGAN; D. DECEMBER 5, 1975 IN ANNAPOLIS, MARYLAND) was an American historian, who won the 1963 Pulitzer Prize for *History of Washington, Village and Capital, 1800–1878* (1962). She completed a bachelor's degree at Smith College in 1919 and a Master's degree at Mount Holyoke College in history in 1925. After graduation, Green served as a part-time instructor at Mount Holyoke from 1925 to 1932. Going on to complete a PhD at Yale University in 1937, she became instructor in the history department at Smith College in 1938 and head of the Smith College Council of Industrial Relations in 1939. During WWII, Green accepted the position of historian at the U.S. Armory at Springfield. After the War, Green became a consulting historian for the American Red Cross in 1946, chief historian of the Army Ordnance Department in 1948, and then served as historian at the research and development board, Office of the Secretary of Defense. In 1954, under a six-year grant from the Rockefeller Foundation, Green became director of American University's Washington History Project. – Joseph Carvalho III

Cathi Hanauer

(B. OCT. 5, 1962 IN NJ) of Northampton is a novelist and also editor of *The Bitch in the House* and *The Bitch is Back, Older, Wiser, and Getting Happie*r collection of essays. Her novels *Gone* (2012), *Sweet Ruin* (2006), and *My Sister's Bones* (1996) are among her best selling works.
– Mary Ellen Lowney

Marion Harland

[See entry for Mary Virginia Hawes Terhune]

Harriet Elizabeth Henshaw

(B. MAR. 2, 1817 IN WORCESTER, MA; D. MAR. 2, 1896 IN LEICESTER, MA) was a "writer of distinction in the Revolutionary years," according to Worcester County historian John Nelson. She was the author of *The Hundredth Town*, and *Early New England Diaries*. – Joseph Carvalho III

Caroline Lee Whiting Hentz

(B. JUNE 1, 1800 IN LANCASTER, MA; D. FEB. 11, 1856 IN MARIANNA, FLA) was an American novelist and author, most noted for her opposition to the abolitionist movement and her widely read *The Planter's Northern Bride*, a rebuttal to Harriet Beecher Stowe's popular anti-slavery book, *Uncle Tom's Cabin*. She was a major literary figure in her day. – Joseph Carvalho III

Holly Hobbie

(NÉE DENISE HOLLY ULINSKAS) author of children's books (from CT, lives in Conway, MA)

Mary Jane (Hawes) Holmes

(B. APRIL 5, 1825 IN BROOKFIELD, MA; D. OCTOBER 6, 1907) MARY JANE HOLMES) was a bestselling and prolific American author who published 39 popular novels, as well as short stories. Her first novel sold 250,000 copies; and she had total sales of 2 million books in her lifetime, second only to Harriet Beecher Stowe. On August 9, 1849 Hawes married Daniel Holmes, a graduate of Yale College from New York City.
– Joseph Carvalho III

Isabelle Katherine Hornibrook

(B. NOV. 16, 1858 IN IRELAND; D. 1941 IN BEVERLY, MA) immigrated from Ireland in 1891 and settled in Worcester, MA and was a prolific and popular writer of boys and girls camping and scouting tales, eg. *Girls of the Morning-Glory Camp Fire* (1916), *Camp Fire Girls in War and Peace* (1919), *Pemrose Lorry, Sky Sailor* (1924), among many others.
– Joseph Carvalho III

Gwendolyn L. Ifill

(B. SEPT. 29, 1955 IN QUEENS, NY; D. NOV. 14, 2016 IN WASHINGTON, D.C.)
was a highly regarded television host and newspaper journalist who grew up in Springfield, MA and graduated from Classical High School while her father served as the pastor of the Bethel AME Church in the city. Ifill worked as a journalist for the *Baltimore Evening Sun* from 1981 to 1984, the *Washington Post* from 1884 to 1991, and the *New York Times* covering the White House from 1991 to 1994. She became the first African-American woman to host a national political television talk show when she became the moderator of the PBS program "Washington Week in Review" in October of 1999. Ifill also famously served as moderator for two vice-presidential debates: Republican Vice-President Dick Cheney vs. Democrat U.S. Senator from North Carolina, John Edwards on Oct. 5, 2004; and Democrat U.S. Senator from Delaware, Joseph Biden vs. Republican Governor of Alaska, Sarah Palin on Oct. 2, 2008. In February of 2016, she and Judy Woodruff became the first team of women to moderate a Democratic presidential debate, Hillary Clinton vs. Bernie Sanders.
– Joseph Carvalho III & Wayne E. Phaneuf

Libby Klekowski

(BORN: MAY 8, 1941 IN BEAUFORT, NC)
is a historian, documentary film producer, and author who lives in Leverett, MA. Among her publications are three books she co-wrote with her husband Dr. Ed Klekowski: *Eyewitnesses to the Great War* (2012), *Americans in Occupied Belgium, 1914-1918* (2014); and *Edith Wharton and Mary Roberts Rinehart at the Western Front 1915* (2017). She was co-produced with her husband and others five PBS (WGBH, WGBY) documentaries: "Under Quabbin," "The Great Flood of 1936," "Dynamite, Whiskey and Wood," "Model T's to War," and

"Yanks Fight the Kaiser", the last four also shown nationally through American Public Television. Active in the Amherst community, Klekowski has served as President, Amherst Town Committee for International Students (1997-2000) – a non-profit organization whose function is to welcome international students to Amherst at a town-sponsored reception, link interested students with host families, and fund Round the World Women; Chairwoman of Round the World Women (1990-2002), a volunteer organization that provides a twice-weekly program for international women through which they are introduced to local areas of interest and are linked to Amherst volunteers who help them adjust to life in a new country; president of the Amherst Woman's Club – 2006-2010 and 2012-2014; and since 2005 she has served as Chair of the Alice Maud Hills Preservation Fund which raises money to preserve the historic 1864 Leonard M. Hills house.
– Joseph Carvalho III

Martha Joanna Reade (Nash) Lamb

(B. AUG. 13, 1829 IN PLAINFIELD, MA ; D. JAN. 2 , 1893 IN NYC) author, historian. After her marriage to Charles Lamb, she moved to Chicago in 1857 and helped to found the Home for the Friendless and the Half-orphan Asylum. After she divorced Lamb, she moved to New York City in 1883 and purchased the *Magazine of American History*, becoming its editor. – Plainfield Historical Society

Mary Sawyer

(B. 1806 IN STERLING, MA) Sterling, Massachusetts is the setting of Sarah Josepha Hale's famous poem, "Mary Had a Little Lamb". Mary Sawyer, the subject of the historically true poem, lived in Sterling.

Leah M. Lamson

award winning journalist, managing director of the New England High School Journalism Collaborative, former editor of *Worcester*

Telegram & Gazette, named the first woman to serve as editor at the newspaper, Simmons College, '76, founding member of the Women's Initiative and a member of the United Way of Central Massachusetts Governance Committee, Judiciary-Media Committee of Massachusetts Supreme Judicial Court, New England Newspaper and Press Association, New England Society of Newspaper Editors, YWCA OF Central Massachusetts, Yankee Quill Award in journalism and Judith Vance Weld Brown Spirit of Journalism Award recognizing the accomplishments of an "outstanding woman in journalism." – Wayne E. Phaneuf

Above: Martha J. Lamb

Rose Hawthorne Lathrop

(B. LENOX, MA MAY 20, 1851; D. JULY 9, 1926)
was an American writer. As Mother Mary Alphonsa in the 1900s, she was a Roman Catholic religious sister, social worker, and foundress. – Joseph Carvalho III

Kelly Ann (Shaw) Link

(B. AUG. 7, 1969 IN MIAMI, FLA)
of Northampton, MA is an author whose book *Get in Trouble* was a 2016 Pulitzer Prize finalist in fiction. She is the co-founder of Small Beer Press in Easthampton, MA and co-edits the occasional "zine" *Lady Churchill's Rosebud Wristlet*. – Mary Ellen Lowney

Elinor Lipman

(B. OCT. 16, 1950 IN LOWELL, MA)
lived in Northampton, MA for many years is an award-winning novelist, and essayist. Lipman received the New England Book award for fiction in 2001. Her novel *Then She Found Me* was adapted to a 2008 feature film directed by Helen Hunt. Lipman also writes a weekly column "I Might Complain" for *Parade*. – Joseph Carvalho III

Allison (McCrillis) Lockwood

(B. OCT. 15, 1920 IN NORTHAMPTON, MA)
is an author and historian who began her career as an advertising copywriter at John Wiley Company, New York City, 1945-1946. Director of public information State University of New York, Buffalo, 1958-1960. Associate professor English Montgomery College, Rockville, Maryland, 1966-1978. She also served on the Northampton Historical Commission, and was a trustee of Historic Northampton. Two of her books of note were: *Passionate Pilgrims: The American Traveler in Great Britain, 1800-1914*; and *Children of Paradise: A Northampton Memoir*. Her second husband was Richard Garvey, noted Springfield journalist and local historian. A Smith College graduate (Class of 1943), enlisted in the Women's Army Corps during her senior year. Lockwood spent WWII interviewing prisoners of war and working with soldiers in Army hospitals. Her book *Touched By Fire* is a tribute to the men and women who served in WWII from Northampton.
– Joseph Carvalho III

Jacqueline T. Lynch

(B. APR. 22, 1962) of Chicopee, MA is the author of *Comedy and Tragedy on the Mountain: 70 Years of Summer Theatre on Mt. Tom, Holyoke, Massachusetts*, and several other non-fiction books on local history and classic films, as well as novels. She is a playwright whose plays have been produced around the United States and in Europe, and has published articles on history in regional and national publications, and currently writes a syndicated column on classic films, "Silver Screen/Golden Years". Locally, she is a former columnist for the *Holyoke Transcript-Telegram*, the *Westfield Evening News*, as well as assistant editor for the former *Chickuppy & Friends Magazine*. She is a native of Chicopee, and a graduate of Westfield State College. – Joseph Carvalho III

Louise L. Mace

(B. JUNE 9, 1894 IN NY; D. JUNE 1965 IN JACKSONVILLE, VT) was a journalist for the *Springfield Union* and the *Springfield Republican* for 42 years. *Theater Arts Magazine* recognized her as America's foremost critic of drama and movies. Mace's importance centered on the fact that during her tenure the Court Square Theatre in Springfield was "the sounding board" for a great many of the most important American plays which were presented there "to test their probable success in New York. As one historian noted, Mace was "writing reviews that undoubtedly influenced the history of theater in America."
– Joseph Carvalho III

Patricia "Patty" M. MacLachlan

(B. MAR. 3, 1938 IN CHEYENNE, WYOMING; GREW UP IN CONNECTICUT) is an American children's writer, who is best known for the 1986 Newbery Medal-winning novel *Sarah, Plain and Tall* which was later adapted as a TV movie. She was a visiting lecturer at Smith College beginning in 1986. She received the National Humanities Medal in 2002 for her body of work. She lives in Western Massachusetts. – Mary Ellen Lowney

Annie Russell (Dunster) Marble

(B. AUG. 10, 1864 IN WORCESTER, MA; D. NOV. 23, 1936 IN WORCESTER, MA) local historian and author of *From 'Prentice to Patron: The Life of Isaiah Thomas* (1935). – Joseph Carvalho III

Jane Anne Maroney

(B. AUG. 19, 1923 IN WESTFIELD, MA; D. MAR. 24, 2012 IN WESTFIELD, MA) was the first woman to serve as a city editor at the *Springfield Newspapers*. A native of Westfield, she graduated from Westfield High School in 1942 and continued her education at American International College in Springfield. She began her career in journalism as a general assignment reporter in the Westfield bureau of the *Springfield Union* in 1946, later joining the city staff in Springfield. Her career as a reporter included covering Springfield City Hall, regional politics and writing a column, "Stray Bits." She served as an assistant night city editor at the *Union* before being promoted to city editor in 1969. Later in her career, she was an editorial writer for the newspapers until her retirement in 1992.
– Cynthia G. Simison

Caroline Atherton (Briggs) Mason

(B. JULY 27, 1823 IN MARBLEHEAD, MA – JUNE 13, 1890 FITCHBURG, MA) She was educated at Bradford Academy in Bradford, Massachusetts, and began writing when she was very young. In 1852, her family moved to Fitchburg. Her first poems were published in the *Salem Register* under the name "Caro." Mason was also published in *The Congregationalist*, *The Liberal Christian*, *The Monthly Religious Magazine*, *The Independent* and *The Christian Union*. She also contributed significantly to the hymnology of the Unitarian church. In 1891, she published *Lost Ring and Other Poems* in 1891. One of Mason's early poems, "Do They Miss Me At Home?" was set to music by S.M. Grannis and published by mid-1852. According to historians of the Civil War era, It obtained "immediate and widespread popularity" in the United States and in England. Its popularity carried into the Civil War, where Mason's lyrics,

Above: Caroline Atherton Mason

written as a homesick girl away from home at school, "readily translated to the plight of the soldiers on both sides, and was among the songs soldiers would sing."
– Joseph Carvalho III

Ellen Meeropol

(B. APRIL 15, 1946) an Easthampton, MA resident, is an author/novelist, teacher, and nurse practitioner. Her books focus on her "passions for medicine and social justice." A resident of Western Massachusetts, her books include *House Arrest* (2011), *On Hurricane Island* (2015), and *Kinship of Clover* (2017). She is a founding member and current

Board President of Straw Dog Writers Guild. After working as a day care teacher and a women's reproductive health counselor, Ellen became a registered nurse and then a nurse practitioner, working at a children's hospital in western Massachusetts for 24 years. In 2005, Meeropol was given the Chair's Excellence Award from the Spina Bifida Association of America for her advocacy around latex allergy and spina bifida.
– Joseph Carvalho III

Sarah Anne (Huyler) Morewood
(B. SEPT. 15, 1823 IN PASSAIC, NJ; D. OCT. 16, 1863 IN PITTSFIELD, MA)
was a poet and "literary figure" who was a close friend of her neighbor Herman Melville. She and her husband, John Rowland Morewood, moved to the Berkshires in 1850. During the early years of the American Civil War she was so active and generous in her support of local regiments that two military camps were named after her.
– Joseph Carvalho III

Leslea G. Newman
(B. NOV. 5, 1955) is the author of 70 books for readers of all ages including the children's books, *A Sweet Passover; Matzo Ball Moon; Runaway Dreidel;* and *Here Is The World: A Year of Jewish Holidays.* Her picture book *Ketzel, the Cat Who Composed* received the Massachusetts Book Award and the Sydney Taylor Gold Medal. *Gittel's Journey: An Ellis Island Story,* and *Welcoming Elijah: A Passover Tale with a Tail* are forthcoming. She is a former Poet Laureate of Northampton, MA. She authored the ground breaking children's book *Heather Has Two Mommies* in 1989. – Ray Kelly & Joseph Carvalho III

Gail Ward Olmsted
(B. OCT. 8, 1955 IN CT)
of Charlton, MA is a novelist and professor at Springfield Technical Community College. Her most recent book is *Second Guessing* (2018).

Dori L. Ostermiller
(B. APR. 4, 1964 IN LOS ANGELES, CA)
of Florence, MA is a novelist who also runs the "Writers in Progress" Writing Center in Florence. Her first novel, *Outside the Ordinary World* (2010), was an Indie Best Notable pick and an MLA "must-read" book published in seven countries. Her work has appeared in numerous literary journals, including *The Bellingham Review, Roanoke Review, Alligator Juniper, BellowingArk, Peregrine, Calliope, Roanoke Review, Chautauqua Literary Journal* and the *Massachusetts Review,* among others. – Mary Ellen Lowney

Hilary B. Price
(B. DEC. 4, 1969 IN WESTON, MA) of Florence, MA is the originator, and author/illustrator of the very popular nationally syndicated newspaper humor series, "Rhymes With Orange". The youngest woman to ever have a syndicated strip, Price began her daily newspaper comic strip in 1995 and it has won "Best Newspaper Panel" from the National Cartoonists Society four times since then. It appears in over 400 newspaper internationally.
– Joseph Carvalho III

Olive Chapin (Higgins) Prouty
(B. JAN. 7, 1882 IN WORCESTER, MA; D. MAR. 24, 1974 IN BROOKLINE, MA)
was an author and novelist. She authored *Now, Voyager* (1941) which was made into a motion picture. Her "greatest and critical success" was the novel, *Stella Dallas* published in 1922. According to film historian Jeanne Thomas Allen, *Stella Dallas* "enjoyed a particularly long life in numerous media forms" including a Broadway play, a silent film starring Belle Bennett which was later re-done as "talkie" starring Barbara Stanwick by Goldwyn, and also as a weekly radio serial that ran from 1938 to 1953. – Joseph Carvalho III

Linda Roghaar
(B. SEPT. 11, 1947)
is a publisher and essayist based in Amherst, MA. She established the Linda Roghaar Literary Agency, LLC in 1996 representing authors, specializing in non-fiction.
– Mary Ellen Lowney

Ruth Sanderson
(B. 1951 IN MONSON, MA)
is an illustrator and author of children's and young adult books. The Library of Congress catalog includes over 90 books by Sanderson, including multiple editions of certain titles. One of her most highly regarded work is *The Enchanted Wood,* which won the Irma

Simonton Black Award and a Young Hoosier Book Award. Sanderson is especially known for her distinguished fairy tale illustrations.
– Joseph Carvalho III

Stacy Madeleine Schiff
(B. OCT. 26, 1961 IN ADAMS, MA)
is an American non-fiction author, served for a number of years in the late 1980s as a senior editor at Simon & Schuster, and was a guest columnist for the *The New York Times*. Almost every book she has written has been greeted with acclaimed from the critics and most have received Awards, the most important was her 2000 Pulitzer Prize for her 1999 book, *Vera* (Mrs. Vladimir Nabokov). Among the many awards for her work, the Academy Award in Literature from the American Academy of Arts and Letters in 2006, the George Washington Book Prize for *A Great Improvisation: Franklin, France, and the Birth of America* in 2006, the EMMA Award for Journalistic Excellence in 2010 for *Who's Buried in Cleopatra's Tomb?*, the BIO Award from the Biographers International Organization, and the 2015 Newberry Library Award. – Joseph Carvalho III

Vera Shlakman
(B. JULY 15, 1909 IN MONTREAL, CANADA; D. NOV. 5, 2017 IN NEW YORK CITY)
was a professor of Economics and Marxism. Dr. Shlakman wrote the landmark study *Economic History of a Factory Town: A Study of Chicopee, Massachusetts* (1935). Her doctoral dissertation at Columbia University on nineteenth century women factory workers was the foundation of this book on the conflicts between labor and capital. A native of Montreal, Canada, Dr. Shlakman received her bachelor's and her master's degrees at McGill University. She received a fellowship at Smith College in Northampton, and in 1938 began teaching at Queens College in New York. Among other Jewish educators, she was targeted over left-wing politics by the

New York City Board of Education, New York state officials and courts during the McCarthy era. Dr. Shlakman pled the First and Fifth amendments in a September 1952 public hearing of the United States Senate Internal Security Subcommittee regarding accusations of being a member of the Communist Party, and was fired. In 1980, City University apologized to professors, and the city paid financial restitution. She died at 108 years of age; her book on the factories of Chicopee influenced a generation of historians.
– Jacqueline T. Lynch

Catharine Maria Sedgwick
(B. DEC. 28, 1789 IN STOCKBRIDGE, MA; D. JULY 31, 1867 IN BOSTON, MA)
was an American novelist of what is sometimes referred to as "domestic fiction". With her work much in demand, from the 1820s to the 1850s, Sedgwick made a good living writing short stories for a variety of periodicals. She became one of the most notable female novelists of her time. She wrote work in American settings, and "combined patriotism with protests against historic Puritan oppressiveness." Her topics "contributed to the creation of a national literature," enhanced by her detailed descriptions of nature. Sedgwick created "spirited heroines who did not conform to the stereotypical conduct of women" at the time. She promoted "republican motherhood."
– Joseph Carvalho III

Opposite page: Hilary Price
Top left, this page: Vera Shlakman
Top right: Catharine Maria Sedgwick
Bottom right: Cynthia Propper Seton

Cynthia Propper Seton

(B. OCT. 11, 1926 IN NEW YORK CITY; D. OCT. 23, 1982 IN NORTHAMPTON, MA) was an American writer and feminist. Following a 12-year career as a columnist for *The Berkshire Eagle* in Pittsfield, Massachusetts, she began writing essays and fiction, producing five novels and three essay collections. Her third novel, *A Fine Romance*, was a finalist for the 1977 National Book Award for Fiction. – Joseph Carvalho III

Eleanor L. Shea

(B. NOV. 12, 1915 IN NYC; D. JULY 7, 1992 IN HOLYOKE, MA) was a respected journalist and newspaper editor who for many decades was the "Woman's Editor" of the *Holyoke Transcript-Telegram* beginning in the early 1960s. – Joseph Carvalho III

Anita Shreve

(B. OCT. 7, 1946 IN DEDHAM, MA; D. MAR. 29, 2018 IN NH) Best-selling American writer, was awarded a O. Henry Prize in 1976 for one of her very first stories *Past the Island, Drifting*. She taught creative writing at Amherst College in 1999, and lived in Longmeadow, MA in the carriage house of the Young Estate from 1994to 2009, where she wrote *The Pilot's Wife* (1998), *Fortune's Rock* (1999), and *The Last Time They Met* (2001). – Joseph Carvalho III

Cynthia G. Simison

(B: MARCH 6, 1956 IN NORTHAMPTON, MA) a native of Northampton and alumna of Northampton High School, received her bachelor's degree in political science and newspaper journalism from the S. J. Newhouse School of Public Communication in Syracuse, New York, in December 1976.

As a child, Cynthia wanted to be a sports writer and with a loyalty to the Boston Red Sox which she still has today, she hoped she might one day become a sportswriter covering her beloved team. During her junior and high school years, she was a part-time sportswriter and librarian for the *Daily Hampshire Gazette*.

While at the Newhouse school, she completed an internship at the *Syracuse Post-Standard* and also was a three-year summer intern at the *Springfield Daily News*. She joined the *Daily News* staff as a reporter in 1977, doing stints as the chief of the Westfield and Connecticut bureaus, as court reporter and as a metro editor. The newspaper's award-winning series, "World War II – 50 Years Later," published from 1991 through 1995 was overseen and written by her.

She later worked as managing editor of special projects which included the development of the weekly Plus Papers. The Republican appointed Cynthia its managing editor in May 2006. During her tenure, the newspaper was three times named the best newspaper in New England and the annual Outlook economic development special section she plans has repeatedly been named the best business section in New England by the New England Newspaper & Press Association.

Active in the community, for the past 20 years, Cynthia has overseen Toy for Joy,

(This page) **Left:** Anita Shreve. **Right:** Cynthia G. Simison
(Opposite page) **Left:** Jean Stone.
Right: Suzanne Strempek-Shea

The Republican's annual collaboration with the Salvation Army to assist needy families at Christmas. A past president of the Valley Press Club, Cynthia continues to be a member of the club's Scholarship Committee. She is also a member of the board and clerk for the Food Bank of Western Massachusetts and a board member for Northampton Dollars for Scholars. She is a past board member of the Pioneer Valley Board of the Red Cross and the YMCA of Greater Springfield. She was the first board member from Western Massachusetts to serve the BoSox Club, the Boston Red Sox booster organization begun by Dominic DiMaggio in 1967.

Cynthia's career with the *Springfield newspapers*, beginning as an intern to the present vital position as managing editor, has made her highly respected and loved by the community. It has endeared her to the columnists whose work she edits and who are quoted as saying "her editing makes me look good." – Barbara Bernard

Susan Stinson

(B. OCT. 17, 1960 IN TX) of Northampton, MA, is currently the writer in residence at Forbes Library, the public library in Northampton, where she runs writing rooms, discussion groups and workshops for writers, and curates a Local History/Local Novelists reading series. Stinson is the author of the novels *Fat Girl Dances with Rocks, Martha Moody, Venus of Chalk*, and *Spider in a Tree*. In 2011, Stinson was awarded the Outstanding Mid-Career Novelist Prize from the Lambda Literary Foundation, which is the largest cash award for lgbt writers. The award honored Susan's work as a whole, which, the foundation wrote, "delves deeply and poetically into stories of the marginalized, and with particular power on issues like body size and body image." She has also received the Benjamin Franklin Award, as well as grants and fellowships from Vogelstein Foundation, the Massachusetts Cultural Council, and the Money for Women/

Barbara Deming Fund, as well as writing residencies at the Banff School of Fine Arts, the Blue Mountain Center, the Helene Wurlitzer Foundation, Norcroft, and the Millay Colony. – Mary Ellen Lowney

Jean Stone

(B. 1949) of Amherst, MA is a novelist who also writes under the pen name "Abby Drake." Her first novel was *Sins of Innocence*. Other titles include *Birthday Girls, Places by the Sea, Tides of the Heart, First Loves, Ivy Secrets, Beach Roses, Good Little Wives*, and *Trust Fund Babies*. – Ronni Gordon

Suzanne Strempek-Shea

(B. DEC. 7, 1958 IN MA) is the author of six novels: *Selling the Lite of Heaven, Hoopi Shoopi Donna, Lily of the Valley, Around Again, Becoming Finola*, and *Make a Wish But Not for Money*. She has also written three memoirs, *Songs From a Lead-lined Room: Notes - High and Low - From My Journey Through Breast Cancer and Radiation; Shelf

Life: Romance, Mystery, Drama and Other Page-Turning Adventures From a Year in a Bookstore*; and *Sundays in America: A Yearlong Road Trip in Search of Christian Faith*, all published by Beacon Press. Suzanne is also the author of *This is Paradise: An Irish Mother's Grief, an African Village's Plight and the Medical Clinic That Brought Fresh Hope to Both*. She also is a co-author of *140 Years of Providential Care: The Sisters of Providence of Holyoke, Massachusetts*. With Elizabeth Searle, she is co-editor of *Soap Opera Confidential: Writers, Soap Opera Insiders and Others on Why We'll Tune in Tomorrow as the World Turns by the Guiding Light of Our Lives*.

Winner of the 2000 New England Book Award, which recognizes a literary body of work's contribution to the region, Suzanne began writing fiction in her spare time while working as reporter for the *Springfield* (Massachusetts) *Newspapers* and *The Providence* (Rhode Island) *Journal*.

Her freelance journalism and fiction has

appeared in magazines and newspapers including *Yankee*, *The Bark*, *Golf World*, *The Boston Globe*, *The Irish Times*, *The Philadelphia Inquirer*, *Organic Style* and *ESPN the Magazine*. She was a regular contributor to *Obit* magazine.

Suzanne is a member of the faculty at the University of Southern Maine's Stonecoast MFA program in creative writing and is writer-in-residence and director of the creative writing program at Bay Path University in Longmeadow, Mass. She has taught in the MFA program at Emerson College and in the creative writing program at the University of South Florida. She runs Bay Path University's annual Summer Writing Seminar in Dingle, Co. Kerry, Ireland. She lives in Bondsville, Mass., with award-winning former Springfield Newspapers journalist and columnist Tommy Shea, co-author of *Dingers: The 101 Most Memorable Home Runs in Baseball History*. – Mary Ellen Lowney

Rhonda Renee Swan

(B. MAR. 15, 1964 IN SPRINGFIELD, MA; D. DEC. 15, 2015 IN SPRINGFIELD, MA) joined *The Republican* as a reporter in May 1987. She worked at the newspaper for 14 years, rising to religion editor and then city editor in the late 1990s, the first African American to hold either post. After working in Virginia, Delaware and Florida, Swan returned to *The Republican* in early 2015 and wrote as a guest columnist until her death. To honor her memory, her family established a scholarship fund for awarding scholarships for journalism majors at Swan's alma mater, the University of Massachusetts at Amherst. – Joseph Carvalho III & Cynthia G. Simison

Claire (Coburn) Swift

(B. APR. 2, 1876 IN WORCESTER, MA; D. JAN. 30, 1963 IN ST. LOUIS, MO) was a journalist beginning her writing career in 1899. She was the author of *Our*

Little Swedish Cousin, part of the popular contemporary "Little Cousin Series" of books. Living in St. Louis, Swift was also a vocal member of the Missouri Equal Suffrage League, and was a member of the Board of Governors of Consumer's League of Missouri. - Joseph Carvalho III

Chrysler R. Szarlan

(B. AUG. 25, 1960) of Wilbraham, MA is a novelist whose debut novel *The Hawley Book of the Dead* was named an NPR Best Book of 2014. – Mary Ellen Lowney

Amy Elizabeth Tanner, M.D.

(B. MAR. 21, 1870 IN OWATONNA, MN; D. FEB. 1, 1956 IN WORCESTER, MA) a Worcester physician, authored numerous books and articles on psychology. Among her more noted works were *The Child* published in 1904 and *Studies in Spiritism* published in 1910. – Joseph Carvalho III

Eva March Tappan

(B. DEC. 26, 1854 IN BLACKSTONE, MA; D. JANUARY 29, 1930 IN WORCESTER, MA) noted children's author. While attending Vassar, graduating in 1875, she served as the editor of the *Vassar Miscellany*. Early in her writing career, she wrote about famous personages from English history, eg. William the Conqueror, Queen Elizabeth I, and Alfred the Great. One contemporary critic declared that "her juvenile books and fairy tales are almost unrivalled." – Joseph Carvalho III

Sabrina Tavernise

(B. FEB. 24, 1971 IN HARTFORD, CT; RAISED IN GRANVILLE, MA) is a journalist who writes for *The New York Times*. She had notably reported from political "hot spots" in Lebanon, and Russia. She also served four years as a war correspondent for *The New York Times* during the Iraq War. – Joseph Carvalho III

Top: Rhonda Renee Swan
Above: Sabrina Tavernise

Mary Virginia Hawes Terhune

(PEN NAME MARION HARLAND)
of Virginia, lived in Springfield for six years in the 1880s during which time she published four of her books *Daughters of Eve* (1882); *Handicapped* (1882); *Judith* (1883); and *Our Village Mystery* (1884). – Joseph Carvalho III

Martha Downe Tolman

(B. MAR. 2, 1838 IN FITCHBURG, MA; D. APR. 18, 1918 IN FITCHBURG, MA) poet.
– Joseph Carvalho III

Juanita Torrence-Thompson

(B. IN SPRINGFIELD, MA)
is an actress, poet, author, and columnist. In 2006 living in Queens, NY, she assumed the editorship of the international poetry magazine, *Mobius*. – Elizabeth Roman

Elizabeth Lois (Jones) Towne

(B. MAY 11, 1865 IN PORTLAND, OREGON; D. JUNE 1, 1960 IN HOLYOKE, MA)
founder, publisher, and editor of *The Nautilus* magazine. Established in 1900 and published from Towne's Cabot Street Holyoke home, *The Nautilus* became the leading periodical of the fledgling "New Thought" movement, precursor to today's New Age Movement, according to biographer/historian Tzivia Gover. Towne served as editor until 1951. As a journalist, she was a frequent contributor to the *Holyoke Daily Transcript and Telegram*; and in 1926 she also assumed the duties of editing the *International New Thought Alliance Bulletin*. That same year, she became the first women elected to the Holyoke Board of Aldermen and the first married woman to serve in that post in the state of Massachusetts. – Joseph Carvalho III

Mary Vardoulakis

(B. 1923) wrote the first novel by a Greek American about the Greek diaspora. She wrote *Gold in the Streets* (1945) while a

student at Wellesley College, winning the Intercollegiate Literary Fellowship sponsored by publisher Dodd, Mead. Set in Chicopee, Massachusetts, her protagonist, George Vardas arrives from Crete in 1906 to work in the factories. As the Greek immigrant community grew in this mill town, they encounter hostility from Polish immigrant factory workers, until both learn to work and live together. Vardas eventually finds a new home in Hartford, Connecticut. A Hartford native, Mary Vardoulakis was the daughter of Greek immigrants, and herself spent four years in her childhood from 1932 to 1936 in her parents' homeland. Though she also published short fiction, this was her only novel. – Jacqueline T. Lynch

Charlotte S. (Edwards) Warner

(B. JAN. 28, 1828 IN SPRINGFIELD, MA; D. JAN. 12, 1916 IN SPRINGFIELD, MA) Springfield poet and author. – Joseph Carvalho III

Above left: Mary Virginia Hawes Terhune
Above right: Eva March Tappan

Edith Wharton

(NÉE EDITH NEWBOLD JONES;B. JAN. 24, 1862; D. AUG. 11, 1937) lived in Lenox, MA, was an American novelist, short story writer, and designer. Her novels and short stories realistically portrayed the lives and morals of the late nineteenth century, an era of decline and faded wealth. She won the Pulitzer Prize for Literature in 1921, and was the first woman to receive this honor.

Emmeline Blanche (Woodward) Harris Whitney Wells

(B. FEBRUARY 29, 1828 IN PETERSHAM, MA; D. APRIL 25, 1921 IN SALT LAKE CITY, UT)
was an American journalist, editor, poet, women's rights advocate and diarist. She served as the fifth Relief Society General President of The Church of Jesus Christ of Latter-Day Saints (LDS Church) from 1910 until her death. – Joseph Carvalho III

Charlotte Frances Wilder

(B. DEC. 12, 1839 IN TEMPLETON, MA; D. DEC. 3, 1916 IN MANHATTAN, KS) was an American writer. She was one of the most widely known writers in Kansas, and the author of many religious books, including for juvenile audiences, and a contributor to church papers and magazines. In 1867, Wilder and her husband set up their home in Manhattan, Kansas – Kansas being the new anti-slavery state. Manhattan came to be known as "Mrs. Wilder's Home." For the next fifty years she was an important leader in her church community, and in "every civic reform movement." At her death, she was vice-president of the State Federation of Clubs. Her contributions to the Methodist press included the *Central Christian Advocate*, *Epworth Herald*, *Zion's Herald*, and the *Methodist Review*. She was the author of *The Land of the Rising Sun* (1877) and *Sister Ridenour's Sacrifice* (1883). – Joseph Carvalho III

Jane Hyatt Yolen

(B. FEB. 11, 1939 IN NEW YORK CITY) a resident of Western Massachusetts, is a writer of fantasy, science-fiction, and children's books, and a poet. Soon after graduating from Smith College, her first book, *Pirates in Petticoats*, was published. She has written over 37 books, including *The Bird of Time* (1971), *The Simple Prince* (1978), *Cards of Grief* (1985), *Sister Light, Sister Dark* (1989), *White Jenna* (1990), *Briar Rose* (1992), *The Devil's Arithmetic* (1993), *Armageddon Summer* (1998), *Wild Wings: Poems for Young People* (2002), *Sword of the Rightful King* (2003), and *Stone Angel* (2015); and edited eight short story anthologies, three of which received the World Fantasy Award for Anthology/Collection in 1984, 1986, and 1987. Her "Pit Dragon Chronicles" series include: *Dragon's Blood* (1982), *Heart's Blood* (1984), *A Sending of Dragons* (1987), and *Dragon's Heart* (2009). Among her many awards for her writings are: the Caldecott Medal, the 1987 Special World Fantasy Award for *Favorite Folktales From Around the World*; the 1992 The Catholic Library Association's Regina Medal for her body of children's literature; the 1993 World Fantasy Award for Best Novel for *The Devil's Arithmetic*; 1999 Nebula Award for Novelette *Lost Girls;* the 2009 World Fantasy Award for Life Achievement; and the 2017 Damon Knight Memorial Grand Master Award. – Jane Kaufman & Joseph Carvalho III

Above: Edith Wharton
Center: Emmeline Blanche Harris Whitney Wells

CHAPTER FIVE

WOMEN IN
Politics, Law and Government

BY MARSHA MAROTTA, PH.D.

Department of Political Science,
Westfield State University

While Americans were debating the rights of women through most of U.S. history, individual women from Western and Central Massachusetts were working hard to improve the lives and fortunes of their sex, their families, and themselves. In ways large and small, they instigated and nurtured a long and rich tradition of participation that shaped the public world and their private lives through politics, law and government service.

This was no easy task. The dominant discourses over the last several centuries set limits on what women could do. Through the notion of Republican Motherhood, the ideology of separate spheres, and the Cult of Domesticity, the strictures of the 18th and 19th centuries called for women to be virtuous, supportive and moral contributors to the family while men moved in the public world of business and politics.

Yet many women knew that the dominant discourses and cultural attitudes did not accurately describe their lives or aspirations, and they joined to shape the discourses, often at great personal sacrifice. They questioned assumptions, critiqued their circumstances, and found creative ways to generate avenues for their ideas and their leadership. The Anti-Slavery, Temperance, and Votes-for-Women movements launched decades of battles for

what many women believed was the promise of the Declaration of Independence – that women be able to exercise the same rights and privileges as men. They questioned the divisions between public and private matters, and fought their way into new opportunities.

For women and families of color, there were additional layers of constraints. They participated in the movements, although often they were not as visible as white women. Other intersectionalities such as class, religion, education, and citizenship status also played a role in the extent to which individual women participated and received credit for their work.

Even after women won the right to vote and won changes in laws through a second women's-rights movement in the 20th century, cultural views about women's roles lagged. Many entered politics, law or government service at a time when attitudes toward women made winning and earning those positions more difficult. At first they served their communities, work that was not considered politics since it usually did not involve political parties. Yet their service opened new doors and helped change the definition of what constituted the political. New organizations and political action committees developed to encourage and fund women candidates for political office, and more women entered law and public service.

The women included in this chapter broke records, from being the first woman to register to vote in Springfield, first woman police chief in New England, first woman district attorney in Massachusetts, to the first woman to be elected as governor of any state in the nation without following her husband into the office.

They have served as leaders in court law on clergy sex abuse and bullying. Their many accomplishments took place from Pittsfield to Worcester, and from Boston to New Orleans to Seattle.

They have opened doors and set new benchmarks for men as well as women over hundreds of years, and continue to do so today. They do not necessarily share philosophies, definitions, preferred methods or specific goals. What connects them is a commitment to political, economic and social justice, and a belief that the principles we live by are contestable and can be changed.

Each generation in their everyday behaviors and practices has built on an inspiring past and provided scaffolding for the future, so that in the 21st century there are fewer and fewer barriers, fewer and fewer "firsts." But inequities continue as women, especially women of color, continue to be underrepresented particularly at the most powerful levels of law, politics and government. For that reason, we continue to recognize their energy and determination, and look to future generations to imagine and sustain the work toward equal opportunity and equal representation at all levels.

Politics and Government
Massachusetts
Women in Congress

BY SHANNON YOUNG

Although Massachusetts was one of the first states to send a woman to Capitol Hill, with Lowell Republican Edith Nourse Rogers entering Congress in 1925, the state has lagged behind others in electing female candidates – a trend activists and others are looking to reverse.

Ahead of the 2018 election, Massachusetts, a state known for its progressive politics, had sent a total of just six women to Congress – half of whom were elected in 2007 or later. U.S. Rep. Nicola "Niki" Tsongas, a Lowell Democrat who entered Congress after a 2007 special election, said the drought of female lawmakers representing Massachusetts in Washington played a major role in her decision to run for office.

"I could not tolerate the fact that women had not been elected to Congress from Massachusetts for 25 years," she said. Tsongas, whose district includes much of the same region that repeatedly returned Rogers to Washington, acknowledged that while Merrimack Valley voters have a history of "breaking gender barriers," other parts of Massachusetts have been slower to embrace female lawmakers.

"There probably are a whole host of reasons (for the lack of women sent to Congress in Massachusetts.) I think, among other things, members would get elected and hold office for a good number of years. There just weren't the opportunities," she said.

Recent elections, however, suggest barriers that previously prevented women from seeking or winning political office are crumbling, she said.

"I think there's a seed change in Massachusetts, and it's not just at the congressional level," Tsongas said, pointing

the women holding high-level positions throughout the state's government.

Since Tsongas entered Congress, Elizabeth Warren, a Democrat, became the first woman to represent Massachusetts in the U.S. Senate after defeating Scott Brown in 2012. One year later, Katherine Clark, D-Melrose, won the special election for U.S. Sen. Ed Markey's former House district – a seat she retained in 2014 and 2016.

Clark, who has helped recruit female Democratic candidates for 2018, said women are running in more than half of the districts where the party hopes to flip congressional representation from red to blue – something she attributed in part to President Donald Trump's election and the recent "#MeToo" movement.

Despite that, women still account for less than a quarter of all congressional lawmakers, the congresswoman noted.

"I hope that barrier will really start to move and that we'll get more toward equal representation in the next few election cycles. I think there's a real possibility as we see women voters energized and motivated like we haven't seen before," she said.

Gail Jackson-Blount, the Massachusetts Women's Political Caucus board president, said her organization has seen a rise in the number of female candidates, even in races where they face strong incumbents.

"Historically, I think that people have been made to feel that it's not (their) turn yet, that they've maybe been told, 'You need to wait your turn,'" she said. "Women today are saying, 'Well, this is the time – I'm not going to not run because of someone who's been in the seat for 20 years.'"

Amy Diamond, the group's Berkshire County chapter president, said MWPC is working throughout the state to help female candidates across the political spectrum overcome historic barriers, like fundraising.

Tsongas, who is not seeking re-election in 2018, said she's "very proud" to see women among the candidates vying for her congressional seat.

Rogers, whose 35-year tenure spanned from 1925 to 1960, is one of the longest serving women in the history of the U.S. House, according to congressional archives. Margaret Mary Heckler, a Wellesley Republican, became the second woman to represent Massachusetts in Congress – the first to do so without succeeding her husband – in 1967; and Boston Democrat Louise Day Hicks was elected to Congress in 1970.

Frances Perkins
(NÉE FANNIE CORALIE PERKINS,
B. APR. 10, 1880 IN BOSTON, MA;
D. MAY 14, 1965 IN NEW YORK CITY)
spent much of her childhood in Worcester, MA where she graduated from the city's Classical High School. Perkins graduated from Mount Holyoke College with a B.A. in Chemistry and Physics. While at Mount Holyoke, she was an active participant in a special Economic History course survey of the working conditions in the neighboring industrial city of Holyoke, MA. In 1904, she accepted a position teaching physics and biology at the Ferry Hall School. During her hours away from the classroom, she would visit the settlement houses in Chicago and on behalf of the poor residents would confront employers to collect unpaid wages that these workers had been cheated out of, or otherwise denied.

Perkins would later continue this "one-woman crusade" in Philadelphia and later in New York City where she received a fellowship from the Russell Sage Foundation. One of her first projects was the stunning report on the poor conditions in New York City's "Hell's Kitchen." Earning her Masters in economics and sociology from Columbia University, she published a very influential article entitled, "Some Facts Concerning Certain Undernourished Children," in 1910. That year, she was appointed secretary of the

TIME Magazine cover of Frances Perkins

New York Consumers League. In that role, Perkins exposed sweatshop conditions and was instrumental in the passage of the 54-hour Bill in the New York Legislature. During this period she was also active in the Women's Suffrage movement and frequently spoke at public events in support of that women's rights effort. In 1918, New York Governor Alfred E. Smith appointed her as a member of the New York Industrial Commission. She was put in charge of the Bureau for Mediation and Arbitration, reorganized the Factory Inspection Division, and settled strikes with unions. In 1928, Gov. Smith appointed her as Industrial Commissioner for the state of New York.

When Franklin Delano Roosevelt was elected president in 1932, He selected Perkins to serve as Secretary of Labor. During Roosevelt's New Deal era, Perkins was "a guiding force" in implementing many of the public works and relief acts aimed at lifting the nation out of the Great Depression. Perkins served during the war years of WWII and helped oversee the critical relationship between labor and business in order to keep America's "Arsenal of Democracy" producing at a record rate. When Harry Truman assumed the Presidency after Roosevelt's death, He asked Perkins to continue in her role as Secretary of Labor. After her service in government, Perkins served as a professor at Cornell University's School of Industrial and Labor Relations.
– Joseph Carvalho III

Jean Ankeney
(B. MAR. 29, 1922 IN FOOCHOW, CHINA;
D. MAY 14, 2005 IN ST. GEORGE, VT)
was an American politician, teacher, and public health nurse. Born in China to American missionaries, Ankeney grew up in Williamstown, MA. She was a teacher and public health nurse. In 1975, Ankeney moved to Vermont and lived in St. George, Vermont. From 1993 to 2002, Ankeney served in the Vermont State Senate and was a Democrat.

Jeanne Florence (Freeman) Bass-Latta
(B. DEC. 12, 1929 IN SPRINGFIELD, MA; D. SEPT. 1996 IN SPRINGFIELD, MA) served as Model Cities director for Springfield, project director for the Springfield Community Partnership and Prevention Alliance, and as the city's

Human Services director beginning in 1975. She also served as president of the U.S. Conference of Human Service Officials. Bass was the 1994 Ubora Award honoree. – African Hall Steering Committee, Springfield Science Museum, Springfield Museums & Joseph Carvalho III

Alice Winifred Bebka

(B. OCT. 2, 1923; D. MAY 1, 1987 IN MILLBURY, MA) was the first woman to serve on the Board of Selectmen for the town of Sutton, MA, elected in 1981.

Sheri Ruth Bemis

(B. DEC. 19, 1962 IN FAIRFAX, VA; GREW UP IN RHODE ISLAND) was the first woman in Massachusetts to serve as a full-time fire chief when she was appointed Fire Chief of the Oxford (MA) Fire Department, appointed in 2010. Now living in Southbridge, MA, and retired from the Fire Department, Bemis teaches at Anna Maria College. – Cynthia G. Simison

Mary Katherine (Egan) Boland

(B. MAY 21, 1939 IN SPRINGFIELD, MA) serves as Senior Counsel at Egan, Flanagan and Cohen, PC, a Springfield, MA law firm started by her father James Egan in 1924. At the forefront of women admitted to the Bar, Mary was one of six women in her class at Boston College Law School (1965). After being awarded a Ford Foundation Fellowship, she returned to Springfield, practicing law in the areas of commercial real estate, banking,

estate planning, and nonprofits. She was active in Springfield community boards serving as President of the Springfield City Council and was a thirty-year Trustee of the MassMutual Life Insurance Company Investment Funds. Mary married the Hon. Edward P. Boland, a thirty-six year member of Congress, and raised four children. –Ted & Rosemary Brown

Tricia Farley-Bouvier

(B. IN PITTSFIELD, MA) is the Massachusetts state representative of the 3rd Berkshire District. She served as a Pittsfield City Councilor from 2004-2008, was elected in a special election to the Massachusetts House of Representatives in 2011. She serves as Vice Chair of the Joint Committee on Labor and Workforce Development. She also sits on the Joint Committee on Children, Families and Persons with Disabilities, the Joint Committee on Ways and Means, the House Committee on Technology and Intergovernmental Affairs, and the House Committee on Ways and Means. – James Gleason & Joseph Carvalho III

Helen Andrews Bowditch

(B. AUG. 3, 1908 IN NEWTON, MA; D. OCT. 12, 2004 IN WORCESTER, MA) was a life-long advocate and activist for programs supporting the development of the youth of Worcester, MA. She was elected to the Worcester School Committee in the 1950s and was the top vote getter in eight successive elections. She retired in 1971, having amassed more votes over her career than any other person in Worcester history. Fourteen years later, in 1985, she was elected chairperson of the committee to overhaul the city charter. She and her husband Bob were jointly awarded the prestigious Isaiah Thomas Award for community service. The Helen A. Bowditch Health Center was named in her honor. – Joseph Carvalho III

Top: Tricia Farley-Bouvier
Bottom: Mary Katherine (Egan) Boland

Emma E. Brigham

(B. JUNE 10, 1872 IN VERMONT; D. JULY 7, 1973 IN SHORT HILLS, NJ), a Republican, was the first woman to be elected (1922)to the Springfield Common Council. In 1924, she was elected to the Board of Aldermen in Springfield, and in 1928 was elected to the Massachusetts Legislature from Springfield's Ward 4. She held that post for eight years and was known as "the Grande Dame of the Republican Party." – Joseph Carvalho III

Alice Driscoll Burke

(B. JUNE 18, 1892 IN THE VILLAGE OF WHITINSVILLE, NORTHBRIDGE, MA; D. MAY 14, 1974 IN SPRINGFIELD, MA) was elected mayor of Westfield in 1939 becoming the first female mayor in New England. Known locally as "Ma Burke," she went on to serve three more terms as mayor. Burke became known as the "Grand Dame of Westfield" for her active role and many contributions to the community. She entered politics in 1934 when she won a seat on the Westfield School Committee. Her last elective office was that of councilwoman-at-large in 1973. – Joseph Carvalho III & Cynthia G. Simison

Rita K. Burke

(B. AUG. 15, 1952) of Amherst served as director of the Amherst Public Safety Communications Center. She helped create the Massachusetts Public Safety Communications Academy, the first state training program for dispatchers. – Diane Lederman

Karen L. Cadieux

(B. JUNE 7, 1954) served as the second mayor and first woman mayor of Easthampton, MA from Nov., 2013 to 2017. Prior to becoming mayor, Cadieux served as assistant to her predecessor, Mayor Michael Tautznik for 17 years. – Joseph Carvalho III

Adelaide Augusta (Hosmer) Calkins

(B. MAY 22, 1831 IN WEST BOLYSTON, MA; D. JAN. 2, 1909 IN SPRINGFIELD, MA) was manager of the Springfield Home for Friendless Women and Children from its founding to the 1880s. She lobbied the Massachusetts General Court (Legislature) for indigent mothers and their children not to be separated into separate Almshouses as was the previous practice. She was appointed to the first advisory board for women to the Massachusetts State Board of Charities. She was also one of the first two women to be elected to the Springfield School Committee at a time when Springfield was one of the, if not the first city to have a woman in that elective office. – Joseph Carvalho III

Above: Emma E. Brigham. **At right:** Alice Driscoll Burke.

Top: Gale D. Candaras. **Above:** Elizabeth Cardona.

Jennifer M. Callahan

(B. AUG. 24, 1964 IN SUTTON,MA)
was the first woman of the Blackstone Valley district elected as a Massachusetts State Representative, serving from 2003 to 2011. In 2016, she was appointed as the first woman town administrator of Millville, MA.
– Joseph Carvalho III

Gale D. Candaras

(B. JAN. 1, 1949 IN BROOKLYN, NY) was the Democratic member of the Massachusetts Senate from 2006 to 2015 representing the 1st Hampden and Hampshire District. Graduating from Western New England University School of Law in 1983, Candaras moved to Wilbraham to practice law. She served for six years on that town's Board of Selectmen before being elected to served the Massachusetts House of Representatives in 1996. Candaras served five terms as State Representative.
– Joseph Carvalho III

Elizabeth Cardona

(B. IN SPRINGFIELD, MA). Fluent in English, Spanish and proficient in Arabic, Cardona served as the Senior Director and Civic Engagement Advisor to Gov. Deval L. Patrick during his tenure. Currently Cardona is the executive director of multicultural affairs at Bay Path University in Longmeadow. Cardona was a founding board member for CHICA Project, a Massachusetts statewide Latina youth leadership, mentoring and coaching program. – Elizabeth Román

Gailanne M. Cariddi

(B. NOV. 1, 1953 IN NORTH ADAMS, MA; D. JUNE 17, 2017 IN BOSTON, MA) was a Democratic member of the Massachusetts House of Representatives for the First Berkshire district from 2001 to June 2017. Prior to her service in the legislature, Cariddi served on the North Adams City Council.
– Joseph Carvalho III

Helen Roberta Caulton-Harris

(B. DEC. 7, 1951 IN SPRINGFIELD, MA)
is the City of Springfield's Director of Health and Human Services, first appointed by the mayor on April 1, 1996. She was appointed by Governor Paul Cellucci as one of two Western Massachusetts representatives to serve on a statewide committee to examine the healthcare delivery system in Massachusetts. Caulton-Harris was also appointed by U.S. Health and Human Services Secretary Donna Shalala to the National Committee on Interdisciplinary Health and Community Based Linkages. In 1999, Caulton-Harris received the AIDS Action Community Service Award from the AIDS Action Committee and the Rebecca Lee Award from the Harvard School of Public Health and Massachusetts Department of Public Health. In 1999, Caulton-Harris received the Dorothy Jordan Pryor Award for Community Service from Springfield Technical Community College. She was the 2016 Ubora Award honoree.
– Joseph Carvalho III

Harriette L. Chandler

(B. DEC. 20, 1937 IN BALTIMORE, MD of Worcester, MA is a Democratic Massachusetts state senator for the 1st Worcester district who began serving as acting Senate President on Dec. 4, 2017, becoming Senate President on Feb. 8, 2018. From 1995 to 2001 she was a member of the Massachusetts House of Representatives prior to being elected to the Massachusetts Senate in 2001, becoming the first woman from Worcester ever to be elected to the Massachusetts Senate. Prior to becoming Senate President she was the Senate Majority Leader. Chandler was the second woman in Massachusetts history to serve as Assistant Majority Leader and is also the second woman in Massachusetts history to serve as Majority Leader. Chandler also served as the Senate Majority Whip,

Assistant Majority Whip, Vice-Chair of the Joint Committee on Public Health, Assistant Vice-Chair of the Senate Committee on Ways and Means, Vice-Chair of the Joint Committee on Federal Stimulus Oversight, and the Vice-Chair of the Joint Committee on Veterans and Federal Affairs. During her last two terms in the House, she was the Chair of the Joint Committee on Health Care. She is also the Co-Chair of the Caucus of Women Legislators, Vice President of the 2015-2016 Executive Board of the Women's Legislative Network of the National Conference of State Legislatures (NCSL), and a State Director of Women in Government. – Shira Schoenberg & Joseph Carvalho III

Frances [aka "Fannie"] Jeannette (Guilford) Clary

(B. MAR. 10, 1857 IN ASHFIELD, MA; D. 1932 IN WILLIAMSBURG, MA) who lived in Williamsburg, MA, led the effort to charter the Williamsburg Grange in 1900 and was very active in both the Woman's Suffrage movement and in the Temperance movement a staunch advocate for prohibition. Clary was nominated in 1904 on the Prohibition ticket for Massachusetts Secretary of State, the first woman in Massachusetts to receive a statewide nomination for a state office. She was too far ahead of her time to be elected with universal Women's suffrage over a decade away. – Ralmon Jon Black, Williamsburg Historical Society

Cheryl A. Coakley-Rivera, J.D.

(B. FEB., 1964 IN SPRINGFIELD, MA) as the daughter of the late Barbara Rivera, a social activist and director of the New North Citizens Council for 31 years, Coakley-Rivera grew up attending community meetings, rallies and protests in Springfield's North End neighborhood. In 1998, while working as a lawyer, Coakley-Rivera ran for and won the 10th Hampden District seat on the House of Representatives. She became the first Latina to serve on the Massachusetts Legislature. After 15 years of representing the district Coakley-Rivera resigned to accept an appointment as an assistant clerk in the Hampden County Superior Court Clerk's office, becoming the first Hispanic to serve in that position. – Elizabeth Román

Martha Mary Coakley

(B. JULY 14, 1953 IN PITTSFIELD, MA; GREW UP IN NORTH ADAMS, MA) is a former Attorney General of Massachusetts. Prior to serving as Attorney General, she was District Attorney of Middlesex County, Massachusetts from 1999 to 2007. Coakley was the Democratic nominee in the 2010 special election to fill the United States Senate seat long held by Ted Kennedy. Coakley was defeated 52% to 47% by Republican Scott Brown in what was widely considered an upset. She won reelection as the Attorney General in the 2010 general election. Coakley was the Democratic nominee for governor in 2014, but lost to Republican Charlie Baker.

Mary J. (McMahon) Fitzgerald

(B. JUNE 7, 1890 IN HOLYOKE, MA; D. 1923 IN HOLYOKE, MA) became one of the first women in Massachusetts to be appointed as a policewoman. She began her short tenure in 1917 in the Holyoke Police Department. – Joseph Carvalho III

Mary (Lavo) Ford

(B. SEPT. 11, 1944 IN MA) served as Mayor of Northampton, MA from 1992 to 1999. She was the first woman to serve as mayor of Northampton. – Joseph Carvalho III

Jane (Famiano) Garvey

(B. FEB. 2, 1944 IN BROOKLYN, NY; RAISED IN HAMPSHIRE COUNTY, MA) is a former government transportation and public works official, now an American business executive, currently serving as the chairman of Meridiam

Top: Harriette L. Chandler. **Above:** Cheryl A. Coakley-Rivera.

103

Top left: Mary Ann Glendon with Laura and President George W. Bush. Top right: Kerry Gilpin. Above: Anne M. Gibbons.

North America. She was the first female Administrator of the U.S. Federal Aviation Administration from 1997 to 2002.
– Joseph Carvalho III

Anne M. Gibbons

(B. 1927 IN SPRINGFIELD, MA ; D. 2015 IN HOLYOKE, MA) of Holyoke was the second woman to be appointed as a judge in Western Massachusetts. In her pioneering judicial career, Gibbons served on a commission, chaired by U.S. Attorney General Archibald Cox, that led to legislation to reform Massachusetts courts. She was part of Gov. William Weld's Commission on Domestic Violence that changed the way the police and courts handled domestic violence cases. She also worked on special projects under the U.S. Department of Justice addressing legal services in rural areas, mental health issues of prisoners, and alternative sentencing for women. Gibbons retired in 1997 as presiding justice of Ware District Court. She had been appointed to the district court by Governor Michael Dukakis in 1977, after serving as assistant city solicitor for Holyoke from 1972 to 1977. – Anne-Gerard Flynn

Kerry Gilpin

(B. 1972 IN KINGSTON, MA) is the second woman to serve as superintendent of the Massachusetts State Police. Col. Kerry Gilpin was named by Gov. Charlie Baker in November 2017. Gilpin, a 23-year veteran of the State Police, served as deputy division commander of the Division of Standards and Training. She is the second woman to lead the State Police. Marian McGovern served as the superintendent of the State Police from 2009 to 2012, Gilpin joined the Massachusetts State Police in 1994. She earned a bachelor of Science in Criminal Justice from Western New England College in Springfield and lives in Hampden, MA.
– Wayne E. Phaneuf & Scott J. Croteau

Mary Ann Glendon

(B. OCT. 7, 1938 IN PITTSFIELD, MA) was the U.S. Ambassador to Holy See from Feb. 29, 2008 to January 20, 2009. She is the Learned Hand Professor of Law at Harvard Law School. In 1995, she was the Vatican representative to the international 1995 Beijing Conference on Women sponsored by the United Nations On June 26, 2013 Pope Francis named Glendon a member of the Pontifical Commission of inquiry for the Institute for Works of Religion (IOR), which is also known as the Vatican Bank. Glendon was the recipient of the 2005 National Humanities Medal.
– Joseph Carvalho III

Eleanor Mary Goggins

(B. MAY 6, 1893 IN PITTSFIELD, MA; D. APRIL 28, 1983 IN PITTSFIELD, MA) was a prominent public official in Pittsfield, MA. She worked at Pittsfield City Hall beginning in 1914. She was appointed City Assessor in May of 1946, one of the first women to hold that post in Western Massachusetts. – Joseph Carvalho III

Above: Governor Ella Grasso at Fort Drum, N.Y. as she visited with Connecticut Army National Guardsmen in training. She takes a look at an M-16 rifle held by Bill Childs of Manchester, CT. With her is Lt. John Knowlton of Manchester. (Submitted photo)

Inez C. Goss

(B. NOV. 10, 1899 IN NORTH ADAMS, MA; D. JUNE 20, 1984 IN HOLYOKE, MA) Served on the Board of Alderman of Holyoke, MA in the 1940s and 1950s, one of the first women elected to that Board. She later became the service coordinator for the Holyoke Soldiers Home. Goss was very active in veterans organizations and served as president of the American Legion Auxiliary, and president of the George C. Clarke V.F.W. Post Auxiliary where she held county, state, and National offices, including her appointment as National Patriotic Instructor. – Joseph Carvalho III

Stephanie B. Grant

(B. SEPT. 9, 1880 IN WORCESTER, MA) In 1908 became the first Worcester woman admitted to the Massachusetts Bar. She went on to serve on the Worcester School Committee in 1911. – Joseph Carvalho III

Ella Rosa Giovianna Oliva (Tambussi) Grasso

(B. MAY 10, 1919 IN WINDSOR LOCKS, CT; D. FEB. 5, 1981) served as the 83rd Governor of Connecticut from January 8, 1975 to December 31, 1980. She was the first woman elected to this office and the first woman to be elected governor of a U.S. state without having been the spouse or widow or a former governor. Grasso graduated from Mount Holyoke College in South Hadley, MA in 1940, and in 1942 began her work as Assistant Director of Research for the War Manpower Commission of Connecticut. In 1952, she was elected to the Connecticut House of Representatives, Democrat, serving until 1957. The next year, she was elected Secretary of the State of Connecticut and served in that post until 1970. In 1970, Grasso was elected as a Democratic Representative to the U.S. Congress and served until 1974 when she left Congress to run for Governor of Connecticut. President Ronald Reagan posthumously awarded her the Presidential Medal of Freedom in 1984, and the National Women's Hall of Fame inducted her in 1993. She was a member of the inaugural class inducted into the Connecticut Women's Hall of Fame in 1994; the Ella Tambussi Grasso Center for Women in Politics is located there.
– Wayne E. Phaneuf

Margaret A. (Oldham) Green

(B. MAY 2, 1896 IN PA; D. DEC. 21, 1975 IN ALEMEDA, CA) was one of the first women to serve as a Holyoke City Alderman, serving "At-Large" from 1934 to 1945. During this time, she also served at various times as vice-chairman of the Republican State Committee, and the Republican National Committee. – Joseph Carvalho III

Eileen P. Griffin

(B. MAR. 10, 1921 IN SPRINGFIELD, MA; D. OCT. 11, 2001 IN SPRINGFIELD, MA) was admitted to the Massachusetts Bar Association in 1949. From 1949-1951 she was the secretary to the former Governor of Massachusetts, Paul Dever. From 1951 to 1967 she practiced law privately in Springfield and from 1964 to 1973 she was appointed to the District Court of Eastern Hampden as the Presiding Justice & was the first female Justice in Western Massachusetts. From 1973 to 1986 she was appointed as the Associate Justice of the Massachusetts Superior Court from which she retired on November 30, 1986. She served on the Springfield City Council from 1962 to 1964, the Board of Trustees at Westfield State College from March 1987 to March of 1997, serving as the Chairman of the Board from 1990-1992. She served on the Board of Trustees of the Springfield Library & Museum Association from 1992-2001. – Joseph Carvalho III

Cele Hahn

(B. 1942 IN IOWA; D. APR. 11, 2014 IN PUERTO VALLARTA, MEXICO) was about as outside as an outsider could be to Westfield politics back in 1994. She'd never run for public office, wasn't a native to the Whip City AND was a member of the media. Sixteen years previously, Westfield's 4th Hampden District had been carved out in a redistricting effort, giving the city just one seat in the state Legislature instead of its historic two seats. A young Republican lawyer, Steven D. Pierce, had come out of nowhere in 1977 to defeat Democrat rivals, even though, more often than not, the city's voters elected Democrats to serve as mayor, state representative and senator. Pierce was succeeded by another GOP candidate (and native son), Michael Knapik, and Knapik, in 1994, was going to move on, running for the state Senate seat being vacated by then-Sen. Shannon P. O'Brien from Easthampton.

Enter Cele Hahn. She and her husband, Curt Hahn, were transplants to Westfield and the owners of radio station WNNZ. Curt's family traced its roots to Hadley, and he and Cele first came to the Springfield area from Michigan in 1978 when they purchased what was then WLDM. They created WNNZ in 1987, and Cele was the host of a popular talk-radio show; so popular was her show that "Talkers" magazine once listed her among the 100 most influential talk-radio hosts in the country. Originally from Iowa where she earned a bachelor's degree in journalism from the University of Iowa, she started out as a newspaper reporter in Miami, Huntington, West Virginia, and Albany, New York. Truth be known, she probably loved writing more than anything else she did in life. Her blog, which readers can find online at celehahn.org, includes the quotation, "All I ever wanted to do was write."

Cele Hahn never shied from anything in which she believed. She had one of those no-nonsense approaches to life and to politics. In this case, she took on a legion of opponents, including two former mayors and a longtime city councilor, John Rhodes, George Varelas and Barbara Russell, and won, decisively.

She went on to serve four terms in the Legislature; she never had another opponent and left the Legislature in 2002.

At the Statehouse, she served on several committees including the Long-Term Debt and Capital Expenditures, the Insurance Committee and the House Ways and Means Committee. In 1999 she was named Legislator of the Year for Mental Health and Immigration Services. She was named Conservationist of the Year 2000 by the Hampden Conservation District. Hahn was a also member of the American Legislative Exchange Council's national task force on commerce and economic development and served as vice president of the National Order of Women Legislators in 1999. In 2002, she and her husband retired from public life and moved to Puerto Vallarta, Mexico. – Cynthia G. Simison

Adelaide "Addie" Frances (Gillette) Hayden

(B. FEB. 27, 1875 IN PLYMOUTH, VT) who lived in Fitchburg, MA was the first female lawyer in Worcester County, Massachusetts.
– Joseph Carvalho III

Jessica L. Henderson

(B. FEB. 2, 1967 IN SPRINGFIELD, MA) is Springfield's first African-American police lieutenant, promoted in 2016. In 2017, she was honored with Springfield's Stone Soul Legacy Award. – Chris Dondoros

Mary Clare Higgins

(B. FEB. 1, 1955) served six terms as mayor of Northampton, 2000-2011. Before becoming mayor, Higgins worked in early childhood education, served as an at-large Northampton City Councilor [1994-1999], and was a Commissioner on the board of the Northampton Housing Authority appointed by Mayor David Musante in 1991.
– Joseph Carvalho III

Iris Shirley (Kaufman) Holland

(B. SEPT. 30, 1920 IN SPRINGFIELD, MA; D. JULY 19, 2001 IN LONGMEADOW, MA) Republican from Longmeadow, MA, was the first female legislator from Western Massachusetts (1972), and in 1979 became the first woman to hold a position of leadership in the Massachusetts House, specifically as House Minority Whip. – Joseph Carvalho III

Ann (Wallace) Holt

(B. FEB. 21, 1943) was born in Springfield and lived and went to elementary school in Indian Orchard. After attending Classical High School and MacDuffie School for Girls, in Springfield, she obtained a B.A. degree in Art from the University of Massachusetts. She then earned a J.D. degree at Suffolk University Law School and an L.L.M. in Law, Psychiatry and Criminology at George Washington School of Law. After law school, she worked as a criminal appellate attorney for the United States Department of Justice. During a 39-year career she represented the United States in petitions and briefs before the Supreme Court as well as before a majority of the federal courts of appeals. She presented oral arguments before three-judge appellate panels across the country and in Puerto Rico and St. Croix. Significantly, she wrote and successfully argued a case before twenty-four Fifth Circuit Judges—the largest assembly of federal appellate judges in the country. United States v Michael, 645 F.2d 252 (5th Cir. 1981) (en banc). The issue involved whether the warrantless installation of a beeper on the exterior of a vehicle while it is parked in a public lot, and the subsequent monitoring of its signals as the automobile travels on public roads constitutes an unreasonable search and seizure. Subsequently, Ann wrote a successful petition for a writ of certiorari involving the same issue to the United States Supreme Court. United Ststes v. Knotts, 460 U.S. 276 (1983). She also was the contact attorney for numerous United States Attorney offices, including Boston and Springfield.

Top: Mary Clare Higgins. **Above:** Ann (Wallace) Holt

At the same time, Ann established a company to sell her hand-painted clothing and hand-knit sweaters. She also pursued art in the evenings as a student at the Yellow Barn Studio in Glen Echo, Maryland. In 2001, she became a Yellow Barn instructor teaching drawing and painting with oils, acrylics, gouache, and pastels. In addition, along with two painting colleagues, she organized a "Paint to Cure" art event to

Top: Mary Elizabeth Hurley. **Above:** Bertha Knight Landes. **Center:** Iris Shirley Holland.

benefit breast cancer research and a "Paint Out and Party Down" event to support the renovation of the Yellow Barn.

Ann continues to teach painting classes at Plaza Artists Materials in Rockville, Maryland. She is also a full-time artist, specializing in portrait, landscape, still life and figurative paintings. Ann paints immediately or directly— "au premier coup" (at first stroke) or "alla prima"(at first attempt). She believes that a painting should not serve simply to showcase the technical prowess of the painter, but instead should allow the viewer to be an integral participant in the realization of the artist's vision. Her recent awards include the Art League of Virginia Award.

Mary Elizabeth Hurley

(B. JUNE 22, 1950 IN SPRINGFIELD, MA) is the District 8 member of the Massachusetts Governor's Council, elected in 2016. From 1995 to 2014, Hurley served as a Judge at the Chicopee District Court. After her retirement from the bench, she returned to private practice with the law firm of Cooley Shrair of Springfield where she served as a principal after her mayoral years. A life-long Democrat, she was Springfield's first woman mayor, serving in that post from 1989 to 1991. Hurley's background of community service includes work as a trustee of Elms College, the Springfield Library and Museums Association, Springfield College, and Holyoke Community College, as well as service on the boards of directors for the Sisters of Providence Health System, Springfield Symphony Orchestra, and the Alcoholism and Drug Services of Western Mass. Inc. She is also a recipient of the Massachusetts Bar Association's Public Service Award. – Joseph Carvalho III

Susan M. Labrie

(B. MAR. 4, 1964) of Williamsburg, MA was appointed Fire Chief of the Goshen Volunteer Fire Department in 2006, the first woman to serve as fire chief in Massachusetts. Prior to her appointment, she had served 17 years in that volunteer fire department – Cynthia G. Simison & Joseph Carvalho III

Nicole M. LaChapelle

(B. APR.1, 1967 IN MA) was elected mayor of Easthampton, MA in 2017.

Bertha Knight Landes

(B. OCT. 19, 1868 IN WARE, MA; D. NOV. 29, 1943 IN ANN ARBOR, MICHIGAN) was the first woman to be elected mayor of a large U.S. city, Seattle, WA. in 1926. – Joseph Carvalho III

Mary F. Lathrop

(B. 1880 IN MA) was one of the first two women appointed as police officers in the Springfield Police Department along with Elizabeth O'Connor in 1918. Officer Lathrop also served for a time as president of the New England Policewomen's Association. – Joseph Carvalho III

Gladys Lebron-Martinez

From being an outreach coordinator, case manager and director of health and human services for Nueva Esperanza, a Holyoke social services agency, to serving on the city's school committee, Lebron-Martinez has made it her goal to empower the Latino community through information and education. For many years she organized a health fair which has now become a block party where the community can gather to eat, dance, network and get information about city services. She is now a member of the Holyoke City Council serving Ward 1. – Natalia Arbulu & Elizabeth Román

Marian J. McGovern
(B. FEB. 17, 1954) first woman commander of the Massachusetts State Police, the oldest statewide law enforcement agency in the country. She grew up in Worcester, became a trooper in 1979 after working in the Westboro District Court Clerk's office. She earned a master's in Criminal Justice from Westfield State University in 1988. She worked as a road trooper in barracks in Northampton and Holden, as a drill instructor at the Massachusetts State Police Academy, at the state police crime lab, and in media relations for the department. She became the first woman trooper to be assigned full time to a detective unit, working violent crimes in the Worcester District Attorney's office for 20 years. She earned promotions to sergeant, lieutenant, lieutenant colonel, and deputy superintendent. In 2009 she was promoted to colonel by then-Gov. Deval Patrick, making her superintendent of the department, the first woman to achieve the post. She retired in 2012 after more than 33 years of service. – Marsha Marotta

Virginia "Ginny" Morse Martinez
(B. CA. 1922 IN MILFORD, MA; D. JUNE 25, 1992 IN NEW ORLEANS, LA), was a long-term Louisiana Republican Party official who is credited with having landed her party's 1988 national convention in her adopted home city of New Orleans, Louisiana where delegates nominated the Bush-Quayle ticket. Martinez was the Louisiana Republican National Committeewoman from 1977 until her death in 1992. – Joseph Carvalho III

Chirlane Irene McCray
(B. NOV. 29, 1954 IN SPRINGFIELD, MA) is a writer, poet, editor, and communications professional/speechwriter. She attended Longmeadow High School and was the only African-American student at that time. Graduating from Wellesley College in 1972, McCray moved to New York City to work for *Redbook*. Her poetry is included in *Home Girls: A Black Feminist Anthology*. Entering politics in 1991, she worked as a speechwriter for New York City Mayor David Dinkins. During the Clinton Administration, McCray worked for the New York Foreign Press Center as a public affairs specialist. In the late 1990s and early 2000s, she worked as a speechwriter for a number of New York Democratic politicians. She is the wife of New York City Mayor Bill de Blasio, and during his 2013 mayoral campaign she edited his speeches and helped interview candidates for staff positions. In 2014, Mayor de Blasio appointed McCray as chair of the Mayor's Fund to Advance New York City. In 2015, she led the launch of ThriveNYC, a plan to overhaul New York's mental health and substance abuse services. – Joseph Carvalho III

Annie L. McTier
(B. JULY 20, 1859; D. JULY 28, 1924 IN SPRINGFIELD, MA), vice president of the Negro Political Union, was the first woman to register to vote in Springfield, MA, Aug. 3, 1920. She "sat on the steps of Springfield City Hall for hours in order to be the first woman in the city to register to vote after the passage of the Women's Suffrage Act." One hundred and fifty-three women registered to vote in Springfield that day. – Kathleen Mitchell

Paula Marie (Connelly) Meara
(B. MAR. 23, 1945 IN SPRINGFIELD, MA) was the first woman to serve as chief of police in New England. She was appointed in February of 1996 by Springfield Mayor Michael Albano. Meara began her career in the Springfield

Police Department as a police officer in 1974. Progressively moving up through the ranks of the Department, she was promoted to sergeant in 1985, to lieutenant in 1987, and captain in 1992. Meara served as Police Chief until her retirement on June 20, 2005. She later served as the Chairperson of the Springfield Casino Site Committee. – Joseph Carvalho III

Linda Jean Melconian
(B. MAR. 28, 1949 IN SPRINGFIELD, MA) served as a Massachusetts state senator representing the greater Springfield area from 1983 to 2005. A life-long Democratic Party member, she was the first woman to hold the post of Majority Leader of the Massachusetts Senate. A college intern to U.S. Congressman Edward P. Boland (D-MA), Melconian began her public service career in 1971 as legislative assistant counsel to U. S. House of Representatives' Majority Leader Thomas P. Tip O'Neill (D-MA). After "Tip" O'Neill was elected House Majority Leader and Speaker, Melconian became the first woman staff professional to merit standing U. S. House Floor privileges in all three majority leadership offices. She held staff positions including chief legislative assistant, speechwriter, House Floor scheduling and Member assistant, advisor on domestic and foreign policy and select/special committee assignments, and Assistant Counsel to the Speaker. She is now a Senior Fellow in the Moakley Center for Public Management. – Joseph Carvalho III

Ellen Brown Merriam
(B. DEC. 2, 1833 IN OTIS, MA; D. 1916 IN SPRINGFIELD, MA) was one of the founders of the Y.W.C.A. in Springfield and was a major fundraiser for the funding required for the organization's first building. In 1886, she was also one of the first two women to be elected to the Springfield School Committee at a time when Springfield was one of the, if not The first city to have a women in that elective office. – Joseph Carvalho III

Effie Maud Aldrich Morrison

(B. JAN. 2,1876 IN MONSON, MA; D. MAR. 29, 1957 IN MILLVILLE, NJ) originated the concept and instigated the plan of the first senior housing project in the United States. She was a deputy director of the Cumberland County Welfare Board in New Jersey. She received several awards for elderly programs.
– Joseph Carvalho III

Kate (Horan) Moynihan

(B. IN HOLYOKE, MA) was one of the first women to serve in a Massachusetts police department, as a police matron in the Holyoke Police Department from 1891 to 1916.
– Joseph Carvalho III

Mary Margaret O'Reilly

(B. OCT. 14, 1865 IN SPRINGFIELD, MA; D. DEC. 6, 1949 IN WASHINGTON, D.C.) educated in the parochial schools of the Springfield Dioceses, worked in the U.S. government for 36 years with the last fourteen years serving as assistant director of the U.S. Mint. When in 1936 Secretary of the Treasury Morganthau insisted that she was "indespensible," President Franklin D. Roosevelt issued an executive order to allow her to serve beyond the mandatory retirement age of 70. Serving until 1938, she retired that year. In 1934, she was asked to advise the Chinese government on the establishment of their new mint.   – Joseph Carvalho III

Gladys Oyola

After years of serving the City of Springfield as a bilingual education program coordinator and directing the Spanish Language Election Program, Oyola was hired as the city's Election Commissioner in 2010. She became the first Hispanic ever to hold the position. Oyola remains passionate about voter registration and ensuring there are sufficient bilingual poll workers at every polling location.
– Peter Goonan

Melinda M. Phelps

(B. JULY 15, 1956) is a lawyer at the Bulkley, Richardson and Gelinas law firm in Springfield, MA. She is a graduate of Mount Holyoke College, Class of 1978; and Western New England College School of Law, J.D. (1983). A longtime resident of Springfield, she served as a Springfield police commissioner, Springfield Technical Community College Foundation board member, Mount Holyoke Club of Greater Springfield past president and Western Massachusetts Electric Company board member. Phelps has also chaired several successful state and federal election campaigns and was named the Best Lawyers® 2012 Springfield, and Massachusetts Personal Injury Litigation (Defendants) Lawyer of the Year. Melinda is currently a board member of DevelopSpringfield, member of the Massachusetts Council of School Attorneys, trustee of Springfield Museums, board member of the Spirit of Springfield, and a member of the WGBY Board of Tribunes. She is a fellow of MassINC's Gateway Cities Innovation Institute, an organization dedicated to revitalizing former manufacturing centers in Massachusetts. Phelps has also served as chair of the United Way of Pioneer Valley's 2011 fundraising campaign, served as a city prosecutor and community development counsel for the city of Springfield. – Wayne E. Phaneuf & Joseph Carvalho III

Elaine A. Pluta

(B. AUG. 27, 1943 IN HOLYOKE, MA) first woman to serve as mayor of Holyoke, MA, 2009-2011.

Karyn Polito

(BORN NOVEMBER 11, 1966 IN SHREWSBURY, MA) is an American Republican Party politician from the state of Massachusetts. She is the 72nd and current Lieutenant Governor of Massachusetts, since 2015. From 2001 to 2011 she was a member of the Massachusetts House of Representatives representing the Eleventh Worcester District – consisting of the town of Shrewsbury, and precincts 1 and 4 of the town of Westborough, both in the county of Worcester.
– Joseph Carvalho III

Top left: Karyn Polito. **Top right:** Melinda M. Phelps.

Elizabeth A. Porada

(B. SEPT. 1, 1933 IN NORTHAMPTON, MA) was the first woman from Western Massachusetts to serve on the Appeals Court, and only the 4th woman to be named to the court created in 1972. She traded in a thriving law practice in Northampton to become a district judge in 1978. She served as Superior Court judge from 1982-1990. Porada also served as an assistant prosecutor in the 1970s for the Northwestern District Attorney's Office. Judge John F. Moriarity once observed that Porada was "a superb trial judge," and "one of the hardest working judges we have had on the superior court." She served as Associate justice on the Appeals Court of Massachusetts from 1990 to 2003, and "Recall Justice" from 2003-2004. Porada has been a resident of Hatfield, and Amherst. – Cynthia G. Simison & Joseph Carvalho III

Ruth Baker Pratt

(B. AUG. 24, 1877 IN WARE, MA; D. AUG. 23, 1965 IN GLEN COVE, LONG ISLAND, NY) was the first U.S. Congresswoman to be elected in New York, serving from 1929 to 1933. In 1925, she became the first woman to serve as a member of the board of aldermen of New York City. Pratt was a member of the Republican National Committee 1929-1943; delegate to the Republican National Conventions in 1924, 1932, 1936, 1940; delegate to the Republican State conventions in 1922, 1924, 1926, 1928, 1930, 1936, and 1938. Spratt also served as president of the Women's National Republican Club from 1943 to 1946.
– Joseph Carvalho III

Mary R. Regan

(B. MAY 28, 1956 IN WESTFIELD, MA) is the first woman to serve as fire chief in the city of Westfield, and the second to serve as a full-time fire chief in the entire state. She was promoted to this post in 2011, after having served in the department since 1987. Leading up to her promotion as chief, she moved up the ranks, first as a captain in 1997, and then as deputy

chief in 2004. She was also the first woman to hold that post in the city of Westfield. Mary attended Westfield schools, and has lived in Westfield her entire life. Mary was particularly proud to serve with her brother, Kevin Regan, the longest serving fire fighter in the Westfield Fire Department. [Kevin was tragically killed in an accident in Yarmouth, MA on December 27, 2014.] Regan retired in 2018.
– Thomas and Susan Sawyer & Ted LaBorde

Sara J. Robertson

(B. JULY 22, 1934 IN LONG BEACH, CA) was a Worcester School Committee member (1969), president of the Worcester League of Women Voters, and the first woman to serve as Worcester's mayor (1982-83). She also taught at Becker College and Worcester State College (now Worcester State University) during the 1980s. – Leah Lamson & Joseph Carvalho III

Mary S. Rogeness

(B. MAY 18, 1941 IN KANSAS CITY, KS) of Longmeadow, MA represented the 2nd Hampden district in the Massachusetts House of Representatives from 1991–2009 and was a

Top left: Ruth Baker Pratt
Top right: Mary R. Regan (photo courtesy of The Republican/Mark M. Murray)
Above: Gladys Oyola

member of the Longmeadow School Committee from 1982–1988. A life-long Republican Party member from 1999–2003, she was the Assistant Minority Whip and from 2003–2009 she was Assistant Minority Leader. – Joseph Carvalho III

Carmen A. Rosa

(B. JULY 31, 1959) of Springfield, MA, in 1993 became the first Latina woman to be elected to the Springfield School Committee. She beat her nearest opponent by almost 4,000 votes. An active committee member, Rosa went on to serve on the state's Education Reform Review Commission.
– Elizabeth Román

Elsie Sweeley Ruther (B. FEB. 24, 1894
IN PA; D. JAN. 25, 1972 IN LUDLOW, MA) was the first woman in the Commonwealth of Massachusetts to be appointed as a truant officer. She was appointed to the Springfield School Department Truant Officer position in the 1920s. – Joseph Carvalho III

Elizabeth D. "Betsy" (Boudreau) Scheibel (B. MAY 1, 1955 IN SOUTH HADLEY,
MA) was the first woman district attorney in the Commonwealth of Massachusetts. In

1993 she became the District Attorney for the Northwestern District and served in that capacity until January 2011. A graduate of Mount Holyoke College (1977) and Western New England College School of Law, she began her career in the Hampden County District Attorney's office in 1980 with much of her caseload involving the prosecution of child sexual assault cases. As Northwestern district attorney, Scheibel had a jurisdiction of forty-seven Massachusetts cities and towns, a staff of about 100, a budget of almost $5 million. Scheibel was the prosecutor at the center of the Phoebe Prince case, which made international headlines. Fifteen-year-old Prince committed suicide in January 2010 after reportedly being relentlessly bullied at South Hadley High School — Scheibel's alma mater. As Northwestern district attorney, Scheibel brought charges against six of Prince's fellow students and alleged bullies. Scheibel also served on Massachusetts' Medicolegal Commission, and the Governor's Commission on Mental Retardation. She also served as the State Director of the National District Attorney's Association. During her career, she also served two terms as president of the Massachusetts District Attorneys Association, and was a ten-year member of the Massachusetts Victim Assistance Board, a Trustee of Westfield State University, beginning in 2016 has served as a Trustee for the University of Massachusetts system. – Joseph Carvalho III

Katie L. (Galluzzo) Stebbins

(B. FEB. 19, 1971) is the vice-president of Economic Development for the University of Massachusetts system. She previously worked as the Assistant Secretary for Technology, Innovation and Entrepreneurship in Massachusetts Governor Charles Baker's Executive Office for Housing and Economic Development. A former Springfield resident, Stebbins was a municipal planner for the city of Springfield and also worked as a project

consultant for the Holyoke Innovation District. She founded Your Friend in Springfield Consulting, a private economic development and project management firm.
– Joseph Carvalho III

Grace Mary Stern
(B. JULY 10, 1925 IN HOLYOKE, MA; D. MAY 15,1998 IN HIGHLAND PARK, IL) was elected as an Illinois state legislator. – Joseph Carvalho III

Ellen Story
(B. OCT. 17, 1941) of Amherst was the Massachusetts State Representative for the 3rd Hampshire District from 1992 to 2017. She is the recipient of the Sarah Levine Service award, Family Planning Council Western Massachusetts, and Special Recognition award, Hampshire County Council Social Agencies in 1991; Legislator of the Year award, from the Women's Bar Association in 2001; and the Jan Wood Award from the Council of Social Agencies in 2016. Prior to her election to state office, she was a member of the Amherst Town Meeting, and Associate Director of the Family Planning Council of Western Massachusetts from 1973 to 1991.
– Joseph Carvalho III

Constance M. Sweeney
(B. JAN. 21, 1950) is a Hampden County Superior Court justice who served as Springfield's first female City Solicitor from 1982 to 1984. In 1986, Massachusetts Gov. Michael S. Dukakis appointed her to the bench. A 2002 New York Times headline referred to her as the "Tough Judge at [the] Center of Boston Archdiocese Suits." The article stated: "in what is easily the most challenging and closely watched case of her career, overseeing the civil suits against the archdiocese that have rocked the largely Catholic city of Boston and sent tremors through the Roman Catholic Church nationwide. And she is unsparing. 'If the tone of this endorsement is harsh, so be it,' she wrote in her court order, 'The court simply will not be

Above left: Constance M. Sweeney. Above right: Ellen Story.

toyed with.'" With her actions, Judge Sweeney sparked the national debate about clergy sex abuse when she ordered the release of 10,000 documents from 84 lawsuits concerning John J. Geoghan, a former priest convicted of molestation. For the first time, the landmark decision allowed a comprehensive look at the archdiocese's handling of abuse cases. Sweeney later ordered the release of more than 11,000 pages of documents concerning accusations of abuse against "scores of priests" from the archdiocese. – Joseph Carvalho III & Wayne E. Phaneuf

Jane Maria Swift
(B. FEB. 24, 1965 IN IN NORTH ADAMS, MA) is an American politician and businesswoman who served as the 69th Lieutenant Governor of Massachusetts from 1999 to 2003 and Acting Governor from 2001 to 2003. She is the only woman to perform the duties of governor of Massachusetts, doing so from April 2001 to January 2003. At the time she became acting governor, Swift was 36 years old, making her the youngest female governor or acting governor in U.S. history. Since leaving elected office she has worked in the private sector as a consultant and executive in education technology, as well as serving on corporate and non-profit boards, teaching and lecturing on topics pertaining to women and leadership, and supporting philanthropies that address issues of importance to women and girls. In 2011, she became the CEO of Middlebury Interactive Languages.
– Joseph Carvalho III

Barbara L. Swords
(B. JUNE 14, 1926 IN SPRINGFIELD, MA; D. DEC. 21, 2012 IN WESTFIELD, MA) was one of the longest serving members of Westfield City Council, one term as an at-large council and ten terms as Ward 4 councilor, from 1985 through 2007. Swords also worked as a volunteer with the Westfield chapter of the American Red Cross, and worked at Noble Hospital from 1968 to 1988. Her years of service to the community was recognized by the Greater Westfield Chapter of the American Red Cross in 2008 when they presented Swords with their "Outstanding Community Spirit Award."
– Cynthia G. Simison & Joseph Carvalho III

Above left: Kateri Walsh. Above right: Linda M. Tyler. Below left: U.S. Senator Elizabeth Warren of Massachusetts attends a hearing on Capitol Hill in Washington, D.C. (Olivier Douliery/Abaca Press/TNS)

Linda M. Tyer

is the current mayor of Pittsfield, MA, assumed office in January of 2016. Previously, she had served as Pittsfield City Clerk, and as the city's Ward 3 Councilor. A graduate of Bay Path University, Tyer is also the founding member and past president of the Samuel Harrison Society in Pittsfield.
– Joseph Carvalho III & James Gleason

Pearl (Leonard) Wallace

(B. OCT. 14, 1910 IN YONKERS, NY; D. APR. 9, 1995 IN SPRINGFIELD, MA) of Springfield (Indian Orchard) and Longmeadow, MA was a noted attorney in Springfield and one of the founders of the successful Wallace & Wallace law firm retiring in 1989 after 45 years of legal work. One of the earliest women to join the Hampden County Bar Association and one of its longest-tenured members. Wallace was one of the most respected women legal professionals in the Pioneer Valley during her long career. – Joseph Carvalho III & Wayne E. Phaneuf

Kateri (Bennett) Walsh

(B. SEPT. 9, 1945 IN SPRINGFIELD, MA) one of the longest serving members of the Springfield City Council, serving from 1987-1992, and from 2003 to the present. She has been the chairman of the city's Springfield Women's Commission, and at the state level has served on the Massachusetts Commission on the Status of Women. – Joseph Carvalho III

Elizabeth Ann Warren

(B. JUNE 22, 1949 IN OKLAHOMA CITY, OK) is a U.S. Senator for the Commonwealth of Massachusetts, elected Nov. 6, 2012. A member of the Democratic Party since 1996, she is recognized as one of the nation's top experts on bankruptcy and consumer protections. Her leadership and advocacy led to the creation of the Consumer Financial Protection Bureau. In the aftermath of the 2008 financial crisis, Warren served as Chair of the Congressional Oversight Panel for the Troubled Asset Relief Program (TARP). *TIME Magazine* called her a "New Sheriff of Wall Street" for her oversight efforts. Warren was a law professor for more than 30 years, including nearly 20 years as the Leo Gottlieb Professor of Law at Harvard Law School. She lives in Cambridge, MA. – Joseph Carvalho III

Anne (Everest) Wojtkowski

(B. JAN. 10, 1935 IN PITTSFIELD, MA; D. OCT. 13, 2014 IN PITTSFIELD, MA) was the first female mayor of Pittsfield, MA serving from 1988 to 1991. She was a trained aeronautical engineer. In 1956, Wojtkowski was the first female engineer hired by the Arthur D. Little consulting firm of Cambridge, MA. In 1969, she began teaching at Berkshire Community College. By the time Anne retired as Professor of Engineering and Mathematics in 2004 she had taught over thirty different courses in engineering, physics, mathematics, computer programming and energy. In 1983, Anne joined with Professor Karen Canfield Border to initiate a sex bias suit against the college's administration, alleging lack of promotional and pay equity. Anne's successful analysis of pay discrimination led the Massachusetts Teachers Association to join the suit and expand it to include female faculty and professionals in all Massachusetts community colleges. The settlement of this suit in 1992 for $10.6 million was deemed "the largest settlement of its kind in Massachusetts and a major step nationally in the battle for equal treatment of women in the workplace." – Joseph Carvalho III

Mary Emma Woolley

(B. JULY 13, 1863 IN SOUTH NORWALK, CT; D. 1947) was the first woman to represent the United States at a major diplomatic Conference, the Geneva Conference on Reduction and Limitation of Armaments (1932). [See entry under Education & Educators] – Joseph Carvalho III

CHAPTER SIX

WOMEN IN
Healthcare

BY ANNE-GERARD FLYNN
Author - Journalist

American National Red Cross photograph collection
(Library of Congress)

Today, women have advanced in all areas of medicine and behavioral health. They also work as veterinarians, dentists and in the field of complementary and integrative health. However, health care has always been synonymous with women in Western Massachusetts, as this chapter highlights.

Much of this care has been associated historically with the work of a Catholic congregation of women religious whose institutions served generations of family members throughout the region's four counties and whose members staffed those institutions at all levels.

Other area hospitals and educational institutions, like the Western Massachusetts Hospital School for Practical Nurses, served women in their pursuit of health care careers. Springfield Hospital opened its first training school for nurses in 1892. It awarded its first degrees two years later to Anna B. Rohan, Annie C. Nihill, Katherine J. Duggan, Margaret McGilvary, Sarah M. Laree and Elizabeth Moore. The school became Baystate Medical Center School of Nursing, in 1976, when Springfield Hospital and Wesson Memorial Hospital merged. A year later, the residential

program ended, and the school graduated its last matriculating class, in 1999, as nursing education moved away from diploma programs toward academic degrees. Many nurses today have master's and doctorate degrees, and work in a variety of settings as nurse practitioners.

In its 107-year history, the school awarded diplomas to some 2,906 students. A bronze statute of a nurse done by sculptor Arthur Moses stands in tribute to the school outside the Chestnut Street building on the Baystate Medical Center campus in Springfield. The artist's wife, Bette, a 1960 graduate of the school, served as model.

Area colleges, too, have educated women of science who continued their education in the field of medicine. One example is Dr. Virginia Apgar who graduated Mount Holyoke College with a degree in zoology in 1929. Four years later, she graduated fourth in her class from the College of Physicians and Surgeons at Columbia University in New York City. She was encouraged to study anesthesiology and became interested in obstetrical anesthesia. She went on to develop what has become known as the Apgar score, an internationally recognized test used to evaluate the health of newborns, and an early expert in the field of birth defects.

Another is Dr. Florence Rena Sabin, the first woman elected to membership of the National Academy of Science. Sabin graduated Smith College in 1893 and entered Johns Hopkins Medical School three years later as a member of the fourth class to admit women. She became the first woman to become a full professor on the Hopkins' staff, and did pioneering research on the body's lymphatic system.

Hartford-born Mary Whiton Calkins, an 1885 graduate of Smith College, became the first woman president of the American Psychological Association in 1905.

Women whose names have become well recognized in the field of health care in the last two decades here include Helen Caulton-Harris who has served as Springfield's director of health and human services since April 1996. She oversees the city's compliance with state health regulations – the schools have a high rate of meeting vaccination requirements – as well as the delivery of a broad range of services to city residents, and the coordination of services for emergency situations in this age of bioterrorism and spread of infectious diseases.

Also, Dr. Grace Makari-Judson who chairs the Baystate Health Breast Network at Baystate Medical Center and is co-director of the Rays of Hope Center for Breast Cancer Research. As medical director of what was then Baystate Medical Center's Comprehensive Breast Center in the 1990s, the medical oncologist became the face of encouraging women to take an active role in their breast health. She has seen the center expand, upgrade and evolve in its approach to helping patients across the region

be treated for the disease, as well as assess their risk for it. She is also Professor of Medicine at University of Massachusetts Medical School – Baystate.

There is also Mary Reardon Johnson whose name is synonymous across the state with services to victims of domestic violence. Johnson retired at the beginning of 2016 as executive director of the YWCA of Western Massachusetts after more than three decades of service. The organization she helped grow from a one-room office and one shelter is today the state's largest provider of domestic violence services. Its Springfield headquarters sits on an 11-acre campus and includes a 48-bed emergency shelter, as well as a 28-apartment, supportive housing project for parenting teens and survivors of domestic violence and sexual abuse.

The traditional name recognition for many long-time residents of Western Massachusetts for women in health care would be with a Holyoke-based congregation of women religious.

Under the guidance of Mother Mary of Providence (Catherine Horan), the Sisters of Providence began to establish, in the late 1800s, hospitals in Western and Central Massachusetts, along with nursing schools, homes for the elderly, the orphaned and unwed mothers.

In the last 100 years, members of the congregation have brought their work into the 21st century.

Sister Julie Crane, a registered nurse who much like the first members of her congregation who went door to door to minister to those in need, began a health care ministry to the homeless in Springfield in 1983.

Sister Mary Peter Meckel founded Open Pantry's Loaves and Fishes Soup Kitchen, the Jefferson Street Shelter and the Calhoun Street Shelter, all in Springfield. She holds a master's degree in business administration from Boston College, and worked in that area at three of her congregation's area hospitals – St. Luke's,

in Pittsfield, St. Vincent's, in Worcester, and Providence, in Holyoke.

Sister Margaret McCleary, who celebrated 60 years with the congregation in 1917, founded the Providence Ministries Network. Its components include Kate's Kitchen, Holyoke's first soup kitchen that McCleary opened in 1980; Loreto House, transitional housing for homeless men that McCleary founded in 1987, and the single-room occupancy Broderick House that dates to the same time.

Sister Mary Caritas Geary headed the congregation's Springfield hospital – Mercy Medical – from 1977 to 1993, helping to modernize its delivery of care, particularly in the area of cancer. She joined the congregation in 1947 as a nurse, and now serves as vice president of the congregation headed by Sister Kathleen Popko who was instrumental in Mercy's evolution as well.

Popko, who holds an undergraduate degree in nursing as well as a master of social welfare degree, and a doctor of philosophy degree from Brandeis University, served as president and chief executive of the Sisters of Providence Health System from 1994 to 1997. She helped form that system and laid the groundwork for its integration, along with two other free standing Catholic health care systems, into a more collaborative and pioneering model of delivering care known, in 1998, as Catholic Health Care East.

From 1997 until 2009, Popko, who had served as president of the Leadership Conference of Women Religious and was therefore known nationally to other congregations' members, served on Catholic Health East's senior management team, eight years as executive vice president of the Northeast division, overseeing regional health corporations in five northeastern states, and then four years as executive vice president of strategy and ministry development.

Pictured right: Clara Barton

The network founded by the congregation today includes the 182-bed Mercy Medical Center as well as Weldon Rehabilitation Hospital, both in Springfield; the 126-bed Providence Behavioral Health Hospital in Holyoke, the only dedicated psychiatric care hospital in the region; West Springfield-based Brightside for Families and Children, an outpatient service offering counseling and family support programs; several outpatient substance abuse treatment centers; and the Mercy Continuing Care Network that includes skilled nursing facilities, residential care facilities, and an adult day health program. It is now part of Michigan-based Trinity Health, the second largest nonprofit health care system in the country.

Medicine and Health Care

Clara Barton

(NÉE CLARISSA HARLOWE BARTON, B. DEC. 25, 1821 IN OXFORD, MA; D. APR. 12, 1912 IN GLEN ECHO, MD) founded and was the first President of the American Red Cross, serving from 1877 to 1904. Working as a teacher from 1838 to 1855, she then moved to Washington, D.C. to work in the U.S. Patent Office but was fired by the Buchanan administration for being an anti-slavery Republican. When Abraham Lincoln was elected, Barton returned to the nation's capitol to resume working at the Patent Office. Soon after on April 19, 1861, the Baltimore rioters which attacked the newly arrived Massachusetts troops, Barton rushed to the rail station to help care for 40 of the injured troops. In the early part of the Civil War, Barton began major efforts to secure medical supplies for the union troops, finally receiving permission in August of 1862 from the Army to work on the front lines. Barton was to help care for wounded soldiers, both Union and Confederate, at the Battles of Bull Run, Cedar Mountain, Antietam, and Fredericksburg. In 1864, Gen. Benjamin Butler appointed Barton

Dorthea Lynde Dix

as "Lady in Charge" of the field hospitals of the Army of the James. Her efforts gained her the nicknames "American Nightingale," and the "Angel of the Battlefield." She performed prodigiously under hard conditions at many more battlefields: Fairfax Station, Chantilly, Harpers Ferry, South Mountain, Charleston, Petersburg, and Cold Harbor. After the Civil War, the Lincoln Administration appointed her to run the Office of Missing Soldiers. Subsequently, Barton and her staff were able to locate over 22,000 "missing men." During the summer of 1865, Barton helped find, identify and properly bury the approximately 13,000 men who died in the infamous Andersonville prison camp in Georgia.

Travelling to Europe in 1868, Barton met the leaders of the International Committee of the Red Cross in Switzerland and agreed to serve as their representative for the American branch of the organization in 1869. After assisting with allied efforts during the Franco-Prussian War especially in the aftermath of the Siege of Paris, she was awarded the Golden Cross of Baden and the Prussian Iron Cross. She returned to the U.S. in 1873 and began lobbying for the establishment of the American Red Cross. Becoming president of the organization in 1877, it took until 1882 to create the first local society in 1882 located in Dansville, NY. Under her leadership the Red Cross performed significant humanitarian work with Ohio River flood victims in 1884; tornado victims in Illinois, and yellow fever epidemic victims in 1888; people affected by the Johnstown Flood in 1889; relief work in Turkey after the Armenian massacres of 1897; with P.O.W.s and refugees in Santiago, Cuba during the Spanish American War in 1898-9; and with the victims of the devastating Galveston hurricane in 1900. The National Museum of Civil War Medicine restored the Boarding house Barton lived in which served as her Office which is called Clara Barton's Missing Soldiers Office Museum. In 1975, the National Park Service established the Clara Barton National Historic Site located in Glen Echo, MD. Her home in North Oxford, MA is now a museum as well. – Joseph Carvalho III

Dorothea Lynde Dix

(B. APRIL 4, 1802 IN HAMDEN, ME;
D. JULY 17, 1887 IN TRENTON, NJ)
was an American activist on behalf of the indigent mentally ill who, through a vigorous program of lobbying state legislatures and the United States Congress, created the first generation of American mental asylums. During the Civil War, she served as a Superintendent of Army Nurses. Born in the town of Hampden, Maine, she grew up in Worcester, Massachusetts. In 1831, she

established a school for girls in Boston and operated the school until 1836. Among her many efforts regarding the treatment of the mentally ill, Dix conducted a critical state-wide study in 1840-41 of the scandalous care of the mentally ill in Massachusetts. She documented that people were kept "in cages, stalls, pens! Chained, naked, beaten with rods, and lashed into obedience." Her shocking report and her subsequent lobbying for reform led to the expansion and improvement at the state's psychiatric ("Mental") hospital in Worcester.
– Joseph Carvalho III

Sister of Providence Mary Caritas Geary

Sister of Providence Mary Caritas Geary's resume is long. It would be for the former president and chief executive officer of Mercy Medical Center.

Geary has dedicated her life to advancing the health care ministries of her congregation and advocating for affordable and accessible health care for all. This includes successfully lobbying U.S. lawmakers for restoration of $8 million in Medicare funds to Mercy and other Western Massachusetts hospitals in 1993. A quirk in a tax bill had left the hospitals with a loss of the funds and Geary pressed U.S. Rep. Richard Neal, D-Springfield, and then U.S. Sen. Edward Kennedy, D-Mass. – who at times sought Geary's input on health care reform – to work for their restoration even after President George H.W. Bush vetoed a bill that would have restored the money.

In 1991, she led a national committee of the Catholic Health Association that wrote a 40-page report entitled, "With Justice for All? The Ethics of Health Care Rationing." She spoke out at the time for health care policies that ensured coverage for all populations, including patients with AIDS and "crack babies or those mothers who have crack babies."

Now in her 95th year of life, Geary has spent more than 70 of those years as a member of the Sisters of Providence of Holyoke. Seventeen of them were devoted to helping the structure that replaced the original Mercy Hospital that was built by her congregation, in 1896, developed as a modern health care complex. Facilities added during her tenure as Mercy president include a rehabilitation center, the first inpatient one in the region, a family life birthing center and a surgery center for outpatient procedures within the hospital. She also got approval – after a multi-year effort – for the hospital's first linear accelerator for cancer radiation treatments in 1992.

Geary is well known for her community involvement – she was even called upon, in 1994, to chair one of the many task forces to study and make recommendations for the odor from the Regional Wastewater Treatment Plant at Bondi's Island – and for overseeing the evolution of her congregation's institutions and ministries to meet the region's health care needs and remain vital.

Mercy's cancer center, which underwent a $15 million expansion that opened in 2015, is named after her.

The daughter of immigrants from Ireland's County Cork, she was born Hannah Jean Geary. She became interested in nursing in high school and entered the Sisters of Providence, in 1947, after completing her training at Mercy's School of Nursing.

In her early years, Geary served as a registered nurse and a nursing supervisor at St. Vincent Hospital, in Worcester, which her order founded in 1893 and named after their patron, St. Vincent de Paul. After making her final vows in 1949, her order sent her back to Mercy to concentrate on dietary services.

During this time, she earned a bachelor's degree from Regis College in Weston, and a master's, with a concentration in nutrition, from Tufts University in Medford. She did a dietetic internship at the Frances Stern Food Clinic at New England Medical Center in Boston.

In 1959, she was assigned to be administrative dietitian at Providence Hospital in Holyoke, and in 1966 her congregation sent her to another one of their facilities – St. Luke's Hospital in Pittsfield as administrator.

Geary was administrator of St. Luke's when it merged with Pittsfield General to become what is now Berkshire Medical Center in 1969. She served briefly as its associate director.

She was elected that year as president of her congregation and retained that position for the maximum two-year terms of four years each. She then served as president of Mercy from 1977 through 1993.

During her presidency, Mercy developed one of the first hospitalist's programs in the country to compensate for the hospital's lack of a residency program and to avoid midnight calls to admitting doctors now off their shift.

In the years following her retirement as Mercy president, Geary helped her congregation convert its former Holyoke motherhouse into Providence Place, a 120-unit rental apartment retirement community for active, independent elders that opened in 1999.

She also helped oversee the construction of Mary's Meadow, a skilled nursing care facility on the Providence Place campus that also offers short-term rehabilitation services. It was described at the time it opened, in 2009, as being the first such facility in the state to be based on the "small house" social concept of care rather than a more medical model.

She continues to serve her congregation as vice president with Sister Kathleen Popko president. The congregation has received $2.5 million in state and federal funding to build 36 affordable housing units for

Sister Mary Caritas

119

senior citizens on property it owns in West Springfield.

Additional housing for the region's growing population of seniors is something Geary, whose religious name of "Caritas" means "charity," called for as early as 1988 when she chaired a task force on the elderly as part of Community 2000, an undertaking by United Way and the Community Council of Greater Springfield to evaluate and address regional needs. – Anne-Gerard Flynn

ALPHABETICAL LISTING OF NOTABLE WOMEN IN MEDICINE AND HEALTHCARE:

Sister Mary Alphonsa

(NÉE ROSE HAWTHORNE LATHROP, B. MAY 20, 1851 IN LENOX, MA; D. JULY 9, 1926 IN NEW YORK CITY) founded the first "free home" or hospice for the care of the terminally ill in the United States. – Joseph Carvalho III

Edith E. Baldwin, M.D.

(B. JAN. 20, 1890 IN SPRINGFIELD, MA; D. FEB. 25, 1970 IN SPRINGFIELD, MA) was "one of the most widely known and highly esteemed women physicians of Hampden County." Baldwin was a 1913 graduate of the Women's Medical College of Philadelphia and trained as a pediatrician. She wrote numerous professional articles for the leading medical journals of the time. Conducting a large private practice in Springfield, she was also a visiting physician at the Springfield Isolation Hospital, the Wesson Memorial Hospital in Springfield, and as a visiting physician for the Children's County Aid for many years. – Joseph Carvalho III

Blanche A. Blackman

(B. AUG. 19, 1878 IN KENDALLVILLE, INDIANA; D. FEB. 22, 1950 IN WHITE PLAINS, NY) became superintendent of the Springfield Hospital Training School in 1924. She had served in the Crimea during World War I. During her 21-year tenure at the hospital, nursing school enrollment increased, and work-hour restrictions led to the employment of graduate nurses to handle tasks previously managed by students. Springfield students were allowed to rotate at three affiliated hospitals: Wesson Maternity Hospital; Contagious Hospital in Providence, RI; and McLean Hospital in Belmont, MA for mental health nursing. Blackman retired as Superintendent of Nursing in 1945. Blackman served as the president of the Massachusetts League of Nursing Education; as a director of the National League of Nursing Education; and on the Massachusetts Board of Nurses Examiners. – Thomas L. Higgins, M.D.

Charlotte M. Boney, M.D.

is chair of the Department of Pediatrics at Baystate Children's Hospital, Springfield, MA. She is also Professor of Pediatrics at UMass Medical School-Baystate.
–Thomas L. Higgins, M.D.

Maura J. Brennan, M.D.

is chief of Geriatrics and Palliative Care at Baystate Medical Center in Springfield, MA and Professor of Medicine at University of Massachusetts Medical School – Baystate. She created the geriatrics fellowship at BMC. She is one of the country's first qualified hospice physicians to be certified as a hospice medical director. She has also been medical director of the Springfield Municipal Hospital. – Thomas L. Higgins, M.D. & Anne-Gerard Flynn

Ellen Leis(s)ing Brown, RN

(B. NOV. 8, 1863 IN LEYDEN, MA; D. DEC. 29, 1959 IN GREENFIELD, MA) was instrumental in founding of Franklin County Public Hospital, where she became head nurse. She later

worked for the Red Cross well into her 80s.
– Thomas L. Higgins, M.D.

Mary Brunton, RN

of Longmeadow, was instrumental in making Baystate Medical Center's Intensive Care Unit (ICU) one of the best in the country. Under her direction, the unit achieved the Beacon Award for critical care excellence for an unprecedented eight years in a row.
– Thomas L. Higgins, M.D.

Rose Kate Butler

(B. SEPT. 30, 1877 IN NEEDHAM, MA; D. 1847 IN FRAMINGHAM, MA) served as the executive director of the Holyoke Visiting Nurses Association from 1928 to 1948, leading the organization through its formative years.
– Joseph Carvalho III

Lucia "Lucy" Giuggio Carvalho

(b. 1956) is a trained oncology nurse, and founder of the successful Rays of Hope Walk & Run Toward the Cure of Breast Cancer . The most successful fundraising walk and run in western Massachusetts for breast cancer, Rays of Hope was founded in 1994 and has raised more than $14.2 million to-date. In 2011, the Rays of Hope awarded a $1.5 million grant to establish the Rays of Hope Center for Breast Cancer Research located inside the Pioneer Valley Life Sciences Institute, part of a collaborative effort, between clinicians at Baystate Medical Center and scientists at UMass-Amherst – Manon L. Mirabelli & Joseph Carvalho III

Hazel E. Chipman

[See entry in Chapter on Women in the Military]

Ju-Yu "Ruby" Chueh, Ph. D.

(B. TAIWAN) is the Co-director of the New England Center for Stroke Research at the University of Massachusetts Medical School in Worcester. – Joseph Carvalho III

Ava Jo Collins, MHA, FACHE

is the Chief Operating Officer of Saint Vincent Hospital in Worcester, MA.
– Joseph Carvalho III

Mary Louise (Griswold) Deane

(B. DEC. 2, 1835 IN COLRAIN, MA; D. JAN. 7, 1912 IN GREENFIELD, MA) created the Women's Board of Organized Work (BOOW) at the Franklin County Public Hospital in 1895. This was one of the first hospital auxiliaries in Massachusetts. – Thomas L. Higgins, M.D.

Henrietta B. (Wilcox) Dexter

(B. JUNE 27, 1842 IN SPRINGFIELD, MA; D. MAY 11, 1916 IN SPRINGFIELD, MA) largely through her efforts that the first school for mentally handicapped children was established in Springfield. She was a prominent member of the governing Board of the Baldwinville Hospital Cottages for Children for 20 years. – Joseph Carvalho III

Mary Phylinda Dole

(B. AUGUST 31, 1862 IN SHELBURNE, MA; D. FEBRUARY 23, 1947 IN SHELBURNE, MA) was orphaned at a young age, and was sent to live in Ashfield, MA with her father's cousin in 1871. Dole graduated from Mount Holyoke Female Seminary in 1886, then went on to study at the Women's Medical College of Baltimore, Maryland, where she earned an M.D. degree in 1888. From 1889-1890, Dr. Dole interned at the New England Hospital for Women and Children in Boston, Massachusetts. In 1891, Dole began a private practice in Greenfield, MA. She was "heartily welcomed" into the community by the head of the local medical society largely because she was willing to respond to the emergency calls from the hill towns, which other local doctors found inconvenient. It is said that Dr. Dole was "always ready with her trusty horse and a carriage or sleigh, depending upon the season."

In 1893, she left Greenfield for further study in Germany and France, where she worked at the Pasteur Institute and was present at the first successful trial of a diphtheria vaccine. Dole returned to Greenfield a year and a half later, practicing medicine there until she moved to New Haven, CT in 1906. In 1919, she returned to the Pioneer Valley, relocating to Northampton. From 1901-1907, Dole served as a trustee of Mount Holyoke College. She was President of the Mount Holyoke Club of Franklin County and honorary president of the Mount Holyoke Club of New Haven, CT. On May 7, 1937 the Alumnae Association awarded Dole the Gold Medal for Eminent Service. In 1941, she published her autobiography, *A Doctor in Homespun*. Her papers are held by Mount Holyoke College. – Betsy McKee, Pioneer Valley History Network

Eva Jean (Parmelee) Dollin

(B. 1883 IN MORRISTOWN, NY; D. 1939 IN LONDON, ENGLAND) was a Springfield nurse who volunteered to serve as an Army nurse during WWI, serving overseas in a British military hospital treating severe combat injuries of hundreds of wounded soldiers. The U.S. Army's Adjutant General's Office records state that Parmalee was "awarded British Military Medal, List No. 27, Spt. 3, 1918." The document detailed the acts of gallantry performed: "When knocked down, wounded and badly shaken by explosion of a bomb during a raid of hostile (German) aircraft on the night of September 4, 1917, with great self-sacrifice continued to care for wounded patients in her ward during the remainder of the night." For that act of bravery, Parmalee was awarded the British Royal Red Cross (second class). After the war, she married a British citizen and stayed in England. The last her friends in Springfield heard from her was just before a Luftwaffe bombing raid that destroyed her home in 1939 during the "London Blitz." Eva's father was a doctor and a co-founder of Springfield Hospital. – Joseph Carvalho III

Top left: Dr. Julia Bauman. **Top right:** Clara Mary Greenough. **Bottom left:** Laura Pinkston Koenigs. **Above:** Diane Kelly.

Gladys Fernandez, M.D.

is the manager of Simulation Programs, assistant program director, Baystate Surgical Residency, and interim clerkship director, Department of Surgery, Baystate Medical Center. – Thomas L. Higgins, M.D.

Grace C. Fitzgibbon, M.D.D.O.

(B. JULY 29, 1885 IN HOLYOKE, MA) graduated from the Massachusetts College of Osteopathy in 1918. She was one of the state's first female Osteopaths.
– Joseph Carvalho III

Suzanne Miles Freeman

(B. JAN. 21, 1880 IN NOVA SCOTIA, CANADA; D. AU. 20, 1969 IN NATICK, MA) immigrated to the United State in 1898 and became a naturalized U.S. citizen. She was the Superintendent of the Hahnemann Hospital in Worcester, MA for over 20 years. She graduated from the Massachusetts Homeopathic Hospital Training School in Boston in 1906. In 1909, She was appointed supervisor of the Hahnemann Hospital's Nurse's Training School serving for four years. During her tenure as superintendent beginning in 1913, "She efficiently aided in the development of that institution," from a small medical facility to a hospital, "of generous capacity and well-known usefulness." By 1931, the hospital was admitting over 2,200 patients annually. Historian John Nelson suggests that, "Probably no woman in the State has served longer as superintendent of an institution of this kind." – Joseph Carvalho III

Rebecca L. Glickman

(B. 1865 IN LITHUANIA; D. 1928 IN SPRINGFIELD, MA) helped found in 1912, and was the first president of the Jewish Home for the Aged on Massassoit St. in Springfield until 1920. She emigrated to the United States in the 1880s. – Joseph Carvalho III

Clara Mary Greenough, M.D.

(B. MAR.16, 1872 IN DEERFIELD, MA; D. DEC. 12, 1963 IN DEERFIELD,MA) was a graduate of Smith College and received her M.D. from Northwestern. During and after World War I, she worked in France and Germany, returning to Greenfield, MA in 1920 where she practiced for many years. – Thomas L. Higgins, M.D.

Elizabeth Inga Hansen

(B. DEC. 12, 1886 IN NAPLES, ME;
D. AUG. 10, 1974 IN PINELLAS, FLA)
was the Superintendent of the Harrington Memorial Hospital established in Southbridge, MA in 1931. Among Hansen's hospital management experiences prior to accepting the position heading up the Harrington Memorial Hospital in the early 1930s was her work at a hospital in Colombo, Ceylon (today's Sri Lanka) in 1916 on behalf of the American Board of Commissioners for Foreign Missions.
– Joseph Carvalho III

Harriet Louise Hardy

(B. SEPT. 23,1906 IN ARLINGTON, MA;
D. OCT. 13,1993 IN HOLYOKE, MA)
working as the school physician at Northfield Seminary for Girls, Hardy saved many lives during the hurricane of 1938. Later, she became the first female associate clinical professor at Harvard (1958) and founded the national Beryllium registry; and worked at the NIH. – Thomas L. Higgins, M.D.

Doreen M. Hutchinson, RN

(B. JUNE 24, 1948)
is Vice-president of Operations and Patient Care at Fairview Hospital, Berkshire Health Systems in Great Barrington, MA, appointed in 2000. Prior to that position, she served as Vice-president of Patient Care Services at Fairview from 1994 to 2000.
– Joseph Carvalho III

Diane Kelly, DNP, MBA, RN

of Dalton, MA is the Chief Operating Officer of Berkshire Medical Center in Pittsfield, MA, assuming that position in 2008. Prior to that, Kelly served as Vice President of Quality and Safety for Berkshire Medical Center from 2002-2008. She began working at Berkshire Medical Center in 1985. – Joseph Carvalho III

Catherine Maloney (O'Leary) Kennedy, M.D.

(B. 1845 IN IRELAND; D. APR. 10, 1908 IN SPRINGFIELD, MA) studied medicine at the Women's Medical College in Philadelphia graduating in 1873. She became the first Roman Catholic female physician to practice in Hampden County, Massachusetts when she opened her office in Springfield in 1876. Kennedy maintained her practice in the city for 25 years. Her family came to the United States when she was 14 years old. Her husband Charles G. Kennedy served in the 38th Pennsylvania Volunteer Infantry Regiment and was severely wounded in the head and died several years later from the effects of that wound. It was then that Catherine decided to enter medical school. – Margaret Humberston & Joseph Carvalho III

Laura Pinkston Koenigs, M.D.

(B. OCT. 31, 1955) of Longmeadow, is the vice chair of Education and program director for the Department of Pediatrics at Baystate Children's Hospital, Springfield, MA. She is also Associate Professor of Pediatrics at University of Massachusetts Medical School – Baystate. – Thomas L. Higgins, M.D.

Dorothea (Cross) Leighton, M.D.

(b. September 2, 1908 in Lunenburg, MA; d. August 15, 1989 in Fresno, CA) was an American social psychiatrist and a founder of the field of medical anthropology. She attended Bryn Mawr College, where she studied chemistry and biology graduating in 1930. That year she began work at the Johns Hopkins Hospital as a technician, attending Johns Hopkins School of Medicine, and graduated with her MD in 1936. She married a classmate, Alexander Leighton, in 1937. In 1942, Leighton published a book that compared the Navajo philosophy of health with that of whites. She then served as a physician with the Indian Personality Research Project from 1942–1945. During

this time, she worked with Clyde Kluckhohn and John Adair. Her 1944 book Navajo at the Door, with Alexander Leighton, is considered "the earliest example of applied medical anthropology." Leighton founded the Society for Medical Anthropology while a professor at the University of North Carolina and was its first president. – Joseph Carvalho III

Julia Lewandowska-Bauman, M.D.

(B. 1883 IN POLAND; D. 1944 IN HOLYOKE, MA) was one of Holyoke's most respected obstetricians. According to her biographer Dr. Marcella Kelly, Dr. Bauman "brought more babies into the world than any other [local] physician of her time." Her family immigrated to Chicopee in 1883 where she received her early education. Graduating with her M.D. from the Pennsylvania Women's College in Philadelphia in 1911, she opened her general practice in Holyoke that same year. In 1916, an American Historical Society publication noted that Bauman was "the only woman of Polish extraction east of Chicago engaged in the practice of medicine." In spite of the demands of her practice, she was deeply involved in efforts to improve health and sanitation, serving on the State Tuberculosis Association and, locally, on the Holyoke Municipal League, the Baby's Hygiene Society, the Board of Health, and the Parks and Playgrounds Commission. She also belonged to several professional medical associations and was on the staff of Providence Hospital.

Her leadership among Polish women's organizations extended to the state and national level: she helped organize and lead the Polish Women's Alliance of America and the Federation of Polish Women's Clubs in Massachusetts and was president of the local Polish Women's Club. – Eileen M. Crosby

Wendy Marsh, M.D., MSc

is the Director of the Bipolar Disorders Specialty Clinic; Medical Director of the Depression Specialty Clinic; and Psychiatrist

for MCPAP for Moms, Women's Mental Health Specialty Clinic at the University of Massachusetts Medical School in Worcester, MA. – Joseph Carvalho III

Joanne Marqusee

(B. DEC. 10, 1956) is the President and CEO of Cooley Dickinson Hospital, appointed in 2014. She joined the hospital staff shortly after its affiliation with Massachusetts General Hospital. She and her staff opened the Mass General Cancer Center at Cooley Dickinson Hospital in the fall of 2015. This service provides coordinated care between the emergency department physician at Cooley Dickinson and a neurologist at Mass General, who examines the patient remotely. Before joining Colley Dickinson, Marqusee served as Chief Operating Officer/Executive Vice President at Hallmark Health, which is comprised of acute care hospitals Lawrence Memorial of Medford and Melrose-Wakefield of Melrose as well as a VNA-Hospice and a number of community-based sites. Before

joining Hallmark Health, Joanne was senior vice president, operations, at Harvard-affiliated Beth Israel Deaconess Medical Center in Boston, where she led both clinical and non-clinical departments and held a series of progressively responsible positions starting in 1992. Earlier in her career, Joanne held positions in government, including at the New York City Health and Hospitals Corporation and the New York State Department of Health. – Joseph Carvalho II

Kristin Mattocks, PhD, MPH

is an Associate Professor of Quantitative Health Sciences, Psychiatry and Family Medicine at the University of Massachusetts Medical School and the Associate Chief of Staff for Research & Education at VA Central Western Massachusetts Healthcare System. Dr. Mattocks' research includes understanding access to comprehensive health care for women Veterans, pregnancy and maternity care coordination among women Veterans in VA care and comprehensive research on the Veterans Choice Program to examine network adequacy within non-VA community provider networks.

Maura McCaffrey

served until 2018 as the President and CEO of Health New England, succeeding Peter Straley in 2014. McCaffrey started working at Health New England in 2002 as a pharmacist. Prior to her appointment at President, McCaffrey served as Health New England's Chief Operating Officer. – Jim Kinney

Elizabeth Moore, R.N.

(B.1843 IN GLASGOW, SCOTLAND; D. JUN.18, 1923 IN SPRINGFIELD, MA) was popularly known as "Mother Moore" at the Springfield Hospital where she served for seventeen years, retiring as superintendent of

Bottom left: J. Aleah Nesteby. Top left: Joanne Marqusee. Top right: Maura McCaffrey

the private ward. A graduate of the Women's Training Hospital in New York City, she later became superintendent of the Nursery and Children's Hospital in NYC. She also worked at the Hampden Institute in Hampton, VA before coming to Springfield.
– Joseph Carvalho III

J. Aleah Nesteby, MSN, FNP
is a nurse practitioner at Cooley-Dickinson Hospital. She helped found the transgender program at Baystate before moving to CDH.
– Thomas L. Higgins, M.D.

Jerri Lin Nielsen, M.D.
(NÉE CAHILL; B. MAR. 1, 1952 IN OHIO; D. JUNE 23, 2009 IN SOUTHWICK, MA)
was an American physician with extensive emergency room experience, who famously self-treated her breast cancer while stationed at Amundsen–Scott South Pole Station in

Antarctica until she could be evacuated.
– Joseph Carvalho III

Thu Hoang Pham
(B. FEB. 16, 1961 IN VIETNAM) of Springfield served as project coordinator of the Vietnamese Health Project at Mercy Medical Center in Springfield beginning in 1997, and was honored in 2003 with a Public Health Luminary Award by the City of Springfield. In 2011, the Sister of Providence Health System and Pham were recognized with the 2011 "Inclusive Culture of Excellence award" celebrating the 15th year of the Vietnamese Health Project. – Alex Peshkov

Top: Dr. Jerri Nielsen at the South Pole Station (*The Republican* file, submitted photo). **Above:** Thu Hoang Pham. **Right top:** Sister Mary Providence.
Right: Kristin Mattocks

Nancy Shendell-Falik

St. Vincent Hospital, Worcester, MA

Founded as a small Catholic community hospital by the Sisters of Providence in 1893, the original 12-bed hospital overlooked the city of Worcester from Vernon Hill. The facility was first named after Saint Vincent de Paul, the patron saint of the Sister's order. In 1898, the hospital was incorporated, and in 1899, the Sisters expanded into a 150-bed building to further their ability to care for the community. Despite this incredible expansion, the need for hospital rooms was still quite

great, so the sisters added an additional 60-bed wing in 1918. There was a great need for quality nurses in the area. In response, the Worcester hospital opened a nursing school in 1900. In addition to the nursing school, a residence for both Sisters and student nurses was constructed in 1922. The nursing school flourished for many years, until it was finally closed in 1988. While the nursing school officially closed, the legacy of nursing instruction continues today at Saint Vincent Hospital.

Sister Mary Providence

(BORN MARY HORAN IN ONTARIO, CAN IN 1850; D. 1943 IN HOLYOKE, MA)

served for 18 years as the Superior of the Sisters of Providence which in 1892 became a Springfield Diocesan Order. During her tenure as Superior, General Treasurer, and Assistant Mother Superior, the Order established five general hospitals, among them Mercy Hospital in Springfield. She established the Mercy Hospital Training School in 1900 and was one of the founders and first president of the New England Conference of Catholic Hospitals. – Joseph Carvalho III

Sisters of Providence

The Sisters of Providence, founded in 1892, are an offshoot of the Sisters of Charity of St. Vincent de Paul of Kingston, Ontario, Canada. The Sisters of Charity had ministered to orphans and the sick in Holyoke, MA since 1873. The Sisters of Providence expanded their ministries to care for people in need; to the sick, elderly, homeless, and orphaned children. They built hospitals in Holyoke, Worcester, Springfield, Montague, Pittsfield, and North Carolina. They opened homes for orphans, nursing homes, rehabilitation centers, shelters for homeless people and battered women. They opened soup kitchens as well as a spiritual direction center and a spiritual life center. – Sister of St. Joseph Judith E. Kappenman

Rhoda Rhoades

(B. 1751; D. 25 SEPT. 1841 IN HUNTINGTON, MA; BURIED IN NORWICH BRIDGE CEMETERY)

was a noted "Indian Doctress." According to historian/anthropologist Marge Brushac, Dr. Rhoades was particularly known for a product she called "The Extract." Nineteenth Century local historian Myron Munson interviewed a local resident, a "Deacon Ellis", in the 1880s, who declared, "Old Rhoda could cure anyone outside of the grave, and – almost – those who had lain in it only a little while." – Condensed from Marge Bruchac, *In Search of the Indian Doctress – Rhoda Rhoades*, Pioneer Valley Historical Network website.

Grace Allen (Blodgett) Seelye

(B. OCT. 26, 1867 IN NEWTON, MA; D. JUNE 19, 1953 IN NORTHAMPTON, MA)

was one of the founders of the Visiting Nurse Association in Springfield in 1914, and served as its first president for sixteen years. She continued her involvement with that organization in various capacities for a total of forty years. – Joseph Carvalho III

Nancy Shendell-Falik, RN, MA

Nancy Shendell-Falik, RN, MA, was appointed president of Baystate Medical Center and senior vice president of hospital relations for Baystate Health on October 1, 2015. Joining Baystate Health in July of 2013, she served in the dual position at Baystate Health of senior vice president/chief operating officer, and chief nursing officer for Baystate Medical Center for two years prior to her promotion. Before coming to Baystate Health, Shendell-Falik served as senior vice president for Patient Care Services and chief nursing officer at Tufts Medical Center and Floating Hospital for Children in Boston, MA. Prior to her work in Boston, she served as senior vice president, Patient Care Services, at Newark Beth Israel Medical Center in New Jersey. – Joseph Carvalho III

Ellen (Goodell) Smith

(B. 1835 IN [NORTH] BELCHERTOWN, MA; D. 1906 IN BELCHERTOWN, MA) attended Dr. Trall's Medical College in New York City and graduated with honors in 1861. In 1867, she married Dr. John Brown Smith in Minnesota and the couple went on to establish the first sanitarium and "Turkish Bath" in St. Paul, MN. Smith returned to Belchertown in 1874. During her long career in health care, she worked in several health institutes in New England, the Midwest, and California. She lectured and wrote on health and temperance for over 40 years. She argued for vegetarianism and a healthy life style. Her book, *The Art of Living,* had a large following in the United States and abroad. She also wrote *The Fat of the Land and How to Live on It* in 1896. – Pioneer Valley History Network

Phoebe A. Sprague, M.D.

(B. DEC. 11, 1845; D. NOV. 29, 1904 IN ALBION, NY) began her medical practice in Springfield in 1873, served as City Physician for a time and became one of "the most celebrated early women physicians in Springfield." – Joseph Carvalho III

Amber Angelia Starbuck, M.D.

(B. NOV. 3, 1878 IN GILL, MA; D. MAY 5, 1969 IN MIDDLEFIELD, MA) was appointed as one of the first women's pathologists in the region by the Wesson Memorial Hospital in Springfield, serving from 1907-1910. Concurrently, she was appointed Superintendent of the hospital from 1908-1910. Dr. Starbuck also served as a director of the Society for the Prevention of Cruelty to Children and along with her work as a school physician for three Western Massachusetts School districts, and as the founder of the Agra-Rhetan Highland Health Center aka "The Big House" respite center in Middlefield, MA. advanced children's health in significant ways during her long medical career. – Joseph Carvalho III

Mihaela M. Stefan, M.D.

(B. JUN. 10, 1957) is director of the Perioperative Clinic and Medical Consultation Program for Hospital Medicine at Baystate Medical Center, Springfield, MA. – Thomas L. Higgins, M.D.

Yuka-Marie Vinagre, M.D.

(B. MAY 27, 1965) is the Chief of Critical Care Medicine and Associate Chief Medical Officer of Saint Vincent Hospital in Worcester, MA. – Joseph Carvalho III

Joan M. Vitello-Cicciu, Ph.D., RN, NEA-BC, FAHA, FAAN

(B. JAN. 19, 1949) is the Dean of the Graduate School of Nursing at the University of Massachusetts Medical School in Worcester, MA. – Joseph Carvalho III

Wesson Maternity Hospital

was opened in 1908 in Springfield.

Above left: Dr. Ellen (Goodell) Smith. **Above:** Dr. Amber Angelina Starbuck (Photo from Clifton Johnson, *Hampden County, 1636-1936* (1936)

Katherine B. Wilson

has served as President and CEO of Behavioral Health Network, Inc since 1984. Under Kathy's leadership, BHN has evolved into a primary provider of mental health, substance abuse and developmental disability services in the Pioneer Valley, serving over 40,000 individuals per year and employing over 2,200 professionals/paraprofessionals. Kathy's leadership in local and statewide initiatives is recognized throughout Massachusetts, as she works tirelessly to shape policy to ensure individuals and family have access to the care they need to live healthy, productive lives. Trained as a family therapist, she left private practice when President John F. Kennedy decreed the Community Mental Health Centers Act.

Kathy joined the Department of Mental Health and Mental Retardation team in Western Massachusetts where she helped design community programs and found new homes for residents of Belchertown State School and Northampton State Hospital. Kathy also helped to design the Community Care Mental Health Center into the present organization, Behavioral Health Network.

Under her leadership, BHN has been very successful in ensuring high quality care, participating in research, and meeting performance expectations of funders. Kathy serves on the Board of Directors of the Association for Behavioral Healthcare, Massachusetts' state trade association representing mental health and addiction providers, as well as on the Board of the Association of Developmental Disability Providers, Massachusetts state trade association representing intellectual/developmental disability providers.

In Springfield, BHN intervenes at critical points when an individual is returning to the community from incarceration, or engaged within the judicial or police systems. BHN offers many types of psychiatric and

Katherine B. Wilson

counseling services, as well as specialty programs for individuals with mental health and/or substance use needs.

As the Forensic Service Provider for the Springfield District Court's Recovery With Justice (RWJ) specialty court, BHN works to reduce recidivism and increase diversion from incarceration for qualified offenders as a path to mental health recovery. Under her leadership, BHN has partnered with area police departments and offered Crisis Intervention Training (CIT) which provides officers with skills needed to de-escalate those in a psychiatric crisis, and re-direct them to treatment or support in lieu of jail. – Anne-Gerard Flynn & Joseph Carvalho III

Worcester Hahnemann Hospital School of Nursing

was founded in 1900 and operated until both hospital and school was closed in 1989.

Worcester Society for District Nursing

was organized in 1892 and incorporated in 1899, the seventh such society in the United States. This organization provided nursing services to the sick in their homes, in essence a "visiting nurse" service. By 1908, over one hundred Worcester physicians requested this service for their patients with average nursing visits per day of sixty-four patients under the leadership of its President Harriet E. Clarke. – Joseph Carvalho III

Susie Walking Bear Yellowtail

(B. JAN. 27, 1903 IN CROW, MONTANA; D. DEC. 25, 1981 IN WYOLA, BIG HORN, MONTANA) was the first Native American to become a registered nurse (RN). She was orphaned as a young child in Montana, and apparently had enough promise that missionaries sent her east on scholarship to Deerfield academy; then attended Franklin County Hospital's school of nursing in the 1920s, and then went on to Boston City Hospital. She was one of the founders of the Indian Health Service and from 1930 to 1960 travelled to reservations throughout America, addressing social, educational and health needs with Native Americans. She founded the Native American Nurses Association. – Thomas L. Higgins, M.D.

CHAPTER SEVEN

WOMEN
at Work

BY NANCY CREED
President of the Springfield Regional Chamber of Commerce, Springfield, MA

Many of the women featured in the pages you are about to read paved the way and passed on their wisdom, so that in 2016, it was possible for me to become the first woman president of the Springfield Regional Chamber in its 125-year history. I am proud to be writing an introduction to the following chapter on Women in Business from Western and Central Massachusetts.

I am also proud to be a woman who always knew, as I think many of these women did, that I could succeed in my career because of my talents, drive, determination, and belief in myself.

While today more and more women are starting businesses, I think back to Julia Buxton, an early entrepreneur who began a home business in Agawam, making leather key holders at the turn of the century. From that home-based leather goods business was born Buxton Co., which grew into an internationally known and respected business, now located in Chicopee. Julia's daughter, also named Julia, succeeded her mother as head of Buxton and was the first women to serve on the Chamber's Board of Directors. In fact, Julia was the founder of what is now known as the Professional Women's Chamber. She was the first recipient of the organization's Women of the Year award in 1954.

As President of the Springfield Regional Chamber, and for many years before that, as the Chamber's Vice President of Marketing and Communications, I have had the privilege of working with some of the women featured in the following pages – Sally Fuller; Diane Doherty; Carol Moore Cutting; Kerry Dietz. The Springfield Regional Chamber works to empower women in business and in the community, as all of us work together to make the entire region a vibrant place to live and work. I and the other women who are leading businesses today are paving the way for the next generation of women leaders.

Imagine the conversations that might take place if we could gather all of these women past, present and future in one room. The next best thing is to let yourself be inspired by these women – I know I have been.

Women of Business & Labor "The Mill Girls"

BY JACQUELINE T. LYNCH

In an era when women were financially dependent on men and the poorhouse was a much-feared reality, women factory workers found independence through hard work and created their own revolution in early years of the Industrial Revolution.

Francis Lowell saw in unmarried women a huge untapped labor pool for his new industrial experiment. It was a cotton textile mill in Waltham where the entire process of manufacturing cotton cloth, from the raw bale to the finished bolt, would be done in several steps under one roof. The idea was new, and the hiring of women, rather than men, to operate the weaving, spinning, and carding machines made females the dominant workforce in the cotton, woolen, and silk mills of New England.

The planned industrial city of Lowell was named for him by his partners, the Boston Associates, and the experiment was copied in Chicopee, where the factories sent agents in wagons out to the Berkshires and up into Vermont to recruit vast numbers of female workers, who were usually from about fifteen to twenty-five years old.

The factories boasted a respectable environment for the young ladies. The women would live in company dormitories, upwards of six girls to a room. They ate together in the dining room, and their room and board was deducted from their monthly pay. They were chaperoned by older women the company hired, usually widows who were considered very respectable. The "mill girls" would be required to go to church, and they had a 10 o'clock curfew.

In the 1830s, they worked eleven hours a day, and another eight hours on Saturday, over sixty hours a week. The lack of career

Opposite Page: Workers in Berkshire Mills in Adams, Massachusetts.
Above: 14 year old "Spooler tender," July 10, 1916 at the Berkshire Cotton Mills, Adams, MA. (Lewis Wickes Hine Photograph Collection, Library of Congress)

options for women at this time still made this arrangement a desirable opportunity for women who yearned, or needed, to support themselves and their families.

They changed the American economy, because now that the factories were making cloth so cheaply, people no longer had to weave their own cloth at home, as they had done for centuries.

Mills girls changed society. They married on average a little later than their mothers' generation, and had fewer children than their mothers' generation. They chose spouses most often from among men they either met in the mills or the brothers and cousins of the girls they worked and lived with, and arranged marriages largely became a thing of the past.

The success of the textile mills was copied all over the northeast, and western Massachusetts was well represented in this revolution; the planned industrial city of Holyoke that followed, including the Skinner silk mill, was an important example, but the consequences of overproduction led to falling prices, which prompted the factory owners to make drastic changes.

Above: 15 year old "Drawing-in" on July 10, 1916 at the Berkshire Cotton Mills in Adams, Massachusetts. (Lewis Wickes Hine Photograph Collection, Library of Congress)

The young women were already working eleven hours a day in the 1830s. By the 1850s, they worked thirteen and a half hours a day, plus eight hours on Saturday. They were working over seventy-five hours per week. They were assigned more machines to tend at once, and the speed of the machines was increased, which also increased the danger of the work and the women's exhaustion. Salaries were reduced.

Some strikes occurred, but most were unsuccessful. The few unions that formed had no political clout.

The era of the Yankee mill girl drew to a close not only under these challenges, but under the pressures as well of The Panic of 1857, a financial crash felt most severely in New England. Many factories closed, stores and businesses closed, and other factories went on half time, laid off workers, and cut wages. The Civil War also caused New England cotton mills to close or reduce operations until the hostilities ended, as the raw cotton was unavailable from the South.

Irish immigrants began to flock to the factories, and were followed by many waves of new immigrants from other countries for decades to come. The United States had transformed from a subsistence agricultural economy to an industrial and consumer economy, largely through the hands of women.

Top Left: Group of workers in the Dwight Mfg. Co. Sophie Motralske, (smallest girl), 3 Lawrence Rd. Works in spinning room, Nov. 1911, Chicopee, Massachusetts. (Lewis Wickes Hine Photograph Collection, Library of Congress)

Left: Sophie, a young spinner. Working in Spinning Room #7 . Dwight Mfg. Co., Chicopee, Massachusetts, November, 1911. (Lewis Wickes Hine Photograph Collection, Library of Congress)

(Opposite Page) **Top left:** Suzanne Beck. **Top right:** Persis Foster Albee. **Bottom right:** Patricia Crowell Begrowicz.

Persis Foster (Eames) Albee

(B. MAY 30, 1836 I NEWRY, ME; D. DEC.7, 1914
IN TEMPLETON, MA) was a professional
saleswoman for the California Perfume
Company, which later became Avon Products,
and is considered the first "Avon Lady" due
to her successful marketing techniques and
her recruiting and training of other sales
personnel. She was a pioneer in getting
women to become financially independent.
– Joseph Carvalho III

Suzanne Beck

(B. JULY 8, 1956) is the Executive Director of the
Greater Northampton Chamber of Commerce,
with membership of over 700 Northampton
area businesses and organizations. She
was appointed to that post in June of 1992.
She serves on the Development Advisory
Committee for the City of Northampton; and
on the Board of Trustees for Cooley Dickinson
Hospital. Beck was a founding member of the
Board of Directors for "Leadership Pioneer
Valley." Prior to her appointment as Executive
Director of the GNCC, Beck, a Smith College
graduate, served as Associate Director of
Springfield Central in Springfield, MA from
1983 to 1992. – Joseph Carvalho III

Patricia Crowell Begrowicz

(B. APR. 2, 1959) is the owner and president
of Onyx Specialty Papers Co. in South Lee,
MA. She served as the General Manager for
MeadWestvaco's Specialty Papers Division
headquartered in South Lee, Massachusetts.
She joined the Specialty Papers' business
in 1998 as Vice President of Operations. She
also served as Vice President of Technology
and New Business Development, and Vice
President of Commercial Operations during
her 11 years with the business unit. Begrowicz

joined Mead in 1996 at the Chillicothe Ohio
Research Center as Director of Process
Technologies. Prior to joining Mead, Begrowicz
served with Union Camp Corporation where
she served in various technical roles at the
company's mills in Virginia, South Carolina
and Georgia. In 2017, the Boston Globe listed
her business as one of the top-100 women-led
businesses in Massachusetts.
– Joseph Carvalho III

Betsy J. Bernard

(B. MAY 16, 1955 IN HOLYOKE, MA) was appointed
president of AT&T Corp., the no. 2 job at
one of the nation's largest corporations,
in 2002, moving from a position in which
she had headed the company's $11 billion
consumer division. She was 47 years old at
the time she became the corporation's first
woman president. Bernard credited her

Julia Bessie Buxton

mother, Barbara C. Bernard of Holyoke, with preparing her for success. The elder Bernard was a radio and television show host and newspaper columnist during a lengthy career in journalism.

Betsy attended public elementary school in Holyoke and then graduated from the MacDuffie School. She went on to attend St. Lawrence University, where, during her junior and senior years, took an internship with AT&T. She accepted the company's offer of a permanent job when she graduated. She was convinced to leave AT&T by one of her mentors, David Dorman, who was then chief executive of Pacific Bell. Bernard worked at Pacific Telesis and Pacific Bell Communications before going to U.S. West, another telephone company. In 2001, Dorman recruited her to become president and chief executive of AT&T Consumer, the telephone giant's long distance and local service unit. He then tapped her for the presidency when he became chairman and CEO of AT&T.

During her time at AT&T, Bernard was frequently named one of the 50 most powerful women in business by Fortune magazine.

Bernard's significant board experience spans over 15 years and includes United Technologies, Principal Financial Group, Serco Group plc, URS, Telular, Zimmer Holdings and Sito Mobile. Bernard chairs the strategic issues committee at the Principal Financial Group and is a member of their audit and finance committees. Additionally, she chairs the nominating committee of Zimmer Holdings and serves on its compensation committee. She served as the lead director of SITO Mobile from 20014 through 2017. Bernard serves as a member of advisory boards for GroTech, Innovate Partners and the Silverfern Group.
– Cynthia G. Simison

Catherine (Gibbs) Bodurtha
(B. DEC. 27, 1827 IN BLANDFORD; D. JUNE 9, 1878 IN AGAWAM, MA) owned and operated a uniform business out of her home in Agawam, MA during the Civil War. Employing several women, she made uniforms for local state regiments of the Union Army.
– Robert Magovern

Barbara Bush
(B. DEC. 14, 1916 IN WESTFIELD, MA; D. OCT. 8, 1994 IN WESTFIELD, MA) was a local businesswoman, historian and preservationist. She was the owner of Elm Business Services in Westfield, and worked for a time as assistant director of the Westfield Chamber of Commerce. She also worked for 22 years at the Woronoco Savings Bank and was eventually promoted to Assistant Treasurer. She was an active member of the Westfield Historical Society, and served as president of its board of trustees, and as a member of the Westfield Historical Commission, was a key organizer of the 1969 Westfield Tricentennial Committee. She served on many community boards including the Westfield Athenaeum Board of Trustees. In 1989, Barbara Bush was voted Woman of the Year by the Business and Professional Women's Club.
– Thomas and Susan Sawyer

Julia Bessie Buxton
(B. FEB. 19, 1883 IN WARREN, MA; D. OCT. 1978 IN SPRINGFIELD, MA) mother of six children started in business in a little shop at her home making leather novelties at the turn of the 20th Century. From that little shop, it grew into an internationally known and respected business. At the height of her career, she was referred to as the "Dean of Women Industrial Executives in New England." It is recorded that she still went into the office daily at the age of 82 to sign checks and payrolls. As a suffragette, Buxton was one of the first women elected to the Republican City Committee, and was president of the Springfield District Republican Club. A Westfield State College graduate, Buxton also was an officer of the Women's Auxiliary of Goodwill Industries in Springfield. She served as Springfield College's first female Trustee and was the first woman to serve as director of the Springfield Chamber of Commerce. Buxton established a professorship at Springfield College as well as a trust at Hampden Bank to help worthy Springfield nonprofit organizations. That trust now lives on at the Community Foundation and was transferred in 1999 valued at $3 million dollars. In 1952, Buxton started what has evolved into the Woman's Partnership of the Greater Springfield Chamber of Commerce, and was their first "Woman of the Year" in 1954. The South End Bridge connecting Springfield to Agawam over the Connecticut River is named after her. – Katie Zobell & Joseph Carvalho III

Patricia A. "Tricia" Canavan
(B. JAN. 24, 1969)
is the president of United Personnel in Springfield, MA. In addition to her responsibilities as company president, Tricia serves on several nonprofit boards, including the Baystate Health Foundation, the Springfield Public Forum, the Springfield Chamber of Commerce, Springfield Business Leaders for Education and the Massachusetts Workforce Development Board. In 2017, the *Boston Globe* listed her business as one of the top-100 women-led businesses in Massachusetts. – Joseph Carvalho III

Abbie (Sullivan) Cray
(B. 1849 IN IRELAND; D. 1924 IN HOLYOKE, MA)
overcame becoming widowed with ten children in 1882 to becoming one of Holyoke's most successful businesswomen by 1883. Hard working and astute, Cray built her fortune and credit to the point where she had several apartment buildings built on Dwight Street by 1905. Further expanding her real estate holdings, she had two more apartment buildings built by 1910 on Walnut Street, one of which was called "The Cray."
– Joseph Carvalho III

Carol Moore Cutting
(B. IN ALABAMA)
owner and general manager of Cutting Edge Broadcasting, established the WEIB 106.3 Smooth FM radio station and became the first African-American woman in Massachusetts to operate a radio station. In 2000, she was recognized with a Business Woman of Distinction Award; and in 2010, she and her husband Dr. Gerald B. Cutting were honored by the Urban League of Springfield with their "Urban Influencer" Award. She is board member of the National Association of Black-owned Broadcasters. – Judith Kelliher

Pearl Marion (Smith) Daniels
(B. JUNE 20, 1885 IN NORTHBOROUGH, MA; D. JUNE 20, 1969 IN GRAFTON, MA)
with her husband Herbert, co-founded the Daniel's Rhode Island Red Plant in Grafton, MA in 1916. They owned and operated the company for decades. By 1930s, the company was recognized as one of the most prominent breeders of pedigreed and certified poultry in New England. Pearl Daniels authored numerous articles on breeding techniques for poultry and agricultural publications. She also served on the editorial board of the industry journal of that time, the *New England Poultryman*. – Joseph Carvalho III

Dawn Dearborn is the president of Tantara Corporation in Worcester, MA, serving in that capacity since February of 2000. Prior to that time, she was the principal with The RECTEC Group from 1987 to 2000. In 2017, the *Boston Globe* listed her business as one of the top-100 women-led businesses in Massachusetts. – Joseph Carvalho III

Top left: Abbey Cray. **Top right:** Patricia A. Canavan and her mother, Mary Ellen Scott. **Above:** Dawn Dearborn.

Above left: Diane Doherty. **Above right:** Helen T. Dunbar.

Florence L. (Davio) DeRose

[See entry in this chapter for Jean (Davio) Jinks]

Harriet (Williams) DeRose

(B. MAY 30, 1877 IN NORTH STONINGTON, CT; D. SEPT. 23, 1960 IN NORTHAMPTON, MA) was a celebrated Northampton businesswoman, journalist, and publisher. She moved from Connecticut to Northampton in 1894 to attend Smith College. After graduating in 1898, she joined the faculty of Northampton Commercial College. In 1919, she was hired as the business manager of the *Daily Hampshire Gazette*, a position she held until 1929. That year, DeRose bought the *Hampshire Gazette* and became one of the nation's first female

newspaper publishers. She was active in the management of the newspaper until a few months before her death. The DeRose family owned and operated the newspaper until 2005. – Peter L. DeRose & Joseph Carvalho III

Kerry L. Dietz

(B. DEC. 24, 1952) is a Springfield-based architect. She formed the successful Dietz & Company Architects in 1985. Very involved with community and regional organizations such as the Springfield Museums Association and the Women's Fund of Western Massachusetts, Dietz was also appointed to the City of Springfield's Planning Board in 2001. Throughout her career, Dietz has worked on a variety of project types but

over time has become most known for her work in affordable housing and education. – Joseph Carvalho III

Marion E. Dodd

(B. IN NEW JERSEY; D. 1978 IN NORTHAMPTON, MA) and

Mary Byers Smith

(B. SEPT. 27, 1885 IN ANDOVER, MA; D. FEB. 2, 1983 IN BOSTON, MA) founded The Hampshire Bookshop in Northampton, MA on April 7, 1916. It was one of the first bookselling companies in the U.S. to be founded, owned, and operated by women. Both were alumnae of Smith College, and most of its employees and board members were also Smith alumnae. It operated for 55 years and became a "vital" part of Northampton's downtown business and college district.

Diane (Fuller) Doherty

(B. JULY 21, 1937) of Longmeadow, MA has been the regional Director of the Western Massachusetts Regional Office of the Massachusetts Small Business Development Center Network (MSBDC) since 1992. The MSBDC, part of the Isenberg School of Management at the University of Massachusetts, offers free and confidential business advisory services, training programs and information and referral to small businesses in Western Massachusetts.

Previously, Doherty founded and served as President and CEO of Doherty-Tzoumas Marketing, a full service advertising and public relations firm based in Springfield. Prior to that, she was Executive Director of Downtown Marketing, an organization whose mission was to promote downtown Springfield.

A graduate of Mount Holyoke College, Doherty is a founder of the Women's Fund of Western Massachusetts and serves on the boards of the Pioneer Valley Plan for

Progress, Bay Path University, The Community Foundation of Western Mass, and Tech Foundry. She is also a board member of Digital Divide Data, a US based non-profit corporation that offers employment and educational opportunities to disadvantaged youth in Cambodia and Laos by addressing the technology divide. – Joseph Carvalho III

Helen T. (Clark) Dunbar

(B. NOV. 5, 1888; D. NOV., 1974 IN HOLYOKE, MA) operated the General Motors car dealership of Holyoke from 1943 to the early 1960s; was elected president of the Motor Car Company of New England; and was president of the Purity Springs Water Company in Florida. A generous philanthropist, Dunbar endowed a number of nursing scholarships at Holyoke Hospital among her many charitable works. – Joseph Carvalho III

Jane (Pratt) Fitzpatrick

(B. NOV. 18,1923 IN SHREWSBURY, VT; D. NOV. 9, 2013 IN STOCKBRIDGE, MA) was the founder of Country Curtains in Stockbridge and long-time owner of the Red Lion Inn in Stockbridge, MA. In 1980, she and her husband Jack, purchased Blantyre in Lenox and transformed the former cottage into a country house resort that is often listed as one of the top lodging properties in the U.S. Her philanthropic efforts extended to the Norman Rockwell Museum, the Austen Riggs Center, Tanglewood, the Berkshire Botanical Garden, and the Berkshire Country Day School. She was the recipient of the first Commonwealth Award in 1993, honoring her as a patron of the arts and humanities. From 1998 to 2001, she was recognized in *Working Woman* magazine as CEO and Chair of one of the top 500 women-owned companies in the U.S. Among many awards she and Jack received together was the 1997 Ernst and Young Entrepreneur of the Year for New England. – James Gleason & Joseph Carvalho III

Nancy Jane Fitzpatrick

(B. IN STOCKBRIDGE, MA) is a second-generation hotelier whose family has owned the Red Lion Inn since 1968. For the last 15 years, she has overseen a hospitality business that includes The Red Lion, Jacks Grill, Elm Street Market, and the 47-room Porches Inn at MASS MoCA in North Adams, Massachusetts.

In addition to her roles at The Red Lion and Porches, Nancy is vice chairman of The Fitzpatrick Companies, parent company of Country Curtains and Housatonic Curtain Company and a trustee of the High Meadow Foundation, the family's private philanthropic foundation. [See also entry in Chapter on Philanthropists] – James S. Gleason

Sally C. Fuller

(B. SEPT. 20, 1947 IN MORRISTOWN, NJ) of Wilbraham, MA. Well-respected and successful in the business world with a long career in Communications and Marketing, she joined The Irene E. and George Davis Foundation in 2005 to lead the Foundation's "Cherish Every Child Initiative." In 2009, Fuller was the project director for the Davis Foundation's "Read! Reading Success by 4th Grade" component of the "Cherish Every Child," initiative. Largely through her efforts, Springfield achieved All-America City status for grade-level reading by the National Civic League. The initiative has also been recognized as a "Pacesetter Community" in 2012, 2013, and 2014. Fuller began her career working for the National Security Agency from 1969-1973 before assuming the position of Director of Communications at Westfield State College (now University) from 1973 to 1976. With the Springfield Chamber of Commerce from 1994 to 1998, she then worked for United Bank from 1998 to 2005. Fuller has been an active volunteer for a large number of Greater Springfield-area educational and cultural organizations: WGBY Public Television for New England, the Girls Scouts, Springfield Day

Sally C. Fuller

Nursery, Springfield School Volunteers, and the Ronald McDonald House. She also serves on the board of the Massachusetts Service Alliance. – Joseph Carvalho III

Mary (Babaian) Garabedian

(B. 1911 IN BOSTON, MA; D. JULY 13, 1997 IN PALMER, MA) and her husband Gary M. Garabedian together owned and operated Thorndike Mills Rug Manufacturing Company in Thorndike, MA from 1935 until their children Mitchell (1958), Eddie (1959), and Anna (1970) began to fill leaderships positions in the company. Mary remained active in the company until 1986. She was a 1958 founding member of St. Mark's Armenian Church in Springfield and active in the Women's Guild. – Joseph Carvalho III

Samalid M. Hogan

Hepsibah (Bowman/Crosman) Hemenway

(B. 1761 IN WORCESTER, MA; D. 1847 IN WORCESTER, MA) was raised by her father, "a man of Caucasian and Mashpee heritage," and her mother who was a member of the Nipmuc community on Worcester's Pakachoag Hill where the College of Holy Cross now stands. She married Jeffrey Hemenway in 1789 and raised ten children while workin as a laundress and a baker. After her husband's death in 1819, she continued her business as a caterer for local residents parties and feasts, and as a sought after specialty baker. She became famous for her decorative wedding cakes and boasted a long client list of the wealthiest families in Worcester and immediate surrounding communities. – Joseph Carvalho III

Samalid M. (Maldonaldo) Hogan

(B. BAYAMON, PUERTO RICO) is the regional director of the Massachusetts Small Business Development Center's western regional office. Previously she was the consulting project manager for the Holyoke Innovation District and the senior project manager at the city of Springfield's Office of Planning and Economic Development. She has served as a senior economic development and policy analyst at the Pioneer Valley Planning Commission and founded CoWork Springfield, a networking organization and co-working space. She has a master's degree in entrepreneurship and innovation from Bay Path University. Samalid was recognized and awarded the Grinspoon Entrepreneurial Sprit Award in 2017. She was also recognized as a Women Trailblazer and Trendsetter by the Massachusetts Latino Chamber of Commerce in 2016, and was awarded in 2013 the "40 Under 40" *BusinessWest* award for her leadership and accomplishments. – Natasha Clark & Joseph Carvalho III

Esther Allen Howland

(B. AUG. 17, 1828 IN WORCESTER, MA; D. MAR. 15, 1904 IN WORCESTER, MA) made and designed the first American-made valentines with her first sales being in the City of Worcester. She was a graduate of Mount Holyoke Female Seminary (today's Mount Holyoke College). Her brother took the samples on a sales trip and came home with an astonishing $5,000 worth of orders. Howland began by hiring her friends to assemble the valentines, with her first sales in Worcester on Feb. 14, 1849.In order to capitalize on the Victorians' feeling that romantic sentiments were private and should be kept secret, Esther Howland created separate sheets with a variety of "mottos" that could be pasted inside the card. She published a book of 131 different verses that dealers could use to help customers personalize their valentines. Within a few years, she built her business into a $100,000 a year enterprise, a notable success for any entrepreneur but a truly remarkable accomplishment for a nineteenth-century woman. – Joseph Carvalho III

Jean M. (Davio) Jinks

in partnership with her sister Florence L. (Davio) DeRose owned and ran the successful full-service advertising firm of Design & Advertising Associates in Springfield. Their parents, Silvio and Rose Davio, immigrated as children from Italy in the early 20th century. Jean & Florence are members of the first generation of their family to graduate from college. After graduating from Rhode Island School of Design and working in New York City for two years, Jean and a partner formed Design Associates in 1960 in Springfield, offering design and graphic services. Florence graduated from the Hartford Art School at the University of Hartford, and later joined Jean as sole partner in the renamed Design and Advertising Associates.

At that point, Design and Advertising Associates was the only completely woman-owned advertising agency in Springfield. The agency employed from four to eight employees and offered design, illustration and multimedia services. The agency was purchased by two employees around 2000. – Peter DeRose & Joseph Carvalho III

Dorothy "Dot" G. Lortie

(B. SEPT. 8, 1931) of Springfield is a successful real estate businesswomen. She began her career in 1965 with Marie Kane Real Estate in East Forest Park, Springfield, MA, becoming a partner in the mid-1980s. She opened her own real estate business, Dot Lortie Realty, in 1989. In 2002 she merged her agency with Landmark Realtors, becoming a partner and a director of the company. Lortie was named "Realtor of the Year" in 1987 by the Realtor Association of the Pioneer Valley;

and in 1995 she was named "Woman of the Year" by the Women's Partnership of the Affiliated Chambers of Commerce of Greater Springfield. Over the years, she has also served on a variety of state-wide committees for the Massachusetts Association of Realtors including its political action committee. Among the many community organizations that she has served, Lortie has been the president of the Springfield Exchange Club, and served on the Springfield Historical Commission, the board of the Forest Park Zoo, and the XMain Street Corp. – Marcia Blomberg & Joseph Carvalho III

Joan (Janina) Czupryna-Lupa

(B. JULY 6, 1948 IN STROJCOW, POLAND) educated in Poland she emigrated to the United States in 1964, settling in Ludlow, MA with her husband Henry and their three children. With her husband Henry, they started a landscaping business evolving into construction with the establishment of N.L. Construction, Inc. in 1982, where she is President. Henry's dream was to create a zoo which he did in 1992 with Joan working as a director and then becoming President upon her husband's death in 2013. Lupa Zoo is an 18 acre privately owned zoo recognized regionally and nationally for its efforts on education and conservation. Joan works tirelessly in keeping the legacy of Lupa Zoo and furthering education. – Joanne M. Gruszkos

Nicole Miller

(B. 1952 IN FORT WORTH, TX) a noted American fashion designer was raised in Lenox, MA. Went into business with P.J. Walsh Co. president Bud Kohnheim and started the Nicole Miller Co. Miller's first shop opened on Madison Avenue in 1986. In 2005, Miller began a long collaboration with J.C. Penney designing a line of affordable clothes, handbags, footwear, and fashion jewelry. She also designs a home furnishings collection for Bed Bath and Beyond. Miller and Kohnheim's

label has achieved $650 million in annual sales. – Joseph Carvalho III

Victoria Principal

(NÉE VICKI LEE, B. JAN. 3, 1950 IN FUKUOKA, JAPAN; ATTENDED HIGH SCHOOL IN CHICOPEE, MA). Actor, agent, businesswoman, philanthropist. Principal had a very successful acting career which included her long-running role on the top rated series "Dallas". In 1989 she created a self-named line of skin care products, Principal Secret. In 2013, Principal Secret Skincare, had revenue of more than 1.5 billion dollars to date, an increase of more than a half billion dollars over the revenue up to 2007. Principal also became a best-selling author, writing three books about beauty, skin care, and health: *The Body Principal* (1983), *The Beauty Principal* (1984), and *The Diet Principal* (1987), with her fourth book entitled *Living Principal* (2001).

Frances Wakefield Riggs

(B. CA. 1900 IN SPRINGFIELD, MA; D. AFTER 1963) a well-respected Springfield businesswoman, Riggs served on the Board of Directors of the Standard Electric Time Company of Springfield beginning in 1928, and also served as President beginning in 1940.
– Joseph Carvalho III

Ida R. Rotman

(B. JUNE 14, 1913) with her husband Murray founded the very successful Rotman's Furniture and Carpet Company in Worcester, MA in 1964 which has grown into "the largest store of its kind in New England." Rotmans has been pleased and honored to receive Achievement Awards from The Better Business Bureau, The Chamber of Commerce, SCORE, The *Worcester Business Journal* (Family Business Award) and Clark University School of Management (Corporate Citizen's Award). Having been previously named the National Carpet Association Retailer of the Year, in 2011 Rotmans was also named The

Top: Dorothy "Dot" G. Lortie. **Above:** Frances Wakefield Riggs (Photo from Harry Andrew Wright, *The Story of Western Massachusetts*, 1949).

Mary Ellen Scott

Retailer of the Year by the National Home Furnishings Association. – Leah Lamson & Joseph Carvalho III

Elaine Sarsynski

(BORN AND RAISED IN SOUTH HADLEY, MA) is a graduate of Smith College with a BA in Economics and an MBA in Finance & Accounting from Columbia University. Elaine started her business career at an early age, picking asparagus with her four siblings on the family's vegetable farm in Hadley, Mass. She joined Morgan Stanley (MS) & Co. in New York city after college, earned an MBA from Columbia University then joined Aetna Inc. culminating in the job of corporate vice president of real estate investments. She founded Sun Consulting Group, LLC offering real estate consulting services to the bio technology industry.

Sarsynski served two elected terms as Chief Executive Officer of Suffield Township in Suffield, Connecticut from 2001 to 2005. She joined MassMutual Financial Group in July 2005 as a Managing Director for Babson (rebranded Barings) Capital Management LLC and served as its Portfolio Management Group Head. Sarsynski served as Chief Administrative Officer and Senior Vice President at Massachusetts Mutual Life Insurance Co, from September 1, 2005 to June 2006. She served as the Vice Chairman of various portfolios in MML Funds Complex and served as their Trustee.

Sarsynski served as the Chairman of MassMutual International LLC until February 9, 2017 and served as its Chief Executive Officer. Sarsynski served as an Executive Vice President of Retirement Services at Massachusetts Mutual Life Insurance Company until February 9, 2017. She served as an Executive Vice President at Massachusetts Mutual Life Insurance Co. from June 2006 until her retirement in 2017.

She has been an Independent Director of Horizon Technology Finance Corporation since June 2012. She served as a Director for LIMRA International, Inc. and LIMRA Inc., a Trustee of Hopkins Academy, Hadley, MA.; director of the Employee Benefit Research Institute. – Joanne M. Gruszkos

Mary Ellen (Neelon) Scott

(B. FEB. 12, 1944 IN MELROSE, MA) has been a leader in the Western Mass community for over 25 years. A Massachusetts native, Mary Ellen moved to Springfield, MA from the eastern part of the state in 1980 with her now-deceased husband, Jay Canavan, and their two daughters. In 1984, Mary Ellen and Jay founded United Personnel Services, Inc., a family and woman-owned business. The company's headquarters started in Hartford, CT, but not long after the headquarters moved to Springfield, MA where it remains today. Scott is currently United Personnel's Chief Executive Officer. United provides clerical, accounting, medical office staff, light industrial personnel and executive placement services and employs over 1,000 people a day throughout Connecticut and Massachusetts. United has been the recipient of numerous awards including; Inc. Magazine's top 500 fastest-growing companies award two years in a row, several Chamber of Commerce awards including Small Business of the Year and is a 13-time winner of their annual Super 50/Super 60 award of the area's top performing companies. Every year since 2006, the Company has also been named one of the Top 100 Women-Led Businesses in MA by The Commonwealth Institute.

Prior to founding United Personnel Services, Scott was the Director of Human Resources at Gemini Corporation in Springfield, MA. Gemini was a clothing manufacturer for Izod, William Carter Co., and Oshgosh B'Gosh with over 400 employees in a union environment. Earlier in her career, Ms. Scott worked in various administrative capacities.

In addition to her business community involvement, Scott received the Business Woman of Distinction Award from the Pioneer Valley Girl Scouts in 2000. She has actively served on several non-profit boards including: Springfield Museums Board member, Past President (first woman President), Springfield Chamber of Commerce and past Board member; Past Chair, Past President and Board member Springfield Symphony Orchestra including chairing a successful endowment campaign for the orchestra; Board Member, Springfield Museums; Board Member, Hampden Bank; former Trustee of Health New England, Economic Development Council of Western MA; former Trustee, Community Foundation; Former President, Colony Club; former Board member WGBY (public television) and Springfield Technical Community College Assistance Corporation.

Scott is a resident of Wilbraham where she

resides with her husband, Roy Scott. Her daughters are: Patricia Canavan of South Hadley, MA, President, United Personnel, and Andrea Canavan of Fort Lauderdale, Florida, Vice President, Worldwide Sales Enablement, Citrix Systems. She is also stepmother to Alexander Scott, CPC of Bristol, CT, Funeral Director, Duksa Funeral Homes, and Christopher J. Scott, Esq. of Westfield, MA Legal Counsel for Smith & Wesson.

Scott is a graduate of Cardinal Cushing College, Brookline, MA and received her Advanced Personnel Certification from Elms College, Chicopee, MA. – Joseph Carvalho III & Wayne E. Phaneuf

Christian L. (Annie) Selke

(B. JAN. 10, 1963 IN STOCKBRIDGE, MA) started her home furnishings design business out of her home in Richmond, Mass. with an industrial sewing machine on the dining room table in 1994. Twenty four years later the Annie Selke Cos., is the umbrella for her Pine Cone Hill and Dash & Albert Rug Co. brands and employs 194 people including 149 at the company headquarters in Pittsfield. The 2010 Massachusetts Small Business Person of the Year by the U.S. Small Business Administration winner, she has no plans to move her company from the Berkshires. Selke was a graduate of Miss Porter's School and the University of Vermont, then graduated cum laude from the Fashion Institute of Technology. After graduation she worked in New York City for Saks Fifth Avenue, Conran's and then for Hermine Mariaux Inc., a licensing company for the Museum of American Folk Art. Her marriage in 1989 to Whitney F. Selke brought her back to the Berkshires.

She started working for Country Curtains, based in Stockbridge, while formulating her business Pine Cone Hill. Two years after starting the business in her dining room, she moved into her garage with five stitchers on staff. The company moved four more times before buying the 200,000 square foot mill in Pittsfield where Annie Selke Companies is located today. The company sells to 4,300 wholesale and design customers around the world including Wayfair and Neiman Marcus. In 2017, her and her husband opened a luxury Bed & Breakfast Inn in downtown Lenox, MA. – James S. Gleason

Teresa "Terry" (Struziak) Sherman

(B. 1943 IN CHICOPEE, MA) A registered nurse, Terry holds a BS in Nursing with Highest Honors from American International College and a MS in Nursing Administration from the University of Massachusetts in Amherst, MA. She is Co-Owner, CEO and Program Director for CEU Direct, Inc. offering online accredited health care education programs and is President and Director of Clinical Practices at Professional Medical Home Care. She was Assistant Professor of Nursing at the College of Our Lady of the Elm and Adjunct Assistant Professor at Western New England College. A published contributor to multiple publications, she authors a monthly health column, "Living Well", in the magazine *Zgoda*, a publication of the Polish National Alliance. Terry has testified before the Massachusetts Legislature's Joint Committee on Health Care on eliminating medical waste in nursing homes and jails.

Sherman's introduction to her Polish heritage was through the Polish National Alliance (PNA) at the age of 9, when she began helping her Father, Financial Secretary of PNA Lodge 711 in Chicopee. Upon his death in 1966, at age 23 she was elected to fill his position becoming both the youngest and first woman to serve as officer. This began Terry's rise through various positions and roles at the PNA both regionally and nationally. She has held positions as Sales Representative and Financial Secretary of Lodge 711, Secretary and Commissioner of District 1, delegate and Recording/Financial Secretary to PNA Council 61. On a national level she serves as a Director

Teresa Struziak Sherman

of the PNA Business Board and Director of Region "A". Sherman has received numerous awards from the PNA for her support to Polish Organizations in addition to awards for her community service to multiple organizations and the nursing profession; plus, she was the first woman to receive the Community Service Award from the Kosciuszko Foundation New England Chapter. – Joanne M. Gruszkos

Mary Byers Smith

[See Marion E. Dodd entry in this chapter]

Anna F. (Burns) Sullivan

(B. OCT. 18, 1903 IN HOLYOKE, MA; D. SEPT. 22, 1983 IN HOLYOKE, MA) a labor activist and leader who played a dominant role in organizing a Weaver's Union at the Skinner Silk Factory in Holyoke in 1932. This was the first union to win a contract under Congress of Industrial Organization auspices. In 1938, Sullivan worked as a full-

time organizer for the CIO tasked to travel throughout New England to organize textile workers. In 1950, she ran unsuccessfully for Congress as a labor candidate. She served as the Textile Workers Union of America's Joint Board District Manager from 1946 to 1966, and was a field representative for the Massachusetts Commission Against Discrimination until her retirement in 1972. According to her biographer, Dr. L. Mara Dodge, Sullivan was "heralded as 'Labor's First Lady in Western Massachusetts'."
– Joseph Carvalho III

Grace Lenora (Geer) Belknap/Swan

(B. CA. 1880 IN WORCESTER, MA;
D. MAY 2, 1956 IN WORCESTER, MA)
established the Worcester Mailing Company in Worcester, MA in 1907. She grew the business until it became the largest enterprise of its kind in New England. In the 1930s, her company acquired some of the first photostatic and planographic printing equipment in New England. Grace Swan served as the president and CEO of the company with her husband William J. Swan serving as company vice-president and treasurer. – Joseph Carvalho III

Rita Mae Tremble

(B. JULY 1, 1916 IN SPRINGFIELD, MA;
D. OCT. 15, 2010 IN LONGMEADOW, MA)
was co-founder and head of Valley Communications in Chicopee, MA [the company began as "Valley Cinema" in 1945]. She also served as a Hampden County commissioner and held leadership roles in a number of civic, religious and charitable groups. A Republican newspaper editorial noted that, "She was a hard charger in an era that did not consider hard charging a feminine virtue." – Cynthia G. Simison

Louise Marie (Smith) Trudeau

(B. 1891 IN ST. JOHN, QUEBEC, CANADA, D. SEPT 12, 1961 IN HOLYOKE, MA) immigrated with her family from Quebec and settled in Holyoke, MA. Trudeau was a prominent Holyoke businesswoman who began her career in 1938 as Assistant Treasurer of the Prentiss, Brooks & Company a major grain dealer headquartered in Holyoke. In 1943, she became president and treasurer of the company serving in that capacity until 1958. Known as "one of Holyoke's outstanding business women," she served on the executive Board of the Holyoke Chamber of Commerce for many years. This was at a time when women were rarely if ever in that governing position in regional Chambers of Commerce. She also was very involved with cultural organizations and served as president of the Cercle des Dames Francaise, as president of the Holyoke Council on World Relations, and a leader in the Holyoke Business and Professional Women's Club. – Joseph Carvalho III

Edna Ione (Smith) Tyler

(B. 1861 IN SOUTH HADLEY, MA; D. 1930 IN WORCESTER, MA) established the first public stenography/typewriting office in Worcester on March 4, 1885. A leader in her profession, Tyler established Tyler's Business College in 1900 in Worcester. She was the founder and first president of the Worcester County Stenographers Association in 1887 which met at the Burnside Building in Worcester.
– Joseph Carvalho III

Helen Blake Weyant

(B. JAN. 14, 1900 IN MONTPELIER, VT;
D. SEPT. 3, 1988 IN SPRINGFIELD, MA)
was a widely-respected fragrance executive for the Charles of the Ritz company. She began her career at Carroll's Cut Rate Store and from there she traveled for Helena Rubenstein, Elizabeth Arden, and Mary Chess companies. She then became assistant to the president of Lanvin Parfums of New York, which later merged with Charles of the Ritz. Weyant received the Woman of the Year Award in 1972 from the Philadelphia Cosmetic Association and was also the second woman to ever receive the Hall of Fame Award from the Fragrance Foundation in 1983.
– Joseph Carvalho III

Suzanne S. White

(B. NOV. 16, 1952) is a successful realtor from Longmeadow, MA. She is Owner and Principal of The Suzanne White Group real estate firm of Western Massachusetts and Northern Connecticut. White also serves on the Longmeadow Zoning Board of Appeals.
– Joseph Carvalho III

Edna Rebecca Fontaine (Spies) Williams

(B. APRIL 18, 1903 IN HOLYOKE, MA;
D. JUNE 4, 1997 IN HOLYOKE, MA)
owned and operated the popular Log Cabin Restaurant in Holyoke for sixty years, opening the business in the midst of the Great Depression in 1933. – Anne-Gerard Flynn & Joseph Carvalho III

Mary Ida (Stephenson) Young

(B. JUNE 29, 1864 IN STONINGTON, MD; D. OCT. 31, 1960 IN LONGMEADOW, MA)
was co-founder with her husband Wilbur F. Young of the internationally famous W.F. Young, Inc. manufacturer of popular consumer product, Absorbine, Jr. [See entry in Philanthropy chapter]

Lora Wondolowski

(B. 31 MAY 1969 IN DOWNERS GROVE, ILLINOIS) is the executive director of Leadership Pioneer Valley. She joined Leadership Pioneer Valley in 2011 as its founding director after serving as the founding Executive Director of the Massachusetts League of Environmental Voters (MLEV). Her political acumen, and

TYLER'S BUSINESS COLLEGE

The Modern Commercial School of Worcester

Exercise wisdom in selecting a school. Consider impartially and critically all essential elements of a Real School.

Remember that the Best School is not the one which advertises itself as such. Pay particular attention to facts and throw out all boastful claims that have no Real Value.

Tyler's Business College, now beautifully located in the new Slater Building, offers an exceptional opportunity to young men and women who are desirous of entering the business world, and who appreciate expert instruction, proper surroundings and associations.

Special work, reviewing, examining and completing courses begun in High Schools and other Business Schools are features given careful attention in this school.

The school assists its graduates in obtaining desirable positions, and through this assistance students are enabled to pass direct from the school into business employment without loss of time. Former graduates who may need help in securing positions are always gladly given the needed assistance.

COURSES

Commercial Course
Bookkeeping, Penmanship,
Commercial Arithmetic,
Commercial Correspondence,
Commercial Law,
Spelling and Defining.

Stenographic Course
Pitman or Munson Shorthand,
Typewriting (Sight or Touch Method),
Correspondence, English, Spelling,
Filing, Cataloguing, Mimeographing,
Multigraphing, Letter-press Copying.

Commercial Teachers' Full Course
This course includes all the subjects in above courses and is arranged for High School, Normal School and College Graduates, also teachers who wish to change their line of work.

Civil Service Course
This course prepares for the various Government examinations.

Special Course
This course is open to persons who for reasons cannot take the regular course. The studies and hours are adjusted to suit the needs of the pupil.

Public Stenography, Typewriting, Multigraphing

Terms and more extended information will be given by mail or through interviews at the offices of the school, Slater Building. Office open every week-day and evening during August.

EDNA I. TYLER,
Principal

Telephones : { 5019

Above: Edna Tyler. **Top center:** Lora Wondolowski.
Top right: Rita Mae Tremble.
Bottom left, in circle: Pearl Leonard Wallace.
Bottom center: Mary Byers Smith.
Bottom right: Louise M. Trudeau (Photo from Harry Andrew
Wright, *The Story of Western Massachusetts*, 1949).

strategy earned the organization strong support with members of Congress, the Governor, members of the legislature and the mayor of Boston. Prior to her work with MLEV, she worked for the League of Conservation Voters Education Fund and National Audubon Society in Washington, DC. A resident of Greenfield, MA, Wondolowski was one of the founders of the Friends of the Great Falls Discovery Center in Turners Falls, was a volunteer and board member of Pride Zone Youth Center in Northampton, and was the founder of the Progressive Christian Voice at First Churches of Northampton. She serves on the Connecticut River Watershed Council, Partners for a Healthier Community, and United Way of Pioneer Valley Boards. On May 22, 2018, Wondolowski was honored by the Professional Women's Chamber as the PWC's Woman of the Year. – Joseph Carvalho III

Mary Kay Wydra

(B. AUG. 6, 1965) is the President of the Greater Springfield Convention & Visitors Bureau. Her leadership of the Bureau began in February of 1996 when she was appointed acting executive director, serving for several months before a new Executive Director was appointed by the Board. After serving for several years as Executive Vice-president of the bureau, Wydra was ultimately selected to the position of President of the Greater Springfield Convention & Visitors Bureau in July of 2000, assuming her duties on Jan.1, 2001. Wydra joined the bureau in 1988 as the Convention Services Coordinator. Under her leadership the Bureau has developed numerous innovative marketing efforts to promote Springfield and Greater Springfield area venues, events, and attractions. She instituted the "Howdy Awards" which annually recognize excellence among the staffs of the regional hospitality industry. – Joseph Carvalho III

Pictured left: Mary Kay Wydra

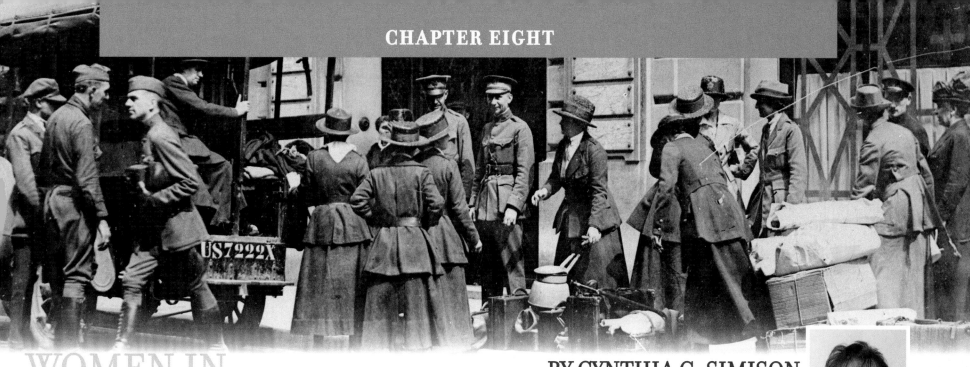

CHAPTER EIGHT

WOMEN IN
Military Service

BY CYNTHIA G. SIMISON
Managing Editor, *The Republican*

Deborah Sampson, of Plympton, Massachusetts, served for over two years as a soldier in Gen. George Washington's Continental Army, disguising her sex and going undiscovered as she fought alongside her male counterparts as Robert Shurtleff. It wasn't until 18 months into her service when she fell ill during an epidemic that Sampson's sex was discovered. She was honorably discharged and would go on to receive a military pension from the Continental Congress.

Other women would follow as they supported their husbands and male family members on America's first battlefields, but it was Sampson who set the stage for women serving in our nation's military. She would not be the only one to disguise herself as a man over the course of American military history.

For many women in the military, during the War of 1812, the Civil War and the Spanish American War, their work would center on service as nurses. Others would be spies, and many would serve in support roles. Their numbers would increase as the military evolved, and the scope of the wars our nation endured unfolded over the past three centuries.

It was not until World War I that women were formally allowed to join the U.S. armed forces. During those pivotal years of 1917 and 1918 in which U.S. troops became involved, more than 30,000 women served as nurses and support staff to the U.S. military. More than 400 nurses died in the line of duty. On the homefront, women answered the "call of duty" by joining the factory workforce in places like the Springfield Armory.

The number of American women serving in the military grew exponentially during World War II as female units were established for all branches of the service, including the Women's Army Corps, Women Accepted for Volunteer Emergency Service (WAVES), a unit of the Naval Reserve, the Marine Corps' Women's Reserve and Coast Guard Women's Reserve

Left: Winslow Homer drawing of women working on packages for Union soldiers during the Civil War.
Above: Smith College WAVES

(SPARS) as well as the Women Airforce Service Pilots (WASPs) and the Army and Navy nurse corps.

Nearly 350,000 women served in uniform from 1941 through 1945, according to the National World War II Museum. They drove trucks, rigged parachutes, were radio operators, repaired airplanes, ferried aircraft across the country for war duty and, as nurses in particular, frequently could be found on the front lines of battle. In the Philippines alone, some 68 service women were taken prisoners of war by the Japanese.

Wrote World War II scholar Stephen Ambrose in his book, *D-Day,* "The contribution of the women of America, whether on the farm or in the factory or in uniform, to D-Day was a sine qua non of the invasion effort."

Rosie the Riveter was the iconic representation of women supporting our military by working to help produce all the materials of war, from aircraft and tanks to guns and ammunition. Ironically, by war's end, most of these women's careers came to an abrupt end when the men who fought the war came home in search of jobs in a peacetime economy.

It was in 1948 that Congress, led by U.S. Sen. Margaret Chase Smith, of Maine, passed and President Harry S. Truman signed into law the Women's Armed Services Integration Act that made it law for women to become permanent members of the armed forces.

In every military conflict since, from Korea to Vietnam to the Persian Gulf and today on active duty in places like Iraq and Afghanistan, women serve in every branch of the military.

In retrospect, the path of women in our nation's military is much like the path we've taken to be recognized simply for our achievements, rather than being defined by our gender. Not until the mid-1970s were women admitted to the military academies. Not until the 1990s could they fly combat missions in fighter jets and serve and command aboard Navy warships.

And, it wasn't until this 21st century that America, saying its military must draw from "the broadest possible pool of talent," decreed women could serve in ground combat roles. Said President Barack Obama on Dec. 3, 2015, "Today, the Defense Department is taking another historic step forward by opening up the remaining 10 percent of military positions, including combat roles, to women. As Commander in Chief, I know that this change, like others before it, will again make our military even stronger."

Today, women like Maryanne Walts, the first woman command chief master sergeant to serve at the Air National Guard's 104th Fighter Wing in Westfield, carry on a proud tradition set by their predecessors.

Walts is an example of women who live among us in Western and Central Massachusetts, serving with National Guard and Reserve units. She and others like her don't see life through a lens defined by gender, but rather defined by a desire to serve our nation in the military, both in peacetime and at war, working to preserve the freedoms which were established as our nation was formed when Deborah Sampson took to the battlefield disguised as a man.

Women on the Home Front in Western Massachusetts During the Civil War

BY JOSEPH CARVALHO III

From the outset of the Civil War, Women on the home front in Western Massachusetts looked for opportunities to contribute to the war effort and support the troops. The Armory Hill Soldier's Aid Society in Springfield was one of the first women's organizations organized by women to support the war effort. More "aid societies" would soon spring up throughout the city, and in all the major towns and cities of the Valley. As regiments filled with their husbands, brothers, sons, friends and neighbors prepared to march off to war, women's groups were often mentioned in the newspapers for having presented gifts to regimental officers and troops from their community.

In October of 1861, as the 27th Massachusetts Volunteer Infantry Regiment prepared to head south to the battlefields of northern Virginia, the "ladies of Chicopee" presented a range of martial gifts. Commander of the Regiment's company from Chicopee, Captain R.R. Swift received an Ames sword and a revolver "Suitably inscribed from his friends in Chicopee." Lt. J.S. Atcheson received a revolver and a "sash" made by the ladies. While $75 was donated for the use of "the rest of the outfit," and aid society member, Mrs. D.H. Webster supplied the entire company with "excellent soap in cakes of convenient size." The community also presented Regimental Colonel H. Lee with "a fine horse and equipments." This type of "off to war" martial gift-giving happened in varying degrees of magnitude and generosity throughout the Valley in the early part of the war. As the war progressed and

the full reality of battle and hardships of camp life in the Union army, the women's efforts soon turned to providing materials for the health and medical care of the soldiers. Several days after Christmas in 1861 as families back in Springfield received letters from the troops detailing casualties and poor camp conditions, the Armory Hill Ladies Soldier's Aid Society responded by meeting at Mrs. William Ritchie's house on High Street to help assemble "boxes" of stockings, bandages, linen wrappings, and other clothing essentials for the troops. This sort of activity was soon repeated throughout

Above: Civil War Winslow Homer drawing of Thanksgiving Day Nov. 24, 1864.
Right: Nurses Merrick and Wolcott, left and right at center, at Brigthwood camp near Washington D. C. during the Civil War, 1861.

the region by other "ladies soldiers aid" groups.

The Armory Hill group stepped up their efforts and on March 4, 1862, they held a "Soldiers' Benefit Festival" at Springfield City Hall inviting "patriotic people one and all." The proceeds amounting to $362 were "applied to the purchase of articles for the benefit of our sick and wounded Volunteers." Soon after other groups began to organize and step up their charity work for the soldiers. The "Ladies Union Society" was organized with the help of Mrs. Porter King on Grays Avenue "to work for the soldiers." By May 1, of that year, "Ladies of the Universalist Society" began meeting on a regular basis "for the purpose of sewing for the soldiers." Not to be outdone, the "Ladies of the First Church" sent a "large box of garments, delicacies, and other articles necessary for hospital use" to the 10th Massachusetts Volunteer Regiment on May 6th. On June 23rd, the Springfield Horticultural Society pledged the proceeds of their Fall "Horticultural Fair" to the Ladies Soldiers' Aid Society.

Meanwhile women's sewing circles sprang up around the region making stockings and bandages for the troops, an activity that would continue throughout the war. Ladies aid societies also began to send boxes of supplies to individual regiments on a fairly regular basis until the federal government established the U.S. Sanitary Commission at which time these Aid boxes were sent to the Commission for review and for distribution. There were many ad hoc charity events that funneled their proceeds to the various ladies soldiers' aid societies. One such event was an "Old Ladies Tea Party" held in Chicopee in January of 1863 which raised an astonishing $555 for the town's soldier's aid society- an amazement which was commented upon in several eastern Massachusetts newspapers. Another event was held by Springfield firefighters, which raised $550 from their "Firemen's Ball" on New Year's Eve.

To coordinate the efforts of the many civic and church-based ladies soldiers' aid organizations, an Association of Ladies Soldiers' Aid Societies was formed in Springfield. Their meetings and activities were organized by a revolving committee of individuals, but always with one from every aid society in attendance so as to maintain a united and organized effort. The pooled efforts were impressive. The *Springfield Republican* reported on February 2, 1863, that the Association packed and forwarded to the Sanitary Commission in New York : "4 barrels and 2 boxes of clothing for hospital use, containing 135 flannel shirts, 144 cotton shirts, 111 pair of cotton flannel drawers, 134 pairs of stockings, 5 bed quilts, 3 sheets, 1 bed sack, 12 pillows, 6 pillow cases, 88 towels, 53 handkerchiefs, 3 dressing gowns, a box of dried apples, a box of second-hand clothing and stockings." The article also noted that the effort was assisted by "a large and valuable contribution of articles from the ladies of Wilbraham."

From January to April, the Springfield Ladies Aid Society Association had donated over $3,000 worth of cloth which they had worked into bandages and garments for the troops. The *Springfield Republican* praised the Association as "a most efficient and beneficial organization," but alerted the community that "its funds are now gone." Samuel Bowles wrote a supportive editorial on April 16, 1863 declaring that "The hearts and hands of the ladies are eager and ready as ever; but the men must put them in funds to buy material, or they will have to stop, and the best working organization our blessed women ever had will go to pieces." Bowles pleaded, "This should not, must not be. They must be kept together and kept at work. Never were their labors more necessary of more efficient than now." He concluded with the exhortation to the public, "Our citizens should put their hands in their pockets, fill up the exchequer again, and bid the noble women go ahead and God Speed!" Fortunately, the public responded and the women of the Society would continue to receive funding from private sources throughout the war for their work on behalf of the troops.

The final phase of the War with General Grant's relentless war of attrition as he marched the Army of the Potomac south to Richmond witnessed increasing volume of casualties. Although they kept a steady stream of clothing and hospital materials flowing to the Sanitary Commission, the various Ladies Soldiers' Aid societies could not keep up with the overwhelming need of the men on the front lines. In addition, Springfield had become a major convalescent and medical treatment site for wounded union soldiers few of whom were from Springfield. As of December of 1863, the "Soldier's Rest" in Springfield had cared for 9, 243 men (over 5,500 were soldiers from Vermont Regiments) and expended more than $10,000 in Building and fuel costs since its establishment in 1861. To remedy, the situation a large "Soldiers Fair" was organized and held at City Hall from Dec. 19-22, 1864. Run by several Prominent local businessmen, the Fair was assisted by the women of the aid societies. In connection with the Fair, A daily newspaper was published called *The Springfield Musket* with Mrs. John Hooker, Mrs. E.D. Rice, Mrs. T.M. Brown, and Mrs. F.B. Hixon serving as editors. The sales of the "Musket" alone raised $1,100. The proceeds from the four day fair was over $18,000.

As the war drew to its close, the women's charitable efforts began to turn to the major social problem of caring for the widows and orphans of union soldiers who had died. To ameliorate the suffering and deprivations faced by this tragically growing segment of the population, a "Home for Friendless Women" was established in March of 1865. Still providing care and materials for the troops remaining in the field, the ladies Soldier's Aid Societies began to transition into the charitable social needs of post-war Springfield. The widows and children of the troops would continue to be the beneficiaries of their good work.
[excerpted from *A Not So Civil War, Vol. I (The Republican,* 2015)]

Smith College and the First U.S. Naval Training School for Women

BY CYNTHIA G. SIMISON

The city of Northampton played host to more than 9,000 WAVES during World War II when Smith College became the site of the country's first Naval Training School for women.

Twenty-eight classes were trained over the course of the 2 1/2 years that the Navy set up shop at Smith.

Dubbed "sailorettes" by the media, they drew more publicity than Calvin Coolidge when he lived in town, according to the *Sunday Republican* in 1942.

The women double-bunked at the Hotel Northampton.

Paradise Pond became their "private ocean."

They marched up and down Main Street between the hotel and Smith College several times daily. They dined at the famed Wiggins Tavern. And they were outfitted in designer uniforms by Filene's in a special branch store on King Street.

It was in early June of 1942 that Smith President Herbert Davis first discussed the possibility of training women for the Navy with his Board of Trustees, according to records in the College Archives.

In notes of that meeting, it was reported that the Navy preferred to use one of the "Seven Sisters" women's colleges, such as Smith, "for the sake of its atmosphere and prestige." Trustees voiced concern that the "Navy (might) swallow the college or vice versa."

It was eventually voted to welcome the Navy to the campus but limit the use of college housing to 500 trainees. In July, Davis announced the plans to the student body and said that the hotel would be used to house additional WAVES candidates.

Students who had been living in three

Above left: Smith College WAVES at dormitory. **Above right:** Smith College WAVES drilling.

dorms - Capen, Northrop and Gillett - gave up their rooms. In true Navy style, the living quarters later were nicknamed "SS Capen, Northrop and Gillett."

Half of the Alumnae House on Elm Street was converted for office use by the school with Sophia Smith's furniture moved to an attic for safekeeping, according to newspaper clippings from the time.

Boxing champion and former Marine Gene Tunney oversaw preparation of the schools physical education program.

In September, an initial class of 120 women officers, the "Zero Group" that included Northampton's own Margaret T. Clifford, was hurried through training in 20 days to provide teachers for those who would follow.

The first class of 900 seaman trainees arrived on Oct. 6, 1942.

"Warm welcome," said Davis in a radio speech given to the community days before that, "We shall give them a warm welcome because we believe in the great importance and urgency of the tasks they are being trained for and we are proud to have the honor of sharing the campus with them."

The trainees followed a four-month

concentrated course with a curriculum that included one month of naval indoctrination and three months of specialized training in the specific duties for which they were selected. The school at Smith provided the indoctrination segment of the course.

Reveille was at 6:15 a.m., and taps was at 10 p.m. In between, the trainees had four recitation classes, two study periods, drill, athletic and recreation period and an evening lecture. They marched to and from meals and classes in groups. Weekly leaves ran from noon on Saturdays to dinner time on Sundays.

They were trained in Navy discipline, history, etiquette, phraseology and policy and were familiarized with ships and craft. Successful completion of the Smith course meant appointment as a reserve midshipman. Once the additional three months of training was completed, the women would be commissioned as ensigns.

In November, a midshipmen's school was added at Mount Holyoke College with the South Hadley campus transformed just as Smith had been.

The Smith school graduated its last class on Dec. 21, 1944. In an address to those last

WAVES who passed through Northampton, Vice Admiral Randall Jacobs, chief of naval personnel, told the women, "You have been brought into the Navy because of a demonstrated need we know you can fill... With your help, we can hit the enemy harder, with your help we may, God willing, make this long war a little shorter."

He also delivered a message to Smith and to the city, saying the Navy was "grateful to Smith College for the use of its facilities and to the people of Northampton for accepting us so graciously into their community. This school could not have been more fortunately located."

Speeches, notes, photographs and clippings from newspapers and magazines are among the scores of documents that trace the history of the school which are maintained in the College Archives.

Women of the Springfield Armory, World War I & II

BY PAUL ANTHONY, PIONEER VALLEY HISTORY NETWORK

Women in the factory workforce from World War I up through World War II had to face many challenges. They had to constantly fight poor working conditions, low wages compared to their male counterparts, discrimination, and a host of other obstacles along the way. Many of these women decided to move into these factory jobs for the needs of the country within these war periods themselves. The men were all off to war and there was a need for the manufacturing of the war time goods that the men needed to continue fighting overseas. There were many women who answered the "call of duty" on the homefront throughout both time periods. Women in these jobs consisted of 20% of the workforce in World War I and in World War II women consisted of 35.4% of the total workforce.

WORLD WAR I ARMORY WOMEN

The United States entering into the First World War caused a change within the working structure on the homefront. Due to many of the men enlisting into the military or being drafted to serve their country caused a large shortage of laborers within the American workforce. Many of these men worked within the growing industrial center of the US from the large economic boom of the industrial revolution. To counteract the shortage of laborers the industrial center saw the need for women to enter the workforce in order to not only supply their male counterparts with food rations, ammunition, and other necessary items they may need in the battlefield; but also the general laborers within other sectors of the workforce too. Springfield and the armory is a prime example of the need for women within the industrial sector to assist in supplying the men fighting the war.

By November of 1918 the shift and need of female laborers grew to 748 female employees which consisted of 18% of the total workforce within the Armory. Some of the women that worked at the armory during World War I worked their way up to higher positions. Miss Helen E. Moriarty was one example. She was a "forewoman" at the armory throughout the American involvement in World War I and was in charge of 53 other girls on the factory floor. She was also one of the first female workers that were employed by the armory at the turn of the 20th century; she resigned to take a secretarial course in late 1918.

The World War I era was a pioneering time for women in the workforce throughout the United States. Within the Springfield Armory women took important roles over from the men that were being sent overseas to fight in the war in Europe. These women took over the roles within the factory itself assembling many of the parts needed to supply the American troops with guns and other munitions.

This change in roles helped women to really begin asserting their independence within the workforce. Many of these women took jobs as filers, drillers, and inspectors during World War I. Their working conditions were generally poor. They did not even receive their own separate restrooms until January of 1918; an excerpt from the January issue of *The Armorer* gives the details of the new restrooms:

"The ever-increasing number of Uncle Sam's women workers will undoubtedly be much pleased to learn of the new restrooms which are being prepared for them."

"New two story buildings are now nearing completion at both the Hill and Watershops Plants where ample provision has been made for toilet, locker and restroom accommodations. Each building is to be in charge of a matron and will shortly be ready for use."

Women Armory workers also fought to create a much safer workplace for themselves. They brought attention to work safety and eventually changed the factory workplace from a safety standpoint for future generations to follow.

WORLD WAR II ARMORY WOMEN

The World War II era of women working at the Springfield armory was drastically different from that of the women of the prior generation. During World War II women represented the majority of people hired into the armory. In June of 1942, women represented 20% of the labor force and by the following year in June of 1943 it doubled to 43% of the total workforce in the armory. The amount of women hired by the armory was staggering between 1942 and 1943, as the demand grew for weapons in the war increased exponentially and the shortage of skilled men went down due to the draft. Between September and October of 1942 some 1600 women were hired by the Springfield Armory to account for the ever-increasing demand of weapons on the battlefield. The drastic increase of female workers during

World War II posed new questions to the factories that they worked in and the government: what to do with the children of the women working in the war industry?

CHILD CARE

Childcare during the World War II era posed a problem to many women that wanted to support the war effort by working in the war industry, but could not find a way to do so with young children. Alyssa Parks, author of *Child Care During World War II for the Springfield Armory*, said:

"Day care became a site of patriotism for many Americans. Such centers provided working mothers with the security that their children would be safe while they worked in factories across the country.

This held true for the Springfield Armory as well. The armory made it relatively easy for working mothers to contribute to the war effort overseas by manufacturing guns for the military. The innovation of providing onsite day care facilities to the mothers employed by the armory was influential in getting more working mothers to work for the war effort."

EMPLOYMENT TRAINING

By using federal and state funds the armory was able to develop fast and valuably significant training programs that prepared the new female workforce to enter the war industry. This was not met with open arms though, much of the management staff was very skeptical of women being able to fill the necessary gaps in the industrial sector because they thought the women would not have the necessary knowledge to get the work done. The skepticism is where the famous propaganda tool of "Rosie the Riveter" came into play that was fashioned by the US Government to urge the women into heavy war industry. Incorporated in

with the Rosie the riveter posters women also began the W.O.W. (Women Ordinance Workers) movement within the industrial war sectors throughout the country. The Springfield Armory was no exception to the WOW movement. Many of the mothers and young women working in the armory gave up their dresses and aprons for what were called "womenalls" with all their jewelry and handkerchiefs wrapped on their heads and got down and dirty in with the remaining men.

Top right: A young woman in full compliance with safety dress code, including wearing goggles, at a mill grinding machine at the Springfield Armory. (Springfield Armory Archives) **Right:** Stocking shop operations during World War II at Springfield Armory. (Springfield Armory Archives)

American Red Cross workers of the Smith College Unit about to leave Paris in camions to open a canteen at Chateau Thierry to serve wounded American soldiers as they come in from the front. From left to right standing they are: Miss Edna True, Miss Elizabeth Bliss, Dr. Agnes Hopkins, Miss Anna Rochester, Mrs Barrett Andrews, Miss Dorothy Brown and Mrs. Ruth Hill Arnold. Left to right, sitting in the camion: Miss Mary Goodman Stevenson, Miss Anne Chapin and Miss Marie Wolf. (Courtesy Library of Congress Archives)

ROLES OF THE WOMEN IN THE ARMORY

The roles that women played in both the World War I and World War II era were crucial to the war effort overseas as well as keeping life at home continuing on as it should have. Many of the women who went into the Springfield Armory took on many of the manufacturing roles once previously held only by men. Some women who worked there prior to the war starting were either office workers or inspectors for the parts and completed M1 rifles that the men worked on to put out.

Women workers in America in the time periods of World War I and World War II impacted one another. The Springfield Armory through the women of the World War I era made many strides to improve safety within the workplace, which had a direct result on the efficiency and manufacturing capabilities of the armory itself. Productivity increased, the overall working conditions in the armory increased, and although after the end of the war many of the "non-essential" women who were not the sole financial support of their families were laid off, these women workers laid the groundwork for the next generation of women who provided the vital component of the nation's defense work force during World War II.

Women in the Military or in Service during Wartime

Deborah Sampson

(B. DEC. 17, 1760 IN PLYMPTON, MA; D. APR. 29, 1827 IN SHARON, MA) In May of 1782, Deborah Sampson did something truly remarkable. She disguised herself as a man and enlisted in the Continental Army under the name Robert Shurtleff. Her motivations are not entirely clear. She may have wished to escape from a town where she was increasingly in conflict with the authorities. She may have seen soldiering as a way to provide for herself and live independently. She may have been fired with patriotism at a time when there was a desperate need for new recruits. A nineteenth-century biographer suggested that her enlistment represented a rebellion against gender restrictions: "Very justly did she consider the female sphere of action, in many respects, too contracted."

Whatever her reasons, Deborah Sampson dressed as a man and traveled to the Worcester County town of Uxbridge, where no one knew who she was. Using the name Robert Shurtleff — no proof of identity was required — she appeared before a recruiter there on May 20, 1782, and enlisted in the Continental Army for a term of three years. The minimum height was 5' 5" — she was 5' 7" — and she apparently satisfied the other requirement — soldiers needed a minimum of two opposing teeth for ripping open paper cartridges. On May 23, she passed inspection in Worcester and was judged ready and able to serve. She received a bounty of 60 pounds, a healthy sum for the times.

Deborah Sampson's physical attributes helped her disguise her sex. She had a muscular build, and her limbs were strong and well proportioned. Her breasts were small, and she could easily bind them with a cloth. Her jutting jaw and a prominent nose also aided her masquerade. Her lack of facial hair did not give her away, since recruiters were signing up adolescents who had not yet begun to grow beards. From her many years of farm work, she no doubt had the physical strength and familiarity with male tools to carry off her deception.

After her enlistment in Worcester, she went to West Point with the Light Infantry Company of the Fourth Massachusetts Regiment. During the autumn and winter of 1783, her unit patrolled the "no man's land" between Loyalist-controlled Manhattan and the areas of Westchester held by the Patriots. According to later testimony from her commanding officer, she "was in several skirmishes and received two wounds, a shot remaining in her to this day."

Deborah Sampson

In the late spring of 1783, Sampson served as a servant to General John Paterson. She accompanied the General to Philadelphia, where she became seriously ill. While she lay unconscious, the doctor discovered that his patient was a woman. Neither the doctor nor General Paterson revealed her secret. She was nursed back to health, and then quietly — and honorably — discharged from the Army. Deborah Sampson returned to Massachusetts, married Benjamin Gannett, Jr., a struggling farmer, and had three children. In 1792, she successfully petitioned the state legislature for back pay due her as a Continental soldier in a Massachusetts regiment. The story leaked out, and the press seized on it.

Deborah Sampson Gannett was by no means the only woman to serve disguised as a man. Many whose deception was discovered were publicly humiliated and some were even prosecuted — it was a crime to impersonate the opposite sex — but one historian has concluded that women often served "undetected and even . . . detected with no one giving a damn." What made Deborah Sampson unusual was that she was celebrated for her service. – *MassMoments*, Mass Humanities

Face of Defense: Female Fighter Pilot Continues Family Legacy

BY AIR FORCE SENIOR MASTER SGT. JULIE AVEY, 104TH FIGHTER WING, MASSACHUSETTS AIR NATIONAL GUARD

Air Force Maj. Ashley Rolfe, a member of the Massachusetts Air National Guard, is making history at the 104th Fighter Wing here as the first female fighter pilot in the wing's 70-year history.

Having grown up near Tyndall Air Force Base in Florida as an Air Force "brat," Rolfe wanted to follow in her father's and grandfather's footsteps to carry on the family legacy of military service.

"The noise of the sonic booms would shake the entire room," Rolfe recalled. "I thought it was the coolest thing in the entire world. So I made my dad take me to all the air shows, and I would drag him from pilot to pilot and ask them, 'How did you become a pilot?'"

DETERMINED TO BECOME A FLIER

Most of them said the most direct path was the Air Force Academy, she said. "So, I was a 10-year-old girl in 5th grade saying, 'I'm going to be a fighter pilot,'" she added. "I was usually shorter than everyone else, and people were usually saying, 'OK, little girl.'"

Rolfe did go on to graduate from the U.S. Air Force Academy and serve in the active-duty

Air Force Maj. Ashley Rolfe is the first female fighter pilot for the Massachusetts Air National Guard's 104th Fighter Wing based at Barnes Air National Guard Base in Westfield, Mass. Rolfe is an Air Force Academy graduate and combat veteran who has served in the Air Force for 11 years. (Massachusetts Air National Guard photo by Senior Master Sgt. Julie Avey)

Air Force for 11 years. In addition to serving at Tyndall, she has been stationed as a fighter pilot at Kadena Air Base in Japan and Nellis Air Force Base in Nevada. She has deployed twice, most recently to Afghanistan for six months. During her swearing-in ceremony to join the Air National Guard's 104th Fighter Wing, she thanked the wing's airmen for a warm welcome.

"I'm really excited to get to know everyone here," Rolfe recalled saying at the time. "Hopefully, you don't necessarily just see me as a 'chick,' but you see me as one of the pilots or one of the 'bros.'"

"I think it is really awesome to hire our first female to the 104th Fighter Wing," said Air Force Lt. Col. William Bladen, 104th Operations Group commander. Bladen said he's known Rolfe since around 2012.

Rolfe said she flew T-38 aircraft in an aggressor role as part of the F-22 Raptor fighter program at her previous duty assignment at Tyndall before coming to the 104th. Becoming a fighter pilot wasn't easy, Rolfe said. "For anyone going into flying fighters, it's a challenge -- a lot of hard work, a lot of studying, and a lot of practice, [and] getting into the fighter pilot culture," she said.

F-15 FIGHTER PILOT

Rolfe graduated from pilot training in 2007, fulfilling her lifelong dream to become an F-15 Eagle fighter pilot.

"I was the only girl in my first half of pilot training," Rolfe said. "But then, I ended up transitioning after the first section of training. Once I went to the T-38s in Columbus, Mississippi, there was another girl in my class. She ended up being one of my bridesmaids, and we're still very close. We were competitive, but still became lifelong friends, and she ended up going to [F-15E] Strike Eagles. We were a little nervous when we first met, because we are both type-A personalities, and who knew how that meshing was going to work? But it worked out great."

Women first entered pilot training in 1976 and fighter pilot training in 1993. The Air National Guard has 195 female pilots. Of those, 10 are fighter pilots.

Kadena was Rolfe's first duty assignment, where she served as the 67th Fighter Squadron as the only female F-15 pilot.

"At first, the guys were hesitant, because they hadn't had a female in the squadron for a few years," Rolfe recalled, "but it didn't take long until I became just one of the 'bros.' They were very accepting and gave me just as much crap as I could give them. Brotherly love, pretty much, and [they] treated me as a little sister, picking on me."

'Fiercely Independent' Daughter
Rolfe said she has a year-and-a-half-old daughter.

"She's already a fiercely independent little girl," Rolfe said.

"I just want to impart you don't have to be limited by what other people say," Rolfe said. "There was a high school football and baseball coach at my school when I was a senior. I had been telling people, 'I want to go to the Air Force Academy. I want to be a fighter pilot,' and blah-blah. He straight-up told me, 'You won't ever be a fighter pilot, because you are a girl.'"

Rolfe emphasized that she wants her daughter "to know even though someone might say you can't do that, do the research and realize, 'No kidding, if you put your mind to it, you can most likely do this.'"

Rolfe added, "Like my mom, she said I couldn't fly off the dining room table when I was 2 and a half. I broke my arm doing it [anyway], and that's the kind of thing my daughter got from me. I'm having to tell her, 'Don't stand on that rocking chair.'"

ALPHABETICAL LISTING OF WOMEN IN THE MILITARY OR IN SERVICE DURING WARTIME:

Alleen V. (Dudley) Augustus
(B. SEPT. 19, 1922 IN SPRINGFIELD, MA; D. MAY 6, 2014 IN SPRINGFIELD, MA) served in the U. S. Navy during WWII, achieving the rank of Seaman First Class serving from June 1, 1942, to Oct. 26, 1945. She was the first woman Commander of Hampden County District 3 American Legion Post 463, a member of American Legion Post 430 and former Commander for two years. Augustus also served as a Silver Hair Legislator, and Trustee for GAR Hall in Springfield. In 1999, she was presented with the "Courage Award" by the National Puerto Rican Woman's Association.
– Joseph Carvalho III

Caroline Asenath Grant Burghardt
(B. JUNE 10, 1831 IN GREAT BARRINGTON, MA; D. FEB. 6, 1922 IN WASHINGTON, D.C.) was a Union nurse during the American Civil War. Working as a governess in New York at the outbreak of the Civil War, Burghardt reported to Bellevue Hospital where she was accepted for nurse training by the board of surgeons on April 19, 1861. After her training, she traveled to Washington on June 8 to begin acting as a nurse for the Union Army. Burghardt served as a nurse until September 6, 1865. During her years of service, she was stationed at numerous field hospitals during and after the Battles of Antietam, Gettysburg, and Winchester; and at Army hospitals at Fortress Monroe, and Alexandria. Dorothea Dix composed a "testimony of hospital services" regarding Burghardt's work during the war praising her "superior fidelity and skill." After the war, she was employed by the U.S. Treasury.
– James Gleason & Joseph Carvalho III

Above: Mildred "Millie" Beatrice Dunbar (right) with City Councilor Kateri Walsh (left). **Top right:** Alleen V. Augustus. **Bottom right:** Gen. Marie Field.

Gertrude M. Carney

(B. MAR. 6, 1922) of Springfield, MA served in the U.S. Navy WAVES during World War II with the rank of Pharmacist's Mate Second Class. She served at the Navy medical facilities at Bethesda, Maryland and Portsmouth, Virginia caring for sick and wounded servicemen and women. – Anne-Gerard Flynn

Hazel E. Chipman

(B. AUG. 8, 1913 IN HARTLAND, ME; D. DEC. 20, 1996 IN SPRINGFIELD, MA)
graduated as a registered nurse from the Wesson Memorial Hospital School of Nursing and worked at the Wesson Memorial Hospital before enlisting in the Army during World War II. She served with the 200th Hospital Ship Complement, with the rank of first lieutenant (Dec. 14, 1943- Sept. 17, 1947). She received European, American, and Pacific theater ribbons, and a Victory Medal. She lived in Springfield from 1926, and belonged to the Wesson Hospital Auxiliary and American Legion Post 185 in Feeding Hills. She also was a longtime part-time bookkeeper for Archie Construction Company.
– Joseph Carvalho III & Cliff McCarthy

Mildred "Millie" Beatrice Dunbar

(B. OCT. 29, 1920 IN SPRINGFIELD, MA; D. SEPT 2018 IN SPRINGFIELD, MA) is a World War II veteran and community activist. Dunbar enlisted in the Women's Army Corps as an aviation cadet on Feb. 15, 1943. Before being discharged in 1946, she had attained the rank of staff sergeant. Prior to enlisting, she worked at the Indian Motocycle factory in East Springfield. After the war, she worked at the U.S. Armory and was a union officer. She was among the community leaders who fought to keep the Armory open prior to its closing in 1968. Her life-long interest and love for her community inspired her to be one of the more prolific "letter to the editor" writers to the *Springfield newspapers*. She would often try to include positive thoughts about contemporary events and local projects as well as sound advice and was a vocal advocate for veterans. Dunbar was one of the founders of American Legion Pioneer Valley Women's Post 463. In 1988, the Springfield NAACP recognized her with an award for her volunteer work with the local African-American organizations and institutions. In 1992, Dunbar was recognized as Springfield Veteran of the Year.
– Joseph Carvalho III & Elise Linscott

Margaret (Clifford) Dwyer

(B. FEB. 23, 1912 IN NORTHAMPTON, MA; D. JAN. 13, 2006 IN HADLEY, MA)
was the first woman from Hampshire County to train with the WAVES in Northampton. In 1942, following a twenty-day training course she was commissioned an ensign and assigned as a company commander in charge of Gillett House on the Smith College campus. Later she was transferred to the U. S. Naval Training School in the Bronx, N. Y. where she was the first regimental commander when the school opened for the training of enlisted women. She spent the last three years of her service in the Office of Naval Operations, Office of Naval Intelligence, in Washington, D.C. and was discharged with the rank of Lieutenant Commander. In 1947, following military service in WWII, she returned to her teaching position at Northampton High School where she remained until 1954. She taught mathematics and English and wrote a weekly article for *The Daily Hampshire Gazette*. From September 1933 to June 1942 she taught at the Hawley Junior High School in Northampton.
– Joseph Carvalho III & Cynthia G. Simison

Parthenia Little (Dickinson) Fenn

(B. SEPT. 20, 1798 IN PITTSFIELD, MA; D. APR. 10, 1878 IN PITTSFIELD, MA)
became sole "director and manager" of the informal women's soldiers aid society of Pittsfield during the Civil War. She organized the preparation and delivery of food, medical supplies and other useful items to be sent to the soldiers of Pittsfield and Berkshire regiments during the Civil War. She was known to personally visit the military encampments at David's Island. It is said that "long before the war closed, the name of Mrs. Fenn was one of those most familiar by the camp-fire and hospital," of the soldiers of Pittsfield. Fenn's entire life had been "noted for kindly services to the sick and suffering." As a teenager during the War of 1812, she volunteered her services to care for sick and wounded soldiers. In the next decade, she provided care for injured and sick Greek patriots during the insurrection against the Ottoman Empire in 1824. – Joseph Carvalho III

Marie T. Field

(B. IN HOLYOKE, MASS.) became the first female brigadier general in the history of the Massachusetts National Guard, in 2002.

Then a resident of Lenox, Field had been a member of the Air National Guard's 104th Fighter Wing at Barnes Regional Airport in Westfield since 1988. At the time of her promotion, she became one of only eight women generals in the National Guard throughout the nation.

"It's humbling in a surprising sort of way," said Field, who started her military career as a flight nurse with the Air Force Reserve in 1978. "I am kind of in uncharted territory. There's a tremendous amount of responsibility to be a role model."

Along with her promotion, she was appointed to the Air Guard's top nursing position in the country as assistant to the chief nurse of the Air Force.

In her civilian life, Field worked as newborn intensive care clinical educator at Brigham and Women's Hospital in Boston.

At the 104th, Field served as medical squadron commander for the 104th for four years. Even that position was groundbreaking

in its way as it was relatively rare for a nurse to be named a medical squadron commander. She had joined the Air Force Reserves in 1978, serving as an aeromedical evacuation nurse and flight nurse instructor. Her time with the Air Reserve included duty at Westover Air Reserve Base in Chicopee before joining the Air Guard in 1988. She retired in 2008.
– Cynthia G. Simison

Constance Ray Harvey

a member of the Class of 1927 at Smith College was awarded the Medal of Freedom for her service to the French Underground in 1941 and 1942 during World War II.
– Fred Contrada

Gloria Heath,

graduate of Smith College, (Class of 1943) flew a B-26 Marauder in the WAVES (Woman Accepted for Volunteer Emergency Service) – Fred Contrada

Roselle M. Hoffmaster

was a Class of 2000 Smith College graduate who enlisted in the U.S. Army and was promoted to the rank of Captain serving in Iraq. She died on active service in Iraq in September of 2007.
– Fred Contrada

Anne Sophia (Clapp) Merrick

(B. NOV. 18, 1818 IN NORTHAMPTON, MA;
D. MAY 2, 1879 IN SPRINGFIELD, MA)
served as a field hospital nurse during the Civil War. She was the widow of famed Springfield inventor Solyman Merrick who died in 1852. When typhoid fever broke out in the ranks of the 10th Massachusetts Volunteer Infantry Regiment in the fall of 1861, Merrick volunteered to serve as a nurse in the 10th Regiment's field hospital. She was joined by Helen Wolcott as the only two nurses for the regiment. Capt. Newell of the 10th reported that, " The addition of Mrs. Merrick and Miss Wolcott to the hospital staff, has proved a valuable one and has done much to mitigate

the asperities of sickness in the camp. They have engaged in their duties with zeal and earnestness, having already gracefully and successfully adapted themselves to the peculiarities of their novel position."
– Wayne E. Phaneuf & Joseph Carvalho III

Margaret Ann "Peg" (White) Parda

(B. JAN. 2, 1924 IN NORTHAMPTON, MA;
D. DEC. 14, 1991 IN NORTHAMPTON, MA)
was a World War II Marine Corps veteran and founder of the Western Massachusetts Chapter of the Women Marines League. She also was a member of the Westfield Marine Corps League, vice commander of American Legion Post 28 in Northampton, and chaplain of the American Legion Post 28 Auxiliary. In her honor, the Women's Marines Chapter of Western Massachusetts carries her name.
– Joseph Carvalho III

Shirley "Penny" (Beach) Seip

(B. JUNE 5, 1922 IN SPRINGFIELD, MA;
D. NOV. 13, 2015 IN LONGMEADOW, MA)
was the first woman applicant in Springfield for the "Lady Leathernecks" during WWII with the United States Marines from Springfield. Shirley went to Boot Camp at Hunter College in New York City. She then went to Henderson Hall to work at the Navy Annex in Washington, D.C. Shirley studied at the Sound, Motion Picture School in Brooklyn Navy Yard. Upon her graduation, she was stationed at Quantico Air Base attaining the rank of Sergeant. Seip was a charter member of the American Legion Pioneer Valley Women's Post 463, and a life member and officer of the Women's Marine Association. – Joseph Carvalho III

Smith College Relief Unit of WWI

The Grecourt Gates at Smith College are a replica of the gates to a French chateau where the Smith College Relief Unit had its headquarters in 1917. The unit, made of up of Smith graduates, went to France to help rebuild villages destroyed early in the Great

Top: Capt. Roselle M. Hoffmaster
Above: Shirley B. Seip

War. Shortly after they arrived, the German army swept through the region once more, forcing the Smith women to help evacuate the villages. The gates, erected in 1924, stand outside College Hall on Elm Street.
– Fred Contrada & Joseph Carvalho III

Ernestine Stowell, M.D.

(B. OCT. 20, 1921 IN NEW HAVEN, CT; D. JULY 20, 2017 IN HOLYOKE, MA) was a resident of South Hadley for nearly 50 years with more than 30 years of service in the Marine Corps, a decade as a college development officer and more than 20 years as a practicing chiropractor are among the highlights of a long and distinguished career that spanned more than 70 years.

  She attended Mount Holyoke College, where in 1943 as a senior she awakened each morning to strident orders of drill sergeants training the first officer class of Women Marines called to emergency service in World War II. While a student at Mount Holyoke she also attended summer sessions at the Yale School of Fine Arts where she studied sculpture, which was an area of particular interest, and later attended the New York School of Interior Design.

  After graduating from Mount Holyoke with a Bachelor of Arts degree in art history, she enlisted that fall in the Marine Corps Women's Reserve and in November was called to basic training at Camp Lejeune, N.C., where she would later graduate from Officer Training School.

  She worked in the intelligence field and was assigned to General A.A. Vandegrift – then commandant of the Marine Corps – in his private map room in the Navy Annex in Washington, D.C. At the time, Marines were training for the battles of Iwo Jima and Okinawa, and she prepared the invasion maps for those campaigns. All was top secret, and those involved were told that if anyone asked about their duties they were to say, "We are camouflaging pigeons." Later she was officer

in charge of recreation and conducted a sports, educational and recreation program for 700 women at Parris Island. S.C.

  In 1946 she was released to inactive duty as a second lieutenant and took a position in public relations and advertising in New York City with Gommi Associates, a commercial photography firm specializing in food styling. It was a position that fit well with her art major at Mount Holyoke. During this period she was a member of the American Institute of Interior Decorators.

  At about the same time she joined a Marine Reserve Company at Ft. Schuyler in the Bronx and later became commanding officer. She conducted a Personnel Classification Training School for 50 women reservists attached to a male battalion of 300 Marines. In 1954 she was one of 32 people – and the only woman – representing all of the armed services to serve on the Military Staff of the Hon. John D. Lodge, then governor of Connecticut.

  After leaving New York she was employed by Mount Holyoke College in 1962 as a field worker for its Capital Fund Campaign as the liaison between the college and the volunteer alumnae. At the end of a successful $13 million fund raising campaign she was awarded the Alumnae Association's Medal of Honor.

  In 1968 she was asked to arrange for the 25th reunion celebration of Women Marines, the organization which trained its first two officer classes at Mount Holyoke College in 1943. The first five directors of Women Marines attended the celebration – probably the last time they all were together. She continued working for Mount Holyoke as a development officer until 1973. In a letter of commendation after the event Col. Barbara J. Bishop, then director of Women Marines, wrote "When arrangements have been perfection, what can one say? With my great thanks for your efforts which truly were 'above and beyond' – even for that rare avis, a Woman Marine."

  When she left Mount Holyoke College in 1973, she entered the National College

of Chiropractic in Lombard, Ill., where she received degrees of Bachelor of Science and Doctor of Chiropractic as well as a Meridian Therapy Certificate for 100 hours of clinical acupuncture training. Shortly after graduation in 1977, she returned to South Hadley where she opened a private practice. After beginning her practice she entered the University of Bridgeport in Connecticut and in 1979 was awarded a Master of Science degree in Biology and a certificate in clinical nutrition. She was licensed in both Massachusetts and Connecticut. She retired in 2003.

  Long interested in nutrition and natural healing she continued her studies in those fields while conducting her practice. She visited Europe, particularly Germany, at least annually where she studied with practitioners of advanced homeopathy and other areas of natural healing.

  After serving in the Marine Corps Reserve for more than 30 years she was retired in 1981 with the rank of colonel. In the late 1980s she joined the Women Marines Association and served two terms as president of the Western Massachusetts unit. She later served as Area Director for the national Women Marines Association. She also was a member of the Westfield River Valley Detachment of the Marine Corps League, the American Legion and Women in Military Service to America. At the time of her death she was president of her class at Mount Holyoke College.
– Cynthia G. Simison

Maryanne Walts

is the first woman to be promoted to Command Chief Master Sgt. of the 104th Fighter Wing, Air National Guard at Barnes Air National Guard Base in Westfield, MA, appointed April of 2014. Entering the Air Force in 1981, she served four years of active duty before transferring to the Massachusetts Air National Guard in 1985. In 2009, Chief Walts became the interim Force Support Superintendent. There she assisted with the

Left: Lt. Col. Margaret White, U.S. Army National Guard.
Above: Maryanne Walts

merging of the Military Personnel Flight and the Services Flight. She transitioned back to the Logistics Squadron in 2010, as the Logistics Readiness Squadron Superintendent. She was promoted to Chief Master Sergeant on June 29, 2012. As command chief, she is responsible for all matters influencing the health, professional development, military readiness, morale and welfare of assigned enlisted personnel and their families. In the role, she serves as an advisor to the wing commander, providing updates of all personnel issues regarding enlisted staff. – Cynthia G. Simison

Sarah Wells

(B. JULY 26, 1701 IN DEERFIELD, MA; D. OCT. 10, 1783 IN DEERFIELD, MA) of Deerfield provided medical care for wounded and sick soldiers from that town who had served at Fort Massachusetts 1748-49. She was recognized for her service during King George's War (1744-48; aka War of Jenkins' Ear) by the Massachusetts Bay colonial government.
– Joseph Carvalho III

Margaret White

is a Lt. Col. Of the U.S. Army Massachusetts National Guard. In February 2014, she became the first woman to lead a Massachusetts National Guard unit deployed at Joint Task Force Detention Center on Naval Base Guantanamo Bay. Her command is composed of the 211th Military Police Battalion the Massachusetts Army National Guard, and will included soldiers from the 747th Military Police Company, based in Ware, MA. A retired police officer, White joined the National Guard in 1981. – Joseph Carvalho III

Helen C. Wolcott

(B. SEPT. 26, 1826 IN NORTHAMPTON, MA; D. DEC. 18, 1910 IN AGAWAM, MA) was a hospital matron in the 10th Massachusetts Volunteer Infantry Regiment during the Civil War. [see also entry for Anne Sophia (Clapp) Merrick in this Chapter]
– Joseph Carvalho III

World War I Posters

The
GREATEST MOTHER
in the WORLD

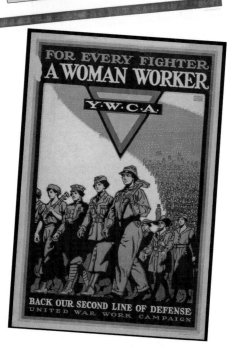

World War II Posters

CHAPTER NINE

WOMEN IN
Science, Technology, Engineering and Mathematics

BY ELLEN SAVULIS

Curator of Anthropology,
Springfield
Science Museum,
Springfield Museums

The fields of science, technology, engineering and mathematics (STEM) have been predominantly male professions over the centuries; however, women have made significant contributions since ancient times. Gazing through microscopes and telescopes, women have participated in humanity's quest to explain the universe. Women have broken sound and gender barriers, discovered the first evidence of dark matter, and inspired the environmental movement.

The involvement of women in the field of medicine occurred in several early civilizations. The study of natural philosophy in ancient Greece was open to women such as Theano (6th century B.C.), a mathematician, physician and a student of Pythagoras and Aglaonice (1st or 2nd century B.C.), an astronomer who predicted eclipses.

In Egypt, women were involved in applied chemistry, such as beer-making and preparing medicinal compounds. Hypatia of Alexandria (c. 350-415 A.D.), was a well-known teacher of astronomy, philosophy and mathematics. She is credited with writing treatises on geometry and algebra, and inventing a hydrometer, astrolabe and a water distiller.

During the European Middle Ages, convents were important places for the education of women. Some communities provided opportunities for women to contribute to scholarly research. For example, German abbess Hildegard of Birgen (1098-1179) was a philosopher and botanist.

With the growth of nunneries, there was a backlash from the male clergy hierarchy. Many orders closed which prevented the advancement of women's education. In the 11th century, the first universities emerged and women were generally excluded from formal education.

In the 17th and 18th centuries the emergence of modern science saw developments in mathematics, physics, astronomy, biology and chemistry which transformed society's views about nature. During this period, 17th century German astronomer Maria Winkelmann was the first woman to discover a comet. The first known woman to earn a chair in scientific studies was Italian physicist Laura Bassi (1711-1778). The first 18th century German woman medical doctor was Dorothea Erxleben.

During the 19th century, women were excluded from most formal scientific education, but they began to be admitted into learned societies. The rise of women's colleges provided jobs for women scientists and opportunities for education. Marie Curie, (1867-1934), a pioneer in the study of radiation, received a Nobel Prize for physics in 1903 and another for chemistry in 1911.

During WWII, a shortage of male workers prompted government and industry to hire women in science and engineering. When men returned from the service, women's status in STEM fields worsened. Discrimination began to manifest itself in policies and culture with a disapproval of women who combined a career and raising a family.

Throughout history, women have been kept from full participation. Often, the barriers to entering these fields are raised in grade school and continue to impede women long after they graduate from college. A number of organizations have been set up to combat the stereotyping that may discourage girls from taking courses in STEM. The American Association of University Women was established in 1881. Sigma Delta Epsilon was created in 1921 as a women's scientific organization. The Society for Women Engineers was established in 1950 as an educational and service organization. The Association for Women in Science, founded in 1971, is one of the most prominent global organizations for professional women

Previous page: Cornelia Maria Clapp
Above: Elizabeth Lee Hazen (left) and Rachel Fuller Brown (right)

in science. One goal is to empower pre-professional college and graduate women in science, technology, engineering and mathematics to stay on the career track. Boston's WISE (Women in Science and Engineering), established in 1976, and similar groups brought together women to lobby for anti-discrimination measures and financial support for female students. Since 1901, 48 women have been awarded the Nobel Prize.

Scientists, and Inventors

Lynn Petra (Alexander) Margulis
(B. MAR. 5, 1938 IN CHICAGO, IL; D. NOV. 22, 2011 IN AMHERST, MA)

has formulated what is now generally accepted as the likely explanation of the origin and evolution of life on earth. Sometimes branded a maverick for her disregard for scientific dogma, she has made profound contributions to our understanding of the development and structure of life forms.

In an age of narrow specialties, Margulis' research has cut a wide swath across disciplines as disparate as molecular and cellular biology, medicine, climatology, geology and paleontology. Her interdisciplinary collaborations are legend in the scientific community.

A gifted and dedicated teacher, Margulis applies her scientific principles to her pedagogy. Her symbiotic model of evolution is mirrored in the lab and classroom, where her students work in collaborative groups. Through her work and her example, she has inspired a generation of students to question conventional wisdom and push back the limits of knowledge.

Lynn Margulis was not a scientist who remained cloistered in the laboratory. She was the author or co-author of 23 books that range from highly specialized professional literature to children's books to lucid popular science. Her best-known work for general readers, The Gaia Hypothesis, co-authored with British scientist James Lovelock, details the ways in which life has shaped the surface and atmosphere of the Earth. She has also participated in the development of science teaching materials at levels from elementary school to graduate school.

Margulis was the Distinguished University Professor of Geosciences at the University of Massachusetts at Amherst. Among her honors are Sigma Xi's Proctor Prize for Scientific Research in 1999 and the National Medal of Science in 2000. In 2001, she was honored with a Commonwealth Award by the Massachusetts Cultural Council; and awarded the Darwin-Wallace Medal in 2008. NAS presented her with a Public Service Award for Astrobiology in 2010. – excerpted from her citation from the Massachusetts Cultural Council.

Henrietta Swan Leavitt
(B. JULY 4, 1868 IN LANCASTER, MA; D. DECEMBER 12, 1921) was an American astronomer who discovered the relation between the luminosity and the period of Cepheid variable stars. A graduate of Radcliffe College, Leavitt began her career in 1893 working at the Harvard College Observatory as a "computer" examining photographic plates in order to measure and catalog the brightness of the stars. She received little recognition in her lifetime, working in relative anonymity. However, it was her discovery that first allowed astronomers to measure the distance between the Earth and distant galaxies. Leavitt explained her discovery: "A straight line can readily be drawn among each of the two series of points corresponding to maxima and minima, thus showing that there is a simple relation between the brightness of the variables and their periods." That revolutionary theory, the "period luminosity Law" was used by astronomer Harlow Shapley in order to posit the first estimates of the scale of the universe. It was after Leavitt's death that Edwin Hubble used the luminosity–period relation for Cepheids together with spectral to determine that the universe is expanding. – Joseph Carvalho III

Margaret Eloise Knight
(B. FEB. 14, 1838 IN YORK, ME; D. OCT. 12, 1914 IN FRAMINGHAM, MA)

has been called "the most famous 19th Century Woman inventor." Working as a young girl in a Manchester, NH cotton mill, she witnessed a fellow worker injured by a steel-tipped shuffle

KNIGHT INVENTED A MACHINE THAT COULD FOLD AND GLUE PAPER TO FORM THE FLAT-BOTTOMED BROWN PAPER BAG, A FAMILIAR DESIGN STILL USED TODAY

which shot out of a mechanical loom. A few weeks later, she invented a safety device for the machine that was adopted by not only the mill she was working for, but many other mills in Manchester. She was only twelve at the time. Poor health in her early 20s precluded her from continuing work at cotton mills, she moved to Springfield, MA in 1867 to work for the Columbia Paper Bag Company. A year later, Knight invented a machine that could fold and glue paper to form the flat-bottomed brown paper bag, a familiar design still used today (the original bag-making machine is in the collections of the Smithsonian Institution). The man she hired to create a patent model of the device stole her design and patented it himself. She sued him and won her case in 1871. She then established the Eastern Paper Bag Co., and began receiving royalties from her patent. During her lifetime she successfully filed and was granted 87 U.S. patents for inventions which ranged from "lid removing pliers," a "numbering machine," a window frame and sash design, and several devices related to rotary engines that she patented between 1902 and 1914. Knight was inducted into the National Inventors Hall of Fame in 2006.
– Joseph Carvalho III

Margaret Eloise Knight (1838–1914) applied for a patent using this model to demonstrate her machine that folded and pasted flat-bottomed paper bags. She was granted patent number 220925 for the invention in 1879. Her concept continues to be used in the manufacture of today's paper grocery bag.

Her first patented invention, inspired by her work at a Springfield, Massachusetts paper company, was her machine for improvement in paper-feeding; it was given patent number 109224 in 1870. She received 26 patents for inventions having to do with the paper bag, shoe manufacturing, and rotary engine industries.

While many women had innovative ideas during the 19th century, it was difficult for them to secure patents under their own names. Knight's inventions are celebrated because they demonstrate women's participation in the American patent system.

DATE MADE: ca 1879 · PATENT DATE: 1879-10-28 · MAKER: Knight, Margaret E.
PHYSICAL DESCRIPTION: metal (overall material), wood (overall material)
MEASUREMENTS: 6 3/8 in x 6 3/4 in x 12 3/16 in; 16.2052 cm x 17.145 cm x 30.9372 cm
ID NUMBER: 1980.0004.01 · ACCESSION NUMBER: 1980.0004
CATALOG NUMBER · 1980.0004.01 · PATENT NUMBER: 220925 ·
CREDIT LINE: Pravel, Gambrell, Hewitt, Kirk, Kimball, and Dodge
DATA SOURCE: National Museum of American History, Kenneth E. Behring Center

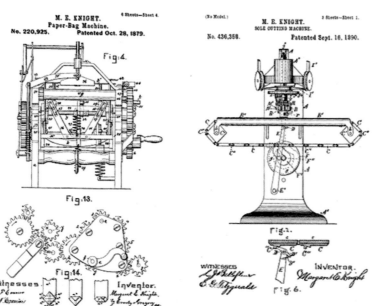

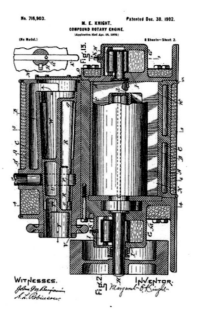

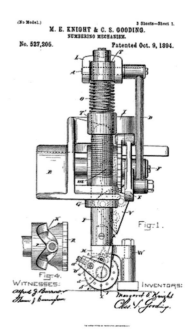

Mary Ann Allard Booth

(B. SEPT. 8, 1843 IN LONGMEADOW, MA; D. SEPT. 15, 1922 IN SPRINGFIELD, MA) was a noted scientist and microscopist. She maintained a fully equipped laboratory at her home in Springfield, MA where she prepared and stored microscope slides. She was especially noted for her preparation of diatoms and pollens and was elected as one of the first female Fellows of the Royal Microscopical Society in 1889. Booth was also a Fellow of the American Association for the Advancement of Science. She donated a series of her photomicrographs to the Springfield Science Museum (Springfield Museums Association, Springfield, MA). – Joseph Carvalho III

Myrtle Claire Bachelder

(B. MARCH 13, 1908 IN ORANGE, MA; D. MAY 22, 1997) was an American chemist and Women's Army Corps officer, who is noted for her secret work on the Manhattan Project atomic bomb program, and for the development of techniques in the chemistry of metals. – Joseph Carvalho III

Sarah "Tabitha" Babbitt

(B. DEC. 9, 1779 IN HARDWICK, MA; D. DEC. 10, 1853 IN HARVARD, MA) was an early American Shaker tool maker and inventor, including inventions for the circular saw, spinning wheel head, and false teeth. Some historians contest whether she was the first to invent the circular saw. She became a member of the Shakers at the Harvard Shaker community in Massachusetts. Babbitt, having realized a round blade would be more efficient, is credited with inventing the first circular saw used in a saw mill in 1813. The circular saw was hooked up to a water powered machine to reduce the effort to cut lumber. It is said

that she was watching men use the difficult two-man whipsaw when she noticed that half of their motion was wasted. Confusing the definitive origins of the circular saw, Babbitt did not patent the circular saw at the time that she created it. It was then patented in the United States by two French men three years later who purportedly learned about the saw in Shaker newspapers. It is also claimed that Babbitt invented a process for the manufacture of false teeth and an improved spinning wheel head. As a Shaker, Babbitt never patented any of her inventions. – Joseph Carvalho III

AN EFFICIENT WORKER IN THE VAN-GUARD

Miss Mary A. Booth began as an amateur, and now is one of the most trusted workers in the field of parasite study by means of photomicrographs. She has mapped out many fields for investigation and further study with her simple apparatus.

Top left and right: Mary Ann Allard Booth
Above: Myrtle Claire Bachelder

Florence Bascom

(B. JULY 14, 1862 IN WILLIAMSTOWN, MA; D. JUNE 18, 1945) was the second woman to earn her Ph.D in geology in the United States, and the first woman to receive a Ph.D from Johns Hopkins University. She was also the first woman hired by the United States Geological Survey. Bascom was known for her innovative findings in the field, and led the next generation of notable female geologists. – Joseph Carvalho III

Rachel Fuller Brown

(B. NOVEMBER 23, 1898 IN SPRINGFIELD, MA; D. JANUARY 14, 1980 IN ALBANY, NY) was a chemist best known for her long-distance collaboration with microbiologist Elizabeth Lee Hazen in developing the first useful antifungal antibiotic, nystatin, while doing research for the Division of Laboratories and Research of the New York State Department of Health. Both Brown and Hazen received many awards for their collaborative work, the first major prize being the Squibb Award in Chemotherapy in 1955. Royalties for nystatin totaled $13.4 million. As Brown and Hazen would not accept any of the money for themselves, the philanthropic Research Corporation used half for grants to further scientific research and the other half to support what became known as the Brown-Hazen Fund. Rachel Fuller Brown was inducted into the National Inventors Hall of Fame in 1994. In 1920, Brown received her B.A. in Chemistry from Mount Holyoke College and her Ph.D from the University of Chicago. – Joseph Carvalho III

Cornelia Maria Clapp, Ph.D.

(B. MAR. 17, 1849 IN MONTAGUE, MA; D. DEC. 31, 1934 IN MONTAGUE, MA) was a noted zoologist, and marine biologist. During her lifetime, Clapp was "rated as one of the top zoologists in the United States." She graduated from Mount Holyoke Seminary in 1878 and then earned both the first and second Ph.D.s from Syracuse University in 1889 and from the University of Chicago in 1896. In 1888, Clapp began her work at the Marine Biological Laboratory at Woods Hole, MA. Later, she returned to Mount Holyoke College to help organize the Department of Zoology, becoming professor of zoology in 1904. – Joseph Carvalho III

Catherine Grace "Cady" Coleman

(BORN DECEMBER 14, 1960 IN CHARLESTON, SC) of Shelburne, MA is an American chemist, a former colonel in the United States Air Force, and a former NASA astronaut. She is a veteran of two Space Shuttle missions, and departed the International Space Station on May 23, 2011, as a crew member of Expedition 27 after logging 159 days in space. She holds a degree in Chemistry from M.I.T. (1983) and a doctorate in Polymer science and engineering from the University of Massachusetts/Amherst (1991). Coleman served as Chief of Robotics for the Astronaut Office, to include robotic arm operations and training for all Space Shuttle and International Space Station missions. STS-93 on Columbia (July 22 to 27, 1999) was a five-day mission during which Coleman was the lead mission specialist for the deployment of the Chandra X-ray Observatory. Designed to conduct comprehensive studies of the universe, the telescope will enable scientists to study exotic phenomena such as exploding stars, quasars, and black holes. Mission duration was 118 hours and 50 minutes. She is also an accomplished flute player and on April 12, 2011, she played live through video link for the audience of Jethro Tull's show in Russia in honor of the 50th anniversary of Yuri Gagarin's flight. She played the duet from orbit while Anderson played on the ground in Russia. In 2015, Coleman was elected as a member of the board of directors for the Hollywood Science Fiction Museum. She is married to the internationally acclaimed glass artist Josh Simpson. – Joseph Carvalho III

Esther Christine (Kisk) Goddard

(B. MAR. 31, 1901 IN WORCESTER, MA; D. JUNE 4, 1982 IN WORCESTER, MA) was the wife of the famed Worcester scientist, Robert H. Goddard, who was an American engineer, professor, physicist, and inventor who is credited with creating and building the world's first liquid-fueled rocket. Esther became enthusiastic about rocketry and photographed some of Goddard's work and aided him in his experiments and paperwork. After her husband's death, Esther laboriously sorted through Goddard's voluminous papers and secured an additional 131 patents on his ground-breaking work. In 1957 a claim of patent infringement was made by Mrs. Goddard on behalf of her late husband against the United States Government, specifically regarding the technologies being developed in building the Redstone and Jupiter missiles at Redstone Arsenal in Huntsville, Alabama.

In response, a detailed engineering assessment was made of the 40 Goddard patents in question by the ARMY, (later NASA) engineers and indeed, it was found that there were many infringements. In 1960, the litigation was settled with a sizeable award from NASA to the Goddard Estate.
– Joseph Carvalho III & Wayne E. Phaneuf

Louise Freeland Jenkins

(B. JULY 5, 1888 IN FITCHBURG, MA; D. MAY 9, 1970) was an American astronomer who compiled a valuable catalogue of stars within 10 parsecs of the sun, and edited the 3rd edition of the *Yale Bright Star Catalogue*. She graduated from Mount Holyoke College in 1911, then she received a Master's degree in astronomy in 1917 from the same institution. From 1913 to 1915 she worked at the Allegheny Observatory in Pittsburgh. Afterwards, she was an instructor at Mount Holyoke from 1915 to 1920. She was noted for her research on the trigonometric parallax of nearby stars. She also made valuable contributions to Astronomy with her research about variable stars. – Joseph Carvalho III

Grace L. (Pettis) Johnson

(B. 1869 IN CT; D. FEB. 25, 1965 IN SPRINGFIELD, MA) was largely responsible for organizing and developing the Science collections of the Springfield Science Museum of the Springfield Museums Association. The growth of this collection led to the creation of a separate building for Science in 1899. She authored seven editions of *The Birds of Springfield and Vicinity* and in 1941 was awarded the William Pynchon Medal. – Joseph Carvalho III

Laurie A. Leshin, Ph.D.

(B. AUG. 5, 1965) is the 16th President of Worcester Polytechnic Institute, Worcester, MA, the first female president in the college's history. An accomplished academic and administrative leader, geochemist, and space scientist, Leshin was appointed in June

(Opposite page) **Far left, top and bottom:** Catherine Grace "Cady" Coleman. **Top right:** Florence Bascom. **Above:** Laurie A. Leshin

Above: Emily Hitchcock Terry
Above right: Henrietta Swan Leavitt

of 2014. In 2003, she became the Director of Arizona State University's Center for Meteorite Studies, which houses the largest University-based meteorite collection in the world. During her time on the faculty at ASU, she spearheaded the formulation of a new School of Earth and Space Exploration. In 2004, Leshin served on President Bush's Commission on Implementation of United States Space Exploration Policy, a nine-member commission charged with advising the President on the execution of his new Vision for Space Exploration.

From 2005 to 2007, Leshin was the Director of Sciences and Exploration Directorate at NASA's Goddard Space Flight Center, where she oversaw science activities. From 2008 to 2009, she was the Deputy Center Director for Science & Technology at Goddard. In this position, she oversaw strategy development at the Center. Starting in 2010, Leshin served as the Deputy Associate Administrator for NASA's Exploration Systems Mission Directorate where she played a leading role in NASA's future human spaceflight endeavors. From 2011 to 2014, Leshin served as Dean of the School of Science and Professor of Earth & Environmental Science at Rensselaer Polytechnic Institute. In February 2013 President Obama appointed her to the Advisory Board of the Smithsonian National Air and Space Museum, and she was appointed by former Secretary of Transportation Ray LaHood to the Advisory Board of the US Merchant Marine Academy. She serves on the United States National Research Council's Committee on Astrobiology and Planetary Science, and as Chair of the Advisory Board for the Thriving Earth Exchange of the American Geophysical Union.

Leshin received the NASA Distinguished Public Service Medal in 2004 for her work on the Presidential Commission and the Outstanding Leadership Medal in 2011 for her work at NASA. In 1996, she was the inaugural recipient of the Meteoritical Society's Nier Prize, awarded for outstanding research in meteoritics or planetary science by a scientist under the age of 35. The International Astronomical Union recognized her contributions to planetary science with the naming of asteroid 4922 Leshin. – excerpted from WPI sources & Joseph Carvalho III

Maria L. Owen

(B. 1825 NANTUCKET, MA; D. 1913 SPRINGFIELD, MA) noted botanist. Among her many writings was the still respected *Flora of Nantucket*. Moving to Springfield, she founded the Botanical Club of Springfield. – Joseph Carvalho III

Jennie Maria Arms Sheldon

(B. JULY 29, 1852; D. JANUARY 15, 1938 IN DEERFIELD, MA,) She attended high school in Greenfield, Massachusetts, was an American entomologist, educator, historian, author, and museum curator. She worked closely with zoologist Alpheus Hyatt at the Boston Society of Natural History, and she was the curator of the Memorial Hall Museum in Deerfield, MA for a quarter of a century. – Joseph Carvalho III

Nettie Maria Stevens

(B. JULY 7, 1861 IN CAVENDISH, VT; D. MAY 4, 1912 IN BALTIMORE, MD) graduate of Westfield Normal School was an early American geneticist. In 1906, she discovered that male beetles produce two kinds of sperm, one with a large chromosome and one with a small chromosome. When the sperm with the large chromosome fertilized eggs, they produced female offspring, and when the sperm with the small chromosome fertilized eggs, they produced male offspring. This pattern was later observed in other animals including humans. It is now known as the XY sex-determination system. The Nettie Maria Stevens Science and Innovation Center at Westfield State University, Westfield, MA was named in her honor in 2017.
– Joseph Carvalho III

Emily (Hitchcock) Terry

(B. NOV. 9, 1838; D. FEBRUARY 6, 1921) was the youngest child of geologist and Amherst College professor and president Edward Hitchcock and his artist wife Orra White Hitchcock. Emily was a scientist, like her well-known father, Edward Hitchcock, and an artist, like her mother, Orra White Hitchcock. Both Orra and Emily were field botanists and primarily scientific illustrators. From 1865 to 1866, Emily attended the co-educational Cooper Union College where the study of science and art were equally emphasized.

Emily Hitchcock married Reverend Cassius Terry (Amherst Class of 1867) on May 18, 1870. By June 1872, the Terrys went to live in St. Paul, Minnesota, where Cassius was Pastor of Plymouth Church. There she botanized and painted. Emily was Minnesota's "first botanical artist and her paintings represent the first portrayal from nature of Minnesota's flora."

Her husband died in 1881 and in 1884, she returned from Minnesota to Northampton and became Matron of the Smith College student residence, Hubbard House, where she remained for 25 years, until 1909. There she botanized, gardened and made conventional flower and fern

Above: Janice Elaine Voss
Bottom left: Jennie Maria Arms Sheldon
Bottom right: Nettie Maria Stevens

173

Stephanie Wilson

herbaria. The Vermont countryside was her summer retreat, and she was an authority on the ferns of Vermont.

For more than 35 years, Emily made botany the center of her life. In June 1913, Emily presented her American Flowers painted herbarium of 142 watercolor flowers and grasses made between 1850 and 1910 to the Department of Botany at Smith College. It is the most significant expression of her scientific skill and artistic talent. Today American Flowers is an important part of the Mortimer Rare Book Room collection. – Daria D'Arienzo, Pioneer Valley History Network

Janice Elaine Voss

(B. OCTOBER 8, 1956 SOUTH BEND, INDIANA; D. FEBRUARY 6, 2012 IN SCOTTSDALE, AZ) was an American engineer and a NASA astronaut. She flew in space five times, jointly holding the record for American women. She was part of the 1990 NASA Group, and her missions as a "missions specialist" were STS-57 (1993); STS-63 which was the first Shuttle rendezvous with the Mir space station (1995); STS-83 (1997); STS-94 (1997); and STS-99, aka the Shuttle Radar Topography Mission, where she and her fellow crew produced what was at the time the most accurate digital topographical map of the Earth (2000). She graduated from Minnechaug Regional High School in Wilbraham, MA in 1972. – Joseph Carvalho III

Stephanie Wilson

(B. SEPT. 27, 1966 IN BOSTON, MA) Wilson's family moved to Pittsfield when she was a year old. She grew up in Pittsfield and graduated from Taconic High School in Pittsfield in 1984. She graduated from Harvard in 1988 with a degree in engineering science, and a Masters in aerospace engineering from the University of Texas in 1992. After graduation, Wilson began working for the Jet Propulsion Laboratory in Pasadena, CA. She was selected as an Astronaut candidate in April of 1996 and began training at the Johnson Space Center in August of that year. During her time at Mission Control, she served in the Astronaut Office CAPCOM Branch, working in Mission Control as a prime communicator with on-orbit crews. Wilson has flown on three shuttle missions: STS-121 (2006); STS-120 (2007) that delivered the Harmony connecting module to the International Space Station; and STS-131 (2010) in which Wilson was responsible for robotics for spacewalking support using the space station robotic arm and for robotic removal of the "Leonardo" Multi-Purpose Logistics Module from the payload bay of Discovery. For the return to Earth, Wilson robotically installed Leonardo, which was packed with more than 6,000 pounds of hardware, science results and used supplies, inside Discovery's payload bay. In 2013, Wilson was honored by the Johnson Space Center's Innovation Group Achievement Award, and its prestigious Director Commendation Award. – Joseph Carvalho III

CHAPTER TEN

WOMEN AND THE
Artistic Heritage
of Western and Central Massachusetts

BY HEATHER HASKELL
Vice President and Director of Art Museums,
Springfield Museums

Women have played a pivotal role in the creative economy of Western and Central Massachusetts for well over 200 years. The following biographies describe the accomplishments of the many women whose contributions to the visual arts continue to be celebrated today.

Although of diverse backgrounds and ways of participating in and supporting the arts, all of these women forged their own paths, pursuing successful careers in male-dominated fields. While many women artists have been traditionally associated with crafts and decorative arts, the artists discussed here are representative of the many others who have worked, often without acclaim, to enhance their own lives, and that of their communities, through creative expression.

Due in part to its central location between Boston and New York City, artists from around the nation have historically traveled to Western and Central Massachusetts to seek inspiration from the beautiful local scenery. In the city of

Springfield, the celebration of the arts reached its height between the Civil War and World War II. The late 19th century was a time of prolific production in American art, in part because of the quickly growing population in the area and the subsequent increase in commerce, industry, and transportation. City dwellers, seeking to escape from their busy urban setting, often traveled to the Massachusetts countryside to reenergize. The Pioneer Valley, especially Mount Tom and the Oxbow above Holyoke, had a long-standing reputation as picturesque and was a particularly popular place in which to paint. As early as 1836, renowned painter Thomas Cole journeyed to the region to create his most famous landscape painting titled "View from Mount Holyoke, Northampton, Massachusetts, after a Thunderstorm—The Oxbow," which is now in the collection of the Metropolitan Museum of Art. In October 1877, *Potter's American Monthly* extolled the Valley in poetic terms, "The valley of the Connecticut River is noted not only for its charming scenery, but for the great number of its beautiful towns. These dot and adorn this stream of flowing crystal like pearls threaded with a cord of silver."

Lithography firms, like the one owned by Nathaniel Currier & James Merritt Ives, made the beauty of the Massachusetts landscape available to everyday Americans across the country. From 1834-1907, the company, known as "the printmakers to the people," produced over 8000 prints documenting the American landscape, including the Oxbow, pastimes and noteworthy contemporary events. Interestingly, among the artists employed by Currier & Ives, Frances (Fanny) Flora Bond Palmer (1812-1876) was one of the most intriguing and most productive. Palmer spent over two decades with the firm, supporting her family and relatives, at a time when it was unusual for a woman to work outside the home. In addition to supervising a staff of 12 women on how to hand-color the prints, Palmer designed at least 170 of the firm's finest and most popular images, often creating the designs "in the field" and accurately recording the flora and fauna she saw in her scenes. The Michele and Donald D'Amour Museum of Fine Arts holds one of the largest collections of Currier & Ives prints in the nation and frequently features the work of Fanny Palmer in special exhibitions.

Springfield-born Belle Townsley Smith (1845-1928) also contributed to the growing awareness and support of art in Western and Central Massachusetts. Married to avid collector George Walter Vincent Smith, the couple founded the city's first Art Museum. While George collected American paintings, including examples by local women artists Ruth Payne Burgess (1865-1934), Harriet

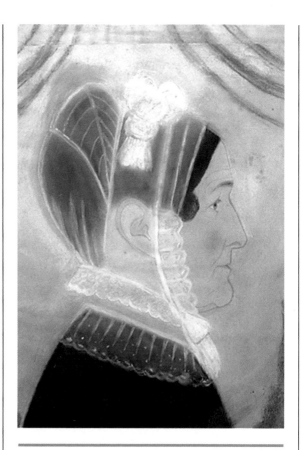

Above: Ruth (Henshaw) Bascom.
(Opposite page) **Center:** Orra White Hitchcock
Right: Jessie Richmond (Tarbox) Beals

Randall Lumis (1870-1953) and Marie Danforth Page (1869-1940), Belle focused on building an important collection of textiles and fine lace and producing scholarship on the lace tradition. When the Museum opened in 1896, Belle's collection of Italian, Spanish and French lace was prominently displayed. Although her name is not included on the Museum, now called the George Walter Vincent Smith Art Museum, Belle served as director after George's death in 1923. During her tenure, she supervised the construction and installation of a new wing on the building

as well as continued to add to the collection. Interestingly, both she and George mandated that a woman serve as director of the Museum and after Belle's death, curator Eleanor Wade and assistant curator Cordelia Sargent Pond both served as directors of the Museum during the 20th century.

Today, the Pioneer Valley boasts one of the highest concentrations of artists and craftspeople in the United States, creating a supportive environment for woman artists to experiment, create, and exhibit. Like their earlier predecessors, many of the women discussed here have had a role in teaching about the arts, serving as mentors for the next generation of women to find their creative voices. From an itinerant folk artist whose father served with George Washington, to a celebrated scientific illustrator, to 21st century visual artists and entrepreneurs, the intriguing biographies of these noteworthy women reinforce our collective sense of pride in the region's artistic heritage.

Art and Artists

Ruth (Henshaw) Bascom

also known as "Aunt Ruth" (B. DEC. 15, 1772 IN LEICESTER, MA; FEB. 16, 1848 IN ASHBY, MA) considered to be America's premier portrait folk artist and pastelist, producing over one thousand portraits from 1789 to 1846. Bascom married first, at about 32 years of age, to Dr. Asa Miles, but he died a year or more after their marriage. She made her first portrait in 1801, but she did not begin creating portraits regularly until after 1818. Bascom worked with a variety of materials, including pastels, pencils, cut paper, and foil. Some of her initial works were layered pieces of paper that represented the head and neck, clothing, and accessories placed over a background. She also made pastel portraits on one sheet of paper in the latter part of her career. – Joseph Carvalho III

Orra White Hitchcock

(B. MAR. 8, 1796 IN SOUTH AMHERST, MA; D. MAY 26, 1863 IN AMHERST, MA)
is the valley's "most often published woman artist." When Orra is recognized it is usually through the work of her husband, the noted geologist Edward Hitchcock (1793-1863), native of Deerfield, pastor at Conway, professor and then president of Amherst College. Orra made hundreds and hundreds of illustrations for Edward's scientific publications, including detailed landscapes of the Connecticut River Valley for his Massachusetts geological survey volumes, as well as striking custom designed charts that illustrated his local discoveries and his classroom lectures. Her work is a remarkable chronicle of the scenic and botanically and geologically diverse Pioneer Valley.

Orra was a prodigy, excelling in the natural sciences, and her artistic talent blossomed early. From 1813 to 1817, as preceptress, Orra taught the young girls at Deerfield Academy the sciences and the fine and decorative arts. Orra was a scientist in her own right, earning the reputation as one of the valleys "most distinguished naturalists." Orra's first published work was a wood engraving of the "Falls on Connecticut River, at Gill, Mass.", a drawing she created for Edward's article in *Port Folio* in December 1818.

Orra White married Edward Hitchcock on May 31, 1821. The couple moved first to Conway where Edward served as pastor and then in 1826 to Amherst, where they spent the rest of their lives.

Orra made drawings for more than 200 plates and 1000 woodcut illustrations for Edwards' various professional publications. Many appear in the 1833 *Report on the Geology of Massachusetts* and its successor, the 1841 *Final Report*. The large and dramatic classroom charts of geologic strata, prehistoric beasts, fossils and dinosaur footprints she drew, most between 1828 and 1840, took up thousands of

feet of cloth. Edward considered them "indispensable aids."

The current revival of interest in Orra White Hitchcock and her work is marked by a series of recent publications that chronicle her life and art: "The 'Union of the Beautiful with the Useful": Through the Eyes of Orra White Hitchcock," by Daria D'Arienzo in the *Massachusetts Review,* Summer 2010; *Orra White Hitchcock: An Amherst Woman of Art and Science*, [catalogue of a 2011 exhibition at the Mead Art Museum] by Robert Herbert and Daria D'Arienzo. – Daria D'Arienzo, Pioneer Valley History Network

---

ALPHABETICAL LISTING OF WOMEN ARTISTS:

Edith Ella Baldwin

(B. MAR., 1848 IN WORCESTER, MA; D. DEC. 24, 1923 IN NORTHFIELD, MA) was a noted painter of portraits and miniatures, a craftswoman and author. Her works were exhibited in the United States and in Paris during her lifetime. – Joseph Carvalho III

Jane Ellen (Bitgood) Barrientos

(B. JULY 20, 1953 IN AGAWAM, MA) award-winning Trompe l'Oeil artist, and art teacher. She established the Barrientos Studio/Gallery in West Springfield, MA in 1985. – Joseph Carvalho III

Jessie Richmond (Tarbox) Beals

(B. DEC. 23, 1870 IN HAMILTON, ONTARIO, CANADA; D. MAY 30, 1942 IN NEW YORK CITY) One of the first professional women photographers in Western Massachusetts. Began her career in 1880s while working as a school teacher in Williamsburg, MA; she later moved in 1893 to Greenfield, Mass. In

1905, she and her husband Alfred T. Beals established a photography studio in New York City. According to her biographer, Ralmon Jon Black of the Williamsburg Historical Society, Jessie was often commissioned for portraits of artists, writers, and actors and soon "became part of the Greenwich Village bohemian culture." – Pioneer Valley History Network

Cotelle R. (Nirenstein) Berman

(B. CA. 1910 IN SPRINGFIELD, MA;
D. FEB. 23, 1942 IN SPRINGFIELD, MA)
Springfield artist/oil and charcoal, won several awards from Art Museums in Massachusetts, New York, and Pennsylvania. Her career was cut short by polio and she died young "before reaching the full maturity of her artist powers," as one art historian observed.
– Joseph Carvalho III

Lark Grey Dimond-Cates

(B. SEPT. 12, 1953 IN KANSAS) is an artist, sculptor, author. She is the sculptor of all of the bronzes which make up the Dr. Seuss National

Memorial Sculpture Garden at the Springfield Museums in Springfield, MA. Dimond-Cates is also the sculptor of the U.S. Congressman Edward P. Boland memorial in downtown Springfield. Her book *Dr. Seuss, Springfield, and the Kettle of Bronze* (2017) chronicles her life as the step-daughter of Theodor Seuss Geisel ("Dr. Seuss") and her artistic career culminating in the creation of the large assemblage of sculptures depicting Dr. Seuss characters emplaced throughout the large Dr. Seuss National Memorial Sculpture Garden which opened in 2002. Dimond-Cates also donated a large amount of Dr. Seuss historical material to the Springfield Library Association in 2017 to help establish The Amazing World of Dr. Seuss Museum in 2017. Her current home and art studio are located in Rancho Santa Fe, California. – Joseph Carvalho III

Josephine E. (Mapp) Edmonds

(B. OCT. 5, 1921; D. MAY 12, 2014 IN SPRINGFIELD, MA) is an artist from Springfield who "played a pivotal role in bringing the work of black artists to Springfield and helping them gain recognition for their talents." A 1998 Ubora Award honoree, Edmonds was the art exhibition coordinator at the Afro-American Cultural Center at American International College where she established a monthly series of exhibitions featuring art by local, national, and international minority artists. She moved from New York to Springfield in 1956. Edmonds was also a co-founder of the Afro-Art Alliance, an organization of local black artists. – African Hall Steering Committee, Springfield Science Museums, Springfield Museums

Elizabeth "Eliza" Goodridge

(B. JAN. 9, 1798 IN TEMPLETON, MA;
D. FEB. 20, 1882 IN READING, MA)
was an American painter who specialized in miniatures. She was the younger sister of Sarah Goodridge [See entry]. It is presumed that Goodridge probably began her career

Above: Lark Grey Dimond-Cates
Above center: Josephine E. Edmonds

in Boston working with her sister, but spent most of her life in the central part of Massachusetts. She lived in Templeton, Massachusetts, and made several extended trips to Worcester in the 1830s and 1840s, during which time she lived with and painted members of the Foster Family. The American Antiquarian Society's portrait collection contains the largest representation – 12 images – of Eliza Goodridge's known work. The Worcester Art Museum also houses several of Goodridge's miniatures. Goodridge's landscapes include "View of Mount Holyoke, Massachusetts and the Connecticut River, ca. 1827," and "View of Round Hill, Northampton, Massachusetts, 1824," in the Worcester Art Museum. In 1849, Goodridge married Colonel Ephriam Stone, who owned a general store and sawmill in Templeton.
– Joseph Carvalho III

Sarah Goodridge
(B. FEB. 5, 1788 IN TEMPLETON, MA;
D. DEC. 28, 1853 IN BOSTON, MA)
also referred to as Sarah Goodrich, was an American painter who specialized in portrait miniatures. She studied for a time under Gilbert Stuart in Boston. In 1825, Stuart sat for her and later claimed that her portrait was "the only true likeness of him ever done." A successful artist, Goodridge supported herself and her family for 30 years on her art commissions. With her eyesight failing, she gave up painting in 1851. She was the older sister of Elizabeth Goodridge [see entry for Elizabeth Goodridge]. – Joseph Carvalho III

Nancy Graves
(B. DEC. 23, 1939 IN PITTSFIELD, MA;
D. OCT. 21, 1995 IN NEW YORK CITY)
was a sculptor, painter, printmaker, and filmmaker noted for her focus on natural phenomena. At the early age of 29, Graves was given a solo exhibition at the prestigious Whitney Museum of American Art, the youngest woman to have done so at that

time. "Camels", her most famous sculpture, was first exhibited at the Whitney Museum of American Art. Graves began creating "open-form Polychrome" sculptures in 1980. Another of her distinctive sculptural approaches were her "aerial landscapes" primarily based upon maps of the moon and similar source material. Her works can be found in the collections of major museums around the world, including National Gallery of Art (Washington, D.C.), the Brooklyn Museum of Art, the Smithsonian American Art Museum, the National Gallery of Australia (Canberra), the Walker Art Center (Minneapolis), and the Museum of Fine Arts (St. Petersburg). – Joseph Carvalho III

Above: Elizabeth Goodridge
Right: Sarah Goodridge

Above: Rosa Ibarra
Left: Fay Kleinman

Rosa Ibarra
(B. IN PUERTO RICO)
is an artist who uses oil on canvas along with sea glass, and gold, copper and silver gilding in her paintings. Ibarra was part of the Michele & Donald D'Amour Museum of Fine Arts' first ever Hispanic Heritage Month exhibit. She continues to exhibit her work in galleries and museums in the United States and abroad.
– Elizabeth Román

Mary Ann (Douglass) Johnson
(B. 1821 IN WESTFIELD, MA; D. FEB. 26, 1906 IN WESTFIELD, MA)
was a prolific and very successful 19th Century portrait artist from Westfield. Educated at the Westfield Academy, Mary Ann Douglas married William A. Johnson, a brick mason and local contractor in 1839. Her husband began making church organs in 1846 and became quite famous. Mary Ann began selling her paintings in 1843; working in both oil and crayon, she gained regional fame for her portraits. She kept a careful catalog of sales which totaled more than a thousand paintings. At the peak of her career in the 1860s and 1870s, she was annually selling between one and two thousand dollars worth of commissioned work per year. While most of her work were portraits, she also did local landscapes – a few are on exhibit in the Westfield Athenaeum, Westfield, MA.
– Kate Deviny

Dorothy Stratton King
(B. 1909 IN WORCESTER, MA;
D. JUNE 14, 2007 IN ARLINGTON, VA)
was an American painter and printmaker. She was a founding member of the Washington Printmakers Gallery in Washington, D.C.
– Joseph Carvalho III

Fay Kleinman
(B. NOV. 29, 1912 IN NEW YORK CITY; D. FEB. 21, 2012 IN BECKET, MA) was an American painter.

She was also known by her married names, Fay Skurnick, and then Fay Levenson. The medium of most of the works Kleinman created is oil on canvas, but she also produced some mixed-media work and watercolors. She exhibited in museums in New York and Massachusetts and in galleries throughout the country. She was the co-founder of the Becket Arts Center in Becket, Massachusetts. – Joseph Carvalho III

Helen Estelle Knox

(B. DEC. 29, 1890 IN SUFFIELD, CT; D. APR. 20, 1963 IN SPRINGFIELD, MA) was a "widely recognized" artist, and watercolorist. She graduated from Smith College in the Class of 1913. Her paintings "won critical acclaim" at exhibitions held at Stockbridge, MA, and New York City art galleries as well as exhibitions by the Springfield Art League. – Joseph Carvalho III

Clara Wells Lathrop

(B. MAY 22, 1853 IN NORTHAMPTON, MA; D. JUNE 15, 1907 IN NORTHAMPTON, MA) was a highly regarded painter whose work was exhibited in galleries in New York and in Paris during her lifetime. She was a graduate of Smith College in the Class of 1886 and later became an instructor of Art at Smith from 1906-1907. – Heather Haskell

Kay (Guinn) Life

(B. JUNE 28, 1930) is an artist and children's book illustrator living in Westfield, MA. – Joseph Carvalho III

Harriet (Randall) Lumis

(B. 1870 IN SALEM, CT; D. 1953 IN SPRINGFIELD, MA) was a widely acclaimed Springfield artist. Harriet was educated at the Connecticut Literary Institution in Suffield, CT. In 1892, she married Fred Lumis, an architectural and structural engineer already established in Springfield. Just a year after her marriage,

Harriet enrolled in the Springfield School Department's Evening Free Hand Drawing School. For the next five years she studied under the tutelage of local instructors including Roswell Shurtleff, an important local painter. In 1910, she attended summer school with Leonard Ochtmann at Mianus, Connecticut, an experience which profoundly affected her development. In her home at 28 Bedford Road, Harriet set up her studio and by 1913 was listed in *Who's Who in Art*.

Harriet Lumis was also instrumental in supporting Springfield's arts organizations. In 1918, she and other local artists established the Springfield Art League, dedicated to the support of artists in the Springfield area. At 50 years of age, Harriet entered the Breakenridge School of Art in East Gloucester. Soon afterward she was "elected" to the National Association of Women Painters and Sculptors. In 1924, her floral oil titled "Phlox" was accepted for display by the National Academy of Design.

She also helped form the Academic Artists Association to "promote and encourage the showing of realistic works of art in the Museum of Fine Arts at Springfield, and to promote the interest of artists who work in a traditional or realistic manner." – Staff of the Lyman & Merrie Wood Museum of Springfield History, Springfield Museums, Springfield, MA

Jane F. Lund

(B. OCT. 14, 1939 IN QUEENS, NY) of Ashfield, MA is a noted artist whose "medium of choice" is pastel and the winner of several awards throughout the 1980s, Lund has had numerous solo exhibitions, including several held at Forum Gallery. Her work has also been included in a wide range of group exhibitions, dating from her 1973 contribution to the New Talent: New England Show at the DeCordova Museum in Lincoln, MA. Other group exhibitions include the 1980 exhibition Three Woman Show: Contract Point, held at the Springfield Museum of Art; the inaugural

exhibition at the Fitchburg Art Museum, titled Monocular Vision: New England Realist Artists in 1989; the Exactitude exhibition at Forum Gallery in 1996; and The Figurative Impulse show held at the Miami Dade Community College in 1998. – Heather Haskell & Joseph Carvalho III

Susan Mikula

(B. MAR. 7, 1958 IN NEW JERSEY) is an artist who works with a mix of old and new photographic technologies, She works with available light, and modifies vintage cameras to create her photographic art. Mikula lives in New York City and in West Cummington, MA. Her work has been shown in solo and group exhibitions in New York, San Francisco, Miami, Los Angeles, and in Northampton, Pittsfield, Westfield, and Provincetown Ma. She also had a solo presentation at Volta 13 in Basel, Switzerland from June 12-17, 2017. Published catalogs of her work include: *Susan Mikula: Kilo* (2017); *Susan Mikula: u.X.* (2014); *Susan Mikula: American Bond* (2011); and *Susan Mikula: Photographs, 2008* (2008). Her work can be found in private collections in the United States and Europe, as well as in the Permanent Collection of the U.S. Embassy, Nuevo Laredo, Mexico, Art in Embassies, U.S. Department of State. – Joseph Carvalho III

Kathleen Nichols-Simpson

was born in Springfield, MA and spent her childhood in the communities of East Longmeadow and Wilbraham. After graduating from the MacDuffie School for Girls, Simpson obtained her B.A. from Smith College. She started her career at the Springfield Museums as an intern in the Education Department of the George Walter Vincent Smith Art Museum and Museum of Fine Arts. The internship evolved into a position as Education Assistant and Simpson later was appointed to the position of Director of Museum Education when the Art, History and Science Museums were centralized

of her adult life in Paris, France as an artist and collector and spent the summers in her hometown of Fitchburg, Massachusetts. Norcross painted Impressionist portraits and still-lifes, and is better known for her paintings of "genteel interiors."

According to one of her biographers, "Her father provided her a comfortable living, under the proviso that she would not sell her paintings." With a life mission to provide people from her hometown the ability to view great works of art, Norcross collected art, made copies of paintings of Old Masters, and systematically documented decorative arts from the 12th through the 19th century." Her funding and art collection were used to establish the Fitchburg Art Museum.

In 1924, her works were shown posthumously in Paris at the Louvre and Salon d'Automne, where Norcross was the first American to have had a retrospective. Her works were also shown the following year at the Museum of Fine Arts, Boston.

Chrystina (Xtina) Geagan Parks

(B. MAR. 2, 1976 IN SPRINGFIELD, MA) is an African wildlife photographer and nature filmmaker, an emerging conservationist, and an expedition leader who works in undiscovered areas of Africa to protect critically endangered species from extinction. One of her first work experiences was to work alongside senior executives in Sales, Marketing and Feature Film Distribution at TriMark Pictures in Hollywood. A career in Development, Marketing and Public Relations followed. She worked as a Media Relations Manager for BDA Sports, one of the top sports marketing agents for the NBA where she managed public relations for the biggest names in the sports world.

Her love of the arts brought her to switch careers. She went from being a marketing coordinator to the Director of Development for the Springfield Museums in Springfield, MA where she managed the marketing and

---

under one administration. Simpson continued her professional development by earning a graduate degree in Educational Administration from the University of Massachusetts, Amherst. In 2010, Simpson was named Vice President of the Springfield Museums. In her role as Vice President, Simpson coordinated the Museums' successful application for Accreditation from the American Alliance of Museums. Simpson also coordinated and wrote the City's application to obtain a state-designation for the Springfield Central Cultural District. In 2015, Simpson was appointed President of the Springfield Museums. Working in tandem with the Board of Trustees, she was responsible for overseeing the $7,000,000 "Seuss in Springfield: Building a Better

Quadrangle" Capital Campaign for campus-wide improvements to the Quadrangle and its historic museum buildings. With funding from the Campaign, she and her staff successfully opened a fifth museum, The Amazing World of Dr. Seuss, in June of 2017. The museum garnered national and international media attention and doubled ticketed attendance to the Museums in less than one year. – Joseph Carvalho III & Wayne E. Phaneuf

Eleanor Norcross

(NÉE ELLA AUGUSTA NORCROSS, B. JUNE 24, 1854 IN FITCHBURG, MA; D. OCT. 19, 1923 IN FITCHBURG, MA) was an American painter who studied under William Merritt Chase and Alfred Stevens. She lived the majority

advertising departments, and membership fundraising. She was the Director of Membership and the Visitor Experience at the Autry National Center, the Museum of the American West, and the Southwest Museum of the American Indian. Geagan Parks is the creator and owner of the film production company, Xtina Studios, and her new wildlife and nature photography gallery, ROAM: A Xtina Parks Gallery is based in North Adams, MA on the campus of Mass MoCA. The gallery showcases Geagan Parks' extensive body of work, as well as exhibit well known photographers and African artists from around the world. The gallery is aimed to increase awareness of the global efforts being made by nature/wildlife photographers, artists and organizations to save wildlife and habitat from extinction. – Joseph Carvalho III

Irene E. Parmalee

(B. 1847 IN GUILFORD, CT; D. AUG. 29, 1934 IN LOS ANGELES, CA) was a successful career portrait artist who opened and operated a studio in Springfield, MA from 1875 to 1929. She was one of the first women to attend the Yale Art School. Among her many works held in the collection of the George Walter Vincent Smith Art Museum in Springfield, MA are highly regarded portraits of Samuel Bowles III (1896), publisher of *The Republican*; Horace Smith (1881), co-founder of Smith & Wesson; Charles M. Merriam (1890), publisher of Merriam-Webster dictionaries; Dr. Josiah Gilbert Holland (1896), noted journalist, historian and author; and Everett Hosmer Barney (1903), inventor of the clamp-on skates – "the man who put America on skates." – Joseph Carvalho III

Cordelia Caroline (Sargent) Pond

(B. JULY 25, 1885 IN GARDNER, MA; D. FEB. 25, 1967 IN AGAWAM, MA) served as one of New England's first female Art Museum Directors as Director of the George Walter Vincent Smith Art Museum in Springfield (part of

the Springfield Museums Association). She received the region's highest recognition with it's Pynchon Award Medal in 1941 for her 46 years of service to the Museum with 20 years as its director. She was responsible for instituting the Museum's education program which served up to 14,000 children annually. – Joseph Carvalho III

Deborah Rubin

(B. APR. 17, 1948 IN CHICAGO, IL) of Amherst, MA is one of the foremost floral watercolor painters in the United States. Her works include seascapes and cityscapes. She has been honored by over 20 awards for her paintings over her career. – Heather Haskell

Top left: Deborah Rubin
Top right: Cordelia Caroline (Sargeant) Pond
Bottom left: Irene Parmalee

Helen Ruth Schmidt

(B. 1911 IN HOLYOKE, MA; D. 1956 IN HOLYOKE, MA) was a noted watercolorist and poet who painted a significant number of the most important architecture of Holyoke, MA.
– Joseph Carvalho III

Janice Selma Throne

(B. 1925 IN BRONX, NY; D. FEB. 28, 2016) of Longmeadow, MA was an important promoter of art and artists in Western Massachusetts. Throne began her working career as a writer and photographer with *Women's Wear Daily* which included an interview with Eleanor Roosevelt. Later in life, she opened the Thronja Fine Art Gallery in Springfield where for many years she helped and promoted a wide range of local artists with national and international reputations. She is credited with rediscovering the woodcuts of local artist Asa Cheffetz and co-authored a catalogue of his work with master print-maker Barry Moser entitled *New England Engraved: The Prints of Asa Cheffetz* for a retrospective at the Springfield Museum of Fine Arts, Springfield Museums.
– Heather Haskell & Joseph Carvalho III

Jane Trigere

(B. NOV. 29, 1948) of South Deerfield is an artist, journalist, and former museum director. She created the Deerfield Arts Bank [art gallery] which operated from 2014-2016 and mounted eleven major exhibitions during that period. She and Ken Schoen are the leaders of the Jewish Historical Society of Western Massachusetts. Trigere has also published a study about the history of the Synagogues of Springfield, MA.
– Jane Kaufman

Mabel Rose Welch

(B. MAR. 26, 1871 IN NEW HAVEN, CT; D. JAN. 1, 1959 IN WILBRAHAM, MA) was a noted painter of miniatures who

(Opposite page) Belle Townsley Smith and George Walter Vincent Smith
Top: Janice Selma Throne, **Above right:** Belle Townsley Smith, **Above left:** Denise Holly Ulinskas

won the Silver Medal of the Pan-Pacific Exposition in 1915. Among her many awards, the Pennsylvania Society of Miniature Painters presented to her its Medal of Honor in 1920, she received a similar award in 1933 from the Brooklyn Society of Miniature Painters; and received the Lindsey Morris Sterling Prize for Miniatures from the National Society of Women Painters and Sculptors in 1937. She lived in Wilbraham for most of her life. – Joseph Carvalho III

Rosemary Tracy Woods
(B. IN PHILADELPHIA, PA)
of Springfield, has served as the executive director and chief curator of the Art for the Soul Gallery in Springfield, MA. She has owned the gallery since 2002. Woods is an active promoter of contemporary African-American artists and the art of the Harlem Renaissance. In 2010, Tracy was awarded the Unsung Heroine Award from the Massachusetts Commission on the Status of Women. She also received a special recognition from former Governor Deval Patrick for her work with the arts. A social justice advocate, she worked on Connecticut Gov. Lowell Weicker's commission to enforce regulations of the then new Americans with Disabilities Act. Woods was recognized for her outstanding achievement by the State of Connecticut as a coordinator of diversity programs. Woods worked with artists with disabilities, and created a state-wide art contest for children that still continues today in Connecticut. – Sarah Platanitis & Joseph Carvalho III

Rosemary Tracy Woods (Dave Roback/ *The Republican*)

ALTHOUGH MOST NOTED FOR HER WATERCOLOR ILLUSTRATIONS, SHE PAINTED IN OIL AND WAS A CHILDREN'S PORTRAIT ARTIST. IN 1948, SHE WAS GIVEN A CALDECOTT MEDAL FOR HER ILLUSTRATIONS OF *ROGER AND THE FOX* WRITTEN BY LAVINIA R. DAVIS AND AGAIN IN 1950 FOR *THE WILD BIRTHDAY CAKE.*

HILDEGARD H. WOODWARD

Hildegard H. Woodward
(B. FEB. 10, 1898 IN WORCESTER, MA; D. DEC., 1977 IN HAWLEYVILLE, CT)
was the author and illustrator of many children's books. She was educated at the School of the Museum of Fine Arts, Boston and in Paris. Her portfolio includes numerous works of fiction and humor for adults. Although most noted for her watercolor illustrations, she painted in oil and was a children's portrait artist. In 1948. she was given a Caldecott Medal for her illustrations of *Roger and the Fox* written by Lavinia R. Davis and again in 1950 for *The Wild Birthday Cake.* She began to lose her sight in the 1960, but didn't stop painting. Ultimately losing her sight, she developed a method of "painting by touch." Her papers are held at the University of Southern Mississippi and the Children's Literature Research Collection at the University of Minnesota house copies of her original artwork. – Joseph Carvalho III

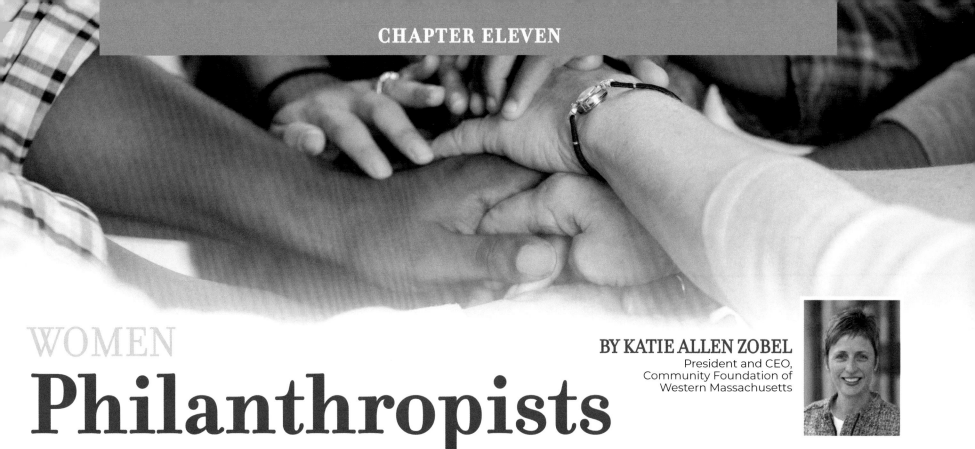

CHAPTER ELEVEN

WOMEN
Philanthropists

BY KATIE ALLEN ZOBEL
President and CEO,
Community Foundation of
Western Massachusetts

In a region known for its innovators and trailblazers, it's not surprising to find that same entrepreneurial spirit in the region's philanthropy. Sparked by passion and purpose, Massachusetts women have been expanding hearts and minds for generations as they seek new ways to improve the lives of others and bring additional resources to their communities.

As a result of their efforts, you can find libraries, museums, animal shelters, parks, colleges, preschools, historic homes and an internationally known music festival that were all started by women.

And every year, local women continue to design and fuel projects and programs that close a gap, fix a problem, or meet a need.

Ann Radcliffe established the first endowed scholarship at Harvard in 1643 so that men without the means could also receive an education. Sophia Smith was the first woman to endow a college for women, anywhere in the world, and she did so with a bequest of nearly $400,000. Mary Lyon went door-to-door asking neighbors and strangers to invest in her cause, and her tireless efforts launched Mount Holyoke College. In the middle of the Great Depression, Gertrude Robinson Smith

founded the Berkshire Symphonic Festival that would go on to become Tanglewood. When Mountain Park, a treasured amusement park in Holyoke was closing after nearly 100 years in operation, the beloved carousel was destined for the auction block. Holyoke resident Angela Wright stepped up to the task and helped raise the money to preserve the carousel. Twenty-five years later, it is still delighting tens of thousands of visitors every year.

Our modern interpretation of the word philanthropy often focuses on individuals that generously give money away and are frequently lauded for doing so with lavish galas and names on buildings. If you go way back to the Greek, philanthropy has nothing to do with money and everything to do with love, care and compassion for others. This chapter highlights a few of the women in this

Helen Nell Storrow

region who put others before themselves. These women voluntarily gave their time, energy and expertise, as well as their financial resources, to pursue a vision of a brighter, healthier, more vibrant tomorrow. They are true philanthropists—caring for humanity first.

It is worth noting that the women in the pages that follow are representative of so many other women who will forever be anonymous but to whom we owe a debt of gratitude for the tasks they took up and the sacrifices they made, quietly and without accolades, in service to their community. We celebrate the women

in this chapter along with so many others who have given generously of themselves for the benefit of others, helping shape a region I am proud to call my home, where community is a value and philanthropy is a verb.

Philanthropists

Helen Nell (Osborne) Storrow

(B. SEPT. 22, 1864 IN AUBURN, NY; D. NOV. 10, 1944 IN LINCOLN, MA) was the daughter of Eliza Osborne who was a socially-conscious Quaker whose aunt Lucretia Mott was an outspoken abolitionist. Lucretia was one of the organizers in 1848 of the now famous Seneca Falls convention which focused on women's rights and even demanded that women be allowed to vote. Their family friends included such nationally known figures as Susan B. Anthony and William Lloyd Garrison.

Helen was first introduced to the city of Springfield when she attended Howard's Boarding School there in the 1880s. It is possible that Springfield was chosen because Helen's oldest sister Emily had married Frederick Harris, a successful and influential business man of that community. A part of fashionable education of young ladies in the late 19th century was travel in Europe and Helen participated in style. Her visit to Switzerland resulted in a life altering moment. While hiking in the mountains of Zermatt, Helen met her future husband James Storrow who was also hiking on the same path. It wasn't until eight years after that first chance meeting that Helen Osborne married James. Because of her sister's ties with Springfield, the now Mrs. James Storrow kept in touch with the happenings in the Pioneer Valley. When the Eastern States Exposition was started in 1916 it was organized as a livestock exhibition. Appealing to the men on the farm but not

their entire family. To correct this oversight the Trustees of the Exposition created what was then called the "Home Department." With her experience in organizing Girl Scout training, establishing regional camps for that same group, organizing relief efforts for Belgium during World War One, and funding the Saturday Evening Girls of the Boston Settlement movement for Eastern European immigrants, Helen Storrow was asked to head this new effort as chairman of that department. In the capacity as chairman she organized displays and exhibits which represented the old and new in the area of homemaking in the 1920s. One exhibit of note was a room dedicated to the process of voting. Women had just received the right to vote in the United States – a fact that would have made Helen's great aunt very happy even if it was eighty years after the Seneca Falls convention had advocated for it.

The theme for the Exposition in 1930 was to be "Two Hundred Years of Agriculture in New England 1630 to 1930." The idea was put forward of decorating one of the temporary buildings in an Early American style in order to present a more attractive setting for the handicrafts displays. In 1926, This initial concept was translated into the even more exciting thought of moving an authentic Early American home to the grounds. Helen liked the idea and shared it with Philip Gilbert who was a Trustee of the Eastern States Exposition as well as Commissioner of Agriculture for Massachusetts. As a result, Storrow accepted the gifted 1794 Gilbert House in West Brookfield arranged for it to be disassembled, and moved to the West Springfield fairgrounds in 1927.

The old farmstead proved so popular with the Fair going public that Storrow expanded the idea of moving just one building to incorporate a recreated village where youth and their families could see how people lived in the 19th century.

Finally, when the buildings had been

located, she presented her proposition to the Exposition Board of Directors — she would purchase and restore the buildings if the Exposition would provide the land. From her original purchase of the Gilbert House, her final cost for all the structures that were moved totaled nearly $350,000 when the project was completed.

Helen had created what she called "The New England Village" and in the first few years she and her friends helped to furnish the buildings through loans of period pieces. She staffed the buildings with guides comprised of Girl Scouts who annually competed to earn the privilege of staying at the Village throughout the Fair. The girls were housed in a bunkhouse type setting that was located in the clearstory attic of the Potter Mansion. The original Aunt Helen's Herb Garden was planned, planted and given to Helen Storrow Village in 1935 by the New England Girl Scouts as a gift of appreciation and affection. This was a secret garden, planned as a surprise gift. It was a real Girl Scout project – the first of its kind in the world. Five thousand Girl Scouts from Massachusetts, Maine, Connecticut, New Hampshire, Rhode Island and Vermont contributed to the garden. After Helen's death in 1944, the Trustees renamed the Village in her honor, "Storrowton." – Dennis Picard (Retired Director of the Storrowton Village Museum, Eastern States Exposition), Pioneer Valley History Network

Philanthropists Lois B. Green and Meridith D. Wesby

BY LEAH LAMSON

In 2002 two Worcester philanthropists gathered a group of women to talk about the role they play in charitable giving money and the possibility of creating a support structure around girls in the area. Lois B. Green and Meridith D. Wesby had attended a conference in Florida focused on the creation of women's leadership groups associated with United Ways across the country.

Both women were well-known and respected in the social services and non-profit arenas. Green had more than five decades of community involvement serving as a consultant to many nonprofit boards as well as filling in as interim president and chief executive officer of the United Way of Central Massachusetts.

Wesby was vice president/administrator of the Fred Harris Daniels Foundation, a family foundation incorporated in 1949 to award grants in Worcester for sustainable change and to help people become more self-reliant in their community.

They brought the idea back to Worcester and with 25 founding members created the Women's Initiative, part of the United Way of Central Mass. Its mission is to ignite positive change for girls through philanthropy and women's leadership. Since its founding, the Women's Initiative has raised more than $4 million and helped address the needs of more than 8,500 adolescent girls throughout Central Massachusetts.

S. Prestley and Helen Blake (*The Republican*, file photo)

Helen Davis Blake

and her husband S. Prestley Blake are major donors to numerous institutions in Springfield, MA and in Florida. Helen was honored with the first ever President's Philanthropy Award for her nearly 40 years of dedicated service to Springfield College on Oct. 23, 2015. The Award was in recognition of her service as a college trustee has included serving as vice chair and secretary of the board and as a member of the Executive Committee and the committees on Trustees, Audit and Compliance, Academic Affairs, Business Affairs, Development and Institutional Advancement, Investment and Student Affairs.

She was the co-chair of "Leadership for the 21st Century: The Campaign for Springfield College," which raised $44.5 million and became the most successful campaign in college history. Pres Blake, co-founder of Friendly Ice Cream Corp., and his wife Helen have given millions to area colleges and charities. – Jonathan Stankiewicz, Wayne E. Phaneuf, & Joseph Carvalho III

Emma M. (Wilder) Anderson

(B. MAY 9, 1903 IN NEWTON, MA; D. SEPT. 24, 1998 IN SPRINGFIELD, MA) of Longmeadow, MA was

Margaret Celeste Champion

a Springfield area philanthropist who donated the land for the Pioneer Valley Montessori School in Springfield, MA in 1964. She and her husband, Richard, founded the 32-acre "Camp Wilder" in the Sixteen Acres neighborhood of Springfield in 1940. Emma served as the camp director for over 40 years. In 2002, the camp was sold to the City of Springfield. Emma Anderson was also a co-founder of the World Affairs Council of the Pioneer Valley and was a Pynchon Award recipient in 1983. She was also the Greater Springfield Chamber of Commerce's "Woman of the Year" in 1979 and she was also a gubernatorial appointee to the White House Conference on Children and Youth. – Peter Goonan & Joseph Carvalho III

Mary Constance Breck

(B. JAN. 19, 1909 IN SPRINGFIELD, MA; D. NOV. 22, 2009 IN LONGMEADOW, MA) was a noted philanthropist and community volunteer. After graduating from Bay Path Institute, now known as Bay Path University, she went to work full time at her father's company. Working alongside her father and her brothers, Edward and John, Breck Shampoo became the world's best-selling shampoo in the 1950s. At the time John H. Breck, Inc. was sold in 1963 to the American Cyanamid Company, she was company Treasurer. In 1964 Constance retired but continued her involvement with professional and charitable organizations. She was a member of the Ladies of the Equestrian Order of the Holy Sepulchre of Jerusalem, a member of the Quota Club International and a past president of its Springfield Chapter. She was a member of the Cosmetic Career Women, and a board member of the Carew Hill Girls Club, serving as treasurer for many years. She was a past member of the Women's Division of the Chamber of Commerce and also served as treasurer of the USO of Greater Springfield, Inc. and worked on a volunteer basis for the Job Corps program as sponsored by WICS (women in community service). She was a Corporator of American International College and a Board member of Wesson Memorial Hospital and the Springfield Girls' Clubs. In recognition of her support of nursing, education, care for the aged, and contributions to cultural, civic and professional activities she was awarded an Honorary Degree of Doctor of Laws by St. Anselm's College, Manchester, New Hampshire in June of 1969 and an Honorary Degree of Doctor of Humane Letters by Bay Path College in May of 1994. – Joseph Carvalho III

Margaret Celeste "Marge" (Belcher) Champion

(B. SEPT. 2, 1919 IN LOS ANGELES, CA) captivated audiences as the live action model for Walt Disney's "Snow White," and later as she danced with her husband Gower in numerous film, television and Broadway hits such as "Show Boat," "The Marge and Gower Champion Show," and "Three for Tonight" with Harry Belafonte. Her extensive talents include directing and award-winning choreographing. A Berkshires resident, Champion is a true patron of the arts. She generously gave not only financial support, but equally important, lends her national reputation, time and vision to both cultural organizations in the Berkshires and to young artists at the beginning of their careers. An active member of the board of Jacob's Pillow Dance Festival, Champion donated an 18th century barn from her property to the Pillow in 1996. Champion also has served on the Advisory Board of the Berkshire Theatre Festival and has been a member of the Executive Committee for the Williamstown Theatre Festival, where she helped to select nominees for the Boris Sagal Fellowship for Directors, which she endowed. Champion was inducted into the National Museum of Dance's Mr. & Mrs. Cornelius Vanderbilt Whitney Hall of Fame in 2009. In 2013 she received The Douglas Watt Lifetime Achievement Award at the Fred and Adele Astaire Awards ceremonies. She was also honored by the Massachusetts Cultural Council in 1997 with a Commonwealth Award. – Joseph Carvalho III

Dorcas Chapin

(APR. 11, 1801 IN CHICOPEE/SPRINGFIELD; D. NOV. 14, 1886 IN SPRINGFIELD, MA) wife of Chester W. Chapin, bequeathed $25,000 in 1885 to the Springfield Hospital Association for the creation of a new hospital. In 1884, she also gifted $10,000 to the Church of the Unity on State Street in Springfield. – Joseph Carvalho III

Michele D'Amour

is the Educational Partnership Administrator for Big Y Foods Inc., a family-owned supermarket chain that currently operates 80 locations throughout Massachusetts and Connecticut. The chain includes 70 supermarkets, 39 pharmacies, Fresh Acres Market, Table & Vine Fine Wines and Liquors, and five Big Y Express gas and convenience locations, employing over 12,000 employees.

Michele began working for Big Y as a cashier while working her way through college. A graduate of Westfield State College, she holds a Master's Degree in Education from American International College. She has had a variety of teaching experiences and has also worked at the college level supervising student teachers. In her role as Educational Partnership Administrator, along with other responsibilities, D'Amour has been responsible for managing a variety of community educational initiatives.

D'Amour currently serves as Chairperson of the Board of Pope Francis Preparatory School and is on the board of Assumption College. Michele served for several years as Chairperson of the Board on the Parent Television Council, a national, non-partisan education organization advocating responsible entertainment and remains on the board as a member at large, she also has served on several other boards and committees.

Inspired by Pope John Paul II's encyclical on Faith and Reason, Michele & her husband, Donald, co-founded the Fides et Ratio grant competition for small Catholic Colleges, as well as the on-going Fides et Ratio summer faculty seminars under the auspices of the Faith and Reason Institute in Washington D.C. Along with the Faith & Reason Seminars, the couple has demonstrated their commitment to faith, health, education and the arts through many philanthropic gifts, including the Michele & Donald D'Amour

Above left: Irene Davis (Courtesy the Davis Family). **Above right:** Michele and Donald D'Amour.

Museum of Fine Arts, The D'Amour Cancer Center, Assumption College, Community Music School of Springfield, Pope Francis Preparatory School and St. Michael's Academy. Michele D'Amour has received recognition for her philanthropic work including an honorary doctorate of human letters from Assumption College, The National Catholic Education Association's Elizabeth Seton Award and the Association of Fundraising Professional's Outstanding Philanthropist Award.
– Joseph Carvalho III & Wayne E. Phaneuf

Irene E. Davis

(B. IN 1893 MISSOULA, MT; D. IN 1984 SPRINGFIELD, MA) was a philanthropist who along with her husband George Davis supported cultural, educational, human service and religious organizations throughout Hampden County. Irene spent some of her childhood in an orphanage after her father was killed in a train wreck until her mother was able to fully support the family. Her early life experiences shaped her compassion to help those in need. She believed that those with resources should give back to their community. In fact, she was so intent on helping others that she often handed out cash to the needy and gave anonymously to organizations. Rather than giving toys to her grandchildren at the holidays, she donated to an organization in their name. This planted the seed of giving and her legacy still lives on today through the Irene E. & George A. Davis Foundation, which was named in her honor and continues to support nonprofit organizations in Western Massachusetts. – Laurel Davis Ferretti

Catherine A. Dower, Ph. D.

(B. MAY 19, 1924 IN SOUTH HADLEY, MA; D. FEB. 17, 2017 IN HOLYOKE, MA) was a highly regarded music educator at Westfield State University in Westfield, MA. She was honored by Westfield State University with Professor Emerita status for her life's work as one of the University's longest tenured and dedicated faculty members. In gratitude for Dower's $1.1 million gift to establish a center for the performing and fine arts, the

Catherine A. Dower Center for the Performing & Fine Arts at the University was established. Her gift was the largest private donation in the University's history. – Cynthia G. Simison & Joseph Carvalho III

Above: Dorothy Dwight.
Above right: Catherine Amelia Ewing

Nina Larrey (Smith) Duryea

(B. AUG. 11, 1869 IN BOSTON, MA; D. 1951 IN STOCKBRIDGE, MA) of Stockbridge, MA, founded Duryea War Relief during WWI to aid European refugees. She was decorated for her work by several European governments.
– James S. Gleason

Dorothy Elizabeth (Rathbun) Dwight

(B. MAY 16, 1903 IN MADISON, NJ; D. SEPT. 20, 1992 IN SARASOTA, FLA) spent her adult life in Holyoke, MA as one of the city's most active and generous volunteers for social welfare agencies and non-profits, including "Mrs. Frederick's Neighborhood Settlement," the Red Cross Blood Mobile, the Boy and Girl Scouts, and Holyoke Hospital. In addition to founding the Holyoke Mental Health and Speech Clinics, Dwight served on the board of directors for the Holyoke Child Welfare agency, the Girl Scouts, the VNA, and the Holyoke Taxpayer's Association.
– Joseph Carvalho III

Catherine Amelia (Fay) Ewing

(NÉE CATHERINE AMELIA FAY, NICKNAMED "AUNT KATY", B. JULY 18, 1820 IN WESTBOROUGH, MA; D. APR. 4, 1897 IN MARIETTA, OH) was an American educator, missionary, philanthropist, and social reformer. In 1857, she took in children from the Washington County Infirmary organizing the first children's home in the state of Ohio.

Ewing taught school in Ohio before becoming a missionary among the Choctaw. Ten years later, upon her return to Ohio, she founded a home for destitute children. Through her efforts, the Ohio Legislature passed a bill in Columbus, which entitled every county to establish a children's home. Ewing also authored a comprehensive historical report on the origin and growth of the children's home movement in Washington County – Joseph Carvalho III

Amelia A. (Kousch) Ferst

(B. MAY 15, 1920 IN WESTFIELD, MA; D. NOV. 27, 1997 IN WESTFIELD, MA) Both Albert and Amelia Ferst left an enormous legacy that Westfield will benefit from generations to come, from the Amelia Park complex off South Broad Street that supports Amelia Ice Rink, Children's Museum, Amelia Park Garden, the Albert and Amelia Ferst Boys and Girls Club and an outdoor skateboard park to the Interfaith Center on the campus of Westfield State University and Samaritan Inn homeless shelter on Free Street. "Between Al and Millie, they did more for Westfield, especially the kids, than any other individual," former Mayor Richard K. Sullivan said. "Al's first love was

Millie but his second was Westfield," he said. She and her husband Albert Ferst established the Albert & Amelia Ferst Charitable Foundation to continue their charitable works after their passing. – Ted Laborde & Joseph Carvalho III

Nancy Jane Fitzpatrick

(B. 1947 IN BERKSHIRE COUNTY, MA) Entrepreneur, community leader, and philanthropist, Fitzpatrick became chair of Berkshire Creative in 2008, an economic development and support organization serving the Berkshire County region of Western Massachusetts. Her record of community service reaches from Boston to the Berkshires and beyond, and includes organizations such as the Berkshire Museum, Berkshire Natural Resources Council, Boston Symphony Orchestra, Hancock Shaker Village, Massachusetts College of Liberal Arts, Mass Cultural Council, MASS MoCA Foundation, and the Trustees of Reservations. Her philanthropic activity, as both a trustee of the Fitzpatrick family High Meadow Foundation and as a private individual, continues to leave an indelible mark both within and outside the county and the state.

Fitzpatrick is a second-generation hotelier whose family has owned The Red Lion Inn since 1968. For the last 18 years, she has overseen a hospitality business that includes The Red Lion, The Porches Inn at MASS MoCA, Elm Street Market, and most recently The Wigwam Cabins. A graduate of Smith College, Fitzpatrick was honored with a Commonwealth Award from the Massachusetts Cultural Council in 2011. – Joseph Carvalho III

Janee Armstrong Friedmann

(B. JANUARY 11, 1937 IN WILKES-BARRE, PA; D. MARCH 21, 2007 IN LONGMEADOW, MA) was a passionate volunteer devoted to promoting the importance of arts, culture and education. A longtime volunteer at the

American Red Cross, she was president of the following organizations: Early Childhood Center of Springfield, the Junior League of Greater Springfield, Richard Salter Storrs Library in Longmeadow, the Springfield Symphony Orchestra, and the Springfield Public Forum. Friedmann served as chairman of the following organizations: Board of Trustees of the Springfield Museums Association, the Edward R. Murrow Society of WGBY, the Society of William Rice at the Springfield Museums, and the President's Society of the Baystate Health Foundation. During her lifetime of service to the Greater Springfield community, Friedmann was an active and very successful fundraiser for numerous capital campaigns, special projects, and annual funds for all of the major cultural institutions based in Springfield, MA. In recognition of her work on behalf of the community, she was the recipient of many awards, including: YWCA Women of

Above: Nancy Jane Fitzpatrick. **Right:** Janee Armstrong Friedmann (Courtesy Cynthia Campbell/ Friedmann Family)

Above left: Helen (Smith) "Bunny" Fuller. **Above right:** Audrey Geisel (Courtesy *The Republican*)

Achievement Award in 1998, Outstanding Volunteer Fundraiser from the Western Mass Chapter of the Association of Fundraising Professionals in 2001, the William Pynchon Award in 2001, and Mary Alice Rogers Award for Volunteerism from WGBY-TV in 2006.
– Joseph Carvalho III & Cynthia Campbell

Helen (Smith) "Bunny" Fuller

(B. MAR. 23, 1917 IN SPRINGFIELD, MA; D. NOV. 8, 2013) of Longmeadow was a philanthropist and active community volunteer in the Great Springfield region. She was a trustee for over 20 years at the Springfield Library and Museums Association serving as its Chairman during the late 1980s and early 1990s. Fuller served on the board of trustees of American International College for over 25 years, and was a founding trustee of the Community Foundation of Western Massachusetts. Well educated, Fuller attended MacDuffie School for Girls in Springfield; graduated

from Miss Hall's School in Pittsfield in 1935; graduated from Smith College in 1939 , attending the Sorbonne, Paris 1937-38; and held a Masters from American International College. Throughout her life, Helen served as an inspiration to others, demonstrating leadership through thoughtful and inspired action and being content to share the credit for her accomplishments with others. These attributes were confirmed in 1991 when she was recognized as a William Pynchon Award recipient by the Advertising Club of Springfield, and honored as Woman of Distinction by the Pioneer Valley Girl Scouts in 1999. – Joseph Carvalho III & David M. Fuller

Audrey (Stone) Geisel

(B. AUG. 14, 1921 IN CHICAGO, IL) is the wife of the late Theodor Seuss Geisel, aka "Dr. Seuss" of Springfield, MA. She was the major donor of funds to create the Dr. Seuss National Memorial Sculpture Garden at the Springfield

Museums in Springfield, MA which opened in 2002 and has had over 3 million visitors to date. She and Dr. Seuss Enterprises approved and supported the creation of The Amazing World of Dr. Seuss Museum at the Springfield Museums which opened in 2017.
– Joseph Carvalho III

Lucy Douglas Gillett

(B. NOV. 20, 1856; D. APR 21, 1949), daughter of Edward Bates Gillett and Lucy Fowler Gillett of Westfield, MA. Lucy Douglas Gillett contributed to the First Congregational Church throughout her life. She was a philanthropist who often donated to the YMCA, Westfield Women's Club, Westfield Library, and the Aged People's Home.

She was one of the charter members of the Hopefully Well Affected Club and was one of the founders of the Westfield Women's Club as well as one of the founders of the Young People's Agricultural Society. She became Vice President and an officer of the Home Department of the Hampden County Improvement League in 1916. She was heavily involved with the 4-H clubs and served on the Women's Advisory Council of Massachusetts State College.

Gillett served for over 40 years as director, vice-president, chairman of various committees including steering and membership of the Hampden County Improvement League. She also led the Lightbearers 4-H Sewing Club at the First Congregational Church in Westfield, and "hundreds of girls in this city took their first stitches under her direction." At the First Church, she served on many committees, supplied the attendance award Bibles, the promotion certificates & prized for the annual Recognition Day exercises for the church school's pupils and endowed that custom. Gillett purchased a residence for the pastor. Miss Lucy was active in the Women's Union at First Church, especially in their missionary work where "countless persons... have been

beneficiaries of her work in this field."

"Her benefactions to the YMCA have been among her largest" She left $100,000 as a nucleus of the construction of a new building; she bought the Henry Taylor house and its large tract of property and gave it to the YMCA. Gillett also purchased the former First Congregational Church parsonage and gave it to the YMCA. – Kate Deviny

Alice Lord (Coonley) Higgins

(B. AUG. 15, 1906 IN LAKE FOREST, IL; D. JAN. 19, 2000 IN WORCESTER, MA), wife of Worcester industrialist Milton Prince Higgins II whose father founded the Norton Co., was Clark University's first woman trustee (1962), and first female chairman of the Board at the university in 1967, is reported to be the first woman to chair a university board in the United States. She and her husband were generous philanthropists for Worcester cultural institutions including the Worcester Art Museum. – Leah Lamson & Joseph Carvalho III

Irene (Mennen) Hunter

(B. NOV. 15, 1918 IN NEWARK, NJ ; D. OCT. 1, 2008 IN MANCHESTER, VT) was a philanthropist who gave millions to local arts and education projects and who dedicated herself to growing the arts in Berkshire County. She lived in Williamstown, MA for fifty years. She and her husband James "Bing" Hunter were known for their generous donations over the years to Massachusetts Museum of Contemporary Art, Jacob's Pillow, public television, the town of Williamstown, the Congregational Church and the Williamstown Theatre Festival. In 1999, their $1 million donation helped establish the black box theater at MoCA, which was named the Hunter Center for the Performing Arts. Hunter also supported the Bennington Museum, the New England Tropical Conservatory, Bennington College and a number of schools in the Manchester area. She also gave to the Emma Willard School, a girls school in Troy, N.Y., which she attended, and the Vermont Symphony as well. – Joseph Carvalho III

Top left: Helen E. James School in Williamsburg, MA.
Top center: Helen E. James
Above: Lucy D. Gillett

195

Left: Helen Bigelow Mirriman. **Above:** Esta Manthos (Courtesy Lyman & Merrie Wood Museum of Springfield History)

Helen Eliza (Field) James

(B. FEB. 3, 1837 IN COLRAIN, MA; D. 1906 IN WILLIAMSBURG, MA), philanthropist, has been referred to as "The Benevolent Angel of Williamsburg (MA)." She used the large trust fund left to her by her brother Marshall Field, the "Merchant Prince of Chicago," to fund many town improvements to Williamsburg, and to establish the Helen E. James School which served high school students from Williamsburg, Haydenville, Westhampton, Goshen, and Chesterfield. She also gave very generously to hundreds of worthy projects in the Pioneer Valley and the Berkshires including the Red Cross, the Visiting Nurses, the Children's Home, and to Cooley-Dickinson Hospital. – Ralmon Jon Black, Williamsburg Historical Society, Pioneer Valley History Network

Myra Hiatt Kraft

(NÉE MYRA NATHALIE HIATT; B. DEC. 27, 1942 IN WORCESTER, MA; D. JULY 20, 2011 IN BROOKLINE, MA) was an American philanthropist and the wife of New England Patriots and New England Revolution owner Robert Kraft. the daughter of Frances and Jacob Hiatt. Kraft was listed by *Boston Magazine* as one of the 20 Most Powerful Women in Boston, She was president and director of the New England Patriots Charitable Foundation and trustee of the Robert K. and Myra H. Kraft Foundation. She served on the boards of directors of the American Repertory Theatre, the United Way of Massachusetts Bay, Northeastern University, the Boys and Girls Clubs of Boston, and Brandeis University. Kraft and her husband started the "Passport to Israel" Program with the Combined Jewish Philanthropies of Boston which provided financial assistance to Jewish parents to send their children to Israel while teenagers to help promote Jewish identity. To encourage greater understanding between Christians and Jews, Kraft, her husband, and her father Jacob Hiatt endowed two professorships in comparative religion at the College of the Holy Cross and Brandeis University: the Kraft-Hiatt Chair in Judaic Studies at Holy Cross and the Kraft-Hiatt Chair in Christian Studies at Brandeis University. *The International Herald Tribune* credited Kraft with "modeling a new form of engaged giving that is transforming the relationship between philanthropist and philanthropy." – Joseph Carvalho III

Esta C. (Kokiernak) Manthos

(B. JULY 5, 1915 IN WEBSTER, MA; D. OCT. 16, 2016 IN SPRINGFIELD, MA) co-founded the Indian Motocycle Museum in Springfield with her husband Charles Manthos. She donated the entire museum collection of motorcycles, memorabilia, and archives to the Springfield Museums Association for the creation of the Manthos Gallery of Indian Motocycle History at the Lyman & Merrie Wood Museum of Springfield History, which opened in 2010. During World War II, Esta Manthos worked for both the Hartford Ordnance District and the Springfield Ordnance District overseeing the quality of war production, as a member of the Board of Examiners of the Springfield Armory. After the war, she worked for Massachusetts Mutual retiring after 33 years as an underwriter. During that period, she also served as vice-president of the Solar Metal Corporation. – Joseph Carvalho III & John Sampson

Rachel (Capen) Merriam
(B. APR. 5, 1824 IN GAINES, NY; D. AUG. 27, 1899 IN GLOUCESTER, MA; BURIED IN SPRINGFIELD CEMETERY, SPRINGFIELD, MA) According to local historians Roberta Grahame and Catherine Blakeslee, Rachel Merriam "by her personal efforts" secured the funds for the establishment of the Springfield Home for Friendless Women and Children. She served as its president for ten years. She also was one of the founders of the Children's Home on Buckingham Street in Springfield. Her second husband was Charles Merriam, publisher of the famed Webster's Dictionary. – Joseph Carvalho III

Helen Bigelow Merriman
(B. JULY 14, 1844 IN BOSTON, MA; D. JULY 25, 1933 IN CONWAY, NH) was a painter, author, and art collector and one of the founders of the Worcester Art Museum. She and her husband Rev. Daniel Merriman moved to Worcester in 1878 where she soon became very active in the Worcester Art Society and the Worcester Art Students Club. The Merrimans gave a large donation to help establish the Worcester Art Museum and became active members of the museum's board of trustees. Helen Merriman was "a champion of women artists" and was instrumental in having the museum acquire important works of artists Sarah Wyman Whitman and Cecilia Beaux. She also wrote several books about art and spirituality, including *What Shall Make Us Whole?: Or, Thoughts in the Direction of Man's Spiritual and Physical Integrity* (1888), *The Perfect Lord* (1891), *Concerning Portraits and Portraiture* (1891), and *Religio Pictoris* (1899). Remembering her childhood home in New Hampshire, Merriman also donated land and money to found North Conway's Memorial Hospital in 1911. – Joseph Carvalho III

Amy Bess (Williams) Miller
(B. MAY 4, 1912 IN EL PASO, TX ; D. FEB. 23, 2003 IN PITTSFIELD, MA) was a Shaker Scholar who saved and opened Hancock Shaker Village and served as its president from 1944 to 1979. She served as President of Berkshire Athenaeum from 1950 to 1990. Miller wrote four books and co-edited a fifth on Shaker history and society. She was the wife of the publisher of the *Berkshire Eagle*, Lawrence Miller. Miller also served on the Massachusetts Board of Library Commissioners from 1964 to 1970. – James S. Gleason & Joseph Carvalho III

Robyn Ann Newhouse, Ph.D.
(B. NEW YORK CITY; GREW UP IN GREAT NECK, LONG ISLAND) is the Vice-president/community service of *The Republican* (previously the *Union News and Sunday Republican*), serving in that capacity since 1988. She is a licensed clinical psychologist and worked at a range of psychology-related jobs from the mid-1970s to 1988. One of the first women of the Newhouse family to work in newspapers, Robyn Newhouse came to Springfield to train with noted publisher and senior editor of Newhouse newspapers, David Starr. She has been very involved with a wide range of important community organizations and has served on the boards of Bay Path University, the Community Music School of Springfield, The Jewish Federation of Western Massachusetts, the Mak'hela (regional Jewish chorus), the National Guild for Community Arts Education, the NCCJ (now on

Robyn Ann Newhouse, Ph. D. (Frederick Gore Photo)

Top left: Mayor Roger Putnam and Caroline P. Putnam (*The Republican* file photo). **Above:** Gertrude Robinson Smith. **Bottom left:** Belle Skinner.

Advisory Board), the Springfield Symphony Orchestra, and WGBY – Public Television. Her life-long interest in music is reflected in her many years of generous support of the Community Music School of Springfield. The CMS's main performance space, Robyn Newhouse Hall is named in her honor. Among her many awards, she was honored as philanthropist of the year for Hampden County in 2010 by the Association of Fundraising Professionals, received the NCCJ Human Relations award in 2013, and received a Herman Snyder award from Sinai Temple. – Wayne E. Phaneuf & Joseph Carvalho III

Margaret E. O'Donnell

(B. JULY 17, 1898 IN FLORENCE, NORTHAMPTON, MA; D. JUNE 28, 1999 IN FLORENCE, NORTHAMPTON, MA) and her sister Agnes K. O'Donnell (B. SEPT. 17, 1902 IN FLORENCE, NORTHAMPTON, MA; D. JAN. 19, 1997 IN FLORENCE, NORTHAMPTON, MA) both retired Northampton school teachers "of modest means" left their $2.4 million estate to a charitable fund bearing their name to provide scholarships for college, nursing education at Cooley Dickinson Hospital, and a variety of other community causes, managed by the Community Foundation of Western Massachusetts. – William Freebairn

Caroline Piatt (Jenkins) Putnam

(B. NOV. 16, 1892 IN MARYLAND; D. FEB. 12, 1993 IN SPRINGFIELD, MA) founded and funded the Catholic Scholarship for Negroes, Inc. which assisted students of color nationwide. She received the Hoey Award from the NAACP for her contributions to education. Since 2009, African-American and Latino students from Springfield and Holyoke, MA public and charter schools have been the focus of this long-running scholarship fund. She was the wife of Roger Lowell Putnam, who served as Mayor of Springfield, Massachusetts, from 1937 until 1943, and as director of the U.S. Economic Stabilization Administration from 1951 until 1952. – Wayne E. Phaneuf & Joseph Carvalho III

Ruth Isabelle "Belle" Skinner

(B. APRIL 30, 1866 IN WILLIAMSBURG, MA; D. APRIL 9, 1928 IN PARIS, FRANCE) was the daughter of William and Sarah Elizabeth Allen Skinner. In October of 1874 after the disastrous Mill River Flood that wiped out Skinnerville and the Skinner's Unquomunk Silk Mill, the family relocated to Holyoke, MA. Educated in the Holyoke public schools, Belle went on to Vassar and graduated as class president in 1887. She was influenced by her father who had a vision of the greater place women must take in world affairs. After a graduating from Vassar, Ms. Skinner spent a year in France and travelled widely with her family.

In 1902, in collaboration with her sister

Katharine Skinner Kilborne, the Skinner Coffee House was created in honor of their recently deceased father William Skinner. The Skinner Coffee House was a recreation center for women who worked in the Holyoke mills. They offered various cooking and sewing classes; music and art lessons; made books available for reading and even provided rooming for "women and children in transition."

When WWI began in August 1914, Belle's sympathies were with France. In 1918, through field glasses from within the French Lines, Skinner saw the town of Hattonchâtel bombed and taken by the German forces. She declared to a French officer that this was to be her village to adopt. When he protested that there was nothing left but the hill, she replied: "Then I will rebuild what there is of it!" Skinner immediately arranged with the French Government to care for the scattered population until rebuilding could begin. And she resolutely set out to help them restore the village without a thought of failure. In recognition of her efforts in 1919, she received from the French government the Gold Medal of Reconnaissance Française, and in December, 1920 the Cross of the Légion d'Honneur. – Penni Martorell, Wistariahurst Museum, Holyoke (Pioneer Valley History Network)

Gertrude Robinson Smith

(B. JULY 13, 1881 IN MAMARONECK, NY; D. OCT. 22, 1963 IN NEW YORK CITY) was an arts patron, philanthropist and a founder of the Berkshire Symphonic Festival, which came to be known as Tanglewood. At the height of the Great Depression, Smith gathered the human resources and secured the financial backing that supported the festival's early success. Her leadership from the first concerts in August 1934 through the mid-1950s has been recognized as foundational to assuring the success of one of the world's most celebrated seasonal music festivals. – Joseph Carvalho III

Peggy (Giffen) Starr

(NÉE MARJORIE, B. NOV. 17, 1920 IN QUEENS, NEW YORK) Peggy and David Starr have been instrumental in raising millions of dollars for arts and cultural organizations throughout the region, working tirelessly to ensure that the people of Western Massachusetts have healthy and growing artistic, cultural and civic organizations. A supporter of Public Television Broadcasting, Peggy Starr was named a Life Member of WGBY's Board. She persuaded station management to create the Edward and Janet Murrow Society for major donors. The Murrow Society has generated millions of dollars for the station. The Starrs are supporters of The Springfield Museums, the Springfield Symphony Orchestra, New England Public Radio and CityStage. They created a $1 million Arts Endowment at the Community Foundation of Western Massachusetts to provide future funding for the four arts organizations they have worked with for over three decades. Marjorie (Peggy) Giffen married Dave Starr in 1943. They moved to the Springfield area in 1971 when Dave became publisher of *The Republican* and the couple quickly became patrons of the arts and leaders in the community. – Wayne E. Phaneuf & Joseph Carvalho III

Lois Eldridge Stebbins

(B. JAN. 6, 1918 IN TAUNTON, MA; D. FEB. 2015 IN LONGMEADOW, MA) was a quiet philanthropist who supported many organizations in Western Massachusetts including the Springfield Museums, Faith Church, the Springfield Library, Community Music School, Springfield Symphony, Mount Holyoke College, WGBY-TV, New England Public Radio, American International College, and the Society for the Prevention of Cruelty to Animals. She served as the president of the Horace Mann Book Club, was a trustee for Ring Nursing Home and then was a trustee for Glenmeadow a senior living community

Above: Peggy Starr (Courtesy of David Starr)

199

Diane Troderman, with her husband, Harold Grinspoon

in Longmeadow, MA. She attended Mount Holyoke College and then Boston University. Stebbins moved to Springfield and taught at AIC where she met her husband Frederick ("Frick") Stebbins. She loved classical music and played the piano, viola and violin. – Greg Swanson & Heather Cahill

Sarah Williams Storrs

(B. SEPT. 5, 1832 IN AMHERST, MA; D. OCT. 16, 1907 IN LONGMEADOW, MA) is remarkable in the town of Longmeadow's history for her benevolence in establishing the town's library and donating the home site for the Longmeadow Historical Society. She was a direct descendant of both the first and second ministers of Longmeadow's First Church. A bout of whooping cough caused her to lose her hearing in infancy. She was educated at the American Asylum for the Deaf in Hartford, and was such a gifted student that she was asked to remain as a member of the faculty. She taught at the school for 15 years. Sarah retired to her family's ancestral home in Longmeadow. Upon her death in 1907, Sarah left $5,000, the family home, land and her family's collection of books to establish The Richard Salter Storrs Library, "Desiring to perpetuate the memory of a name dear to my family for three generations." The large and important collection of items preserved by Sarah, chronicling her family's role in early Longmeadow, was acquired by the Longmeadow Historical Society. The Richard Salter Storrs Library and the Storrs House Museum are still vital centerpieces of community learning and events today. – Melissa Cybulski

Diane L. Troderman

(B. SEPT. 2, 1941) Philanthropist and educator Diane Troderman, with her husband, Harold Grinspoon, established the Harold Grinspoon Charitable Foundation with a focus on education, funding annual awards for excellence in teaching. Troderman grew up in Brookline and majored in biology at Wheaton College, where she became interested in the ways people learn. She has taught biology and the learning disabled. The Harold Grinspoon Charitable Foundation supports the Entrepreneurship Initiative to foster entrepreneurship education. The two also established the Harold Grinspoon Foundation to promote Jewish life in Western Massachusetts, North America and Israel. Its PJ Library sends free Jewish content books and CDs to families across North America. Troderman was the first chair of the former Hatikvah Holocaust Education Center at the Springfield Jewish Community Center and has served on countless organizations, including the Partnership for Excellence in Jewish Education and the Partnership for Effective Learning and Innovative Education. In addition, she has served on the boards of American Jewish World Service, the Jewish Education Service of North America, Hazon, and was a founding chairman of the Hadassah Brandeis Institute. She is a past president of the Springfield Jewish Federation and Hillel at University of Massachusetts. – Jane Kaufman

Mary E. Walachy

(B. FEB. 15, 1953) is the Executive Director of The Irene E. & George A. Davis Foundation in Springfield, MA since 1997. She also serves as a member of the Board of Early Education and Care, Inc. since 2012. Walachy is a well-respected advocate for early childhood education in Springfield and throughout the state of Massachusetts. Under her direction and leadership, The Davis Foundation launched the successful "Cherish Every Child" initiative which was instrumental in the passage of the Pre-K legislation passed by the Massachusetts legislature. In 2009, She lead the Foundation's expansion of its "Cherish Every Child" initiative to include "Read! Reading Success by 4th Grade" campaign. Walachy also created the "Funder Collaborative for Reading Success," a collaboration of more than 12 funders who have collectively raised over $2 million in support of early literacy and reading success. In 2013, she was appointed by Governor Deval Patrick to the Massachusetts state Board of Early Education and Care. – Joseph Carvalho III

Ruth Dyer Wells

(B. AUG. 17, 1907 IN BOSTON, MA; D. DEC. 13, 1989 IN WHITE PLAINS, NY) was the first director of Old Sturbridge Village in Sturbridge, MA when the museum opened in 1946. She held this role until 1950. Wife of the wealthy George B. Wells, owner of the American Optical Company, she would play a crucial role in

the development of the village for the next 35 years. OSV's predecessor museum, the Wells Historical Museum, was created by the Wells family in 1935 from their substantial family collections. The Wells family ownership of the world famous and very successful American Optical Company in Southbridge, MA provided the means for their philanthropic efforts to preserve New England history, architecture, and culture through the remarkable Old Sturbridge Village. Ruth Wells also donated the land in Charlton, MA where the Cape Hill Nature Center was developed. She was also a member of the American Farm School and was involved in a program in which New England cows were shipped all over the world.

Among her many philanthropic efforts for the town of Southbridge, MA, Wells organized the first community center in Southbridge, which was located across Main Street from the site of the present Arts Center. She spent most of her life in Southbridge except for her last days in a hospital in White Plains, New York. – Wayne E. Phaneuf & Joseph Carvalho III

Cynthia Maria (Hawes) Wesson

(B. AUG. 14, 1825 IN NORTHBOROUGH, MA; D. JULY 18, 1906 IN SPRINGFIELD, MA) was the wife of Daniel Baird Wesson, partner and founder of Smith & Wesson Firearms Co. She was one of the wealthiest women in Massachusetts and was a generous philanthropist. Early in 1900, she and her husband established the Wesson Memorial Hospital (homeopathic) in the house on High Street in Springfield, MA. The hospital building was built by the side of the former High Street home, and they funded the construction of the Wesson Maternity Hospital on the grounds as well. – Joseph Carvalho III

Robin Wheeler

served as Chairman of the Board of Trustees of the Springfield Library & Museums Association and was a primary leader in the

Above: Mary E. Walachy (Ed Cohen Photo)

Merrie Y. Wood (Courtesy of Lyman Wood)

$4.3 million to complete the funding for the Lyman & Merrie Wood Museum of Springfield History which opened in 2010. At the 2010 history museum event honoring the Woods' donation, Merrie Wood said: "I just couldn't think of anything that would be around as long and be as permanent and be as meaningful to as many people as this is." Merrie and Lyman moved to Hampden in 1983 and soon after became very involved in the major cultural and higher education institutions of greater Springfield. In addition to their many years of support of the Springfield Museums, the couple also led the campaign to have Planned Parenthood build a new state-of-the-art facility in Springfield. Major supporters of Springfield College, Western New England and Bay Path Universities, Merrie and Lyman also contributed to the Springfield Symphony Orchestra and Baystate Health along with other community institutions throughout the Pioneer Valley. In recognition of their generosity, Merrie and Lyman were named Philanthropists of the Year in 1994 by the National Society of Fund-raising Executives of Western Massachusetts. As a special tribute, Merrie is buried near the entrance of the Wood Museum of Springfield History. – Joseph Carvalho III

Mary Ida (Stephenson) Young

(B. JUNE 29, 1865 IN STONINGTON, MD; D. OCT 31, 1960 IN LONGMEADOW, MA) was co-founder with her husband Wilbur F. Young of the internationally famous W.F. Young, Inc. manufacturer of popular consumer product, Absorbine, Jr. When Wilbur died in 1928, Mrs. Young took over running the company. She became a major local philanthropist and among her charitable efforts established the W.F. Young Camp for Children in Athol, Massachusetts. [See also entry in Business & Labor Chapter]. – Joseph Carvalho III

creation of the Dr. Seuss National Memorial Sculpture Garden, and many of the key capital improvements at the Springfield Library system and the Springfield Museums during the 1990s. She and her husband Thomas' generous donations to the Springfield Museums were recognized by the naming of the primary changing exhibition gallery

of the Michele & Donald D'Amour Museum of Fine Arts in Springfield, MA in their honor. – Joseph Carvalho III

Merrie Y. Wood

(NÉE MEREDITH, B. OCT. 20, 1937 BORN IN NEW YORK CITY; D. SEPT. 2, 2012 IN HAMPDEN, MA) and her husband R. Lyman Wood donated

CHAPTER TWELVE

WOMEN
in Music

BY SONYA LAWSON, PH.D.
Chair of the Music Department,
Westfield State University

Although many people immediately think of Boston and its citizens when they think of musical prowess, there are actually a plethora of women from Western and Central Massachusetts that are worthy of being recognized. From the mid-1800s until today there have been, and continue to be, women composers, performers, and music educators who have played an important role in the cultural life of this region.

These women run the gamut from concert singers in the 19th century, to popular music entertainers in the 20th and 21st centuries, to classical music enthusiasts and performers, to ground breaking music educators and theorists. Violinists, harpists, bass players, guitarists, pianists are all represented in these pages. Country, opera, pop, folk, and rock singers delight audiences throughout the past two centuries. Jazz and Broadway musicians are also present! Contrary to a belief that not much music outside of symphonies and church takes place in this region, these entries will prove that music of every imaginable sort has been made in a multiplicity of venues.

Not confined to regional success, many of these women were well-travelled, both in the United States and abroad. For example,

in the 1850s, Elise Hensler performed across Europe; Marilyn Crittendon performed in South America in the 1940s as a member of an orchestra; and Carol Denise Fredericks moved to France in 1979 to perform as part of a jazz trio. As you read the biographies of these women you will be impressed with how many of them participated in the cultural life of cities that are far beyond the borders of Massachusetts.

The diverse ethnicities that have been a part of the story of Western and Central Massachusetts since colonial days are well represented in the women portrayed in this book, and the variety of backgrounds can easily be seen in the diverse career and musical choices made by these women.

Women in Music: Composers, Performers, and Music Education

Adele Addison:
Springfield's greatest gift to music

BY RICHARD C. GARVEY

Coming from my tape deck is the magnificent voice of Adele Addison, soloist with the Cleveland Symphony, George Szell conducting. All of this pleasure comes because of a question I recently posed to a man who loves both Springfield and music: Who is the city's greatest gift to music? He unhesitatingly answered: Adele Addison. The tape was hand-delivered.

When I first heard her voice, I am not sure. Her first formal concert that I attended was in Old First Church here more than 50 years ago, but I may well have heard her earlier. I cannot claim to have heard her when she was a soloist with the Chestnut Street School chorus. She won that post because, when the school assembly was singing "God Bless America," her voice caught the attention of the music teacher, Ruth Ray. She enticed her into the glee club.

Certain that the young soloist had a special gift, Ray persuaded Ruth Ekberg, a voice and music teacher who had been educated at Hartt School of Music in Hartford and with private tutors in New York City, to hear her. Ekberg accepted her as a student, and followed her Classical High School career under the tutelage of its music teacher, Hazel Clark.

Being a Gilbert & Sullivan buff, I may have heard Addison when Classical presented those operettas. Ekberg, an officer of the Tuesday Morning Music Club and founder of its Junior Extension, introduced the soprano to more

Adele Addison

audiences, and the Springfield Junior League gave her a scholarship to Westminster Choir School in Princeton, N.J.

After four years of study there, Addison returned to Massachusetts to compete for the vocal scholarship at Tanglewood. The other contestants must have accepted the inevitable when the judges asked for four encores. One of the judges, Rudolph Elie, was the music critic of the Boston Herald, allowing him to become a prophet the next day when his review was published: "Potentially one of the greatest singers to appear so far in America. When she comes to Boston for a recital, you'd better plan to be present!"

The accompanist for the trials was Boris Goldovsky, who could recognize young talent. (He had made his piano debut with the Berlin Philharmonic at 13.) Goldovsky wisely accepted Addison as his pupil at Tanglewood, and also hired her as a soloist with his New England Opera Co., later the Goldovsky Opera Institute and the Goldovsky Grand Opera Theater. Two years later, after summer study at Tanglewood and winter study at the New England Conservatory of Music at Boston, Addison made her debut in Boston and critics competed for superlatives.

After her highly-praised New York's Town Hall debut in 1952, she made annual appearances with the New York Philharmonic. When that orchestra recorded "The Messiah" for Columbia Masterworks, Leonard Bernstein chose Adele Addison as soloist. She later recorded with many major orchestras.

On her many visits here to her parents and to appear in concert, often with the Springfield Symphony, she would also visit Ekberg who died in 1982, six months before Addison's mother died here. The soloist also came in 1963 to accept an honorary doctorate from UMass. She now teaches voice at Manhattan School of Music.

Some may have heard her voice without knowing it. Sam Goldwyn, convinced that Addison "ranks with the greatest singers of our time," persuaded her to provide her singing voice for Dorothy Dandridge who, with Sidney Poitier, appeared in "Porgy and Bess." In that movie classic, you see Dandridge – but you hear Addison.

[Editors' note: This column was written in June of 1997 by the late Richard C. Garvey, former editor of the *Springfield Daily News* and assistant publisher of the *Union-News* and *The Republican*. He was the premiere local historian of Western Massachusetts.]

Brynn Cartelli:

"It's all about women supporting women"

By RAY KELLY

The Cartelli family has been known for decades in Western Massachusetts for their successful Fathers & Sons auto dealerships.

But in 2018, it was all about their daughter.

Brynn Cartelli, 15, of Longmeadow became the youngest contestant to win NBC's popular singing competition "The Voice." In doing so, she took home a $100,000 prize and was signed to a recording deal by Universal Music Group.

Her first single, "Walk My Way," penned by songwriter Julia Michaels, was the first bona fide hit to come from "The Voice." It reached Number 2 on the iTunes chart.

Throughout her time on "The Voice," and in the months that followed, the Longmeadow High School freshman was mentored by pop star Kelly Clarkson.

"Kelly is more than just an inspiration and mentor to me," Cartelli said. "She's a friend. She is almost like family to me now."

Since her win, Clarkson has offered the teenage singer counsel on her choice of producers and songwriters and how to develop into a national recording act, while not losing yourself in the process.

"I really respect what Kelly has done in her career and the way she talks about the struggles she has had as a woman in the music industry," Cartelli said. "It's hard being a young girl breaking into the industry, but I am glad I have people like Kelly to look up to and support me."

She added, "It's all about women supporting women."

As a young singer, Cartelli has been inspired by the vocal abilities of Clarkson, Adele and Beyonce, as well as singer-songwriters like Tori Kelly, Maren Morris and Mary Kate Kestner.

"There are a lot of females out there who do not get the recognition they deserve," Cartelli said.

Cartelli's rise to Season 14 champion is startling for a teenager who until recently was best known for occasional performances at Uno's Courtyard in Springfield or Cisco Brewery in Nantucket. The producers of "The Voice" reached out to her in February 2017 after seeing her perform in a YouTube video. She wowed Clarkson in the televised Blind Auditions in February 2018. Then, she sailed past her competitors in the Battle and Knockout rounds and Live Playoffs to become one of four finalists and later the eventual winner.

"I never expected this to happen," Cartelli said. "I was hoping to just to make it to the finale. It never occurred to me that I would be the winner, even when I got to the Top 2. It never registered in my mind."

Throughout the competition, her parents, Deb and Damon Cartelli, and younger brother, Jack, were there to cheer her on.

In the finale, Cartelli edged past her rivals with the catchy "Walk My Way" and a powerful cover of Adele's "Skyfall."

Her performances on "The Voice" were immediately popular on iTunes and Apple Music.

After her victory, Cartelli returned to Longmeadow High School to close out her freshman year there before beginning work on the recording of her debut album.

She says she wants to continue her education, while still pursuing her goal to establish herself as a successful singer.

Clarkson, who rose to fame on the inaugural season of "American Idol" in 2002, offered career advice to Cartelli at a televised press conference immediately after her win on "The Voice" finale.

"I always tell her to stop and enjoy it, and don't get too overwhelmed," Clarkson said. "It's good to keep the momentum, but not to be

Brynn Cartelli (Photo by Hoang 'Leon' Nguyen)

miserable. I didn't have anybody tell me that, so I'm constantly annoying her with this message: 'It's not worth it unless you're having a good time.' None of it is worth it. Any job would be better. It is not worth it. It is hard. It is a lot of work."

Ameriie

(NÉE AMERIE MI MARIE ROGERS, B. JANUARY 12, 1980 IN FITCHBURG, MA), singer and actress. Ameriie was born to a South Korean mother, artist Mi Suk and African American father, Charles. A few months after she was born, the Rogers family moved to South Korea, where Ameriie lived for three years. Her father, Charles, was a chief warrant officer in the U.S. military, so the family lived in many different places, including Alaska, Texas, Virginia and Germany. Known professionally as Amerie (currently Ameriie), she is an American singer, songwriter, author, actress and record producer. She debuted in 2002 with her highly acclaimed debut album "All I Have". In 2003, she helped develop the BET original series "The Center". – Joseph Carvalho III

Tryphosa Bates-Batcheller

(NÉE TRYPHOSA DUNCAN BATES, B. APRIL 14, 1876 IN NORTH BROOKFIELD, MA; D. JULY 12, 1952 IN GOSHEN, NY) was a well-known American socialite, "club woman" and concert singer. In 1904, she married the wealthy shoe manufacturer Francis B. Batcheller and thereafter retained her maiden name as the first half of her hyphenated married name. The couple left their native North Brookfield, Massachusetts home and set up home in an apartment in Paris, France.
– Joseph Carvalho III

Esther Dale (Case) Beckhard

(B. NOV. 10, 1885 IN BEAUFORT, SC; D. JULY 23, 1961 IN LOS ANGELES, CA) began her singing, stage and screen career by entertaining the troops in musical performances during World War I. Later, she became a regular vocalist for the Springfield Symphony then began a career in radio with New York's RKO, then performed on Broadway for a few years before heading to Hollywood to appear in films.
– Joseph Carvalho III

Marie Lecea Brackman

(B. JAN. 1, 1873 IN HOLYOKE, MA; D. MAR. 8, 1963 IN HOLYOKE, MA) was a well-known soprano who performed in the most famed venues in America including the New York Metropolitan Opera House, Carnegie Hall, and with the Boston Symphony. Also performing in Europe, Brackman's performance elicited this review from *The London Herald*: "Miss Brackman possesses a voice of great beauty, elasticity, and power." – Joseph Carvalho III

Marlyn Crittendon

(B. FEB. 14, 1918 IN SPRINGFIELD, MA; D. JUNE 5, 1993 IN AMHERST, MA) was one of the finest musicians to come out of Springfield. She played her first public concert in Springfield's Symphony Hall when she was only six years old. She showed such promise in her youth that she was accepted as a student of Louis Persinger, the famed teacher of Yehudi Menuhin. Later she won a full scholarship to the Julliard School in New York.

Her career was launched in 1940 when she joined Leopold Stokowski's All American Youth Orchestra to tour the United States and South America. In 1941 she was invited by Eleanor Roosevelt to give a recital at the White House. After that success she was asked to assemble and direct the Breck American Girl Philharmonic Orchestra in 1943 for a nationally broadcast radio program advertising Breck hair products. From 1946 to 1948 she served as a member of the National Symphony Orchestra in Washington, D.C.

After leaving the National Symphony she became concert-mistress of the Springfield Symphony Orchestra, and continued in that position for 28 years. She also served as the orchestra's librarian and as assistant conductor of the Young Peoples Symphony of Greater Springfield. Crittendon was also known as a music teacher. While serving in the Springfield Symphony, she taught violin at Amherst College and Mount Holyoke College. – Staff of the Lyman & Merrie Wood Museum of Springfield History, Springfield Museums, Springfield, MA

Zoë Darrow

(B. 1989) is an accomplished fiddler and musician of rare intensity and expressive range who grew up playing Cape Breton and other Celtic music on a sheep farm in Blandford, MA. She released her first recording in 2001 at the age of 12, with her band the Fiddleheads. In 2007, *Celtic Heritage Magazine* acclaimed Zoë as an artist "destined to add savory spice to the global mix."

A graduate of Mount Holyoke College with a degree in anthropology and music, she has also become a much sought after collaborator, touring and recording with luminaries like banjo innovator Tony Trischka, Bela Fleck's primary banjo guru and an instructor at the Berklee College of Music. With Tim Eriksen and percussionist Peter Irvine she has toured North America and as far abroad as Singapore. – Joseph Carvalho III

Helen Maria Dunham

(B. AUG. 16, 1827 IN PITTSFIELD, MA ; D. JUN. 13, 1902 IN NEWTON, MA) in 1846 became one of the first if not the first woman to serve as a regular church organist in Western Massachusetts at the Pittsfield Congregational Church. – Joseph Carvalho III

Helen Anna (Downing) Ezold

(B. AUG. 18, 1916 IN HOLYOKE, MA; D. SEPT. 9, 2006 HOLYOKE, MA) was a noted pianist and organist who performed on stage and radio during the 1930s to the 1950s. In addition to her instrumental work for Holyoke area churches, Ezold was the official pianist for the American Guild of Music Convention Concerts in New York, Cincinnati, Chicago, and Minneapolis. Ezold also served as the manager of the Holyoke City Band and was the first

woman admitted to the Holyoke Musicians Union, serving as vice-president for seven years. – Joseph Carvalho III

Stacia (Filipiak) Falkowski

(B. 1926 IN INDIAN ORCHARD, SPRINGFIELD, MA) is a noted Springfield violinist who has performed with John Denver, Bob Hope, Perry Como, Bobby Vinton, Wayne Newton, Raquel Welch, Judy Garland, and the Moscow Circus. The daughter of Polish immigrants, Falkowski has also performed in Poland, notably at Wawel Castle and at Wroclaw University. – Joseph Carvalho III

Nicole Margaret Fiorentino

(B. APRIL 7, 1979 IN LUDLOW, MA) is an acclaimed American bass guitarist. Originally a touring member of the alternative rock band Smashing Pumpkins. – Joseph Carvalho III

Carole Denise Fredericks

(B. JUNE 5, 1952 IN SPRINGFIELD, MA; D. JUNE 7, 2001 IN DAKAR, SENEGAL) achieved fame and popularity in Europe and the French-speaking world for her French language

(Opposite page) **Top:** Marlyn Crittendon. **Bottom:** Tryphosa Bates-Batcheller. (This page) **Center:** Carole Denise Fredericks **Top:** Stacia (Filipiak) Falkowski. **Above:** Zoë Darrow

musical recordings. Moving to France in 1979, Paris was to become her home for the next two decades. Between 1990 and 1996, Fredericks was a vital part of the Fredericks Goldman Jones Trio, alongside singer-songwriter Jean-Jacques Goldman, and Welsh-French guitarist Michael Jones. In 2006, Fredericks' life and contribution to the study of French were recognized posthumously by the Northeast Conference on the Teaching of Foreign Languages. Coming from a musical family, she was the sister of the legendary blues musicologist and recording artist Taj Mahal. – Joseph Carvalho III

Ashley Gearing

(B. MAY 15, 1991 IN SPRINGFIELD, MA) is an American country music. At the age of eleven, Gearing's song "Can You Hear Me When I Talk to You?" was a popular recording on the 2003 U.S. Billboard's "Hot Country Singles & Tracks" chart making her the youngest solo artist to enter country music charts, a record previously held by the famed Brenda Lee. Her first full-length album, "Maybe It's Time", was released in 2006. – Joseph Carvalho III

Jessy Greene

(B. IN SHEFFIELD, MA) is a noted violinist, cellist and vocalist now based in St. Paul, Minnesota. She was a former member of Geraldine Fibbers and the Jayhawks. – Joseph Carvalho III

Elise Friederike Hensler

(B. MAY 22, 1836 IN GERMANY; D. MAY 21, 1929 IN LISBON, PORTUGAL) lived in Springfield and attended school here in the 1850s. She became a celebrated international singer, performing in Europe. She married the widowed Prince Ferdinand de Saxe-Coburg and Gotha of Portugal, becoming the Countess of Elba living at the Chateau Cintra. Six years after their marriage, Ferdinand was offered the throne of Spain but fearing that his American wife would not be accepted at the stratified Spanish court, he declined the offer. Biographers Roberta M. Greene and Catherine S. Blakeslee wrote, "Thus a daughter of Springfield was the heroine of as romantic a love story as the modern world has known." – Joseph Carvalho III

Left: Carleen Maley Hutchins
Top: Ashley Gearing
Above: Elise F. Hensler

Irene Higginbotham

(B. JUNE 11, 1918 IN WORCESTER, MA; D. AUG. 27, 1988 IN NEW YORK CITY) was a prolific African-American jazz and popular music songwriter especially active during the 1930s and 1940s. She was a concert pianist at age fifteen and joined American Society of Composers, Authors and Publishers (ASCAP) in 1944. Higginbotham was a composer of nearly 50 published songs, and musicologists have speculated that she probably wrote many other songs that were not published or were published without giving her credit. She used a pseudonym, "Glenn Gibson," to publish her music. – Joseph Carvalho III

Marjorie Hughes

(NÉE MARJORIE CARLE, B. DEC. 15, 1925 IN SPRINGFIELD, MA) is a former singer with the famed Frankie Carle Orchestra. She began singing with the Paul Martin Band in 1946, then became the lead vocalist for her father, Frankie Carle. She recorded with Columbia Records and RKO Radio from 1945 to 1947. In 1950, she moved to the West Coast to pursue a career in radio and television.
– Joseph Carvalho III

Carleen Maley Hutchins

(B. MAY 24, 1911 IN SPRINGFIELD, MA; D. AUGUST 7, 2009 IN WOLFEBORO, NH) was an American former high school science teacher, violinmaker and researcher. She was best known for her creation, in the 1950s and 1960s, of a family of eight proportionally-sized violins now known as the "violin octet", and for a considerable body of research into the acoustics of violins.

According to her biographer, Quincy Whitney, Hutchins' greatest innovation is a technique known as "free-plate tuning." Hutchins was also the founder of the New Violin Family Association, author of more than 100 technical publications, editor of two volumes of collected papers in violin acoustics,

and co-founded the Catgut Acoustical Society, which develops scientific insights into the construction of new and conventional instruments of the violin family.
– Joseph Carvalho III

Meg Hutchinson

(B. 1978 IN SOUTH EGREMONT, MA) is a folk singer-songwriter. She has won numerous songwriting awards in the United States, Ireland, and the United Kingdom, including prestigious competitions at Merlefest, NewSong, Kerrville, Falcon Ridge, Telluride Bluegrass and Rocky Mountain Folks festivals. She has recorded with the noted folk music label, Red House Records.
– Joseph Carvalho III

Storm Large

(NÉE SUSAN STORM LARGE, B. JUNE 25, 1969 IN SOUTHBOROUGH, MA) is a singer, songwriter, actress and author. She attracted national attention as a contestant on the CBS reality television show "Rock Star: Supernova". For many years solely a rock artist, in recent years she has branched out into the theater and cabaret world. A resident of Portland, Oregon, she currently balances performing with her

Top left: Meg Hutchinson (*The Republican* file photo)
Top right: Irene Higginbotham
Right: Marjorie Hughes

Above: Nerissa Nields, left, Katryna Nields, right (*The Republican* file photo, third party submitted). **Top center:** Ethel Lee (Hoang 'Leon' Nguyen photo). **Bottom right:** Sara Gilbert, left, and Linda Perry, right (Photo by John Shearer/Invision/AP)

own band in venues around the country and touring with the Portland-based band Pink Martini around the world. – Joseph Carvalho III

Amy Lee
(B. IN NORTH ADAMS, MA) is a noted saxophonist, composer and arranger. She has played with a variety of musicians and singers, and is best known for being a member of Jimmy Buffett's Coral Reefer Band. – Joseph Carvalho III

Ethel Lee
(B. IN EVERGREEN, ALABAMA) is a jazz singer who began her singing career in 2003 after serving 28 years on the police force of West Springfield, MA. She was the first female and first African-American to be hired by West Springfield. Performing throughout New England, she has performed for major venues and events with her band, the Ethel Lee Ensemble. Over the years she has been a lead vocalist for The Eric Bascom Quintet, and Richie Mitnick & Rhapsody, The Sounds of Music Singers. – Joseph Carvalho III

Mariam Massaro
(B. MAY 15, 1954) is the owner and Director of the Singing Bridge Performing Arts Lodge, West Cummington, MA; owner of Singing Brook Studio in Worthington, MA; a recording artist, singer/songwriter, and musician, leader of the Gaea Star Band. She is the producer and performer for the weekly "Gaea Star Goddess Radio Show". Massaro is also the owner-operator of Wiseways Herbals, maker of natural medicinal and body care products, established in 1988. – Joseph Carvalho III

Ann (Kosakowski) McNamee
(B. MAY 21, 1953 IN SOUTHBRIDGE, MA) is a musical theorist and singer/songwriter based in San Francisco, CA. She is also a retired Professor Emerita of Music at Swarthmore College. Reflecting the change in technology in music, her band Moonalice was the first band without a label to achieve over one

million downloads (over 4.6 million to date) of a song from its own servers, direct from artist (DFA). Since retiring from that band in 2012, McNamee has focused on writing songs for musical theater. – Joseph Carvalho III

Nerissa Franklin Nields

(B. JUNE 2, 1967) of Northampton, MA is a folk musician, author, and member with her sister Katryna Tenney Nields (B. APR. 30, 1969) of the band The Nields. – Joseph Carvalho III

Linda Perry

(B. APR. 15, 1965 IN SPRINGFIELD, MA) is a singer-songwriter and record producer. She was inducted into the Songwriters Hall of Fame in 2015. Perry first gained fame as the lead singer and primary songwriter of the band 4 Non Blondes. In her career, she has founded two record labels and written numerous hit songs for other artists including "Beautiful" for Christina Aguilera, "What You Waiting For?" for Gwen Stefani, and "Get the Party Started" for Pink. Her songs have also been recorded by Adele, Alicia Keys, and Courtney Love. – Joseph Carvalho III

Judith Raskin

(B. JUNE 21, 1928 IN NEW YORK CITY; D. DEC. 21, 1984 IN NEW YORK CITY) has been acclaimed by American music historians as "one of America's greatest lyric sopranos of the twentieth century." Majoring in music at Smith College, she graduated in 1948. It was during those college years in Northampton taking singing lessons that her vocal abilities were revealed. In the ensuing years, She quickly developed her vocal skills winning the Marian Anderson Award for 1952 and 1953. In the 1950s, she began appearing on concert stages throughout America. Raskin received national recognition in 1957 when she sang in the televised American premiere of Poulenc's "Dialogues des Carmelites." In July of 1957, she performed a concert version of Puccini's "La Boehme" with the Symphony of the Air in New York City's Central Park. Soon after, she was asked to join the New York City Opera Company making her debut performance in 1959. The height of her career came on Feb. 23, 1962 when she made her debut at the Metropolitan Opera in Mozart's "Marriage of Figaro." Her performance received universal critical acclaim. In later years, she became an instructor at the Manhattan School of Music. Duiring her life, Raskin recorded for Columbia, London, Decca, RCA Victor, and CRI records. – Joseph Carvalho III & Jane Kaufman

Jeanne Sagan

(B. JAN. 11, 1979 IN SPRINGFIELD, MA) is highly regarded heavy metal bassist and vocalist for the band, Crossing Rubicon. Formerly she was the bassist for the band All That Remains from 2006-2015, and for Acacia Strain from 2003 to 2006. – Joseph Carvalho III

Jane (Lewis) Satterthwaite

(B. JULY 23, 1873 IN NORWOOD, NY) was an American opera singer. She retired from the operatic stage to take charge of the Voice Dept. of the Denver Conservatory of Music. IN 1912, she moved to Boylston, MA and opened a tea room in that "summer home" mansion which became known locally as "Chalet at Rocks." In 1929, She was appointed head of the department of home economics of the Worcester Electric Light Company in Worcester, MA. Her sister was Jessie Dell Lewis (See entry in Actors Chapter). – Joseph Carvalho III

Meta Schaff (Mallary) Seaman Ellis

(B. NOV. 20, 1889 IN LENOX, MA; D. JAN. 15, 1978 IN LONGMEADOW, MA), a graduate of Mount Holyoke College, Class of 1910, noted vocal teacher at regional women's colleges and girls schools, including Mount Holyoke College, Smith College, and McDuffie School for Girls in Springfield. She also was a vocal teacher

Meta Schaff (Mallory) Seaman Ellis

and choral director at American International College for many years. Many vocalists attributed their musical success to her efforts. She was a founding member of the Springfield Girls Club and first president of the Woman's Auxiliary of the Hampden District Medical Society. – Joseph Carvalho III

is now in her eleventh year as conductor of this choral ensemble. – Springfield Symphony Orchestra website.

Emily Burns (Erwin) Strayer

(B. AUG. 16, 1972 IN PITTSFIELD, MA), also known as Emily Robison, is an American songwriter, singer, multi-instrumentalist, and a founding member of the female country band, Dixie Chicks. She has been the lead vocalist of the Court Yard Hounds. – Joseph Carvalho III

Alice (Mikus) Stusick

(B. DEC. 31, 1904 IN CHICOPEE, MA; D. MAR. 18, 1978 IN BOSTON, MA) was an acclaimed harpist who performed with both the Springfield and Hartford Symphony orchestras, as well as the Clearwater (FLA) and Port Richey (FLA) symphonies. A faculty member of the Hartford Conservatory of Music and Arts, she also played for the Amherst Opera Company. Alice married Dr. Stanley S. Stusick, a highly regarded physician of the Greater Springfield area. As soon as her two daughters Veleda and Mary-Alice learned to read music and become proficient in playing the harp, Alice began performing with them as the Stusick Harp & Instrumental Trio. The trio travelled throughout the northeast performing at both large and small venues from the 1950s to the mid-1970s. In 1958, the Stusick Trio performed for President Dwight D. Eisenhower at a special concert at the Eastern States Exposition. – Joseph Carvalho III

Sara Lou "Sally" Willeke

(B. 1907 IN PLAIN CITY, OH; D. MAY 14, 1987 IN LENOX, MA) became the music director of South Mountain Concerts in Pittsfield in 1950 and served in that capacity until 1980. Her husband had served as director from 1918 to 1950. Sally Willeke retired in 1980 and was named "director emeritus." She was a graduate of the Julliard School of Music in New York City and came to Pittsfield in 1929. – James Gleason & Joseph Carvalho III

Above left: Alice Stusick. **Above right:** Mary M. Williston.

Nikki R. Stoia

(B. OCT. 3, 1957) is a coach/accompanist, piano soloist, singer and conductor known for her musical versatility, with a repertoire that encompasses traditional and contemporary classical and popular music. Stoia is presently a Senior Lecturer II in the University of Massachusetts/Amherst Department of Music and Dance, Music Chief Undergraduate Advisor and Associate Dean of Advising for the College of Humanities and Fine Arts. Having served as accompanist for the Springfield Symphony Chorus for nineteen years, Stoia

Dar Williams

(NÉE DOROTHY SNOWDEN WILLIAMS, B. APRIL 19, 1967 IN MOUNT KISCO, NY) is a "pop-folk" singer-songwriter once described in *The New Yorker* as "one of America's best singer-songwriters." She moved to Northampton, MA in 1993 where her songwriting and recording career blossomed and gained national attention. She toured with Joan Baez and has performed and recorded with a "who's who" list of folk singer-songwriters and musicians over the years. Her studio music albums include "The Honesty Room" (1993), "Burning Field" (1995), "Mortal City" (1996), "End of Summer" (1997), "The Green World" (2000), "The Beauty of the Rain" (2003), "My Better Self" (2005), "Promised Land" (2008), "Many Great Companions" (2010), and "In the Time of Gods" (2012). She has also authored *What I Found in a Thousand Towns: A Travelling Musicians Guide to Rebuilding America's Communities,* published in 2017. She now lives in Cold Spring, New York. – Joseph Carvalho III

Mary M. (Quirk) Williston

(B. MAR. 5, 1881 IN LEVERETT, MA; D. MAY 1971 IN HOLYOKE, MA) was a noted lyric soprano who grew up in Holyoke, MA. After her debut at Carnegie Hall as a lyric soprano, success "came almost overnight." A Mount Holyoke College graduate (Class of 1902), Williston toured the United States, Canada, and Europe for many years with various traveling opera companies. After her retirement from the professional stage, she opened and operated music studios in Holyoke and Springfield, MA into her eighties. Williston also was president of the Holyoke Music Club, and served as president of the Quota Club, touring the middle west and New York to organize other Quota Clubs. – Joseph Carvalho III

Sylvia A. Zaremba

(B. JANUARY 15, 1931 IN CHICOPEE, MA, D. JUNE 5, 2005 IN COLUMBUS, OH) attended the

Sylvia A. Zaremba

Curtis Institute of Music in Philadelphia on scholarship. Zaremba achieved fame as a child prodigy and international pianist who was playing concerts at age 6. She played with the Women's Symphony Orchestra of Boston at age 7, with the New York Philharmonic Symphony and with Arthur Rodzinski and the Cleveland Orchestra at age 9. Her formal debut was at age 10 at a New York Town Hall Concert. At age 11, she played in front of an audience of 5,000 in Cleveland. During her teens, she performed with many of the major American orchestras including the Chicago Symphony, Symphony of the Air and the Philadelphia Orchestra. At age 15, she performed Chopin in a nationwide radio broadcast with the New York Philharmonic. Celebrating her Polish heritage, she performed with Leopold Stokowski and the American Symphony live from Carnegie Hall. Zaremba began touring at age 17 performing in the US, Europe and South American with many notable symphonies and orchestras. She recorded on the Unicorn and Realistic labels. Her most memorable performance was in the White House for President Harry S. Truman. Sylvia settled in Columbus, OH where she was chairwoman of the keyboard department at the Ohio State University School of Music until she retired in 1994. In retirement, Sylvia maintained a private teaching studio at her home. – Joanne M. Gruszkos

Kim Zombik

of Northampton, lead singer in a number of Western Massachusetts bands including Live on the Planet, Stash, the Eric Olsson Band, and Unit 7. Now based in Montreal, Canada, Zombik has produced several music solo albums including "The Intimate Sky From Whence You Came" and "Interlude". During her career, she has performed internationally on major stages: from The New York Jazz Session in Irkutsk, Siberia to the Blue Note in Fukuoka, Japan; from the Montreal's International Jazz and Off Jazz Festivals to the Ginza Jazz Festival, Japan. Zombik has also performed with a variety of stellar artists: from jazz bassist William Parker to the funk musician George Clinton and Parliament Funkadelics; and from Joe Hisaishi's Japanese New World Philharmonic Orchestra to New Orleans' Charles Neville. – Joseph Carvalho III

Northampton film maker Nate Ford of 'Hegemony Pictures' films (left) photographs lead singer of the band 'Stash', Kim Zombik of Northampton (right) for Stash' s music video. His parter Jesse Gardon, center, holds a reflector. They are on the railroad bridge above Main Street. (*The Republican* staff photo/ Chitose Suzuki)

CHAPTER THIRTEEN

WOMEN
in Sports

BY M. SUSAN GUYER, DPE, ATC,CSCS,CES,EIM
Chair of the Exercise Science and Sport Studies, Springfield College

Imagine the road yesterdays' women had to travel in their quest for equality to compete. It is difficult from todays' perspective to truly comprehend the double standard that was the norm for these women in terms of access and fairness of opportunity, and marginalized compensation in terms of salaries and stipends. But it is because of their spirit and thirst to compete that these pioneers paved the road for todays' women to enjoy the level of competition and achievement that defines the modern arena of competitive sport.

Serena Williams said, "The success of every woman should be the inspiration to another. We should raise each other up. Make sure you're very courageous: be strong, be extremely kind, and above all be humble." Competing in sports may not define us as women but our athleticism did drive us toward who we became. The arenas of sport allow us to be strong, powerful, and teach us not to be afraid of life's battles. We lift up ourselves and women as a whole when we train our bodies and minds to be powerful in the arenas of organized play and specialized sport. We have become leaders and the inspiration for the girls and young women that will follow this road that we continue to pave. It is an important reminder that, when young girls engage in play, they use the creativity of their minds for imagination and invention, and they develop the rudimentary skills of negotiation and governance. They begin to lay the foundation to become the leaders of their own future. And it is the responsibility of the women of sports today to remember that it was their own thirst for play and the opportunities that followed that helped to cultivate who they became. It is time for the women of today to recognize their responsibility to uphold the pioneering spirit of the women who came before them to maintain a safe and encouraging environment out of which todays play becomes the genesis for tomorrows' skills for success. As Soccer great Mia Hamm said, "Somewhere behind the athlete you've become and the hours of practice and the coaches who have pushed you is a little girl who fell in love with the game and never looked back... play for her."

Women in Sports

Marguerite 'Midge' Martin and the Principal of Equal Access

BY CYNTHIA G. SIMISON

For every step forward that women have taken over the years, Marguerite R. Martin worries the journey to equality of the sexes is still far from being complete.

It was 34 years ago that "Midge" Martin first approached the board of governors at the Longmeadow Country Club, asking if she might be able to tee off early on weekend mornings for a round a golf. Back then, women members were relegated to tee times after 1 on Saturday afternoons and after 11:30 on Sunday mornings.

A financial planner and insurance agent, Martin got nowhere, so she took her case to the Massachusetts Commission Against Discrimination in 1990 and later filed a lawsuit against the Country Club where she and her husband were longtime members. Her challenges attracted national attention and encouraged women across the state to seek changes at other clubs. She even wound up the subject of a chapter in a 1995 book, *The Unplayable Lie: The Untold Story of Women and Discrimination in American Golf*, written by Marcia Chambers and published by Pocket Books.

As her case wound its way to resolution, Longmeadow Country Club changed its rules and reached a settlement in 1997 with Martin for $45,000 to cover the costs of her legal fees. At the time, she remarked, "You know, equal rights shouldn't cost you money."

Fast forward 20 years and Martin, who is now in her 90s, still plays golf, though not as frequently, and still has strong feelings about the equality of the sexes, or the lack thereof in

Marguerite "Midge" Martin

the 21st century.

"The underlying thing is that (sexual discrimination) never goes away. Women have achieved a great deal and been promoted, but it's still a job for women to get ahead. For some reason, the world still looks at men as superior, and women will deny it, as we should," she says.

At the time she filed her discrimination complaint with the state, Martin said, "I'm not a rabble-rouser and not a radical. I'd just like to

have a choice of when I can play and not have it be in the heat of the day. I'd like to be like any other person."

As then, she remains a matter-of-fact person, someone who recognizes her good fortune of having accomplished much in her professional life (she was the first female general agent in the nation for a major insurance company) and of having a wonderful 46-year marriage to a man who loved and supported her being the woman she wanted to be.

Martin grew up in Springfield in the 1920s and 1930s in a family where she was encouraged to be whatever she dreamed and to accomplish all things she set in her sights. It was a time when even civil rights, let along women's rights, were far from being in the forefront of the American consciousness.

As a little girl, Martin remembers, she "came home from school one day and said a black girl had asked me to go to her birthday party. I was little at the time. My mother said, unlike people at the time, 'What would you like to do?' I said, 'I would like to go to that party. I like that girl.'" So, to the party she went. "People were against everything at the time. I was the only white girl at the party. When I got home, my mother asked, 'Did you have a good time,' and I said I did."

With her mother's often unspoken guidance, Martin learned to trust her instincts and be confident in her convictions, she says. "I find women still give in too much these days. People are afraid to stand up (for something) because they don't want to be ostracized. My mother had a way of saying, 'If everybody were jumping off the Memorial Bridge would you do that? She was saying, 'Use your own head.'" Martin graduated from Classical High School in 1943 (or, as she says, 1942-and-a-half) and from Boston University's Sargent College of Health and Rehabilitation Sciences four years later. At her 50th college reunion, she was honored with a "special recognition award" for her accomplishments.

In the ensuing years, she had in 1950

challenged a rule of the Roman Catholic Diocese of Springfield, asking and receiving the approval of then Bishop Christopher J. Weldon to marry her Protestant husband-to-be in the main chapel of Holy Name Church, rather than in the rectory next door where diocesan rule allowed such "mixed" marriages to take place. And, as she began her first career teaching physical education at Brookline High School in the early 1950s, Martin took on another issue of gender disparity in the unfair opportunities offered to girls athletic teams, a situation she had endured herself back at Classical High where she was "class athlete." Her criticism as a teacher led to more gym time and more coaching for the girls' sports teams at Brookline's high school.

As this March observance of women's history month comes to a close, Martin says she thinks women, themselves, "are a big problem" in the ongoing effort to attain equality. "Women don't stand up for their rights as they should," she says. "You always have to remember we are equal, (we) should be treated equally, (and) not sit back and take second place. I've done that all my life. I'm glad I did."

The challenge she made at Longmeadow Country Club, while gratifying in its result also led to great sadness, Martin reflects.

"It was a very hard thing. It was like the world crashed in. Everyone went against me, including the women because they were ruled by their husbands. It was quite a sad thing for me to watch, to see all my friends suddenly shun me. They couldn't look me in the eye."

At the time, Martin says, she wondered of those women, "How can one have a good marriage if he's considered superior to yourself."

She remains a member of Longmeadow Country Club and looks forward to the golfing season ahead, particularly to the renovations being completed at the clubhouse: "I hope to get out a few times. I like the sociability."

Although she no longer works in the true sense of the word, Martin still stays abreast of the financial world, putting her talents to work in handling investments for the College Club of Springfield which maintains a scholarship fund that annually benefits young women from the Pioneer Valley.

As for the future of women's rights, Martin is an optimist. She believes, for instance, there will one day be a woman in the White House, but, "I think it will be a hard battle."

"For some reason, women don't always support women, and men get the vote of the men and some women. Women have to adjust to the fact a woman can be a powerful leader. I was lucky I had a family that practiced that."

Historical Notes:

The First women's gymnastics instruction in the United States was held at Mount Holyoke College in South Hadley, MA in 1862.

First Women's basketball game was played at Smith College, Northampton, MA introduced by Senda Berenson, Director of Physical Education at Smith College. Berenson wrote the first official rules for women's basketball in 1899.

ALPHABETICAL LISTING OF WOMEN IN SPORTS:

Bilqis Abdul-Qaadir

(B. NOV. 11, 1990 IN SPRINGFIELD, MA) holds the record as the leading scorer in Massachusetts girls basketball history. She began playing varsity as an eighth grader at New Leadership Charter School, scoring a total of 3,070 points in her varsity career. She was valedictorian of her class. At 5' 4" tall, she went on to play Division I basketball at the University of Memphis, where she received the United States Basketball Writers of America's "Most Courageous" award in 2011 for being the first NCAA player to play with coverings in

Bilqis Abdul-Qaadir

accordance with her faith. Graduating magna cum laude from Memphis with a degree in exercise science, she spent a fifth year at Indiana State, where she led the Sycamores to a Missouri Valley Conference title and was named the league's Newcomer of the Year. She ranks 10th all-time in a single season for points scored (454), was also named First Team All-MVC, Second Team Scholar Athlete and earned a combined seven conference Player, Newcomer and Scholar Athlete of the Week awards. Looking to play basketball overseas, Abdul-Qaadir started an online campaign called Muslim Girls Hoop Too in protest of a hijab ban by the International

Basketball Federation. She met former President Barack Obama twice as a result of her work as an athlete and activist. In May 2017, the federation repealed its hijab ban. – Jane Kaufman

Kim Adler

(B. SEPT. 1967 IN SPRINGFIELD, MA; GREW UP IN EAST LONGMEADOW, MA) is a champion professional bowler and considered to be "one of the top female bowlers of all time." Adler has won 15 national PWBA titles including the 1999 U.S. Women's Open. In 2004, Adler placed first in the "Classic All-Events" at the USBC Women's Championship. In 2015, she was inducted into the USBC Hall of Fame in the "Superior Performance" category. A hospitalist nurse practitioner, Adler now lives in Taos, New Mexico. – Joseph Carvalho III

Kacey Bellamy

(B. APR. 22, 1987 IN PROVIDENCE, RI; GREW UP IN WESTFIELD, MA) was a 2010 Winter Olympics Women's Ice Hockey Silver Medalist. As a steady hand on defense for the United States women's national hockey team, Westfield's Kacey Bellamy accumulated two silver medals in the 2010 Vancouver and 2014 Sochi Winter Olympics, a gold medal in the Pyeongchang 2018 Winter Olympics, and seven golds in World Championship tournaments. She was part of the CWHL's Clarkson Cup winning-Boston Blades squads in 2013 and 2015 before switching to the Boston Pride of the NWHL, where she won the Isobel Cup. Prior to playing for the Berkshire School, Bellamy played for five years on the Springfield Pics along side her older brother Rob Bellamy. Bellamy was also part of seven gold medal winning U.S.

Above left: Kim Alder
Above right: Stacie Bourbeau
Bottom left: Kacey Bellamy (Courtesy of Frederick Gore, *The Republican*)
Bottom right: Senda Berenson

Women's National Hockey teams for the International Ice Hockey Federation World Women's Championships: 2008, 2009, 2011, 2013, 2015, 2016, and 2017. – Garry Brown

Senda Berenson

(NÉE SENDA VALVROJENSKI, B. MAR. 19, 1868 IN BUTRIMONYS, LITHUANIA; D. FEB. 16, 1954 IN SANTA BARBARA, CA) immigrated to the U.S. with her family in 1875 changing their name to Berenson. Her first teaching position after attending the Boston Normal School of Gymnastics from 1890-1892 was at Smith College in Northampton where she developed the first rules for women's basketball in 1899. A number of her basic rules were still in force in women's basketball for over seventy years. – Joseph Carvalho III

Stacie Bourbeau

(B. JUNE 5, 1977 IN BERNARDSTON, MA) lives in Orange, MA, she was the 2015 U.S. Women's Amateur Billiard Champion. Bourbeau is a two-time New England Ladies American Rotation Champion, and was the 2007 BCA Women's Masters Champion. In 2012, she was inducted into the New England Pool & Billard Hall of Fame. – Joseph Carvalho III

Alice W. Bridges

(B. JULY 19, 1916 IN WATERVILLE, ME; D. MAY 5, 2011 IN CARLISLE, PA), also known by her married name Alice Roche, was an American competition swimmer, who at age 20, represented the United States at the 1936 Summer Olympics in Berlin, Germany. It first appeared that Bridges, who originally was a back-up contestant, had actually won her event. Several hours later the judges reversed their decision and gave the gold and silver to two women from the Netherlands, leaving the bronze for Bridges.

Bridges grew up in Uxbridge, MA. She and her twin sister learned to swim in a pond in Uxbridge, and she later trained at the Olympic pool in nearby Whitinsville, MA. When the

sudden chance arose for her to participate, townspeople raised funds to pay for her travel to Berlin, which she otherwise could not have afforded.

Stasia Milas Czernicki

(B. MAY 18, 1922 IN WEBSTER, MA; D. JAN. 17, 1993 IN WEBSTER, MA) was an American professional candlepin bowler who set the all-time candlepin record for ten strings with 1388 pins. She also shares the world record for women's doubles (2382), mixed doubles (2676), and women's five strings (707). She was world champion eight times, singles queen six times, a member of the women's doubles title team three times, mixed doubles team twice, and a member of the world's women's title team in 1965.

The World Candlepin Bowling Council and World Candlepin Bowling Congress recognized her as Woman Bowler of the Year in 1967, 1968, 1970, 1971, and 1972. In 1987, Czernicki was inducted into the International Candlepin Bowling Association Hall of Fame.

In her honor, the International Candlepin Bowling Association has established the Stasia Czernicki Memorial Award to recognize players who also exhibit fine sportsmanship. Czernicki was the first woman bowler regularly seen on the long-running TV show "Candlepin Bowling", broadcast on Boston's WHDH-TV (later WCVB-TV), Channel 5. Hosts Jim Britt (1958–61) and Don Gillis (1961–96) frequently introduced her as the star of the

show. Her 41–12 match record includes 18 consecutive wins, more than any other female competitor. She was a certified Massachusetts Bowling Association (MBA) bowling instructor and served as director of the MBA Instructors School and as a member of the World Candlepin Bowling Congress's executive board. – Joseph Carvalho III

Marcia Frederick

(B. JAN. 4, 1963 IN SPRINGFIELD, MA) was the first U.S. woman to win a Gold Medal at the World Gymnastic Championships in Stasbourg, France (1978). She is one of 461 athletes to receive a Congressional Gold Medal. – Joseph Carvalho III

Top left: Stasia Milas Czernicki
Top right: Marcia Frederick

Katie Guay

of Westfield, MA was a women's ice hockey official at the 2018 Winter Olympics in Pyeongchang, South Korea. In college, she broke the school record for career goals – 74, in Division I women's hockey at Brown University. – Meredith Perri

Erika Lawler

(B. FEB. 5, 1987 IN FITCHBURG, MA) was a member of the 2009–10 United States national women's ice hockey team. Lawler played prep hockey at Cushing Academy where she won the Betty Davis Award as the top athlete in her class three times. She then played collegiately for the Wisconsin Badgers of the Western Collegiate Hockey Association and won three NCAA titles (2006, 2007 and 2009). She received a Silver Medal in the XXI 2010 Winter Olympics in Vancouver. Lawler played for the Boston Blades from 2005 to 2012. – Joseph Carvalho III

Nancy Lieberman

(B. JULY 1, 1958 IN BROOKLYN, NY) was the first woman athlete to ever play in a men's professional basketball game (1986). She played for the Springfield Fame, Springfield, Massachusetts' professional basketball team that was part of the U.S. Basketball league. – Joseph Carvalho III

Rebecca Rose Lobo-Rushin

(B. OCT. 6, 1973 IN HARTFORD, CT) is a 2017 Naismith Memorial Basketball Hall of Fame Basketball star, and a American television basketball analyst. Lobo was raised in Southwick, MA, and was the state basketball scoring record-holder with 2,740 points in her high school career for Southwick-Tolland Regional High School in Massachusetts. She held this record for 18 years. Lobo was a star player of the University of Connecticut women's basketball team that won the 1995 National Championship with a record of 35-0.

In her senior year, Lobo was the unanimous national player of the year, winning the 1995 Naismith College Player of the Year award, the Wade Trophy, the AP Player of the Year award, the USBWA Player of the Year award, the Honda Sports Award for basketball, and the WBCA Player of the Year award. Lobo was awarded the prestigious Honda-Broderick Cup for 1994-95, presented to the athlete "most deserving of recognition as the Collegiate Woman Athlete of the Year". Lobo played in the WNBA from its inaugural season, for the following teams: the New York Liberty (1997-2002); the Houston Comets (2002); and the Connecticut Sun (2003) where she retired. She also played two seasons in the National Women's Basketball League with the Springfield (MA) Spirit from 2002-2003. She was inducted into the Women's Basketball Hall of Fame in 2010. On April 12, 2003, Rebecca changed her last name from Lobo to Lobo-Rushin after marrying *Sports Illustrated* writer Steve Rushin at the Basketball Hall of Fame in Springfield, Massachusetts. – Joseph Carvalho III

Karen Lende O'Connor

(B. FEB. 17, 1958 IN BOLTON, MA) is a noted American equestrian. She has ridden in five Olympic Games, three World Equestrian Games and two Pan-American Games, winning multiple medals, including a team silver at the 1996 Olympic Games and a team bronze at the 2000 Olympic Games. O'Connor has played an active role in the administration of the United States Equestrian Federation and the United States Eventing Association (USEA). O'Connor and her horses have been honored by multiple organizations for their competition record, and as of 2013, six horses ridden by O'Connor held positions in the list of the top 50 USEA high scoring horses. – Joseph Carvalho III

Opposite Page: Nancy Lieberman
Right: Rebecca Lobo-Rushin (Courtesy Don Treeger, *The Republican*)

Above left: Elena Pirozhkova (AP Photo/Charlie Neibergall). Above right: Lesley Visser (AP Photo/Matt Sayles, file)

Elena Pirozhkova

(B. OCT. 13, 1986 IN NOVOKUZNETSK, RUSSIA; GREW UP IN GREENFIELD) is an Olympic wrestler, and a Gold Medalist wrestler at the Pan Am games in 2008, 2009, and 2010.
– Joseph Carvalho III

Mary Jeanne (Talarico) Tash

(B. JAN. 12, 1951) of West Springfield, MA, a nationally ranked fencer, also served as the women's fencing coach for the Springfield Fencing Club from the 1970s until 1990 when she retired from competition.
– Joseph Carvalho III

Lesley Candace Visser

(B. SEPT. 11, 1953 IN QUINCY, MA; GRADUATED FROM SOUTH HADLEY HIGH SCHOOL) is the first and only woman to be enshrined into the Pro Football Hall of Fame, in 2006. During her 40-year career in sports journalism she has worked for *The Boston Globe*, ESPN, ABC Sports, and CBS. Visser was voted the "No. 1 female sportscaster of all-time" in a poll taken by the American Sportscasters Association, and was elected to the National Sportscasters Association's Hall of Fame in 2015. Among her other "firsts: voted to Sports Writers Hall of Fame; first woman assigned to Monday Night Football; first woman assigned to a super bowl sideline; first and only woman to handle a Super Bowl Trophy presentation; first woman sportscaster to carry the Olympic Torch; first woman honored as a Lombardi Fellow; only sportscaster male or female to have worked on the network broadcast of the Final Four, the Super Bowl, the World Series, the NBA Finals, the Triple Crown, the Olympics, the US Open, and the World Figure Skating Championship. Visser was also named one of the Ten Pioneers of Women's Sports by *USA Today*; named one of the "100 Luminaries in the History of CBS"; and voted to the Radio and TV Hall of Fame. – Joseph Carvalho III

CHAPTER FOURTEEN

WOMEN OF
Stage and Screen

BY TINA D'AGOSTINO
Executive Director, City Stage,
Springfield, MA

I've spent over sixteen years promoting arts and entertainment in Western Massachusetts. Touring productions delight, enthrall, and entertain our community. Artists, actors, singers and musicians have come from communities across the region, the country, and the world — to perform at CityStage and Symphony Hall. The best part of my job is the applause. I love to watch an audience rise to its feet at the end of a performance. I admit, a standing ovation usually brings tears to my eyes.

Even before I began working in this business, I was an avid theater-goer. I have always loved reading playbills and learning about the actors, the producers, the creative teams and their experiences, their inspiration, and their history. It is amazing how many women from Western and Central Massachusetts have graced the professional stage, and entertained the nation through radio, television and film performances since the 19th century. From Eva Tanguay of Holyoke who became the "Queen of Vaudeville" to silent film actress Carol Holloway of Williamstown who appeared in 117 silent films, to Eleanor Powell of Springfield who acted and danced her way to Hollywood fame in the 1930s, to Pittsfield's Elizabeth Banks, of today's most popular Hollywood films, our region has produced some of the nation's most famous actresses and entertainers.

Two extremely talented African-American women from Springfield broke down barriers to rise to the very top of their fields: Cheryl Boone Isaacs who is the 35th president of the Academy of Motion Picture Arts and Sciences, and Ruth E. Carter who is an award-winning costume designer for film and television with over forty films to her credit. Our region has also been the home of American radio stars including voice actress June Foray; actress/comedian Julia Sanderson of Springfield; and Peg Lynch of Becket, who wrote over 10,000 scripts for radio and television in her career. This chapter also celebrates television pioneers such as Springfield's Kitty Broman who began her career in 1952 and hosted her own television show until 1982, to Nina Blackwood who was part of the original "Video Jockeys" for the wildly popular MTV in the 1980s, and

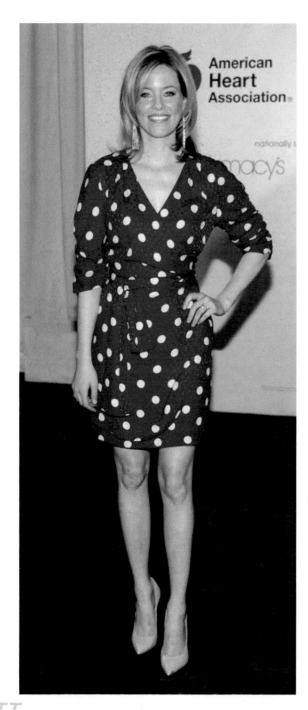

Victoria Principal of Chicopee who rose to fame as the star of the nation's most popular TV series "Dallas". The reader will find many talented women of stage, screen, radio, and television included in this chapter.

ALPHABETICAL LISTING OF WOMEN OF STAGE, SCREEN, RADIO, AND TELEVISION

Karen Jane Allen

(B. OCT. 5, 1951 IN CARROLTON, IL) is an American film, stage and television actress. In film, she is best known for playing Marion Ravenwood in "Raiders of the Lost Ark" (1981) and "Indiana Jones and the Kingdom of the Crystal Skull" (2008). She developed an affinity for knitting, and in 2003, started her own textile company, Karen Allen Fiber Arts, in Great Barrington, Massachusetts. The company sells items Allen knits with a Japanese-made knitting machine. For her work in the textile arts, she was awarded an honorary master's degree from The Fashion Institute of Technology in 2009. Allen also teaches acting at Bard College at Simon's Rock, located in Great Barrington. – Joseph Carvalho III

Annie Baker

(B. APRIL, 1981 IN BOSTON, MA) is an award-winning American playwright who grew up in Amherst, MA. Her first play produced off-Broadway was "Body Awareness" in 2008. Baker's play "The Aliens" premiered in April of 2010 and shared the 2010 Obie Award for "Best New American Play" with her 2009 play "Circle Mirror Transformation". In 2013, her play "The Flick" premiered and received the Obie Award for Playwriting that year. "The Flick" won the Pulitzer Prize for Drama in 2014. – Joseph Carvalho III

Elizabeth Irene Banks

(NÉE MITCHELL, B. FEB. 10, 1974 IN PITTSFIELD, MA) is an actress, director, and producer in film, theater, and television. Banks' filmography is too extensive to list here, except to mention that she has appeared in many of the most popular American films from 2005 to date. She also played a recurring role on the hit television series "30 Rock" in 2010 and 2011. She has co-starred with Paul Rudd in five films, and with Tobey Mcguire in five films including the "Spider-Man" series. Banks also reprised her role of Effie Trinket in the "Hunger Games" movie series, all of which were box office hits. She produced and directed "Pitch Perfect 2". – Joseph Carvalho III

Nina Blackwood

(NÉE NINA KINCKIŃER, B. SEPT. 12, 1955 IN SPRINGFIELD, MA) was part of MTV's original "video jockey" team of hosts in 1981. In 1986, she hosted her own "Rock Report" for the "Entertainment Tonight" television show. Blackwood also hosted the television music program "Solid Gold" from 1986-1988. In 1999, Blackwood and Danny Sheridan created a nationally syndicated radio program, "Nina Blackwood's Absolutely 80's" for the United States Radio Network. She currently hosts a weekday music program for Sirius XM Radio. – Joseph Carvalho III

Kathryn "Kitty" Elizabeth (Flynn) Broman

(B. FEB. 5, 1916 IN PITTSBURGH, PA; D. JAN. 5, 2014 IN LONGMEADOW, MA) became the first woman board member of the National Association of Broadcasters in the 1970s. Hailed as the first lady of Springfield-area television, her long-running show "At Home with Kitty" was a top-rated regional program for WWLP Channel 22 for many years. One of the pioneers of early television, Broman began her career in television broadcasting in 1952 and hosted her own television show until 1982. She served as the president of Springfield Television Corporation. As a broadcaster she won the McCall's "Golden Mike" award for special programming, and served as president of the New England Chapter of the American Women in Radio and Television. In 1984, she and her husband William Putnam purchased and operated Carroll Travel. – Jim Kinney & Joseph Carvalho III

Mary-Ellis Bunim

(B. JULY 9, 1946 IN NORTHAMPTON, MA; D. JAN. 29, 2004 IN BURBANK, CA) was the television producer and co-creator of MTV's "The Real World" and "Road Rules". She was inducted into the Television Academy Hall of Fame in 2012. – Joseph Carvalho III

Jane Burby

(NÉE JANE R. BURBY, B. OCT. 4, 1869 IN HOLYOKE, MA; D. IN 1961 IN WESTCHESTER CO., NY) was an actress who starred in major theatrical

productions for over 50 years frequently on Broadway stages. – Joseph Carvalho III

Ruth E. Carter

(B. APR. 10, 1960 IN SPRINGFIELD, MA) is a award-winning costume designer for film and television with over forty films to her credit. Carter met famed director Spike Lee while working at the Los Angeles Theater Center, and has designed costumes for seven of his films, including "School Daze" (1988), "Do the Right Thing" (1989), "Mo' Better Blues" (1990), "Malcolm X" (1992), "Oldboy" (2013) and "Chi-Raq" (2015). Carter has also worked with noted directors Steven Spielberg and John Singleton. She has earned two nominations for the Academy Award for Best Costume Design for her work on the films "Malcolm X" (1992) and "Amistad" (1997). In 2002, Carter was honored with a Career Achievement Award from the American Black Film Festival. She was also honored with *Essence*'s 2015 Black Women in Hollywood Award.
– Joseph Carvalho III

Above: Kathryn "Kitty" Elizabeth (Flynn) Broman
Right: Ruth Carter (Ed Cohen Photo)

Margaret Celeste "Marge" (Belcher) Champion

[See entry in Chapter on Women Philantropists]

Maura West DeFreitas

(NÉE MAURA JO SNYDER, B. APR. 27, 1972 IN SPRINGFIELD, MA) a television actress, best known for her 15-year portrayal as Carly Snyder on the CBS daytime soap opera "As the World Turns", a role she held from 1995 until the series finale in 2010. She received a Daytime Emmy Award in 2010. – Joseph Carvalho III

Adelaide E. Detchon

(B. 1858 IN MAHONING, OH; D. 1946 IN NORTHAMPTON, MA) was an American lyrical and musical reciter. Her work was praised by Robert Browning and actually had a quatrain written for her by Oliver Wendell Holmes in admiration for her acting and singing performances in the 1880s and 1890s. In her later years, she was more known locally as a Springfield businesswoman who managed the United Art Box Company located in Springfield, MA. – Joseph Carvalho III

Ann Dowd

(B. JAN. 30, 1956 IN HOLYOKE, MA) is a noted film and television actor. She has played roles in several films, including "Green Card" (1990), "Lorenzo's Oil" (1992), "Philadelphi" (1993), "Garden State" (2004), "The Manchurian Candidate" (2004), "Marley & Me" (2008), "Side Effects" (2013), "St. Vincent" (2014), and "Captain Fantastic" (2016). Dowd received the National Board of Review Award for Best Supporting Actress for her role in the film Compliance (2012). Over the years she has appeared in many episodes of the most popular television programs and series such as "Law & Order", "The X-Files", "NYPD Blue",

"Third Watch", "Judging Amy", and "Chicago Hope". In 2017, she began playing Aunt Lydia on the Hulu series "The Handmaid's Tale", for which she won the Primetime Emmy Award for Outstanding Supporting Actress in a Drama Series. – Joseph Carvalho III & Cynthia G. Simison

Mamie L. Duncan-Gibbs

(B. AUG. 3, 1962 IN SPRINGFIELD, MA) is a successful actress with roles in "Black Nativity" (2013) and "Third Watch" (2003). Among her starring roles in musical theater has been her well-received Velma in the hit musical "Chicago". Duncan-Gibbs has appeared on Broadway stages in numerous productions from 1982- 1999. She was one of the original members of the cast of the Broadway hit "Cats", and George C. Wolfe's musical "Jelly's Last Jam". Duncan-Gibbs learned jazz dancing at Springfield's Dunbar Community Center under legendary jazz dance teacher, Frank Hatchett. – Joseph Carvalho III & Elizabeth Román

Meghann Alexandra Fahy

(B. APR. 25, 1990 IN LONGMEADOW, MA) is a television and stage actress known for her "One Life to Live" character Hannah, and Natalie on Broadway's "Next to Normal". – Joseph Carvalho III

June Lucille Foray

(NÉE FORER, B. SEPT. 18, 1917 IN SPRINGFIELD, MA; D. JULY 26, 2017) was a voice actress for radio, theatrical shorts, feature films, television, video games, record albums, talking toys, and a range of other digital media. She was honored with a star on the Hollywood Walk of Fame, and was instrumental in having the category Best Animated Feature instituted by the Academy Awards in 2001. She is best known for such animated characters as Rocky the Flying Squirrel, Lucifer from Disney's "Cinderella", Cindy Lou Who from Dr. Seuss' Grinch television special, Jokey Smurf, and

Top left: Adelaide E. Detchon
Left: Ann Dowd

Granny from the "Fritz Freleng" cartoons, among many others. – Joseph Carvalho III

Sabina H. Gadecki

(B. SEPT. 28, 1983 IN CHICOPEE, MA) is a successful model, television personality, and actress. When she was 18, Gadecki won the Miss Polonia America title, and was chosen as Miss Polonia World the following year. From 2006-2015, she was the television host for the Travel Channel's "World Poker Tour" for five seasons. She has acted in a wide range of television shows from MTV, Lifetime, Comedy Central, NBC, Showtime, and the USA Network. Gadecki has also been featured in major television commercials. In 2015, she appeared in the film "Entourage". – Holly Angelo & Cori Urban

Louise Galloway

(B. 1879 IN MARSHALL, MICH.; D. OCT. 10, 1949 IN BROOKFIELD, MA) celebrated actress of the Broadway stage, who moved to Brookfield, MA in 1912 and married Lindoff A. Bassett of Brookfield in 1914 but retained her maiden name which was also her stage name. – Joseph Carvalho III

Brenda Arlene Garton-Sjoberg

(NÉE BRENDA ARLENE GARTON, B. JULY, 1961 IN INDIANA) of Longmeadow is the director of the Institute for Medias and Non-profit Communication at Western New England University in Springfield, MA. In 1989, she began her long career as a television anchor for WWLP Channel 22 News for over 20 years. Her first television experience after graduating from Quinnipiac University was as a reporter and fill-in anchor for CBS affiliate WSBT-TV in South Bend, Indiana. – Joseph Carvalho III

Elaine Carol Giftos

(B. JAN. 24, 1943 IN PITTSFIELD, MA) Is a retired actress and dancer who appeared on Broadway, television and in motion pictures during her career which spanned from 1969 to 2001. Trained as a dancer by George Ballantine,

Top left: Mamie Duncan Gibbs (*The Republican* file photo)
Above left: June Lucille Foray
Top right: Sabina Gadecki
(Photo by Andy Kropa/Invision/AP)
Right: Brenda Arlene Garton-Sjoberg

Above: Academy of Motion Picture Arts and Sciences President Cheryl Boone Isaacs 88th Academy Awards nominations announcement, Los Angeles, America - Jan. 16, 2014. (Rex Features via AP Images)

Center: Carol Skellie Holloway

she was a member of the New York City Ballet and performed on Broadway stages before moving to California to begin a career in television and motion pictures. Her first television appearance was in the hit show "I Dream of Jeannie". From there, she went on to appear in most of the hit television series of that era: "Bonanza", "The Interns", "Ironside", "Adam-12", "Streets of San Francisco", "Love", "American Style", "The Partridge Family", "The Bob Newhart Show", "The Six Million Dollar Man", "Barney Miller", "Three's Company", "Hawaii Five-O", "Quincy, M.E.", "Knight Rider", "Magnum, P.I.", "Murder, She Wrote", and "Ally McBeal". Her movie credits include: "On a Clear Day You Can See Forever"(1970), "No Drums, No Bugles" (1972), "Everything You Always Wanted to Know About Sex* (*But Were Afraid to Ask)" (1972), "The Wrestler" (1974), "Paternity" (1981), and "Angel" (1984). She is the owner of The Wright Way of Feng Shui and is a nationally known Feng Shui consultant. – Joseph Carvalho III

Carol Skellie Holloway

(B. APR. 30, 1892 IN WILLIAMSTOWN, MA; D. JAN. 3, 1979 IN LOS ANGELES, CA) was an American actress of the silent film era. She appeared in 117 films between 1914 and 1941.
– Joseph Carvalho III

Cheryl (Boone) Isaacs

(B. AUG. 8, 1949 IN SPRINGFIELD, MA) is an American film marketing and public relations executive. In 2013, she was elected as the 35th president of the Academy of Motion Picture Arts and Sciences (AMPAS). She was the first African-American woman to hold that post, and only the third woman to do so. Prior to her election to president, Boone Isaacs represented the Public Relations Branch of the Academy from 21 years. From 1997 to 1999, she was president of Theatrical Marketing for New Line Cinema. At the 2015 Governors Awards, Boone Isaacs launched a new Academy initiative called A2020, which focuses on "improving representation of diversity – age, gender, race, national origin, point-of-view." She has also spearheaded the development of an AMPAS museum developed in conjunction with Los Angeles Museum of Contemporary Art.
– Joseph Carvalho III

Jean Louisa Kelly

(B. MAR. 9, 1972 IN WORCESTER, MA) is an American actress. After making her film debut as Tia Russell in "Uncle Buck" (1989) alongside John Candy, she appeared in a wide range of other films including "The Fantasticks" (1995) and "Mr. Holland's Opus" (1995). From 2000 to 2006, she was known for portraying Kim Warner on the CBS sitcom "Yes, Dear".

Jessie Dell Lewis

(B. MAY 13, 1867 IN NORWOOD, NY; D. FEB. 22, 1934 IN WORCESTER, MA), sister of Jane (Lewis) Satterthwaite, was a successful and widely known theater director. She opened a "studio of expression" in Worcester. Her last grand production was a 300-person/actors pageant, "The Spirit of Worcester" performed on Sept. 29, 1933 at the Worcester Municipal Auditorium. She wrote the pageant script from her hospital bed at the Worcester memorial Hospital from an illness that eventually took her life. – Joseph Carvalho III

Peg Lynch

(NÉE MARGARET FRANCES LYNCH, B. NOV. 25, 1916 IN LINCOLN, NEBRASKA; D. JULY 24, 2015 IN BECKET, MA) was a writer, actress, and creator of radio and television sitcoms. She was the first woman to create, write, star in, and own her own sitcom. During her lifetime, it is estimated that she wrote over 10,000 scripts for radio and television.

Rachel Anne Maddow

(B. APR. 1, 1973 IN CASTRO VALLEY, CA) is a television news host for MSNBC and a liberal political commentator. Maddow began her career by working in radio with her first radio hosting position at WRNX (100.9FM) in Holyoke, MA in 1999. Next, she hosted the "Big Breakfast" radio program for WRSI in Northampton, MA from 2002 to 2004. She left WRSI in 2004 to join the new Air America co-hosting the "Unfiltered" radio program until March of 2005. In April of that year, she launched her very successful two-hour weekday radio program, "The Rachel Maddow Show". In 2008, Maddow began her nightly MSNBC television program, "The Rachel Maddow Show". Among her awards: GLAAD Media Award (2010), Maggie Award (2010), Walter Cronkite Faith & Freedom Award (2010), the 2008 Visibility Award in the category "Lesbian/Bi Woman of the Year (American)," Emmy Award for Outstanding News Discussion & Analysis (2011), and two Emmy Awards in 2017 for Outstanding Live Interview, and Outstanding News Discussion & Analysis. – Joseph Carvalho III

Nora Marlowe

(B. SEPT. 5, 1915 IN WORCESTER, MA; D. DEC. 31, 1977) was an American film and television star. Marlowe was best known for her role from 1973 to 1977 as Flossie Brimmer in 27 episodes of the CBS family drama, "The Waltons". Marlowe also played Sara Andrews in 23 episodes of the CBS sitcom "The Governor and J.J.", starring Dan Dailey. She was cast in films such as "The Thomas Crown Affair", "North by Northwest", and "Westworld".
– Joseph Carvalho III

Julie Elizabeth McNiven

(B. OCT. 11, 1980 IN AMHERST, MA) is a singer and actress mostly known for her recurring roles on the popular television series "Mad Men" and "Supernatural". She also had a recurring role from 2010-2011 on the series "Stargate: Universe", and "Book Club" in 2012. She grew up in Amherst. – Joseph Carvalho III

Above left: Rachel Anne Maddow (Courtesy Judith Roberge, Smith College)
Above right: Jean Louisa Kelly
Bottom right: Peg Lynch

Raquel Obregon

radio personality in the Pioneer Valley for more than 20 years, Obregon's voice is easily recognizable, whether she is hosting New England Public Radio's "Tertulia" or "Cantares Latino Americanos" on WTCC, Springfield Technical Community College's community access radio station. Both of her shows highlight Latin music from around the world. Her WTCC show is one of the only shows in the area that is bilingual, presented this way to attract both Spanish and non-Spanish speaking listeners. – Submitted by New England Public Radio

Jeannine Claudia Oppewall

(B. NOVEMBER 28, 1946 UXBRIDGE, MA) is an American film art director. She has worked on more than 30 movies in such roles as production designer, set decorator and set designer, and has four Academy Award nominations for Best Art Direction for "L.A. Confidential", "Pleasantville", "Seabiscuit" and "The Good Shepherd". Many of her film sets represented different time periods within the 20th century, including the 1930s ("Seabiscuit"), the 1950s ("L.A. Confidential" and "Pleasantville"), and from the 1960s ("The Big Easy", "The Bridges of Madison County" and "Catch Me If You Can").
– Joseph Carvalho III

Kelly Overton

(B. AUG. 28, 1978 IN WILBRAHAM, MA) is a Broadway, film, and television actress. She also wrote, directed, produced and starred in "The Collective" with her husband Judson Pearce Morgan in 2008. In 2016, Overton was cast in the lead role of Vanessa Helsing in the television science fiction series "Van Helsing".
– Joseph Carvalho III

Tina Packer

(B. SEPT. 28, 1938 IN WOLVERHAMPTON, UK) was described by the Massachusetts Cultural

Bridget Moynahan

(B. APR. 28, 1971 IN BINGHAMTON, NY) is an actress and model. She has starred in the CBS television drama series "Blue Bloods" since 2010. As a film actress, she was featured in "The Sum of All Fears" (2002), "The Recruit" (2003), "I, Robot" (2004) and "Lord of War" (2005). Her family moved to Longmeadow, MA when she was seven years old and she lived there until graduating from Longmeadow High School in 1989. – Joseph Carvalho III

Left: Bridget Moynahan (Photo by Ben Hider/Invision/AP)
Above: Julie McNiven

Council as "one of the state's most innovative theater artists." Packer was trained at the Royal Academy of Dramatic Arts, was a member of the Royal Shakespeare Company, and performed in London's West End and in repertory companies throughout Great Britain. As an actress, she appeared in the following films: "Doctor Who" (1963), "David Copperfield" (1966) and "Two a Penny" (1967). She established Shakespeare & Company in Lenox, MA in 1978 as a center for performance, education and training. Over the years she developed a method for training actors that combines traditional British instruction in voice training, movement, stage fighting and clowning with a deep exploration of the language in the text. The Massachusetts Cultural Council honored her with a Commonwealth Award in 1999.
– Joseph Carvalho III

Gretchen Palmer

(B. DEC. 16, 1961 IN CHICOPEE, MA; GREW UP IN LUDLOW, MA) is a television and film actress and singer who began her career in movies and television in 1985. Palmer had recurring roles in the following television series: "The Joe Schmo Show", "The Parkers", and "The Young and the Restless". She has also appeared in the following films: "Fast Forward" (1985), "Crossroads" (1986), "Red Heat" (1988), "When Harry Met Sally..." (1989), and "Trois" (2000). For three years in the early 1990s, Palmer was one of Ray Charles' "uh-Huh" back-up singers for Diet Pepsi commercials. – Nancy L. Nelson & Joseph Carvalho III

Elizabeth Ann Perkins

(B. NOVEMBER 18, 1960) raised in Colrain, MA, is a successful movie and television actress. Her film roles have included "Big", "The Flintstones", "Miracle on 34th Street", "About Last Night...", and "Avalon". She starred in the role as Celia Hodes in the long-running television series "Weeds". – Joseph Carvalho III

Eleanor Torrey Powell

(B. NOV. 21, 1912 IN SPRINGFIELD, MA; D. FEB. 11, 1982) was a dancer and actress made famous by her dancing, especially tap, in musical films of the 1930s and 1940s. She made her Hollywood debut as a featured dancer in the 1935 film "George White's Scandals". During the "Golden Age of Hollywood," Powell was one of Metro-Goldwyn-Mayer's premier dancing stars. Three of her most famous dance performances were in the films "Born to Dance" (1936), "Broadway Melody" (1937), and "Rosalie" (1937). Powell was named the "World's Greatest Tap Dancer" by the Dance Masters of America in 1965.
– Joseph Carvalho III

Top left: Kelly Overton
Top right: Tina Packer (*The Republican* file photo by Mark MacCarthy)
Right: Gretchen Palmer (*The Republican* file photo from "handout" from Palmer)

Victoria Principal

famed television and movie actress, attended Chicopee Comprehensive High School in Chicopee, MA. [See entry in Chapter for Women in Business.]

Chastelyn Rodriguez

(B. MAR. 20, 1983 IN SPRINGFIELD, MA) is an actress, model, and singer. Rodriguez was selected in 2009 from thousands of participants to be part of Univision's third season of "Nuestra Belleza Latina," a Latin reality show and beauty competition watched internationally. She made it to the top nine contestants of the show. Rodriguez has modeled at New York Fashion Week as well as internationally. In 2010, she took the crown as "Miss Diaspora" as winner of the Miss Diaspora Models International Pageant in New York City. – Darlyn Diaz Lindsay

Julia Sanderson

(NÉE JULIA ELLEN SACKETT, B. AUG. 27, 1887 IN SPRINGFIELD, MA; D. JAN. 27, 1975 IN SPRINGFIELD, MA) was a famed actress and singer. As a child actress she appeared in the Philadelphia-based Forepaugh Circus moving to Broadway when she was a young woman where she appeared in Jerome Kern musicals. During her career, she performed on Broadway and in London, England. She and her third husband, Frank Crumit began working as a song and comedy radio team in 1930. From 1930 to 1943, they drove from their Longmeadow home, "Dunrovin", twice each week to perform in New York City for their popular radio show "The Battle of the Sexes." Sanderson retired from the stage after Crumit's death in 1943. The Julia Sanderson Theater in Springfield was named after her. – Joseph Carvalho III

Top left: Eleanor Powell. **Top right:** Victoria Principal. **Bottom left:** Julia Sanderson. **Bottom right:** Chastelyn Rodriguez (*The Republican* file photo by Darlyn Diaz Lindsay)

Renee Ilene Sandstrom

(B. FEBRUARY 15, 1974 WORCESTER, MA), is an American singer and former child actress better known by her stage name, Renee Sands. She is best known for her role as Renee on Kids Incorporated. – Joseph Carvalho III

Chloe Stevens Sevigny

(B. NOV. 18, 1974 IN SPRINGFIELD, MA) is an actress, director, fashion designer, and former model. From 2006-2011, Sevigny played Nicolette Grant in the HBO television series "Big Love", which earned her a Golden Globe for Best Supporting Actress in 2010.
– Joseph Carvalho III

Liza Snyder

(B. MAR. 20, 1968 IN NORTHAMPTON, MA) is a successful television actress known for her roles on the ABC series "Sirens" (1993-1995), and the CBS series comedies "Yes, Dear" (2000-2006), and "Man With A Plan" (2016-).
– Joseph Carvalho III

Lois Maureen Stapleton

(B. JUNE 21, 1925 IN TROY, NY; D. MAR. 13, 2006 IN LENOX, MA) was an American actress in film, theater and television. She was nominated for the Academy Award for Best Supporting Actress for "Lonelyhearts" (1958), "Airport" (1970) and "Interiors" (1978), before winning for her performance as Emma Goldman in "Reds" (1981). She was inducted into the American Theatre Hall of Fame in 1981.
– Joseph Carvalho III

Eva Tanguay

of Holyoke, MA (B. AUG. 1, 1879 IN MARBLETON, QUEBEC, CANADA; D. JAN. 11, 1947 IN HOLLYWOOD, LOS ANGELES, CA) was a hugely popular vaudevillian actress/singer. She was famous for her stage persona as the "I Don't Care Girl." From 1904 to 1915 she was one of the highest paid vaudeville performers of her time and was known as the "Queen of Vaudeville." Her family emigrated to Holyoke

in 1884 where she spent her childhood. At the age of ten, she began touring professionally with a stage production of "Little Lord Fauntleroy". By 1905, she began performing in Vaudeville as a solo act which became her standard for the remainder of her career.
– Joseph Carvalho III

Anne Froelick Taylor

(B. DEC. 8, 1913 IN HINSDALE, MA; D. JAN. 26, 2010 IN LOS ANGELES, CA) was an American screenwriter from 1941 to 1950, and later a playwright and novelist. Her screenwriting career ended when she was identified as a communist by two witnesses at a hearing before the U.S. House of Representatives Un-American Affairs Committee (HUAC).
– Joseph Carvalho III

Uma Thurman

(B. APRIL 29, 1970 IN BOSTON, MA), Oscar-nominated and Golden Globe winning actress, whose father, Robert Alexander Farrar Thurman, taught at Amherst College, grew up in Amherst, MA.

Top left: Uma Thurman (AP Photo/Francois Mori) **Top right:** Chloe Sevigny (AP Photo/Mark J. Terrill).
Bottom right: Lois Maureen Stapleton

Paige Turco

(B. MAY 17, 1965 IN SPRINGFIELD, MA) is a successful television and film actress. In 1987, she made her television acting debut on the CBS soap opera "Guiding Light". Turco's early film career began with starring roles in two "Teenage Mutant Ninja Turtles" movies in 1991 and 1993. She would later star in the Disney production "Invincible" in 2006. From 1994 to 2014, she starred in a number of other CBS television series such as "American Gothic", "NYPD Blue", "Party of Five", "The Agency", and "NCIS: New Orleans". In 2014, she began starring in The CW television series "The 100". – Joseph Carvalho III

Maura West

[See entry for Maura West DeFreitas]

Alicia Roanne Witt

(B. AUG. 21, 1975 IN WORCESTER, MA) is an American actress, singer-songwriter, and pianist. She first came to fame as a child actress after being discovered by David Lynch, who cast her as Alia Atreides in his film "Dune" (1984) and in a guest role in his television series "Twin Peaks" (1990).Witt later had a critically acclaimed role as a disturbed teenager in "Fun" (1994), and appeared in "Mr. Holland's Opus" (1995), in the horror film "Urban Legend" (1998), in "Vanilla Sky" (2001), "Last Holiday" (2006), and the thriller "88 Minutes" (2007). Television appearances include "The Walking Dead", "The Sopranos", "Nashville", "Two and a Half Men", "Friday Night Lights", "Law & Order: Criminal Intent", "Cybill", and "Justified". In addition to acting, Witt is an accomplished pianist, singer, and songwriter. She released her self-titled debut album in 2009. Witt has also appeared in ten Hallmark Channel movies.

Top left: Alicia Witt. Top right: Eva Tanguay.
Bottom left: Maura West (AP Photo/Chris Pizzello).
Bottom right: Paige Turco.

CHAPTER FIFTEEN

OTHER
women of note

This chapter includes an amazing group of women who either didn't fit neatly into one of the previous thematic chapters, or excelled equally in multiple fields of endeavor. We have featured the famed local aviator Maude Irving Tait Moriarty as one of these notable women.

She competed against men and won convincingly on numerous occasions flying the GeeBee airplane, the fastest airplane of its time. She shared the courage and daring of those early aviators and became an inspiration to the future generations of women aviators. Women like Fitchburg's Josephine Wright Chapman was one of the nation's few women architects; Ida Farrar's 46 years of ground-breakiing librarianship at the Springfield City Library earned her a coveted William Pynchon Medal in 1939; and Eliza Roxcy Snow of Becket became one of the most famous women of the early Mormon community. Unusual lives are also celebrated in this chapter such as Lillian Asplund of Worcester who was the last surviving American passenger of the Titanic sinking, and Elizabeth Dickerson Rice of West

Springfield who became Countess Bianciardi of Florence, Italy in the late 19th century. As a footnote to history at the end of this chapter, we have noted the lives of two women from our region whose infamous exploits have merited recognition by other nations.

More importantly, we have also included some of today's notable women who have contributed much to our communities. To be sure, these represent only a small sample of the remarkable women who live, work, and serve in the many towns and cities of Central and Western Massachusetts. However, we felt that it was important to highlight their achievements to illustrate the power of women in our time. – The Editors

Maude Irving (Tait) Moriarty

(B. JULY 10, 1898 IN CHICOPEE, MA; D. OCT. 5, 1982 IN EAST LONGMEADOW, MA)

"There's one thing you don't think about and that's the powder on your nose," Maude Tait said to a *Springfield Republican* reporter about the experience of flying her Gee Bee airplane. Ms. Tait was the first licensed female pilot in Massachusetts and Connecticut to fly solo. Throughout her career as a pilot she set numerous flying records.

She was born in Chicopee in 1898 to James and Mary Tait and educated in Springfield. She was a graduate of the MacDuffie School for Girls and worked as an elementary school teacher, first in Hampden, and then in East Longmeadow. In 1928 she took a leave of absence from teaching to realize her dream of flying. She was no doubt inspired by the activities of her father and his brothers, who sold their dairy business and purchased a plot of land on which they built the Springfield Airport. They were responsible for bringing the Granville Brothers, inventors of the famous Gee Bee racers, to the airfield. The Tait family provided the financial backing as well as the space for the Granvilles to set up production in Springfield.

Surrounded by pilots and the inventors and builders of racing aircraft, Maude Tait soon acquired her pilot's license and never returned to the classroom. She expressed her love of flying in these words: "After learning to fly, you itch to do it on your own. I always felt if others could do it, I could too. I didn't feel daring, just curious and interested in speed and altitude and always wanting to explore their possibilities." Piloting a small plane solo required a cool head, intelligence, and courage – forced landings due to bad weather, running out of fuel, or malfunctions of the aircraft were not uncommon.

Maude Irving (Tait) Moriarty (also on previous page)

In 1929, Tait set an unofficial altitude record for women by flying her Curtiss Robin aircraft at 16,500 ft. That same year she dropped the kick-off football from her plane at the Silvertown's Professional football season opener. Other flying firsts of 1929 included piloting parachute jumper Ted White from Northampton and giving her plucky grandmother a 103rd birthday present of flight. This gave her grandmother the honor of being the oldest person to fly at that time!

In 1931 Maude-Irving Tait reached the pinnacle of her career and achieved national fame as a pilot. She shattered Amelia Earhart's speed record by 10 mph and missed the men's speed record by 1 mph, clocking a speed of 214.9 mph in her Gee Bee Sportster. That same year Tait also won the Aerol Trophy at the National Air Races in Cleveland, Ohio, cementing her position as one of the outstanding women flyers in the nation. At home, in recognition of her barrier-breaking accomplishments, the Advertising Club of Springfield awarded her the Pynchon Medal in 1932. She was the youngest person at that time to be given Springfield's most prestigious honor. Her citation captured the romance and excitement of that time, stating "to have flown your winged ship through the uncharted paths of the sky at a speed greater than any other aviatrix, the Advertising Club recognizes as an extraordinary achievement."

In 1932, Tait married Attorney James Moriarty. She planned to participate in the 1932 National Air Races but was side-lined due to mechanical difficulties with her plane. She didn't return to competitive flying, but her interest in aviation continued throughout her lifetime. She used her fame to promote flying and headed up very successful promotional campaigns to attract young men into the Army Air Corps in World War II. Privately, she still flew her Gee Bee here in the Valley on occasion through the 1940s.

– Paul Anthony & Margaret Humberston, Pioneer Valley History Network website

ALPHABETICAL LISTING
OTHER WOMEN OF NOTE

Lillian Asplund

(B. ON OCT. 21, 1906 IN WORCESTER, MA; D. MAY 6, 2006 IN SHREWSBURY, MA), born to a Swedish immigrant family (father Carl Oscar Vilhelm Gustafsson Asplund and mother Selma Augusta Emilia Johansson), was the last American survivor of the Titanic sinking. In 1907, Lillian's father had taken his family to Småland, Sweden, to help his widowed mother settle problems with the family farm. By early 1912, the family was ready to return to the United States, and Lillian's father booked passage for his family on the Titanic. Lillian, her mother and brother were rescued by the RMS Carpathia, which had arrived at the scene shortly after four o'clock in the morning. Lillian and her brother were loaded into burlap bags and hoisted to the ship's deck.

Elsa Bakalar

(B. 1919 IN ENGLAND; D. JANUARY 29, 2010 IN NORTHAMPTON, MA) was an English-born American garden designer. She moved to Heath, MA in 1977 and wrote about gardening and garden design. She is best known for her 1994 book, *A Garden of One's Own*.
– Joseph Carvalho III

Helen Eva (Allen) Barlow

(BORN SEPT. 8, 1882 IN AMHERST, MA; D. SEP 27, 1946 IN MA) was one of the most active and "most well-known club women in Western Massachusetts." She was one of the most influential leaders in the early to mid-twentieth century in organizing and promoting women's organizations in the region. A Smith College graduate, Barlow served as President of the Longmeadow Women's Club and as President of the Western Massachusetts Women's Club, and was an active committee member for many years with the Federation of Women's Clubs.

Top: Lillian Asplund
Above: Helen Eva (Allen) Barlow

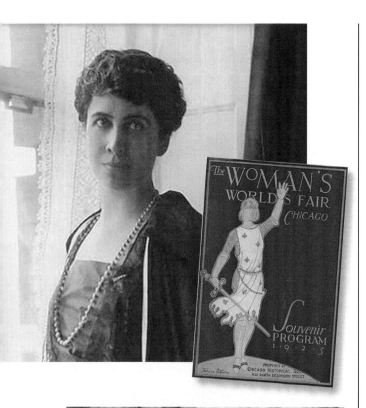

She also served for a number of years as vice-regent of the Daughters of the American Revolution, and as the organization's State Librarian. – Joseph Carvalho III

Josephine Wright Chapman

(B. AUG. 20, 1867 IN FITCHBURG, MA; D. SEPT., 1943 IN SOMERSET, ENGLAND) was one of only 50 women architects in the United States at the turn of the century. A successful architect, the Craigie Arms building in Cambridge, MA, St. Mark's Episcopal Church in Fitchburg, MA, Tuckerman Hall in Worcester, MA, and a number of "grand estate" homes in Washington, DC are among her accomplishments. Some of her work has been listed on the National Register of Historic Places, most notably the Craigie Arms Building. – Joseph Carvalho III

Grace Coolidge
and the Women's World Fair

First Lady, Grace Coolidge organized the first "Women's World Fair, "The World Exposition of Women's Progress" which opened in Chicago on April 18, 1925. – Joseph Carvalho III

Rita Coppola-Wallace

(B. JAN. 28, 1960 IN FT. LAUDERDALE. FLA) is the Executive Director of the Office of Design and Construction at Williams College in Williamstown, MA. To date, has been responsible for the management of over $400 million in capital projects at the College. Prior to joining the administration at Williams in 2013, Coppola-Wallace was the Director of Capital Asset Construction for the City of Springfield from 2007 to 2013. She was a project manager for the City for over 30 years with projects ranging from schools, libraries, parks and all public buildings. Coppola-Wallace also developed and implemented Springfield's extensive lake and pond management program. She conceived and managed the restoration of

the Historic Everett Barney Carriage House at Forest Park in Springfield, and served from 1998 to 2006 as the Executive Director of the Society of Everett Barney & S.E. Barney, Inc. Early in her career, her extensive research of the early history and design of Springfield's famed Forest Park led to its award-winning restoration and its return as a major attraction. – Joseph Carvalho III

Mary Salome Cutler Fairchild

(B. JUNE 21, 1855 IN DALTON, MA; D. DEC. 30, 1921) was a pioneering American librarian and library educator, and a graduate of Mount Holyoke Female Seminary in 1875. She later taught at the college from 1876 to 1878. In 1884, she was hired by Melvil Dewey, the librarian of Columbia College, as a cataloguer. When Dewey opened the first library school, Fairchild taught cataloging. She moved with it when the school moved to Albany. The school was reorganized and named the New York State Library School. She served as vice-director in addition to teaching. Because of Dewey's frequent absences she conducted much of the administration of the school. – James S. Gleason

Ida F. Farrar

(B. JUNE 4, 1867 IN MARLBOROUGH, NH; D. FEB. 9, 1949 IN SPRINGFIELD, MA) was a long time librarian at the Springfield City Library Association organized one of the nation's first reading club for the blind, initially called the Springfield City Library Reading Circle for the Blind (later called simply, the "Saturday Afternoon Club"). Farrar served as the club's president for 27 years. She was awarded the William Pynchon Medal in 1939. She retired from the City Library Association in 1941 after 46 years of service. – Joseph Carvalho III

Top left: First Lady Grace Coolidge
Bottom left: Rita Coppola-Wallace

Janine Fondon

(B. NEW YORK CITY) Professor Fondon earned her undergraduate degree in Sociology and Anthropology at Colgate University and received her master's degree from New York University in Communications and Business/Media Ecology. She has also completed study groups in London and Paris as well as at the University of the West Indies (Barbados). Fondon's career of over 15 years in communications, strategic public relations and multicultural marketing prepared her to be a media ecologist and professor. Fondon, along with her husband Tom Fondon and daughter Nikai Fondon, have worked collectively on consulting projects and their company, UnityFirst.com, an online network that engages communities in current events and topics relating to diversity/inclusion, education, entertainment and technology.
– Joseph Carvalho III

Doris W. Hayden

(B. MAR. 20, 1902 IN BLANDFORD, MA; D. SEPT. 1, 1996 IN BLANDFORD, MA) prolific Western Massachusetts genealogist and local historian, specialized in Western Hampden County and Blandford history and genealogy. She and her daughter Jean H. York transcribed voluminous local records for Blandford and the related families in Western Massachusetts.
– Joseph Carvalho III

Sara Elizabeth Bruce Northrup Hollister

(B. APR. 8, 1924 IN PASADENA, CA; D. DEC. 19, 1997 IN HADLEY, MA) played a major role in the creation of Dianetics, which evolved into the religious movement Scientology. She was the second wife of science-fiction author L. Ron Hubbard, who would become the leader of the Church of Scientology.

Lujuana D. Hood

(B. OCT. 31, 1953) As Director of the Pan African Historical Museum of the United States of America (PAHMUSA), LuJuana Hood has worked in the field of cultural heritage for over 20 years. She emphasizes the 'intangible' cultural heritage such as folklore, tradition and knowledge. In addition to taking students on educational tours to Senegal, West Africa, Ms. Hood directs the African American Heritage Trail Underground Railroad Walking Tour in Springfield, MA which includes reenactors. Hood also directs the Makeda Project. This project focuses on the cultural heritage of African women and investigates how their forced migration into the new world shaped the culture of African Americans and women of the diaspora – and their ability to excel in education, economics, civil rights, the arts and created opportunities when there were none. With a mission to establish the proper representation of Africans and African American culture – and its contribution to world history, the museum programs are open to communities, students and scholars.
– Janine Fondon

Susan Jaye-Kaplan

(B. JAN. 15, 1946) of Longmeadow, MA founded GO FIT, Inc. in 2005 to address the need of economically underprivileged and underserved youth who are not being educated to learn about the benefits of exercise as a means to good health and general welfare. GO FIT, Inc. has been implemented successfully throughout the Pioneer Valley. Jaye-Kaplan also the founded the Pioneer Valley Women's Running Club (PVWRC) in 2000, the only all women's running club in Western Massachusetts and Northern CT. Her leadership and vision helped establish the first annual health and fitness expo at the Naismith Basketball Hall of Fame in Springfield in conjunction with Bay Path University, Bay State Health Systems, Spirit

Top: Ida Farrar
Bottom: Janine Fondon

239

of Women and members of the PVWRC. Jaye-Kaplan has been honored by The Pioneer Valley Girl Scouts as a Woman of Distinction/ Woman of Vision Award in May 2004; the recipient of the President's Citation Award at Commencement Exercise at Western New England College, May 2006; The 2006 Elms College Step Forward Woman of Vision Award; and The Daily Points of Light Award recipient for July 2006 by The Points of Light Foundation and Volunteer Center National Network, in partnership with the Knights of Columbus and the Corporation for National and Community Service; and is the recipient of the William Pynchon Award. – Joseph Carvalho III

Left: Susan Jaye-Kaplan
Above: Edna Mapp and Rebecca Johnson

Edna R. Mapp

(B. JUNE 8, 1913; D. FEB. 16, 2013 IN SPRINGFIELD, MA) was the highly regarded wife of Alexander Ben Mapp. Her numerous community involvements were directed toward the positive development of young people in the Springfield urban community. She was a co-founder of the Springfield Chapter of Jack & Jill, Inc., and served on the boards of the YWCA, Hilltop Child and Adult Services, the Girls' Family Center, and the National Advisory Committee of Camp Atwater. She was an active volunteer in the Read Aloud school program, and frequently cooked and served meals at the Open Pantry, and was a volunteer driver for the ill and handicapped to medical appointments. – Anne-Gerard Flynn

Judith A. Matt

(B. JULY 25, 1943) is the President of the Spirit of Springfield, a non-profit organization responsible for producing many of the staple community events that form Springfield's civic life. Matt was born in Waterbury, CT, moved to Springfield in 1970. In Springfield's downtown area Matt and her husband (John Stumpf) bought and renovated a Victorian row house. While volunteering for and working on numerous projects, the newly elected Mayor of Springfield Richard Neal (now U.S. Congressman) noticed Matt's drive, work ethic, and civic pride. Neal recruited her to plan his inauguration, and then to head up his Mayor's Office of Community Affairs (MOCA). In this position, Matt became responsible for many of the large community events in Springfield, including the city's 350th birthday and the 4th of July Fireworks. When MOCA lost funding, cancelling many of those events, Matt along with the help of several private citizens who felt these events were crucial to city pride, established the non-profit Spirit of Springfield. The Spirit of Springfield is now responsible for the 4th of

July fireworks, Parade of the Big Balloons, the Pancake Breakfast, Bright Nights, and the other major events that make up a lion share of Springfield's civic culture. Along the way she has served as a: Vice Chair at Bay Path College, Director and Vice Chair of the Urban League of Springfield, and as President of the American Cancer Society, American Heart Association, and the Women's Division Chamber of Commerce. Throughout her career, Matt has held to her goal of giving people an opportunity to celebrate and take pride in their city: The City of Springfield.
– Jason J. Alves

Vanessa Otero

is the chief operating officer of the New England Farm Workers Council/ Partners for Community in Springfield, MA. Otero is also a member of the Reginal Employment Board of Hampden County. She is a former member of the Massachusetts Convention Center Authority Board. In 2017, Otero was appointed by Massachusetts Governor Charles Baker to the state's newly formed Latino Commission.
– Damaris Perez-Pizarro

Top left: Vanessa Otero. **Top right:** Porter Phelps house at the Huntington Museum. **Above:** Elizabeth Porter Phelps.

Elizabeth Porter Phelps

(B. NOV. 24, 1747 IN HADLEY, MA; D. JAN. 1, 1817 IN HADLEY, MA), a wealthy Hadley resident, was an early American diarist. Her home is now the Porter-Phelps-Huntington Museum in Hadley, MA.

Elizabeth Dickerson Rice

(B. 22 APR 1835 IN WEST SPRINGFIELD, MA; D. JANUARY 2, 1886 IN VEVEY, DISTRICT DE LA RIVIERA-PAYS-D'ENHAUT, SWITZERLAND; BURIED IN PARK STREET CEMETERY, WEST SPRINGFIELD, MA), daughter of Caleb Rice and Marietta (Parsons) Rice, Caleb was the first Mayor of Springfield and first President of Mass Mutual

Life Insurance Co., frequent writer of Letters to the editor in the Republican, married Prof. "Count" Carol Bianciardi, became Countess Bianciardi of Florence, Italy, wrote a book of poems entitled *At Home in Italy*.
– Joseph Carvalho III

Marion Burbank Rice

(B. SEPT. 9, 1904 IN FITCHBURG, MA; B. APR.12, 1995 IN FITCHBURG, MA), a Denishawn dancer, teacher, choreographer, producer, was a respected American modern dance choreographer, dance teacher and producer.

Dora D. Robinson

(B. AUG. 7, 1951) served as executive director of the United Way of the Pioneer Valley from 2009 to June of 2017. During her tenure, she co-founded the UWPV Women's Leadership Council "to engage local women leaders in supporting financial literacy and health initiatives for women and girls." She has been involved in non-profit leadership in Greater Springfield for over 40 years. For eighteen of those years, Robinson served as president and executive director of the Martin Luther King, Jr. Family Services, Inc. in Springfield. She also served as corporate director of child and family services at the Center for Human Development in Springfield. Robinson is a founding member of the MLK, Jr. Charter School of Excellence in Springfield. She lives in East Forest Park, Springfield, MA. – Joseph Carvalho III

Elizabeth Ann (Katten) Kittredge Rome

(B. JULY 3, 1942 IN SPRINGFIELD, MA) was one of the creators of the Hatikvah Holocaust Education Center and produced its permanent exhibits in 2003. When Hatikvah closed in 2010, she facilitated Hatikvah's Local Survivor exhibit's move to the Lyman & Merrie Wood Museum of Springfield History in Springfield, MA. From 1982 to 1992, she served on the Longmeadow (MA) School Committee. In 1993, Massachusetts Governor William S. Weld appointed her to the State Board of Education. – Jane Kaufman

Eliza Roxcy Snow

(B. JAN. 21, 1804 IN BECKET, MA; D. DEC. 5, 1887) was one of the most famous Mormon women of the 19th Century. A renowned poet, she chronicled history, celebrated nature and relationships, and expounded scripture and doctrine. Snow was married to Joseph Smith as a plural wife and was openly a plural wife of Brigham Young after Smith's death. Snow was the second general president of the Relief Society of The Church of Jesus Christ of Latter-day Saints (LDS Church), which she reestablished in Utah Territory in 1866, serving until her death in 1887. – Joseph Carvalho III

Left: Marion Burbank Rice. **Above center:** Dora Robinson.

Carolyn (Czaja) Topor

(B. MARCH 24, 1937 IN SPRINGFIELD, MA) founded the New England Chapter of the Kosciuszko Foundation in 1997 to foster knowledge and appreciation of Polish culture, history, and traditions among Americans. Since early childhood, Carolyn participated in activities within the Polish community, Polish dance demonstrations and competitions, commemorations and celebrations. Under her leadership, the Chapter became affiliated with Elms College in Chicopee, MA and supported the development of the Polish Center of Discovery and Learning at Elms College serving on its first Board of Directors. Carolyn has served as president of the Chapter since 1998. Each year the Chapter has a Polish Film Festival and a gala celebration to recognize the recipients of Kosciuszko Foundation scholarships and grants and to honor the latest Distinguished Polish-American

Above: Carolyn (Czaja) Topor. **Right:** Eliza Roxcy Snow

awardee. Through the years the Chapter has had lectures, symposiums, art exhibits and concerts at area colleges and museums. In 2008, she received the "Knight's Cross of the Order of Merit of the Republic of Poland (Krzyz Kawalerski Orderu Zasługi Rzeczypospolitej Polskiej)," Poland's highest civilian honor conferred on foreigners and Polish residents abroad for merit rendered to Poland.

A 1958 Phi Beta Kappa graduate of Mount Holyoke College, Topor served as president of the Women's Symphony League during the 1980s, and the Fine Arts Council of the Museum of Fine Arts in Springfield. She has received many awards for her volunteer activities including "Alumnae Medal of Honor" from Mount Holyoke College, Rotary International's "Paul Harris Award for Community Service", Kosciuszko Foundation New England Chapter's "Distinguished Polish American" and Central Connecticut State University Blejwas Endowed Chair/Polish Studies "Polish Medal of Merit." – Joanne M. Gruszkos & Joseph Carvalho III

Janet Troutman-Simmons

(B. JUNE 24, 1927) has a long and distinguished record of Springfield community service. She chaired the Mason Square community committee which resulted in the establishment of the W.W. Johnson Life Center. Working for Senator Edward W. Brooke in his Springfield office, she headed the Domestic Action Program which established the Tri-city Day Camp at Westover Air Force Base which was a nationally recognized program. For many years, she served as the Executive Director of the W.W. Johnson Life Center. Troutman-Simmons was the 2006 Ubora Award honoree. – African Hall Steering Committee, Springfield Science Museum, Springfield Museums

Amanda Barnes Smith

(B. FEB. 22, 1809 IN BECKET, MA; D. JUNE 30, 1886 IN RICHMOND, UT) was a "Mormon pioneer" (Latter Day Saints).

Above: Sarah Elizabeth Thomas
Right: Stamps of Laura Second and Lona Cohen

Claribel Hinsdale Smith

(B. DEC. 11, 1863 IN FEEDING HILLS, AGAWAM, MA; MAR. 14, 1953 IN SPRINGFIELD, MA) appointed the first law librarian of Hampden County with her offices at the Hampden County Court House in Springfield. – Joseph Carvalho III

Sarah Elizabeth Thomas, Ph. D.

is an American librarian best known for her leadership positions in a number of research libraries. In May 2013 it was announced that she had been appointed vice president for Harvard University Library; she took up the post in August 2013. A graduate of Smith College (Class of 1970), Thomas was raised in Haydenville, MA. In 2007, she was awarded the Melvil Dewey Medal from the American Library Association. – Joseph Carvalho III

Julia Carolyn Weston

(B. JULY 25, 1877 IN DALTON, MA; JULY 21, 1937 IN LOS ANGELES, CA) was the Weston Paper Company heiress, and mother of the famous Julia Child of the hugely popular French Chef PBS show. – Joseph Carvalho III

Lucy Wright

(B. FEB. 5, 1760 IN PONTOOSUCK PLANTATION, LATER NAMED PITTSFIELD, MA; D. FEB. 7, 1821 IN WATERVLIET, NY) became the leader in the Shaker community after Mother Ann passed, a rare woman religious leader for early 19th century. – James S. Gleason

Infamous Women:

Lona Cohen

(B. JANUARY 11, 1913 IN ADAMS, MA; D. DECEMBER 23, 1992), born Leontine Theresa Petka, also known as Helen Kroger, was an American spy for the Soviet Union. She was the wife of Soviet spy Morris Cohen.

Laura Secord

(NÉE INGERSOLL; B. SEPT.13, 1775 IN GREAT BARRINGTON, MA; D. OCT. 17, 1868 AT DRUMMOND HILL /NIAGARA FALLS, ONTARIO, CANADA) was a Canadian heroine of the War of 1812. She is known for having walked 20 miles (32 km) out of American-occupied territory in 1813 to warn British forces of an impending American attack. Her contribution to the war was little known during her lifetime, but since her death she has been frequently honored in Canada.

CHAPTER SIXTEEN

This exhibit was presented in collaboration with the University of Massachusetts-Amherst (Dr. Laura Lovett, Department of History) Bay Path University, Pan African Historical Museum of USA's Makeda Project. Co-curators were Janine Fondon and LuJuana Hood. As history-makers and shapers, Fondon and Hood share this exhibit in honor of their own 'intersection' — to document the untold stories of women at various intersecting points of history.

Janine Fondon (Bay Path Chair of Undergraduate Communications and contributor to the "It's Our Movement Now" book project directed by Dr. Laura Lovett) made history with her husband Tom Fondon by creating UnityFirst.com as the first Black-owned online news journal in Massachusetts that shares the untold stories of African Americans and other diverse communities across the state, region and country. Janine's family came to the U.S. via Ellis Island and her aunt Irene Morgan was a civil rights game-changer.

WOMEN'S
special exhibitions
The Intersection: Women of Color On the Move

As Director of the Pan African Historical Museum of the United States of America (PAHMUSA) and Underground Railroad Walking Tour, LuJuana Hood has worked in the field of cultural heritage for over 20 years. Her grandmother, Dr. Elouise Franklin, was a pacesetter who broke barriers as a woman and missionary in a time when women took a back seat to men in the pulpit.

This exhibit shares the intersecting "lines" and worlds of women of color on the move to create a more inclusive world. Women of color were often excluded from success in mainstream society and forced to navigate the side and back road intersections filled with conflict, controversy and commonalities. They broke barriers in civil rights and feminism before it was commonly known and overcame obstacles well beyond our imagination. Anna Julia Cooper lived 105 years – from her birth in slavery to the women's vote in 1920 and the eventual civil rights movement of the 1960s. She inspires us to navigate complex intersections as we are on the move to success today and tomorrow.

QUEENS AND PHARAOHS

Hatshepsut

Hatshepsut, the fifth pharaoh of the 18th Dynasty of Egypt, was born about 1507 BC and reigned from about 1473 to 1458 BC. As one of Egypt's most successful pharaohs, she held a position that few women could claim. She dressed like a male and even appeared with a false beard to show strength. With resentment about her power as a leader, Hatshepsut's stepson, Thutmose III, tried to erase her legacy and minimize her success. Before her reign, she served as queen in the reign of her husband, Thutmose II.

Ndaté Yalla Mbodj

Senegal's Ndaté Yalla Mbodj (1810-1860), who succeeded her sister, Queen Ndjeumbeut Mbodj, was crowned on October 1, 1846, as the last great lingeer, or queen, of the kingdom of Waalo. She led a great army and battled against French colonization and the invasion of the Moors. Though she was eventually overtaken, her bravery remains a symbol of female empowerment, and a statue was erected in her honor. Traditional Wolof society was considered matriarchal, and Lingeer (queens) were ready to represent their countries via politics and the military.

Biblical Queen of Sheba

In the Bible, she is noted as the Queen of Sheba. The Ethiopians call her Makeda. The Yemeni call her Bilqis. Both the Ethiopian and Yemeni people claim her as their own. In 960 BC, she ruled an ancient kingdom located in the area called Ethiopia and Yemen today. She was a ruler of great wealth who controlled major trade routes as well as gold mines. She is a prominent figure in the Islamic Quran and the Ethiopian Kebra Nagast (the Glory of Kings). Her legendary voyage to the grand court of the Judean monarch King Solomon is recorded in the old testament in the Book of Second Chronicles (9th chapter and 9th verse) where she shows the power of her wealth by presenting gifts to Solomon. Known for her beauty, she embodied divine wisdom. Her dynasty was one of power. She was a woman of great magnitude – she was a queen.

INNOVATION

Anna Julia Cooper

MOTHER OF BLACK INTELLECTUALISM
Anna Julia Cooper's life covered many eras. She lived through slavery, the Civil War, Reconstruction, women's suffrage, Jim Crow and the Civil Rights movement. She was one of the most prominent African-American scholars in the United States and a colleague of W.E.B. Du Bois. Upon receiving her Ph.D. in history from the University of Paris-Sorbonne in 1924, Cooper earned a doctorate and became only the fourth African American to do so. She was also a member of the Alpha Kappa Alpha Sorority, Inc. Cooper's most

Top left: Hatshepsut. **Bottom left:** Ndaté Yalla Mbodj.
Top right: Queen of Sheba.

> "THE CAUSE OF FREEDOM IS NOT THE CAUSE OF A RACE OR A SECT, A PARTY OR A CLASS — IT IS THE CAUSE OF HUMANKIND, THE VERY BIRTHRIGHT OF HUMANITY."
>
> - ANNA JULIA COOPER,
> *AMERICAN PASSPORTS*

famous written work – *A Voice from the South* – which included speeches and essays on subjects including women's rights and racial progress, was published in 1892.

Olivia Davidson
TEACHER AND VISIONARY

In 1854, Olivia America Davidson was born free in Virginia and later graduated from Hampton University in 1878. In 1879, she enrolled in the State Normal School at Framingham, Massachusetts (now Framingham State University), and later graduated as one of six honor students in 1881. At the request of Booker T. Washington, she became a teacher and vice principal at Tuskegee Institute on August 25, 1881, and worked diligently as his partner in growing the school. In 1886, she became the second wife of Booker T.Washington, and she continued her role as "Lady Principal." On the campus, a building has been named in her honor. A true pioneer throughout her life, she lived and worked in various areas of the country, including Virginia, Ohio, Mississippi, Alabama, Tennessee, and

Massachusetts. In 1886, Davidson spoke before the Alabama State Teachers' Association with the following theme – "How Shall We Make the Women of Our Race Stronger?" She emphasized that teachers should strive to engage Black girls as the "hope of the race." She died of tuberculosis in 1889 at Massachusetts General Hospital.

SLAVERY TO FREEDOM

Jenny Slew

Born in 1719 to Betty Slew, a free white woman and a man of African descent (most likely a slave), Jenny Slew was one of the first African Americans to sue for her freedom and the first person to win a jury trial. Slew lived a life as a free woman in Ipswich, Massachusetts until

Top center and top right: Anna Julia Cooper
Bottom right: Oliva Davidson

1762 when she was kidnapped from her home and forced into servitude by John Whipple Jr. In 1765, three years after the kidnapping, Slew brought a suit to court to demand her freedom and 25 pounds in damages – thus charging Whipple with violating her freedom. Slew eventually won her case.

Elizabeth "MumBet" Freeman

Elizabeth Freeman (c. 1744-1829), was the first enslaved African American to file and win a freedom suit in Massachusetts. Known as Bet or MumBet, she was among the first slaves in Massachusetts to successfully sue for her freedom, encouraging the state to abolish slavery. The Massachusetts Supreme Judicial Court ruling, in Freeman's favor, found slavery to be inconsistent with the 1780 Massachusetts State Constitution. Her suit, *Brom and Bett v. Ashley* (1781), was cited in the Massachusetts Supreme Judicial Court appellate review of Quock Walker's freedom suit. When the court upheld Walker's freedom

under the state's constitution, the ruling was considered to have implicitly ended slavery in Massachusetts. W. E. B. Du Bois once claimed Freeman as his relative.

Sojourner Truth

Sojourner Truth (Isabella Baumfree) was an African-American abolitionist and women's rights activist. Truth was born into slavery in Swartekill, Ulster County, New York, but escaped with her infant daughter to freedom in 1826.

Truth won three court cases in her time. In 1828, she won her court case to recover her son Peter. In 1835, she became the first Black to win a slander suit in a case against the Folgers. Finally, in 1865, she won a case to desegregate the horse car systems of Washington, DC. In 1843, at age 46, Isabelle adopted the name Sojourner Truth, left New York and traveled to Springfield, MA where she attended camp meetings and held prayer sessions She stayed in Springfield far into the winter before some Springfield friends introduced her to the Northampton Association. This is where she made her home and even met Olive Gilbert, who wrote her memoir. She also met other contemporaries such as Frederick Douglass, William Lloyd Garrison and Wendell Phillips. The Northampton Association supported women's rights and religious tolerance and united around the issue of the abolition of slavery.

In 1850, she purchased a home in what would become the village of Florence in Northampton for $300 and spoke at the first National Women's Rights Convention in Worcester, Massachusetts in 1850.

CIVIL RIGHTS AND WOMEN'S RIGHTS

Maria W. Stewart

Maria W. Stewart (1803-1879) was born Maria Miller in Hartford, Connecticut. She was an African American domestic servant who became a teacher, journalist, lecturer, abolitionist, and women's rights activist. She was the first-known American woman to speak to a mixed audience of men and women, whites and black. Also, she was the first African-American woman to make public lectures, as well as to lecture about women's rights and make public anti-slavery speeches. Her second speech was delivered in 1832.

She moved to Washington, D.C in 1861 to teach. Around 1870, Stewart was appointed to head housekeeping at the Freedmen's Hospital and Asylum in Washington, D.C. Sojourner Truth also held this position before Stewart. The Freedmen's Hospital, founded in 1862, was the first hospital of its kind to provide medical treatment for former slaves and later became a teaching hospital for the Howard University Medical School.

Ana Roque de Duprey

(1853-1933) was a feminist who founded the Puerto Rican League of Women in 1917. She was a key orchestrator of the suffragette campaign in Puerto Rico in the 1920s and noted for her leadership of the Puerto Rican Woman's Suffrage Association.

Jean Denton Thompson

Freedom Rider Jean Catherine Thompson was arrested in Jackson, Mississippi on May 24, 1961. She also participated in the December 1, 1961 Freedom Ride from Baton Rouge, Louisiana to McComb, Mississippi.

Top left: Ana Roque de Duprey. **Top right:** Maria W. Stewart. **Bottom left and right:** Jean Denton Thompson (photo on right courtesy of Daniel Denton)

been recognized by Jamaica (the Jamaican Order of Merit in 1991) and Great Britain (2004- Greatest Black Briton).

Mary Eliza Mahoney

(1845-1926) from Dorchester, MA was first professionally-trained and certified African American nurse in the United States. In 1879, she graduated from nursing school in Boston (New England Hospital for Women and Children) and later(1886), she became one of the original members of what is known as the American Nurses Association (ANA). In 1908, co-founded the National Association of Colored Graduate Nurses. Mahoney was always concerned with women's equality and civil rights. After women won the right to vote in 1920, Mahoney was among the first women in Boston to register to vote.

LAW AND NEW ORDER

Elizabeth Jennings Graham

Elizabeth Jennings Graham, an activist and educator, was born free in New York City to Thomas and Elizabeth Jennings in 1826. Her father was an innovator as the first African American patent holder in the United States and one of the originators who founded New York's Abyssinian Baptist Church. In 1854, Elizabeth Graham insisted on her right to ride on an available New York City horse-drawn streetcar at a time when all such companies were private and most operated segregated cars. Her case was decided in her favor in 1855 and it led to the eventual desegregation of all New York City transit systems by 1865.

Irene Morgan

She came before Rosa Parks. Irene Morgan took a stand by refusing to give up her seat in Virginia (1944) and later won a critical Supreme Court precedent in 1946. Irene Amos Morgan Kirkaldy (1917-2007) boarded a bus in Virginia that was headed to Baltimore

Throughout the 1960s, she continued to be deeply committed to working with several other CORE projects. Also, her sisters Alice and Shirley Thompson were also Freedom Riders. Jean Denton Thompson now resides in Amherst, MA.

MEDICINE

Mary Seacole

Mary Jane Seacole (1805-1881) was a Jamaican businesswoman and "nurse" who provided comfortable quarters as well as medical aid for those wounded servicemen and officers during Crimean War. With knowledge of herbal medicine, she was often compared to nurse Clara Barton. She will be remembered for the help and service she provided. She has

Top left: Mary Seacole. **Bottom left:** Mary Eliza Mahoney. **Top right:** Elizabeth Jennings Graham

but was asked to give up her seat because the driver said it was located in the 'white section.' She was arrested in Middlesex County, Virginia, in 1944 under a state law imposing racial segregation in public facilities and transportation. The NAACP Legal Defense Fund, with William H. Hastie, the former Governor of the U.S. Virgin Islands and Thurgood Marshall, legal counsel of the NAACP, represented her (Irene Morgan v. Commonwealth of Virginia), a case which came before the United States Supreme Court. In 1946, in a landmark decision, the Court ruled that the Virginia law was unconstitutional. Morgan's case inspired the 1947 Journey of Reconciliation, during which 16 activists from the Chicago-based Congress of Racial Equality rode on interstate buses to test the enforcement of the Supreme Court's ruling.

EDUCATION

Otelia Cromwell

In 1900, Otelia Cromwell (1874-1972) became the first African-American graduate of Smith College. She went on to receive a master's degree at Columbia University in 1910 and received a doctorate in English at Yale in 1926. She was an educator and professor at Miner Teachers College, serving as head of its literature department. In 1874, Otelia Cromwell was born in Washington, D.C. to Lucy McGuinn and John Wesley Cromwell. Her father was a journalist, educator, and the first African American to practice law with the Interstate Commerce Commission.

Gloria Johnson Powell

Gloria Johnson-Powell (1936-2017) became the first African American woman to attain tenure at Harvard Medical School. She was a child psychiatrist who played a key role in the American Civil Rights movement. She grew up in Boston, Massachusetts and later

Top: Gloria Johnson Powell. **Bottom left:** Irene Morgan. **Bottom right:** Otelia Cromwell

Executive Assistant to the Branch Manager, Xerox Corporation (Hartford, CT). She recently retired from Mount Holyoke College after 28 years of service to the Office of Human Resources. She has been married to Frederick J. Jackson, Jr. for 54 years.

MILITARY SERVICE

Harriet Ida Pickens and Frances Wills

The first black female Naval Officers Frances Wills and Harriet Pickens were commissioned as officers in the United States Navy on December 21, 1944. They graduated from the Naval Reserve Midshipmen's School (WR) at Northampton, MA. Pickens, born in Talladega, AL, a public health specialist, graduated cum laude from Smith College in 1930 and from Columbia University with a master's degree in Political Science. Her father, William Pickens, a founder of the National Association for the Advancement of Colored People, urged her to join. Frances Eliza Wills was a native of Philadelphia but later lived in New York. She was a Hunter College graduate who had worked with famed African American poet Langston Hughes while pursuing her MA in Social Work at the University of Pittsburgh. She then worked at an adoption agency. Francis Wills Thorpe (her married name)

attended and graduated from Mount Holyoke College in 1958 with a B.A. in economics and sociology. She completed her M.D. in 1962 from Meharry Medical College in Nashville, Tennessee. In 1998, Dr. Johnson-Powell established an endowed lectureship at Mount Holyoke in honor of her mother.

Sophia Hayden

(1868 – 1953) was an American architect and first female graduate of the four-year program in architecture at Massachusetts Institute of Technology. She graduated from MIT in 1890 with a degree in architecture with honors. Sophia Gregoria Hayden was born in Santiago, Chile. Her mother, Elezena Fernandez, was from Chile, and her father, George Henry Hayden, was an American dentist from Boston.

Rosemary Jackson

Rosemary Jackson, from Springfield, MA was a 1961 graduate of Bay Path College (now Bay Path University). She was the first Black Executive Secretary at the Travelers Insurance Company (Hartford, CT) and the first Black

Above: Harriet Ida Pickens (left) and Frances Wills (right)
Above center: Sophia Hayden
Above right: Rosemary Jackson (both photos)

also wrote a book, *Navy Blue and Other Colors*, which was about her experiences as a pioneering naval officer.

Chief Yeoman Edna Young

one of the first enlisted women sworn into the regular Navy During World War II, Edna Young joined the WAVES. By the war's end on Sept. 2, 1945, 70 enlisted Black WAVES joined Pickens and Wills. One of them, Chief Yeoman Edna Young became one of the first enlisted women sworn into the regular Navy on June 6, 1948. Her assignments included tours of duty at Pearl Harbor (Hawaii) and Paris, France (Shape headquarters) – which were also firsts for a black woman. She served her country proudly for more than 22 years. She retired in 1967 after attaining the rank of Chief Petty Officer. Edna Young was once a resident of Springfield, MA and lived on Hancock Street. She was married to U.S.Navy Chief Petty Officer William L. Shannon for 41 years.

FROM GOVERNMENT TO POLITICS

Shirley Chisholm

Shirley Chisholm, in 1972, became the first Black and first official woman candidate from a major party to run for the President of the United States. Chisholm came 100 years after Victoria Woodhull, a white woman who ran in 1872 – 50 years before women could vote. She was technically the first female nominee for President in 1872, but no votes were recorded and her age, at 34, precluded her from holding office. In 1968, Shirley Chisholm became the first Black woman elected to the United States Congress, and she represented New York's 12th Congressional District for seven terms from 1969 to 1983. Shirley Chisholm made her home in suburban Williamsville, New York. She later resumed her career in education and taught at Mount Holyoke College in Massachusetts.

At Mount Holyoke, she taught politics and sociology from 1983 to 1987. She focused on undergraduate courses that covered politics as it involved women and race.

Angela Davis

Born in 1944, Angela Davis was raised in Birmingham, Alabama. In 1961, she entered Brandeis University (Waltham, MA) on a full scholarship. She later became a political activist and master scholar who studied at the Sorbonne in Paris, France.

In her youth, Davis was an active member of her church youth group. As part of the Girl Scouts, she not only earned many badges and certificates but also participated in activities to protest racial segregation in Birmingham. Davis, as a high school junior, won acceptance as part of the American Friends Service Committee (Quaker) program which took

SHIRLEY CHISHOLM for PRESIDENT

UNBOUGHT   UNBOSSED

1972

Top left: Edna Young
Top right: Shirley Chisholm
Bottom right: Angela Davis

College where she became a member of the Combahee River Collective, a Black feminist organization, which inspired her to write prose and poetry.

RELIGION

Jarena Lee

In 1819, in an age when women were prohibited by social and religious customs from preaching, Jarena Lee became the first woman to be authorized to preach by Richard Allen, founder of the African Methodist Episcopal Church. In 1833, the publishing of her autobiography made Lee the first African American woman to have an autobiography published in the United States.

She has been compared to influential African American women of her time, such as Maria W. Stewart and Sojourner Truth.

Pastor Dr. Elouise Franklin

A visionary leader of faith "I will take the ridicule, rebukes and scorn, so that the door can be opened for women in the ministry and so that future generations can walk through the door. She believed that if God could use a man, God could certainly use a woman." Pastor Dr. Elouise Franklin. Pastor Dr. Elouise Franklin (1913 - 1986) was the pastor of the New Hope Church of God in Christ in Springfield MA and Mother E. Franklin Temple Church of God in Christ in Holyoke, MA, a Pentecostal Holiness Christian denomination. In one of her most powerful sermons, she proclaimed: "God sent me to free the woman – now go and do the work God has commissioned you to do." Dr. Franklin was concerned about and worked tirelessly for the social and spiritual welfare of her community. She would work with probation officers, lawyers, judges, and doctors, to help people who had lost all hope by offering a renewed spirit of hope. Hers was a ministry that changed lives for the better through the

African Americans from the South and enrolled them in integrated schools in the North. Davis attended Elisabeth Irwin High School in New York City's Greenwich Village.

Chirlane Irene McCray

First Lady of NYC Chirlane Irene McCray (born in 1954) is a writer, editor, communications professional, and political figure. She has published poetry and worked in politics as a speechwriter. Married to current New York City Mayor Bill de Blasio, she is the First Lady of New York City. She recently launched "NYC Well" is a one-click, onecall connection to counseling, crisis intervention, peer support and referrals to ongoing treatment services serving all five boroughs. McCray was born in Springfield, MA and moved to Longmeadow, MA in 1964. She attended Longmeadow High. In 1972, McCray attended Wellesley

power of Jesus Christ. In her early years in the ministry, she worked in the field as a national and international evangelist as well as a state supervisor for the Women's Department of the Church of God in Christ. She supervised missionary activities in Connecticut, Massachusetts (Second Jurisdiction), New Hampshire and Montreal, Canada. After the death of her husband, Bishop C.W. Franklin, she took the lead as pastor of both churches. At that time, the position of pastor was traditionally held by a man. Pastor Dr. Franklin successfully directed both churches for 20 years. She was a woman before her time – a woman of vision and true trailblazer who broke barriers for other women alongside men who were called to serve. Pastor Dr. Elouise Franklin left a legacy of love.

MATH AND SCIENCE

Evelyn Boyd Granville
Mathematican Evelyn Boyd Granville was born in Washington, D.C. and later became the valedictorian at historic Dunbar High School, which was founded in 1870, as the first public high school for African-Americans in the United States of America. Boyd graduated and entered Smith College in the fall of 1941. She majored in mathematics and physics and was elected to Phi Beta Kappa and Sigma Xi and graduated summa cum laude in 1945. She worked for the U.S. Space Technology Laboratories. Then, in 1962, she worked for the North American Aviation Space and Information Systems Division. While there, she worked on various projects for the Apollo program, including celestial mechanics, trajectory computation, and "digital computer techniques." In 1989, Granville was awarded an honorary doctorate by Smith College. It was the first one given by an American institution to an African-American woman mathematician.

Shirley Ann Jackson
Shirley Ann Jackson (born 1946) is an American physicist and the eighteenth president of Rensselaer Polytechnic Institute. She is the first African-American woman to have earned a doctorate at the Massachusetts Institute of Technology (MIT). Jackson is the second African-American woman in the United States to receive a doctorate in physics.

Dorothy Phillips
Dorothy J. Phillips, Ph.D. recently retired from the Waters Corporation in Milford, Mass. She is a director-at-large for the American Chemical Society (ACS), the world's largest scientific society. Phillips received her B.A. from

Top: Shirley Ann Jackson
At right: Evelyn Boyd Granville

Vanderbilt University and her Ph.D. from the University of Cincinnati. Phillips was the first African-American woman to earn a B.A. degree from Vanderbilt University School of Arts & Sciences and a Ph.D. in biochemistry from the University of Cincinnati. In 2015, Vanderbilt established the Dr. Dorothy J. Wingfield Phillips Endowed Chair to advance research, education, and diversity in the STEM (science, technology, engineering and math) fields.

MUSIC, ARTS AND ACTIVISM

Coretta Scott King

Coretta Scott King met Martin Luther King Jr. while the two were both students in Boston, Massachusetts. In 1954, Coretta earned her college degree at New England Conservatory of Music (Boston) – specializing in voice and violin. She would later marry Martin Luther King Jr. and became a noted community leader in her own right. As Martin Luther King Jr.'s wife, she helped lead the civil rights movement in the 1960s. After her husband's assassination in 1968, Coretta fought hard to establish the Martin Luther King Jr. Holiday – a federal holiday first celebrated in 1986. Coretta Scott King once said in a speech during the National LGBTQ Task Force conference in Atlanta in 2000:

"We have a lot more work to do in our common struggle against bigotry and discrimination. I say 'common struggle' because I believe very strongly that all forms of bigotry and discrimination are equally wrong and should be opposed by right-thinking Americans everywhere. "

Joan Chandos Baez

Joan Chandos Baez (born 1941) of Mexican and Scottish heritage, is an American folk singer, songwriter, musician, and activist whose contemporary folk music often includes songs of protest or social justice. In 1958, her father became part of the MIT faculty MIT and moved his family to Massachusetts. He was later credited as a co-inventor of the x-ray microscope. Once in Massachusetts, Baez began performing near her home in Boston and nearby Cambridge. She also played in clubs, and attended Boston University for about six weeks. In 1958, Baez first performed at the Club 47 in Cambridge, MA. Over the course of her career, Baez has released over 30 albums. In 1980, Baez was given an honorary Doctorates by Antioch University and Rutgers University. She has been noted for her political activism and the "universality of her music".

Meta Vaux Warrick Fuller

Meta Vaux Warrick Fuller (1877 – 1968) was an African-American sculptress who explored her craft in Paris before returning to the United States. Fuller's work often captured created the social commentary of the time. For example, her sculpture of Mary Turner focused on the story of a young, pregnant black woman who was lynched in Georgia in 1918 one day after protesting the lynching of her husband. Warrick preceded the Harlem Renaissance, a movement among African Americans promoting their literature and art. In 1907, Warrick married a prominent physician, Dr. Solomon Carter Fuller, of Liberian heritage, who was one of the first Black psychiatrists in the United States. When they married, he was on staff in the pathology department at Westborough State Hospital in Westborough, Massachusetts. The couple settled in Framingham, Massachusetts.

EXPLORERS

Betty Stringfield

Born in 1911, Bessie Stringfield was known as 'The Motorcycle Queen of Miami.' Born in Kingston, Jamaica, she later moved to Boston Massachusetts. Following the death of her parents, she was adopted by an Irish woman. She taught herself how to ride a motorcycle at age 16 and by age 19, she traveled across the U.S. via motorcycle. She was the first African-American woman to ride 'solo' across the United States via motorcycle. During World War II, she served as one of the few motorcycle dispatch riders for the United States military. She also earned money from performing motorcycle stunts in carnival shows. She has been noted by the Motorcycle Hall of Fame and the American Motorcyclist Association (AMA) for her achievements.

Willa Brown

Born in 1906, Willa Beatrice Brown was teacher and aviator who actively lobbied for civil and women's rights. Her achievements included many 'firsts', including being the first African-American woman to earn her pilot's license in the United States, the first African-American woman to run for the United States Congress, the first African-American officer in

(Opposite page) **Left:** Coretta Scott King. **Right:** Dorothy Phillips
Top left: Joan Chandos Baez
Right: Meta Vaux Warrick Fuller
Bottom left: Betty Stringfield

Above: Crystal Y. Brown Battle
Center: Willa Brown
Right: Elizabeth Hobbs Keckley

the US Civil Air Patrol, and the first woman in the United States to have both a pilot's license and a mechanic's license. She not only lobbied the U.S. government to integrate the U.S. Army Air Corp and include African Americans in the Civilian Pilot Training Program (CPTP), but also co-founded the Cornelius Coffey School of Aeronautics with Cornelius Coffey, which was the first private flight training academy in the United States owned and operated by African Americans. She trained hundreds of pilots, several of whom would go on to become Tuskegee Airmen.

Crystal Y. Brown Battle

Born in New York City, Crystal Y. Brown Battle has lived in various cities across the U.S. from California to Massachusetts. Travel is the norm for Brown-Battle considering her high school years in the Washington, DC area, to college at Penn State in Pennsylvania, and graduate school in Boston at Simmons College. Crystal Brown Battle is a modern-day travel enthusiast and global trekker. She has made it her love and priority to explore every continent in the world before the age of 35. She has recently published "If Passports Could Talk," a book that depicts her travel adventures. Crystal's desire for travel can be traced back to her grandmother, Harriett, a librarian and inveterate traveler who visited many places in the U.S. as well as four continents.

WITH HER STELLAR WORK, [RUTH CARTER] RECEIVED TWO ACADEMY AWARD NOMINATIONS FOR BEST COSTUME DESIGN FOR SPIKE LEE'S "MALCOLM X" IN 1993 AND STEVEN SPIELBERG'S "AMISTAD" IN 1998. ALSO, SHE CREATED THE LOOK FOR GABRIELLE UNION IN "BEING MARY JANE."

FASHION

Elizabeth Hobbs Keckley

Former slave Elizabeth Hobbs Keckley, who was born in 1818, became a successful seamstress who also authored a book as well as fought for civil rights. She was best known as the personal modiste and confidante of Mary Todd Lincoln, the First Lady. Keckley bought her and her son's freedom. She created a fashion business and serviced an elite clientele. Among them were Varina Davis, wife of Jefferson Davis; and Mary Anna Custis Lee, wife of Robert E. Lee. Some of her fashions are held at the Smithsonian.

Ann Cole Lowe

Ann Cole Lowe, born 1898, was an American fashion designer and the first African American to become a noted fashion designer over many decades from 1920-1960. In 1953, Lowe designed the ivory silk taffeta wedding dress worn by Jacqueline Bouvier as she married Senator John F. Kennedy. From Clayton, Alabama, Lowe is the great-granddaughter of a slave woman and an Alabama, plantation owner. All generations of the family were seamstresses.

Above: Ruth Carter
Right: Ann Cole Lowe

Ruth E. Carter

Ruth Carter, from Springfield, MA, is a 1982 graduate of Hampton University's Department of Fine and Performing Arts where she majored in Theatre Arts. She has worked in the entertainment industry for over three decades. Carter was first African-American costume designer to be nominated for an Academy Award. She has worked on several pivotal films: Spike Lee's "Do the Right Thing," "The Butler," "Selma," "Roots" and Marvel's "Black Panther." With her stellar work, she received two Academy Award nominations for Best Costume Design for Spike Lee's "Malcolm X" in 1993 and Steven Spielberg's "Amistad" in 1998. Also, she created the look for Gabrielle Union in "Being Mary Jane."

The Global School®

WILBRAHAM & MONSON ACADEMY

ESTABLISHED 1804

WILBRAHAM & MONSON ACADEMY

The Global School®

Wilbraham & Monson Academy in Wilbraham, Massachusetts, was founded in 1971 with the merger of two historically significant institutions of learning – Monson Academy andWilbraham Academy (formerly Wesleyan Academy). Both schools – Monson Academy, founded in 1804, and Wesleyan Academy (1817) – were created as coeducational academies. Throughout its first century, Wesleyan had an enrollment of approximately one-third female students, an unusually high percentage for the times. Many of the young women who attended Wesleyan contributed extraordinarily to the world as notable alumnae, while a young teacher at Monson Academy in the early 20th century became the first female cabinet member in the United States, an integral part of drafting the New Deal as Secretary of Labor under President Franklin Roosevelt. Although both Monson Academy and Wilbraham Academy closed briefly in the early 20th century due to financial constraints and reopened as male-only academies, male and female boarding and day students were brought together again with the merger of the two institutions into Wilbraham & Monson Academy in 1971. Today's Academy is proudly more than 40 percent female.

Mabel R. Welch
BORN: NEW HAVEN, CONN.; 1871-1959
ATTENDED 1884-1888

Mabel Rose Welch was an American painter of portrait miniatures and landscapes. Welch attended Wesleyan Academy from 1884 to 1888. She then studied at the Art Student's League of New York. Welch moved to Paris for further study, showing her work at the Paris Salon. During her career, she was a recipient of the Levantia White Boardman Memorial Medal; she was a member of the Pennsylvania Society of Miniature Painters, the Woman's Art Club and Art Workers Club. Among her awards were the Medal of Honor of the Pennsylvania Society of Miniature Painters and a silver medal from the Panama-Pacific International Exposition. This award-winning artist's works are held in the collection of The Metropolitan Museum of Fine Arts, Corcoran Gallery in Washington D.C., Brooklyn Museum and the Pennsylvania Museum of Fine Arts.

Mary Ann Allard Booth
BORN: LONGMEADOW, MASS.; 1843-1922
ATTENDED 1857-1859

Mary Ann Allard Booth was a woman ahead of her time. An 1859 Wesleyan Academy graduate, she became one of the early 20th century's leading women scientists and a pioneer in the field of microscopic photography. In 1917, Collier's Weekly acclaimed Miss Booth as one of the world's seven most illustrious women scientists. Elected as one of the first female fellows of the Royal Microscopical Society in 1889, Booth was also a fellow of the American Association for the Advancement of Science. Noted for her preparation of diatoms and pollens, Booth earned a Diploma of Honor in Entomology at the 1884-1885 New Orleans World's Industrial and Cotton Centennial Exposition. In 1901, Booth bought a steam automobile and became the first woman (and second person) in Springfield, MA to own and drive a motor car.

Christine Ladd-Franklin

BORN: WINDSOR, CONN.; 1847-1930
ATTENDED 1863-1865

Christine Ladd-Franklin was Wesleyan Academy's class valedictorian, who specialized in mathematics, psychology and logic. She was the first woman to complete all of the requirements for a Ph.D. from Johns Hopkins University. In 1929, she published "Color and Color Theories," which featured articles and papers she published throughout the previous four decades. Christine's interest in this area began with a study of the horopter in 1886. The innovator and feminist also published books, as well as several papers in the American Journal of Mathematics.

Chloe Clark Willson

BORN: EAST WINDSOR, CONN.; 1818-1874
ATTENDED 1837-1839

Chloe Clark Willson received her academic training at Wesleyan Academy, a seminary that specialized in training Methodist missionaries for service around the world. In 1839, Chloe joined fellow Methodists on the ship "Lausanne," traveling to what was to become the Oregon Territory. Chloe was 21, 4 feet, 10 inches tall and unmarried. Chloe soon married Dr. William Willson and began work teaching in Puget Sound and Willamette Falls. In 1844, the Willsons moved to Willamette Valley, where Chloe became the first and only teacher at the Oregon Institute (subsequently named Willamette University).

Frances Perkins

BORN: BOSTON, MASS.; 1880-1965
TAUGHT AT MONSON ACADEMY, 1903-1904

As Secretary of Labor throughout President Franklin Roosevelt's four terms and the first woman to hold a cabinet position, Frances Perkins designed most of The New Deal social welfare and labor policies, such as Social Security, the minimum wage, the Fair Labor

Ladd-Franklin's Theory of Colour Perception

- Evolutionary-based theory
  - Stage 1: vision sensitive only to achromatic colours ranging from white to black
    - Rods represent the earliest stage of the development of vision
  - Stage 2: emergence of cones sensitive to yellow and blue
  - Stage 3: some of the cones sensitive to yellow undergo a further specialization to become cones sensitive to red and green
- Evidence for her theory comes from the study of colour blindness
  - Studied people unable to see red and green but able to see yellow and blue
  - Law of progressions and pathologies: the last system to evolve is the first to show effects of degeneration

Above: Christine Ladd-Franklin
Right: Chloe Clark Willson

THE CHLOE CLARK
EXPLORER'S PLEDGE

Today, I will be the best I can be.
I will believe in myself.
I will be responsible.
I will help my friends, my school, and my family.
I will be an Explorer!
I'm proud of who I am and who I'm becoming.

Standards Act and protections for unions. She was the only woman present when President Franklin Roosevelt signed the Social Security Act. The sociologist and worker's rights advocate was featured on cover of *TIME Magazine* in August 1933.

Lucy Stone
BORN: WEST BROOKFIELD, MASS.; 1818-1893
ATTENDED: 1839-1841
Lucy Stone was an abolitionist, suffragist, acclaimed speaker and women's rights activist. She organized the State Woman's Suffrage Association of New Jersey, and was elected its first president. Stone also launched a New England chapter of this association and helped found the American Equal Rights Association. In 1850, Stone convened the first women's rights convention held in Worcester, Mass. Lucy also founded The American Woman Suffrage Association in 1869, and was the founder and editor of the *Woman's Journal of Boston*, a paper dedicated to women's rights.

Special thanks to Wilbraham & Monson Academy faculty member Gary Cook for his research; LuJuana Hood, executive director of Pan African Historical Museum USA, for always connecting the dots; and posthumously to Coralie Gray, former WMA librarian. Project and archives coordinated by Janet Moran, Director of Archives at WMA in conjunction with the Marketing & Communications department.

Above: Frances Perkins
Right: Lucy Stone

APPENDIX I
awards & honors

Women William Pynchon Award Winners

YEAR	NAME
1922	Mary Ann Booth
1928	Lucy Walker Mallary
1932	Maude Irving (Tait) Moriarity
1939	Ida F. Farrar
1941	Grace Pettis Johnson
1943	Margaret C. Ells
1945	Hazel (Clark) Steiger
1948	Alice I. Halligan
1950	Sally Leeds
1951	Cordelia S. Pond
1959	Mary J. Foley
1975	Kitty F. Broman
1977	Mary H. Weckwerth
1981	Joan F. Putnam
1982	Rita M. Tremble
1983	Emma M. Wilder Anderson
1983	Sister Mary Caritas
1991	Anne V. Cooley
1991	Helen (Smith) "Bunny" Fuller
1993	Sister Mary A. Dooley

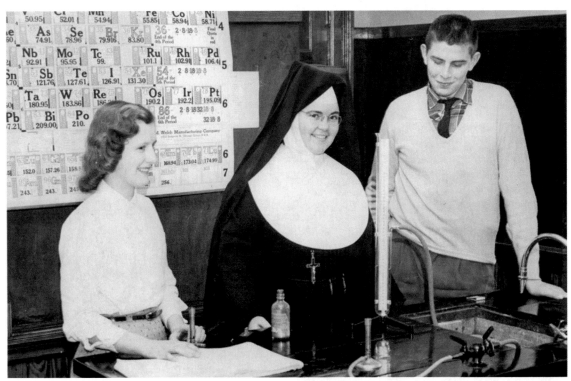

Previous page: Kitty F. Broman

Above: Sister Mary Dooley
Far right: Carol W. Kinsley
Right: Frances Gagnon

(Opposite page) Top left: Brenca Lopez
Bottom left: Anne V. Cooley
Right: Lucy M. Carvalho

(Opposite page) **Top left:** Diane Doherty
Bottom left: Marie M. Stebbins
Bottom center: Jean F. Gailun
Right: Mary Pat McMahon

Top left: Joan Kagan
Bottom left: Kathy Picard
Top right: Jean C. Caldwell interviewing Sen. Ted Kennedy (editor Wayne E. Phaneuf is seen on far left)

1993	Barbara Rivera
1994	Harriet Michaels
1998	Frances Gagnon
2000	Sister Jane Morrissey
2001	Janee Armstrong Friedmann
2003	Carol W. Kinsley
2004	Lucia M. (Guiggio) Carvalho
2006	Brenda J. Lopez
2007	Dr. Carol A. Leary
2008	Diane Fuller Doherty
2009	Susan R. Jaye-Kaplan
2009	Marie M. Stebbins
2010	Barbara C. Bernard
2010	Mary Reardon Johnson
2011	Mary Pat McMahon
2012	Ellen Freyman
2013	Jean C. Caldwell
2013	Jean E. Gailun
2013	Joan Kagan
2014	Kathy J. Picard
2015	Donna Johnson
2015	Sue Ellen Panitch
2016	Michaelann Bewsee
2016	Gale Kirkwood
2016	Angela Wright
2018	Craig Carr
2018	Sally Fuller

Women Visions Community (Worcester) Award Honorees

1951	Mrs. J. Herbert Johnson
1989	Anne M. Morgan
1993	Lois B. Green
2009	Kay Bassett
2010	Mary C. Streeter De Feudis
2011	Dr. Martha Pappas

Top left: Donna Johnson, **Top right:** Gale Kirkwood, **Bottom left:** Michaelann Bewsee, **Bottom right:** Sue Ellen Panitch

Women Visions Citizen of the Year Honoree

1993.....................Annette A. Rafferty

Women Visions Public Service Award Honorees

1994.....................Joan M. Merrill, Ed.D.

1996.....................Roberta R. Schaefer

1998.....................Cynthia M. McMullen, Ed.D.

2001.....................Penelope B. Johnson

2002.....................Magdalen Bish

2004.....................Mary S. Keefe

2007.....................Women Together/
                      Mujeres Unidas

2008.....................Josefina Valez

2009.....................Jean McMurray, *Worcester
                      County Food Bank*

2011.....................Deborah Cary, *Mass
Audubon's Broad Meadow Brook Wildlife
Sanctuary and Conservation Center*

Women and Women-related Visions Cultural Enrichment (Worcester) Award Honorees

1993.....................Virginia Byrne

1995.....................Sima Kustanovich

1997.....................Elizabeth Bishop
*Conference & Poetry Festival, Worcester
County Poetry Association*

1998.....................Stasia B. Hovenesian,
*Hispanics Achieving and Celebrating
Excellence Committee*

2000.....................Worcester Women's History
                      Project

2007.....................Gloria Hall

William G. Dwight Distinguished Service to Holyoke Award: Women Awardees

2017.....................Barbara C. Bernard

2016.....................Helene Alderman Florio

2014.....................Betty Medina-Lichtenstein

2013.....................Doris Ransford

2012.....................Deborah Buckley

2003.....................Clare R. Rigali

2002.....................Sue Ellen Panitch

2000.....................Margaret F. Woods

1998.....................Maril O'Malley

1991.....................Joan Steiger

1985.....................Angela Wright

1980.....................Edna E. Williams

1979.....................Adeline Barowsky

1978.....................Marcelle M. Burgee

1976.....................Alice Childs

1969.....................Lois B. Falcetti

1964.....................Mrs. Donald P. Cooke

1962.....................Dorothy N. Franz

1961.....................Mrs. Richard Weiser

1958.....................Mrs. John N. Hazen

1952.....................Harriet Heywood

1951.....................Esther M. Greeley

1946.....................Frances Frederick

Ubora Award:

Initiated by Dr. Ruth S. Njiiri and the African Hall Subcommittee of the Springfield Science Museum, Springfield Museums Association in 1992, the Ubora Award is awarded annually to an African-American in the Greater Springfield area "who has demonstrated a dedicated commitment to the Community. Ubora is the Swahili word for "excellence."

1994.....................Jeanne Bass

1996.....................Bettye Webb

1998.....................Josephine Edmunds

Above: Dr. Ruth S. Njiiri

2002.....................Barbara Jefferson

2004.....................Barbara Lanier

2006.....................Janet Troutman-Simmons

2007.....................Denise R. Jordan

2008.....................Allyson Gouzounis

2010.....................Zelman "Zee" Johnson

2011.....................Gerry Garner

2013.....................Katie Glasgow

2016.....................Helen Caulton-Harris

Miss Massachusetts
(Winners from Western and Central MA)

1954 ... Nan Cowan, Sterling

1955 .... Jean Dernago, Springfield

1987 ... Rosanna Iversen, Great Barrington

1995 .... Kristen Mastroianni, Wilbraham

2000 .. Rosalie M. Allain, Leominster

2011 ..... Alida D'Angona, Bolton

2013 .... Sarah Kidd of Leominster

2015 .... Polikseni Manxhari of Holden

"Black Women of Excellence 2018" Awards, Urban League of Springfield

Ruth E. Carter
of Springfield: Academy Award nominated costume designer.

Dr. Shirley J. Whitaker, M.D.
Nephrology specialist, Baystate Health, Springfield, MA

Pia Flanagan, J.D.
MassMutual Corporate Secretary, and Chief of Staff to President Roger W. Crandall.

Adrienne Smith, M.S., Ed.D.
Dean of Engineering and Technologies, Springfield Technical Community College, Springfield, MA

Tania Barber, MBA
President and CEO, Caring Health Center, Springfield, MA.

Dr. Tashanna Myers, M.D.
Gynecological oncologist, Baystate Health, Springfield, MA.

Enku Gelaye, J.D.
Vice Chancellor for Student Affairs, UMass, Amherst, MA.

Anika Gaskins
Vice President of Regional and National Marketing, MGM Springfield.

Sheila Goodwin, MBA
Senior Vice President, PeoplesBank

Paulette Henderson, BA
Funeral director and owner, Henderson Funeral Home, Springfield, MA

Cheryl Stanley, Ed.D.
Dean of Education, Westfield State University, Westfield, MA.

Jessica Henderson
Lieutenant, Springfield Police Department, Springfield, MA.

Yvette Frisby, MA
Senior vice president, Urban League of Springfield, Inc., Springfield, MA.

Shadae Thomas-Harris, ED LD
Springfield (MA) Public Schools principal, Harvard University teaching fellow.

Helen Caulton-Harris, RN
Commissioner, Health and Human Services, City of Springfield, MA

Massachusetts Cultural Council– Commonwealth Awards

1993 .... Jane P. Fitzpatrick, Stockbridge, MA

1997 .... Marge Champion, Berkshire County, MA

1999 .... Tina Packer, Lenox, MA

2001 .... Lynn Margulis, Amherst, MA

2011 .... Nancy Jane Fitzpatrick, Stockbridge, MA

Women of Western and Central Massachusetts inducted into the National Women's Hall of Fame in Seneca Falls, NY

Susan B. Anthony

Clara Barton

Emily Dickinson

Dorothea Dix

Abby Kelley Foster

Ella Grasso

Frances Perkins

Sophia Smith

Nettie Stevens

Lucy Stone

Anne Sullivan

Sojourner Truth

Edith Wharton

APPENDIX II

historical articles

published by the Historical Journal of Massachusetts and the New England Quarterly

"Esther Forbes's Rainbow on the Road: Portrait of the Nineteenth Century Provincial Artist," by Kent P. Ljunqquist (Vol. 38. Spring 2010)

"The Allen Sisters: 'Foremost Women Photographers in America'(1880-1915)," by Suzanne L. Flynt (Vol. 37, Fall 2009)

"Mr. and Mrs. Prince: An African American Courtship and Marriage in Colonial Deerfield," by Gretchen Holbrook Gerzina (Vol. 37, Fall 2009)

"Mrs. Elizabeth Towne: Pioneering Woman in Publishing and Politics, 1865-1960," by Tzivia Gover (Vol. 37, Spring 2009)

"Addie Card: The Search for Lewis Hine's 'Anemic Little Spinner'," by Joe Manning (Vol. 36, Summer 2008)

"Anna B. Sullivan, 1903-1983: The Formative Years of a Textile Union Organizer (Holyoke, Massachusetts)," by L. Mara Dodge (Vol. 36, Winter 2008)

"The Enigma of Mount Holyoke's Nellie Neilson (1873-1947)," by Gerald Vaughn (Vol. 28, Summer 2000)

"The Ecstasy of Sara Prentice: Death, Re-Birth, and the Great Awakening in Grafton, Massachusetts," by Ross Beales (Vol. 26, Summer of 1997)

"School Suffrage and the Campaign for Women's Suffrage in Massachusetts, 1879-1920," by Edmund Thomas (Vol. 25, Winter 1997)

"The Tatnuck Ladies' Sewing Circle: A Forum for Women's Political Views in Worcester Massachusetts, 1847-1867," by Laura Wasowics (Vol. 24, Winter 1996)

"Nursing in Massachusetts During the Roaring Twenties," by Mary Ellen Donna, Joellen Hawkins, Ursula Van Ryzin, Alive Friedman, Loretta Higgins (Vol. 23, Summer 1995)

"'As if a Great Darkness': Native American Refugees of the Middle Connecticut River Valley in the Aftermath of King Philip's War," by James Spady (Vol. 23, Summer 1995)

"Women at Work: Views and Visions from the Pioneer Valley, 1870-1945," by Donna S. Kenny (Vol. 13, January 1985)

"Bread and Roses: The Proletarianization of Women Workers in New England Textile Mills, 1837-1848," by Laurie Nisonoff (Vol. 9, January 1981)

"The Massachusetts Suffrage Referendum of 1915," by Robert Granfield (Vol. 7, January 1979)

"Witchcraft in Early Springfield: The Parsons Case," by Christine Wrona (Vol. 6, Fall 1977)

"Rural Medical Practice in Early 19th Century New England," by Joseph Carvalho III (Vol. 4, Spring 1975)

"Housing in Holyoke and its Effect on Family Life, 1860-1910," by Paul N. Dubovik (Vol. 4, Spring 1975)

"Marriage Customs in Colonial New England," by Irene Ktorides (Vol. 2, Fall 1973)

Articles about Women from Western and Central Massachusetts in The New England Quarterly

"Mistress of Her Art: Anne Laura Clarke, Traveling Lecturer of the 1820s," by Granville Ganter (Dec. 2014)

"Sisters in Arms: Incest, Miscegenation, and Sacrifice in Catharine Maria Sedgwick's Hope Leslie," by Erica Burleigh (June 2013)

"Thinking Musically, Writing Expectantly: New Biographical Information about Emily Dickinson," by Carol Damon Andrews (June 2008)

"Martha Dickinson Bianchi: War Poet," by Marcy L. Tanter (June 2007)

"Publishing the Cause of Suffrage: The Woman's Journal's Appropriation of Ralph Waldo Emerson in Postbellum America," by Todd H. Richardson (Dec. 2006)

"'Have We Not a Hymn?' Dickinson and the Rhetoric of New England Revivalism," by Daniel L. Manheim (Sept. 2005)

"Catharine Sedgwick's Cosmopolitan Nation," by Philip Gould (June 2005)

"A Mother and Her Daughters at the Northampton Community: New Evidence on Women in Utopia," by Christopher Clark (Dec. 2002)

"Reading and Writing 'Hope Leslie': Catharine Maria Sedgwick's Indian 'Connections'," by Karen Woods Weierman (Sept. 2002)

"Seventeen Eighty-Three: The Turning Point in the Law of Slavery and Freedom in Massachusetts," by Emily Blanck (Mar. 2002)

APPENDIX III
women in bronze

by Joseph Carvalho III & Wayne E. Phaneuf

Susan B. Anthony bronzes:

Susan B. Anthony having tea with Frederick Douglass, outside the Susan B. Anthony historic home in Rochester, N.Y. sculpted by Pepsy Kettavong and installed in 2001.

"When Anthony met Stanton" statue depicts when Amelia Bloomer introduced Susan B.

Anthony to Elizabeth Cady Stanton In May 1851. Sculpted by Ted Aub, located at the Women's Rights National Historical Park, National Park Service, Seneca Falls, N.Y.

Marble Monument to Elizabeth Cady Stanton, Susan B. Anthony, and Lucretia Mott sculpted by Adelaide Johnson and gifted to the United States on Feb. 10, 1921 by the National Woman's

Party. The marble "portraits" are copies of the individual busts Adelaide Johnson carved for the Court of Honor of the Women's Building at the World's Columbian Exhibition in 1893. The group sculpture created by Johnson was unveiled at the Capitol Rotunda in Washington, D.C. on Feb. 21, 1921 attended by representatives of over 70 women's organizations.

Clara Barton bust at Red Cross Visitors, History and Education Center, Red Cross Square, Washington, D.C. (photo courtesy Rudi Williams, U.S. Dept. of Defense)

Nurses Memorial with Statue of Clara Barton tending to a wounded soldier, Massachusetts State House, Boston, MA.

Dorothea Dix bronze bas relief sculpted by Sheila Levrant de Bretteville and Susan Sellers, part of the Activist Women and Legal wallpaper at the Massachusetts State House, Boston, MA, sponsored by Mass Humanities in 1999.

Lucy Stone statue, by sculptor Meredith Bergmann part of the Boston Women's Memorial, Commonwealth Avenue Mall, Boston, MA, dedicated Oct. 25, 2003.

Lucy Stone bas relief sculpted by Sheila Levrant de Bretteville and Susan Sellers, part of the Activist Women and Legal wallpaper at the Massachusetts State House, Boston, MA, sponsored by the Mass Humanities in 1999.

Sojourner Truth statue, created by Thomas Jay Warren was a gift from the sculptor to the City of Northampton. The statue was installed in Sojourner Truth Memorial Park in 2002.

(Opposite page) Susan B Anthony and Frederick Douglass having tea, statue in Rochester, NY
Above left: Susan B. Anthony statue at Amelia Park in Westfield, MA
Above right: Bust of Clara Barton at Red Cross headquarters   **Right:** Statue of Lucy Stone

Anne Sullivan sitting with Helen Keller, created by Mico Kaufman captures the moment Anne Sullivan successfully teaches Helen Keller her first word – "water." The statue was dedicated on June 28, 1992.

Deborah Sampson statue in Sharon, MA, Lu Stubbs, Sculptor.

TO THE ARMY NURSES
FROM 1861 TO 1865
ANGELS OF MERCY AND LIFE
AMID SCENES OF CONFLICT AND DEATH
A TRIBUTE OF HONOR AND GRATITUDE
FROM THE MASSACHUSETTS DEPARTMENT
DAUGHTERS OF VETERANS

(Opposite page) **Far left:** Statue of Deborah Samson. **Top right:** Nurse statue at the Massachusetts State House. **Bottom center:** Statue of Sojourner Truth outside of the Northampton Chamber of Commerce. **Bottom right:** Sojourner Truth Monument in Battle Creek, Michigan in July 2010.
Above: Statue of Anne Sullivan and Helen Keller

APPENDIX IIII

Women from Western and Central Massachusetts on U.S. Stamps

(Images courtesy U.S. Postal Service)

THANK YOU

The Power of Women
SPONSORS

GOLD:

Baystate Health, Pride

BRONZE:

Bay Path University, Elms College, Springfield Museums

COMMUNITY PROFILE:

104th Fighter Wing, Barnes Air National Guard Base, Behavioral Health Network, Inc., Big Y World Class Markets, Bulkley, Richardson & Gelinas, Holyoke Medical Center, Health New England, Senator Eric P. Lesser, Massachusetts General Hospital, Mercy Medical Center, Congressman Richard E. Neal, New England Farm Workers' Council, PeoplesBank, The Republican, Springfield College, Springfield Regional Chamber of Commerce, Springfield Symphony Orchestra, VA Central Western Massachusetts Healthcare System, The Zonta Club of Springfield

BAYSTATE HEALTH

Since 1870

Baystate Health salutes the many women throughout western Massachusetts who have left an indelible mark on their communities and beyond.

Two women back in the 1800s, both facing resistance, went on to use their influence to change the course of modern medicine. Elizabeth Blackwell, MD, was considered the first woman doctor of medicine in modern times. Shortly after graduating from Geneva Medical College in New York, she met a young Florence Nightingale in London, who was about to defy her family by studying nursing and go on to become the founder of modern nursing.

Thanks to the pioneering efforts of these valiant trailblazers, women everywhere continue to play a central role in healthcare today. According to the Bureau of Labor Statistics, nearly 80% of workers in the healthcare and social assistance field are women. Baystate Health follows that trend with 77% of its workforce being female.

Both women and men at Baystate Health have been providing skilled and compassionate healthcare to the people of western Massachusetts for nearly 150 years. From its earliest beginnings when Springfield Hospital opened its doors, through the multi-hospital partnership that created the modern-day Baystate Medical Center in 1976, to today's ever expanding integrated healthcare system, Baystate Health has grown alongside the many communities it serves.

Today, Baystate Health continues to evolve with Baystate Medical Center recognized as a nationally-distinguished teaching hospital, a center for research, and the home of Springfield's first medical school campus, University of Massachusetts Medical School – Baystate. As the tertiary care referral center for the region, Baystate Medical Center offers a comprehensive range of medical services, including the only Level I trauma center for both adults and pediatric emergencies in western Massachusetts.

Baystate Health

baystatehealth.org

A LEGACY OF WOMEN IN HEALTHCARE

— Since 1870 —

Our mission is to improve the health of the people in our communities every day, with quality and compassion.

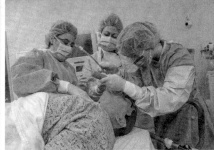

Baystate Health

baystatehealth.org

WELCOME TO PRIDE

Since 1917

Pride has always welcomed diversity and women of all ethnic groups. They have been, and continue to be, a major segment of Pride's workforce. Without these talented, friendly, hard-working, fun-loving women Pride would not enjoy the success that it does. We applaud them..

These numbers alone give some idea of the power of women at Pride.
64% of the senior management team are women.
57% of the middle management team are women.
59% of the store management team are women.
The influence and wisdom of women in the founder's family has always been evident. Each of them have been a major influence in the mission, principles, operations and image of the Pride chain..

Last but not least are our female customers. Pride appreciates their business, their loyalty, and their comments and suggestions over the years. We have adopted and implemented most of the ideas and requests of our female customers at all times. We welcome more. Welcome to Pride!

Pride
Stores & Kitchens

Clockwise from top right - Wilbraham Rd, Burnett Rd, East Longmeadow, Berkshire Ave, Chicopee St, Parker St

POWER OF WOMEN AT PRIDE

— Since 1917 —

Pride owes it's success to women! Beginning in the early days, founder Bob Bolduc relied on women to run the entire operation with him. Together Bob and two women originally worked on all aspects of the business, from managing the phones and staff, dispatching deliveries and schedules, and finally, keeping the books. They grew Pride from one full-service gas station into the large retail chain that we know today.

Throughout our history and into the Pride of today, the face of Pride at all levels has remained female. From store cashiers and managers to middle management and the corporate office, one sees mostly energetic, condent, professional women. Throughout these years women have played major roles in Pride's growth.

Corporate Office

BAY PATH UNIVERSITY

Since 1897

Founded in 1897 as the Bay Path Institute, the University's first location was in the heart of downtown Springfield at the corner of State and Dwight Streets. Students came from all parts of New England, often traveling by trolley or rail, to attend Bay Path's innovative and career-focused programs. For decades it experienced both educational and financial success, becoming one of the most respected and largest business schools in the northeast.

Today, Bay Path's main campus is in Longmeadow, Massachusetts and serves a global student population of over 3,200. A private, four-year women's university, Bay Path offers undergraduate degrees for traditional women, over 30 graduate and doctoral programs for women and men, and accelerated online degree programs for adult women through The American Women's College. The Strategic Alliance division builds on Bay Path's history of providing practical and relevant education, and partners with companies and organizations to offer customized learning experiences and programs.

The University is also a valued contributor to the Greater Springfield community through its Kaleidoscope arts and lecture series, student-led service projects, and the Women's Leadership Conference—an annual event that draws over 1,500 participants and has featured renowned speakers such as former U.S. Secretary of State Madeleine Albright, Maya Angelou, and Barbara Walters, to name a few.

All students, undergraduate and graduate alike, are encouraged to aspire to the University's motto, Carpe Diem—Seize the Day, and become lifelong learners who will have a positive impact on their lives, families, communities, and workplaces.

BAY PATH
UNIVERSITY

588 Longmeadow Street, Longmeadow, MA 01106
800.782.7284

Deepwood Hall, Bay Path University campus

COLLEGE OF OUR LADY OF THE ELMS

Since 1928

Elms College has a long history of women's empowerment, and has always recognized the power of women to do good in this world. In fact, the college was founded 90 years ago by a group of women who sought to empower others to build better lives for themselves, their families, and their communities.

Those women were the Sisters of St. Joseph of Springfield, Massachusetts, an order of nuns who saw a need in the local community for a college dedicated to providing an education rooted in fundamental justice while also welcoming the stranger, the immigrant, the poor, and those of all faiths.

Today, Elms College carries on that spirit by fostering a learning community committed to unity and social justice. The Elms community embraces and respects all people, cultures, and religions, as well as the planet, so that our graduates can effect positive change in our world.

Elms continuously works to add programs, update facilities, and improve access to services; to support all students in their academic and professional endeavors; and to encourage inquiry and reflection, strength of heart, and effective action.

Through undergraduate and graduate academic curricula steeped in social justice and advocacy, a tradition of scholarly excellence, and a variety of extracurricular opportunities in faith development, service, leadership, and community building, Elms College empowers its women and men to change this world for the better, just as the Sisters of St. Joseph have sought to do since their founding more than 350 years ago in France.

291 Springfield Street, Chicopee, MA 01013
www.elms.edu

THE SPRINGFIELD MUSEUMS

Since 1857

A well-established community anchor, the Springfield Museums have a long history of delivering exhibitions that expand visitors' worldview and encourage their curiosity, creativity, and sense of wonder and awe. Our mission since 1857 is to inspire exploration of our connections to art, history, and science through outstanding collections, exhibitions, and programs.

The extraordinary scope of the Springfield Museums' collections—nearly three million objects and documents—range from Chinese ceramics, American and European art, dinosaur fossils, Middle Eastern rugs, historic photographs and manuscripts, Medieval panel paintings, and Native American baskets to technological inventions that changed America. Our special exhibitions, augmented by our partnerships with organizations such as the Smithsonian, allow the Museums to bring even more world-class shows to our visitors. And our programming for all ages allows us to offer hands-on, immersive experiences that for many can be life changing.

In 2017 we expanded our interactive offerings when we opened the first and only museum in the world dedicated to Springfield native Theodor Seuss Geisel, also known as Dr. Seuss. One of the most beloved children's authors of all time, Dr. Seuss revolutionized learning to read by making it fun. We took a leaf from his book with the Amazing World of Dr. Seuss which features family friendly, interactive, bilingual exhibits that facilitate experimentation with sounds, vocabulary, and rhyme through delightful, play-based activities.

The Springfield Museums are stewards of the past, and at the same time we hope to be Museums for the future. We constantly consider how to make our collections relevant to contemporary audiences and contemporary concerns. This kind of innovation is our lifeblood. We hope you visit; it's worth the trip.

Located in the heart of downtown Springfield, Massachusetts, the Springfield Museums offer access to five world-class museums, including the Amazing World of Dr. Seuss Museum and the Dr. Seuss National Memorial Sculpture Garden, all under a single admission.

Home of the Amazing World of Dr. Seuss

SPRINGFIELD MUSEUMS
ART · HISTORY · SCIENCE · SEUSS IN SPRINGFIELD

21 Edwards Street
Springfield, MA 01103

THE 104TH FIGHTER WING

at Barnes Air National Guard Base

The 104th Fighter Wing is honored to highlight two powerful women: Command Chief Master Sgt. Maryanne Walts and Maj. Ashley Rolfe.

Command Chief Master Sgt. Maryanne Walts enlisted in the Air Force in 1981 upon graduating from Westfield High School. She was appointed as the organization's first woman Command Chief in April 2014 because of her distinguished background in logistics, coupled with exceptional people skills and a legacy of building progressive relationships. As the most senior enlisted leader in the Wing, Chief Walts is responsible for about 1,000 enlisted members. She oversees matters influencing the health, professional development, military readiness, morale and welfare of assigned personnel and their families.

A mother of three grown boys, Chief Walts said, "to be successful — not only in the military but also in life — the key is to understand how to balance it all…recognizing when you have to shift is the key. Ask for help when you need help; communicate and collaborate for the greater good."

Maj. Ashley Rolfe is the 104th Fighter Wing's first woman pilot in the Wing's 70-year legacy. In the fifth grade, Rolfe would tell people "I'm going to be a fighter pilot." Rolfe was enthused by the room-shaking sonic booms from military aircraft. "I thought it was the coolest thing in the entire world," she said. Maj. Rolfe was inspired by her grandfather and her father, both fighter pilots.

In high school, a football and baseball coach once said, "you won't ever be a fighter pilot, because you are a girl." Obviously, he was wrong. Rolfe emphasizes that "you don't have to be limited by what other people say."

Maj. Rolfe is a 2005 graduate of the U.S. Air Force Academy and a combat veteran. She served on active duty for 11 years and joined the 104th Fighter Wing in 2016. She has a three-year old daughter and newborn son.

Command Chief
Master Sgt.
Maryanne Walts

Maj.
Ashley Rolfe

BEHAVIORAL HEALTH NETWORK, INC.

Since 1938

Behavioral Health Network, Inc. (BHN) is a regional provider of comprehensive behavioral health services for adults, children and families. BHN began as the Child Guidance Clinic in 1938 and has grown into the largest behavioral health service provider in Western Massachusetts. BHN serves those with life challenges due to mental illness, substance abuse or intellectual and developmental disabilities. Across all BHN programs, staff and caregivers offer support, guidance and tools that help individuals make positive, life-altering changes.

BHN serves approximately 40,000 individuals annually. Services and programming are rendered at 40 locations across the four-county area including two locations in Holyoke. The organization employs over 2,300 individuals.

Services available to the public include many types of counseling programs and services for adults, youth, children, couples and families with the support of our trained Licensed Mental Health Counselors and accredited psychiatrists.

BHN also offers treatment services to medically and psychologically stabilize an individual through the challenging process of early recovery from addiction to opioid/non-opioid substances, alcohol or gambling.

Services also include 24-hour crisis intervention for children, youth and adults experiencing a mental health or addiction crisis. Domestic violence supportive individual and group services are also available.

BHN has three locations in Holyoke: behavioral health services provided at City Clinic, 235 Maple Street, (413) 532-0389, and the Mt. Tom Center for Mental Health and Recovery, 40 Bobala Road, (413) 536-5473; and Developmental Services at 1727 Northampton Street.

bhn
Behavioral Health Network

417 Liberty Street, Springfield, Massachusetts 01104

MARIE COUILLARD D'AMOUR

1876 - 1957

Marie Couillard D'Amour was educated in a one-room schoolhouse in northern Quebec, Canada. Early on, she showed a passion for reading, writing and grammar, and especially the French language. Her love for learning led her to choose teaching as a profession. Marie regarded motherhood as her most important teaching role and dedicated herself to raising seven children. She and her husband, Phillippe D'Amour immigrated to Holyoke, MA in 1906 in search of better opportunity for their family in America. Philippe was a carpenter who shared her commitment to family life. They thrived on hard work and despite difficult financial times, they still sacrificed and made education a priority for their children.

During the Great Depression of the 1930's the D'Amours' eldest son, Paul, opened a small market in Chicopee, Massachusetts. His brother, Gerald, joined him in business. The neighborhood grocery store at an intersection where two roads converged to form a "Y", was operated by Paul and Gerald. The Y Cash Market, was the beginning of Big Y Supermarkets. Together, the two brothers built a family-oriented business, one that strongly values education at all levels.

Marie Couillard D'Amour would be proud of her family's ongoing contribution to education in our community. As a tribute to a woman who strongly valued education, Big Y continues to help employees and students at all levels achieve their educational dreams.

BIG Y WORLD CLASS MARKETS®
2145 ROOSEVELT AVENUE, SPRINGFIELD, MA 01104
WWW.BIGY.COM

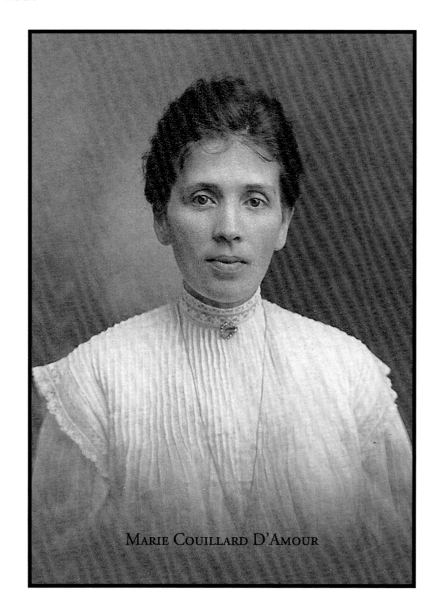

MARIE COUILLARD D'AMOUR

BULKLEY, RICHARDSON AND GELINAS, LLP

Since 1920

In a profession historically dominated by men, Melinda Phelps has demonstrated how women can succeed and lead. For the past 18 years, we at Bulkley Richardson have been able to witness Melinda's talent as a skilled attorney who has achieved exceptional results for her clients. We have learned from her valuable insight and pragmatic problem-solving skills, benefited from her sage counsel and open-door policy, and observed her charisma and grace even under the most challenging of circumstances. She possesses an innate ability to balance determination with empathy and compassion.

Melinda is a celebrated lawyer but an even more dynamic woman. She has earned the respect of colleagues, courts and community leaders and is continually recognized for her tireless commitment to the City of Springfield.

Bulkley Richardson has provided high-quality legal services to local and national clients for nearly a century. Melinda has upheld the firm's standard of excellence and continues to exemplify the level of professionalism that has contributed to Bulkley Richardson's longstanding reputation as a leading law firm in Western MA.

We applaud Melinda for blazing a trail for women in the legal community and for being a true role model to the women of Bulkley Richardson! We have all become better lawyers because of Melinda. But more importantly, we have all become better people because of her.

"Throughout my professional career, I have aspired to represent my clients without alienating adversaries. I have done this, not out of weakness or to avoid unpleasant situations, but because I have a profound respect for my colleagues and their role in the judicial system. I have counted it a great and weighty privilege to represent clients at their most vulnerable moments; they have made me more compassionate, and a better listener. I have enjoyed the life of a litigator: the intellectual challenge of preparing a case for trial, learning from experts and participating in the theater of the courtroom trial." – Melinda Phelps, Partner at Bulkley Richardson

ATTORNEYS AT LAW

BULKLEY
RICHARDSON

BETTER REPRESENTATION

1500 Main Street, Suite 2700, Springfield, MA

HOLYOKE MEDICAL CENTER

Since 1893

From its beginnings in 1893, Holyoke Medical Center has always responded to the healthcare needs of the greater Holyoke community. The hospital has continuously expanded to accommodate an ever-growing population of patients, offering state-of-the-art technological services, as well as routine exams and treatments. It has remained dedicated to attracting exceptional, highly skilled physicians, nurses, and healthcare providers to serve patients with the highest quality of care, compassion and individualized attention that they deserve.

A nationally-accredited hospital, Holyoke Medical Center received the Top Hospital Award from the Leapfrog Group for excellence in quality of care and patient safety in both 2014 and 2016. This full-service hospital provides a complete line of inpatient and outpatient medical and surgical services, including an award-winning Stroke Service, which has been consistently recognized as one of the best in the state by the Massachusetts Department of Public Health and the American Heart Association/American Stroke Association.

Our Mission at Holyoke Medical Center is to improve the health of all people in our community. We do that with honesty, respect and dignity for our patients, visitors and staff. We do that through expert and compassionate care, education and knowledge sharing, community partnerships, fostering innovation and growth and by inspiring hope in all we touch. We do that by being good stewards of our resources and providing efficient and cost effective care to all.

Throughout our history, we are fortunate to have been supported by the hard work and dedication by many powerful women. From our first appointed fundraisers, Anna Maria Whiting and Catherine Taft, in 1891, to our first Superintendent of Nurses in 1893, Clemma Edith Tower, who later became the first embalmer in western Massachusetts, to the first female president of our medical staff in 1974, Dr. Lulu Warner, and to all of the female leaders who have since followed… we pay tribute to you, our own notable women of western Massachusetts.

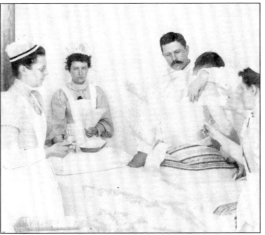

An examination in process in the mid-1890s. The woman on the far left is Clemma Edith Tower.

Dr. Lulu Warner

Holyoke Medical Center

Holyoke Medical Center

HolyokeHealth.com

HEALTH NEW ENGLAND

Since 1985

We are proud to recognize The Power of Women and would like to congratulate all of the women being featured for their strong work ethic and contributions to the communities of Western Massachusetts. We are especially proud to honor Maura McCaffrey, Health New England's first female president and CEO, for her commitment to strong corporate values, deep personal connections and enduring efforts to positively influence the health and lives of those we serve. As a strong champion of women in business, she has made a lasting impact on the health care industry, and business and community partners across the region.

Health New England's story began with a group of local physicians, Baystate Medical Center and two community hospitals who had a vision to start a health plan that would serve the health care needs of the local community. Founded in Springfield, Massachusetts, Health New England's mission still rings true more than 30 years later - to improve the health and lives of the people in the communities we serve.

Health New England was incorporated as a health maintenance organization (HMO) in 1985, and began serving members on January 1, 1986. Growing from just 13 associates and 800 members in 1986, Health New England's 360+ associates now serve approximately 160,000 members.

Today, as part of Baystate Health, Health New England continues to be the most trusted and valued health plan in our region by providing a health care experience that is caring, simplified and affordable, and by acting as a leading corporate citizen.

Health New England serves commercial members in Berkshire, Franklin, Hampden and Hampshire Counties in Western Massachusetts, in Worcester County in Central Massachusetts, and in parts of Connecticut. Through the BeHealthy Partnership, Health New England provides coverage for Medicaid members living in and around Holyoke, Northampton, Springfield and Westfield. Health New England's Medicare Advantage plans offer coverage for seniors living throughout Western Massachusetts.

 Health New England

One Monarch Place, Suite 1500 | Springfield, MA 01144-1500

healthnewengland.org

SENATOR ERIC P. LESSER

Throughout my life I've been surrounded by inspiring women: my mother, a social worker and scholar; my wife, a solo practicing attorney; and my two sisters who are both pursuing their career passions. I'm also the proud father of two young daughters — and I want them to grow up knowing the stories of inspiring women, too. That is why books like this, reminding us of our history, are so important.

We have come a long way — from a time when enslaved women (and men) were led to Springfield on the Underground Railroad by other brave women, to the years when women kept the war effort running in factories across Western Massachusetts, to today, when women are leading local companies and mentoring young women to take on their own leadership roles through organizations like the Women's Fund of Western Massachusetts.

This was a landmark year. We finally passed the Pregnant Workers Fairness Act, prohibiting employment discrimination on the basis of pregnancy. And we enacted paid family and medical leave so that no one is punished for taking time off work to care for loved ones. These steps build on the progress of the last two years.

In 2016, we updated the Massachusetts Equal Pay Act — the first of its kind in the country, passed in 1945 — to implement the country's most aggressive pay equity provisions to date. We also established the Commission on the Status of Women and Girls to recommend policies to help improve their quality of life.

We should be proud of the work we have done, but we still have more to do to achieve true gender equality. Women are changing our communities and our country for the better every single day. We should not only support their work, but celebrate it.

Eric P. Lesser

Senator Eric P. Lesser
First Hampden & Hampshire District

COOLEY DICKINSON HOSPITAL

Massachusetts General Hospital and Cooley Dickinson Health Care congratulate Cooley Dickinson President and CEO, Joanne Marqusee for her steadfast dedication to improving the quality of care and healthcare operations in the Pioneer Valley.

Joanne's professional experience includes over 30 years of leadership roles across a range of health care settings, including community hospitals, academic medical centers, public hospitals, and government agencies. Before joining Cooley Dickinson Health Care as President and CEO in 2014, she served as Chief Operating Officer/Executive Vice President at Hallmark Health, which is comprised of acute care hospitals Lawrence Memorial of Medford and Melrose-Wakefield of Melrose as well as a VNA-Hospice and a number of community-based sites.

Joanne has been a passionate advocate for the healthcare field throughout her career and we are honored to have her leadership.

Cooley Dickinson Hospital, a Massachusetts General Hospital Affiliate, is an acute care community hospital that offers medical/surgical, orthopedic, obstetric/gynecologic, psychiatric, geriatric, palliative, emergency, ambulatory, diagnostic, and rehabilitation services to residents of the mid-Pioneer Valley of Western Massachusetts.

Massachusetts General Hospital is ranked #4 by *U.S. News & World Report* and is the only hospital ranked across all 16 specialties. The oldest and largest hospital in New England, Mass General conducts the largest hospital-based research program in the nation and is designated a Magnet® hospital, the highest honor for nursing excellence awarded by the American Nurses Credentialing Center.

MASSACHUSETTS
GENERAL HOSPITAL

COOLEY DICKINSON
HEALTH CARE
MASSACHUSETTS GENERAL HOSPITAL AFFILIATE

MERCY MEDICAL CENTER

Since 1899

The Sisters of Providence – courageous and pioneering women – came to Western Massachusetts from Canada 140 years ago to care for the poor, the orphans and the immigrants working in the Holyoke mills. From these beginnings, the Sisters built a compassionate, transformative presence, providing health care, food and shelter for the homeless and needy, social services, and care of the elderly and disabled.

At Mercy Medical Center, we answer the call to preserve and strengthen their legacy of care and service. We are part of an extraordinary Mission; a Mission that allows us to make a positive difference in the world around us and a profound difference in the lives of those who need our healing touch.

Fully accredited and nationally recognized as a high quality provider, Mercy Medical Center includes Providence Behavioral Health Hospital, Weldon Rehabilitation Hospital, Brightside for Families and Children, and two outpatient substance abuse treatment centers. Mercy's hallmark programs include the Sister Caritas Cancer Center, Breast Care Center, Family Life Center for Maternity, a highly-acclaimed Emergency Department and a state-of-the-art Intensive Care Unit.

Mercy Medical Center is part of Trinity Health Of New England, an integrated health care delivery system formed in 2015. Trinity Health Of New England is a member of Trinity Health located Livonia, MI, one of the largest multi-institutional Catholic health care delivery systems in the nation.

Ever mindful of the inspiration we derive from the Sisters of Providence, we continue to move forward by focusing on our Mission to serve as a "transforming, healing presence" and our commitment to care for the most vulnerable in our community.

A Legacy of the Sisters of Providence

Top photo: Sisters of Providence at the site of the new Mother House.
Bottom photo: Mercy Medical Center today.

RICHARD E. NEAL

Congressman

Richard E. Neal has long served the citizens of western and central Massachusetts.

A native of Springfield, he began his public service career in 1973 as an Assistant to Springfield Mayor William C. Sullivan. In 1978, he was elected to the Springfield City Council and served as President of the Council in 1979. He was the Mayor of Springfield from 1984 to 1989.

Congressman Neal was first elected to the House of Representatives representing the First Congressional District of Massachusetts in 1988.

He is the Ranking Member of the Ways and Means Committee and serves as the dean of both the Massachusetts Delegation and the New England Congressional Delegation on which he also serves as co-chairman. Congressman Neal is an at large Whips for the House Democrats.

Active in the community he serves, Congressman Neal is the Democratic Leader of the Friends of Ireland caucus. He guest lectures at the University of Massachusetts Amherst and served as a Trustee at Mount Holyoke College for over a decade.

From the early days of the Massachusetts Colony to the present day, women have played an invaluable part of the fabric of Western Massachusetts. We owe much to their sacrifices, their nurturing and their displays of fortitude. As leaders at home, on the farm, in the factory, in business and in politics, they have enriched our lives.

We are proud to pay tribute to them!!

Richard E. Neal

NEW ENGLAND FARM WORKERS' COUNCIL

Since 1971

The organization was established to help the families migrating to New England from Puerto Rico to work at the Connecticut tobacco farms. Since then, families in New Hampshire, Connecticut and Massachusetts have been provided with comprehensive support services that combine career readiness preparation, educational achievement and skills training with the objective of placement in an educational or employment career track.

Our Chairman, Heriberto Flores, tells stories of when the organization employed mostly men. It was given the name "El Gallo" (The Rooster) an emblem of which is still our logo. Roosters have an interesting place in Puerto Rico's history. Some consider it an integral part of the island's folklore and patrimony.

Even as an undergraduate at Smith College majoring in Women's Studies, I could not imagine becoming proof of the empowerment of women of color in this sector. Today, as Chief Operating Officer, I am proud that women make up 64% of our workforce. These women are committed to being change agents and to the improvement of the quality of life of their own families and the families that they serve.

Looking ahead, the achievements of the women in our workforce and of the women we serve will no longer be new but instead common in our organization and community.

Vanessa Otero

CONSEJO DE TRABAJADORES
DE FINCA
DE NUEVA INGLATERRA

PeoplesBank

Commitment to our Customers

PeoplesBank is dedicated to offering quality products and services that will meet the needs of our customers. Through our product offerings and superior customer service our customers will be successful in meeting their financial goals. We are committed to providing service excellence. We strive to make banking with us easy and hassle free and keep that in mind with everything that we do.

Commitment to the Community

Established in 1885, PeoplesBank is one of the area's oldest and most respected community Banks. We take responsibility for our role in the community and we consistently look for ways that we can support the Pioneer Valley and make our area a premier place to live and work. We have demonstrated our passion for the community through our sponsorships and contributions, employee community involvement as well as our commitment to promote more environmentally friendly initiatives.

Commitment to our People

At PeoplesBank, we promote an atmosphere that nurtures growth- that challenges and inspires- and that's committed to excellence. We recognize that our most valuable asset is our vibrant and talented team of colleagues. We believe in giving each of our employees every opportunity to succeed through comprehensive training; a supportive team environment; professional development opportunities; comprehensive, industry-competitive benefits; and the freedom to share ideas and opinions.

A passion for what is possibleᴸᴹ

bankatpeoples.com | 413.538.9500 | #bankatpeoples

At PeoplesBank, we recognize that our most valuable asset is our vibrant and talented team of associates.

Community banks are not known for building green offices, but PeoplesBank opened its third LEED® Gold-certified office in Northampton in 2013.

THE REPUBLICAN AND MASSLIVE.COM

Since 1824

The Republican has been telling the stories of the people who live and work in Western Massachusetts since the newspaper was founded by Samuel Bowles in 1824. The rich history of this region can be found on the pages of the paper, printed day after day, for the past 194 years.

There is perhaps no recorded history of the region as detailed as that told by the journalists whose stories and photos have appeared in the pages of The Republican - and now on our website, MassLive.com.

Western Massachusetts was built by the hard work and dedication of the many ethnic groups who emigrated from their native countries and created new lives here for themselves and their families.

In our Heritage Book Series we tell the stories of these ethnic groups, along with books on significant milestones in Western Massachusetts history.

We began with the "Irish Legacy" in 2012 and continued with "The Struggle for Freedom, The History of African-Americans in Western Massachusetts," "Our Stories, The Jews of Western Massachusetts," "Nuestra Historia, A History of Latinos in Western Massachusetts," "Building a Better Life, The French Canadian Experience in Western Massachusetts," "On Being Italian, A Story of Food and Faith in Western Massachusetts," "Springfield 375 Years," "Path of Fury," on the June 2011 tornado, "A Not So Civil War" Vol. 1 and 2, the "Eastern States Exposition Centennial", "Saving Union Station, A 40 Year Effort Ends in Success", "Polish Heritage - History of a Proud Community in Western Massachusetts", and the book you are holding now, "The Power of Women - Celebrating Women from Western and Central Massachusetts from the 1600s to the Present Day."

We will celebrate the diversity of our local communities by continuing to tell their stories in future Heritage Books.

1860 Main Street, Springfield, MA 01101

SPRINGFIELD COLLEGE

Since 1885

Springfield College has fulfilled its mission—educating leaders who will serve others—since its founding in 1885. Throughout our history, our strongest and most effective leaders have included women from our alumni and faculty bodies. We celebrate the power of women by recognizing our president, Mary-Beth A. Cooper, PhD, DM, who brought to Springfield College a strategic vision for the future grounded in her experience from a distinguished career in higher education administration and community service.

We also pay tribute to Cathie Schweitzer, PhD, our first woman director of athletics; sport psychologist Mimi Murray, PhD, '61, G'67, a mover in the passage of Title IX, National Organization for Women's Person of the Year, Women's Sport Foundation's Pioneer for Girls and Women in Sport in the United States, and National Gymnastics Coach of the Year; Nancy Darsch '73, one of the first WNBA coaches; Pam Hixon '73, Olympic field hockey coach; Erin Pac Blumert '03, Olympic bronze medalist in bobsled; Olympians Nell Jackson '53, Paula Deubel Phillips '57, Kathy Corrigan Ekas '66, and Denise Desautels '77; Shawn Ladda, G'85, past president of the National Association for Girls and Women in Sport; past Professor Margaret Jones, the first female NCAA Division III director of strength and conditioning; Elizabeth Proctor, G'00, the first female NCAA Division I head football strength and conditioning coach; Irene Cucina, DPE'99, past president of the American Association for Health, Physical Education, Recreation, and Dance; former Rhodes Scholar Julia Chevan, PT, PhD, MPH; nationally-renowned foot and ankle surgeon Dr. Judith Baumhauer '83, the first woman president of the Eastern Orthopaedic Association; and Bridget Belgiovine, G'87, former Director of Division III at the NCAA, just to name a few.

Our women are strong because our mission is strong.

SPRINGFIELD
COLLEGE

263 Alden Street, Springfield, MA 01109 • springfield.edu

President Mary-Beth A. Cooper (right) with Professor Mimi Murray

SPRINGFIELD REGIONAL CHAMBER

Since 1879

The Springfield Regional Chamber was founded in 1879 -- a time of unprecedented growth and prosperity for Springfield. Today in 2018, as Springfield is experiencing a similar renaissance, a woman is leading the Springfield Regional Chamber for the first time in its history.

Nancy Creed took the helm of the Springfield Regional Chamber at an exciting time for the region. After having been the organization's Vice President of Marketing and Communications for many years, she became President in 2016, as MGM Springfield was beginning construction, as improvements to streets, roads and I-91 were being made, and as the renovated Union Station opened its doors to restored grandeur, prompting commuter rail service between Springfield and Hartford.

At the heart of all of this is the Springfield Regional Chamber – connecting businesses, championing business growth, convening leaders, and serving as a catalyst for thriving communities.

The Springfield Regional Chamber advocates for businesses on legislative issues, champions existing and emerging businesses in the region through various programs, including its Leadership Institute and "Rise Up Springfield," an innovative collaboration between the city, the Association of Black Professionals and the Springfield Regional Chamber. The Professional Women's Chamber, a division of The Springfield Women's Chamber, empowers business women through leadership, education and networking programs.

The Chamber recognizes and supports women leaders and business owners in our region in all that we do. To the women featured in this book – the women who led the way and those who are leading us into the future – we congratulate you for your hard work and achievements. Our strength lies in our power and our power lies in working together.

connect2
commerce
springfield
Regional Chamber

1441 Main Street, Springfield, Massachusetts 01103

Nancy F. Creed

SPRINGFIELD SYMPHONY ORCHESTRA

Since 1944

The Power of Springfield Symphony Orchestra Women, On and Off the Stage:

The Springfield Symphony Orchestra embraces and celebrates powerful women on and off the Symphony Hall stage. Over the past twenty years, the SSO has been a leading example of a female-forward organization; increasing the number of women hired as performers on stage and as staff members in our offices. We lead by example, choosing women like Susan Beaudry as Executive Director, Masako Yanagita as Concertmaster, Marsha Harbison as Assistant Concertmaster, and Kirsten Lipkins as Director of Education and Librarian.

Giving women a fair and equal opportunity to showcase their power and expertise is something we value and execute in a very practical way through our practice of "blind auditions." Musicians who audition for the Springfield Symphony Orchestra do so behind a screen that conceals their identity from the jury. Studies show that this practice increases the likelihood that women musicians will advance to the next round and, ultimately, reduces gender-biased hiring.

Honoring and empowering women is also a central part of the music we chose for our 75th Anniversary Season. It is our hope that playing the music of American women composers like Amy Beach, Jennifer Higdon, Libby Larsen, Joan Tower, and Augusta Read Thomas will challenge the perception of who actually composes orchestral music; solidifying a place of power and importance for women in the lineage of American orchestral music.

As we celebrate 75 seasons in downtown Springfield, we also celebrate the powerful women both in and outside of our orchestra, who make all that we do better and possible. Brava!

Springfield Symphony Orchestra

1441 Main Street, Springfield, MA

Clockwise from above: Susan Beaudry, SSO Executive Director; Marsha Harbison, first section second violin/Assistant Concertmaster; Romina Kostare, second string; Masako Yanagita, first violin/Concertmaster; Kirsten Lipkens, Director of Education/Librarian

VA CENTRAL WESTERN MASSACHUSETTS

Since 1924

VA Central Western Massachusetts Healthcare System provides primary, specialty, and mental health care, including psychiatric, substance abuse and PTSD services, to a Veteran population in central and western Massachusetts of more than 120,000 women and men.

Edward P. Boland Medical Center is the official name for VA Central Western Massachusetts Healthcare System's Leeds campus in Northampton. In 1992, Congressman Neal submitted a bill which was signed by the President to designate the Department of Veterans Affairs Medical Center located in Northampton, Massachusetts, as the 'Edward P. Boland Department of Veterans Affairs Medical Center.' Congressman Boland was from Springfield and represented the Second Congressional District. He also served in the U.S. Army during World War II. Join us in marking the name of our main campus, and in honoring the Veteran and public servant, Edward P. Boland.

VA Central Western Massachusetts Healthcare System is comprised of eight sites of care: Edward P. Boland Veterans Affairs Medical Center (main campus), Springfield Community-Based Outpatient Clinic (CBOC), Greenfield CBOC, Pittsfield CBOC, Worcester CBOC, Fitchburg CBOC, Lake Ave Clinic, and Plantation Street Clinic.

VA | U.S. Department of Veterans Affairs

VA Central Western Massachusetts Healthcare System
Edward P. Boland Medical Center
421 North Main Street, Leeds, MA 01053

Edward P. Boland Medical Center is the main campus for VA Central Western Massachusetts Healthcare System in Leeds, MA

U.S. Rep. Edward P. Boland, left, with then Springfield Mayor Richard E. Neal in Nov. 5, 1985.

THE ZONTA CLUB OF SPRINGFIELD

Since 1929

Zonta International is a leading global organization of executives and professionals working together to advance the status of women worldwide through service and advocacy. The Zonta Club of Springfield, founded in 1929, 10 years after Zonta International, has a long tradition of local projects promoting women's economic self-sufficiency, legislative equality, and access to education and health. We work to address domestic violence, provide funding for organizations helping women reclaim their lives, and fund scholarships for women returning to college as well as young women demonstrating commitment and leadership in public policy, government, and volunteer organizations.

Zonta members make a difference in the world, while forming friendships with local and international members, united in the goal of improving the status of women. The strength of our shared commitment advances women's legal, political, professional, educational and health status across the globe. If you are a woman looking to make a difference in your community and/or globally, become a member of Zonta. By becoming a member of Zonta, you will have the opportunity to...

• Make a difference in the world today.
• Create friendships and associations with other executives around the world.
• Belong to an international network of executives and professionals representing a diversity of occupations and affording you a global perspective on women's issues.
• Share a commitment to enhance the status of women worldwide.
• Provide service to individuals and their families.
• Fundraise to support important service projects on the local and international level.
• Enrich your life personally, as we pool talents to make the world a better place.

Some of our previous local community service projects have included; Help Our Kids, Gray House, The Period Project, YWCA Women's Shelters, Dress for Success, Weston Rehabilitation Center, Brightside Angels.

ZONTA
CLUB OF
SPRINGFIELD, MA

MEMBER OF ZONTA INTERNATIONAL

EMPOWERING WOMEN
THROUGH SERVICE & ADVOCACY

Please visit our website for more information:
Zonta International | www.zonta.org
Zonta Club of Springfield | www.zontaspringfield.org

INDEX